Mémoires
of Michilimackinac
and the
Pays d'en Haut

Mémoires of Michilimackinac and the *Pays d'en Haut*

Indians and French in the Upper Great Lakes at the Turn of the Eighteenth Century

Edited and translated by José António Brandão

Michigan State University Press · *East Lansing*
Mackinac Island State Park Commission · *Mackinac Island*

Michigan State University Press
East Lansing, Michigan 48823-5245

Mackinac Island State Park Commission
Mackinac Island

Printed and bound in the United States of America.

28 27 26 25 24 23 22 21 20 19 1 2 3 4 5 6 7 8 9 10

Library of Congress Cataloging-in-Publication Data
Names: Brandão, José António, 1957–
translator, editor.
Title: Mémoires of Michilimackinac and the Pays d'en Haut : Indians and French in the upper Great Lakes at the turn of the eighteenth century / edited and translated by José António Brandão.
Description: East Lansing: Michigan State University Press ; Mackinac Island: Mackinac Island State Park Commission, [2019] | Includes bibliographical references and index.
Identifiers: LCCN 2018047631 | ISBN 978-1-61186-325-3 (cloth : alk. paper) | ISBN 978-1-60917-604-4 (pdf)
Subjects: LCSH: Mackinac County (Mich.)—History—18th century—Sources. | Fort Michilimackinac (Mackinaw City, Mich.)—History—18th century—Sources. | Indians of North America—Michigan—Mackinac County—History—18th century—Sources.
Classification: LCC F572.M14 M46 2019 | DDC 977.4/923—dc23 LC record available at https://lccn.loc.gov/2018047631

Cover and book design by Charlie Sharp, Sharp Des!gns, East Lansing, MI
Cover art by Louis Nicolas, from Codex Canadensis, ink on paper, 13¼ × 8½ in. (33.7 × 21.6 cm). *Front cover*: Captain of the Illinois Nation, an unnamed Illinois headman; *back cover*: King of the great nation, Nadouessiouek, an unnamed Sioux headman. Gilcrease Museum, Tulsa, Oklahoma, used with permission.

Michigan State University Press is a member of the Green Press Initiative and is committed to developing and encouraging ecologically responsible publishing practices. For more information about the Green Press Initiative and the use of recycled paper in book publishing, please visit *www.greenpressinitiative.org*.

Visit Michigan State University Press at *www.msupress.org*

This book is dedicated to
David A. Armour
in memoriam

Contents

Preface

This book got its start while I was researching the introduction to *Edge of Empire: Documents of Michilimackinac, 1671–1716* (Peyser and Brandão, eds., East Lansing and Mackinac Island: Michigan State University Press and Mackinac State Historic Parks, 2008, xxiii–xliii). Michilimackinac was central to French ambitions in the interior of North America, and I read and used the three documents offered here to make my case then. I consulted two of the documents, those by Michel Bégon de La Picardière and François Clairambault d'Aigremont, in the original French. Both are part of the French Michilimackinac Research Project (FMRP) collection housed at Western Michigan University. The third document, the *Relation du sieur De lamotte Cadillac,* was to be found only at the Newberry Library in Chicago, but was published in a multivolume work by Pierre Margry in his *Découvertes et établissements des Français dans l'ouest et dans le sud de l'Amérique septentrionale, 1614–1754*, 6 vols. (Paris: D. Jouaust, 1876–1886.) And since the introduction I was writing was to a volume of translated documents, I searched for English translations of the three documents to recommend to readers who might not read French. Translations of all three documents existed.

I quickly realized, however, that there were problems with the published versions of the three documents. A trip to the Newberry with a group of students gave me the opportunity to consult the manuscript version of *Relation du sieur De lamotte Cadillac* and I was immediately struck by the fact that, there, Cadillac's name was spelled differently than Margry had rendered it. A quick comparison of a few pages of the manuscript with Margry's printed version convinced me that he had altered a great deal in preparing the manuscript for publication. I ordered a microfilm copy of the *Relation du sieur De lamotte Cadillac*, added it to the FMRP collection, and used that for my research. The English translation of the *Relation du sieur De lamotte Cadillac* could not be recommended since it was based upon Margry's flawed transcription while those of Bégon's and d'Aigremont's reports revealed that they were based upon heavily redacted versions of the originals and of questionable accuracy. In the end I drew upon the three original reports to make my case about Michilimackinac, but could not shake the disappointment that what most students of the subject had to work with was so deeply flawed.

Intrigued by the questions raised in the treatment of the *mémoires* as they came to be published and translated, in particular that attributed to Antoine Laumet, *dit* Lamothe Cadillac, I determined to see what I could learn about them and if the results warranted new publication. Certainly, the three documents in question here are not the only ones that deal with Michilimackinac in the period from 1690 to 1715. *Edge of Empire* contains many, and the appendix provides a fairly comprehensive list of others, dating to the same period, that have appeared in translation. Nor are the three documents translated anew here the only ones that merit new consideration. Many late nineteenth- and early twentieth-century English translations of French documents were done by amateurs and professionals of widely varying ability, and not all were up to the even relatively lax (by modern standards) scholarly expectations of the periods in which they appeared.

Unfortunately it simply is not feasible to retranslate every relevant document. The three *mémoires* that are the focus of this work seemed to merit new attention because they are a logical follow-up volume to *Edge of Empire*: they were produced by three (at least) different people at about the same time as the documents in *Edge of Empire*; cover, with a different sort of document and perspective, Michilimackinac and the region's French and Native inhabitants at the turn of the seventeenth century; and are self-contained reports with a specific focus upon Michilimackinac, the *pays d'en haut*, its people, and their place in French imperial plans. Thus, that all three of these important *mémoires* have been either questionably translated and/or based upon abridged, or otherwise altered, versions of the central documents in question, are only two of a number of factors that makes reconsidering them appropriate. (The full extent of the problems with the three is discussed in the introduction.) I am glad that others shared my view that the project merited support and, eventually, publication. I am especially grateful for the opportunity to present both the French texts and English translations of these important documents.

The volume is divided into several parts. It begins with an explanation of the approaches used in transcribing and translating the various documents and is followed by the introduction, which examines the history of the three *mémoires* and the problems with extant versions in print, and summarizes what the documents contribute to our understanding of Michilimackinac, the region, and New France in the period 1694 to 1713. This is followed by each of the three *mémoires* in French transcription with an English translation on the facing page. An appendix offers a list of other translated documents that relate to Michilimackinac in this period. The list was compiled by Dr. Keith Widder, formerly of Mackinac State Historic Park and who, with Dr. David Armour and Dr. Joseph L. Peyser, began the FMRP. Keith prepared the list as a way to identify existing resources for research on Michilimackinac and as a guide for Joe Peyser. Having a list of what was already translated would allow Joe to focus upon other relevant, and untranslated, documents. The list was completed in the early 1990s and revised as of summer 2014.

Tyler Miller, Michael Sanders, and Kyle Moerchen—all graduate students in history at Western Michigan University—updated the electronic format of the list, double-checked sources and uniformity of citations, and searched for documents that may have appeared in translation since Keith completed his initial inventory. The list is offered here as a resource to researchers, but no claims are made about the quality and completeness of the translations. Recent works focused upon Michilimackinac and that offer a large number of translated documents about the place, such as those in this series and Timothy Kent's two-volume work (see the bibliography), are not included in the list. All of the latter are aimed at English-reading audiences and are well known for filling in gaps in the existing body of translations related to Michilimackinac.

Acknowledgments

As in all such projects, there is a long list of contributors without whose assistance this book would not have been possible. Western Michigan University granted me a yearlong sabbatical leave to conduct research for the book. My thanks to Wilson Warren, Lynne Heasley, and James Palmitessa of the sabbatical application evaluation committee, and Marion (Buddy) Gray, former department chair, for their endorsement of the project. Mackinac State Historic Parks, with the assistance of a grant from the Florence Gould Foundation, underwrote a portion of my salary for that year. Phil Porter, director of Mackinac State Historic Parks, and Steven Brisson, deputy director of MSHP and codirector of the FMRP, managed to secure funding for me, and the FMRP as a whole, at a time of severe cuts to support in the social sciences. To them I extend a special *merci beaucoup*. A second sabbatical leave, for the semester following my term as department chair, was supported by interim dean Keith Hearit and former provost Tim Greene. I am grateful to them for encouraging my research and to the Peyser Endowment Committee for an additional grant to return to the Newberry during that sabbatical to complete research. Thanks also to the Department of History at WMU for providing summer research assistance, and to Tyler Miller, Michael Sanders, and Kyle Moerchen for their good work.

An initial Joseph L. Peyser Endowment Research Support Grant from the Department of History at Western Michigan University, and a Lester J. Cappon Fellowship in Documentary Editing from the Newberry Library in Chicago, made possible the extended stay in Chicago needed to transcribe the *Relation du sieur De lamotte Cadillac*, collate it with the 1727 edition of the document, and to consult the library's rich holdings. Without the latter, the discussion about this document would not have been possible. The entire staff of the Newberry, both administrators and librarians, could not have been more professional or helpful in making my stay in Chicago stress-free and productive. Still, a special thanks is owed to the staff of the Newberry's Special Collections reading room: every morning, Joy Austria, Dan Fink, and Helen Long "brought around" my "Cadillac" for me. Mr. John Aubrey, Ayer Manuscript Collection librarian, and the participants of the Fellows Seminar for fall 2010, especially Juliana Barr, David Buisseret, Barbara Hanawalt, Jean O'Brien, and Sarah Pearsall, provided research guidance or helpful comments and suggestions on my initial attempts to understand, and explain, the history of the *Relation du sieur De lamotte Cadillac*.

Others, who have read portions of the manuscript and have offered sage advice and corrected errors, include my late dear friend and colleague Catherine Julien, Gordon Sayre, Pierre Lebeau, and Joseph Gagné. The anonymous reviewers for Mackinac State Historic Parks/Michigan State University Press were most helpful, both in terms of spotting small but significant matters of language and by offering suggestions for improving my argument in key places.

For assistance in reviewing the translation I am indebted to Cynthia Running Johnson. She has, with good grace and humor, taken on a project far afield from her own research interests and spared me more errors than I want to admit. Translation, for me at least, is a humbling experience, and it was, indeed, nice to have such a gracious colleague along for it. Still, the translation, as with all else in the book, is my responsibility, and all errors that remain are of my making—again, often against the advice of my betters.

At Michigan State University Press, editors Julie Lohr and Kristine Blakelee have been at their usual supportive best. I am grateful for all their suggestions for improvement and their guidance of the project from start to finish. Ellen White produced the map of the region and peoples of Michilimackinac and Barbara (Bonnie) Fitch Cobb, once again, turned her keen eye to my prose, stifled laughter (I hope) at my seeming inability to get straight "that" and "which," and improved mightily all *that* I wrote. Project editor Amanda Frost, with patience and keen eye for detail, saw the manuscript over the finish line. Thanks also to designer Charlie Sharp for his outstanding cover and design. The skill and care that all involved with this project have applied to it are deeply appreciated. Certainly it is a better book for their efforts.

Lastly I wish to thank Keith Widder for allowing me to publish a portion of his remarkable compendium of published source material on Michilimackinac, and the late David Armour for his continual support of my efforts. Dave brought me into the FMRP and was an unflagging supporter of all that I sought to do, including this project. He died in early 2010 before I had done much more than outline what I wanted to do and why, but I hope that Dave would have been happy with what follows, and the book is dedicated to his memory.

Note on Editorial and Transcription Approach

The documents transcribed and translated in this volume include one that has been published in French transcription and English translation and two that have been published only in English and in much modified form. Therefore I have taken somewhat different approaches in presenting the transcriptions here. In the case of the *Relation du sieur De lamotte Cadillac* I have transcribed the 1718 version of the volume as it appears, and indicated differences between it and Margry's version in the notes. All of Margry's changes were made without informing the reader, and there are far too many to indicate each of them. There are literally dozens of changes per paragraph of the manuscript, and I have confined my notes to changes such as deleted or added words, and especially those that affect meaning or understanding of what the original author wrote/intended and that, of course, impact the translation. I have also collated the 1718 copy of the manuscript with the second version of the manuscript, dated to 1727 based on the date on the cover of the volume in which it is found. I indicate in the notes major variants in word choice, proper names of people and places, and editorial practices such as adding or deleting chapter titles. I have not noted every difference in spelling and punctuation. Neither Bégon's nor d'Aigremont's *mémoires* appear in transcription, and thus there is no need to compare the transcription here to others—it simply reflects the original documents.

The author or copyist of the 1718 *Relation du sieur De lamotte Cadillac* began the first paragraph of a chapter by writing the first word in larger print, either in cursive or block letters. Beginning at page 11, although it was not done consistently, the author or copyist also began making the first word or two of new paragraphs larger. The size of the enlarged first word(s) is not always the same, but it is clear that some effort was made to set that word or words apart. Where the author or copyist used the larger print I have bolded the text, but have kept the font size the same. Up to page 5 in the manuscript, the author or copyist also indented the first sentence of each new paragraph. The practice is abandoned after that, but it is clear, based on where words end on the page, that one paragraph ends and a new one begins. After page 11 the practice of starting paragraphs with words in larger print also helps make clear where one ends and another begins. In Bégon's and d'Aigremont's *mémoires* there are no special characters or features of writing. Each new paragraph is clearly evident by where the preceding paragraph ends while a new one begins with a capital letter in the first word. Sometimes, but not always, the capital letter is made larger than the other letters in the word. For the sake of consistency I have indented the first line of each new paragraph in all three documents.

All paragraphing, spelling, punctuation (or lack thereof) are as found in the document. The 1718 *Relation du sieur De lamotte Cadillac* is replete with grammatical errors. At times, often in the same sentence, the author switches from the plural to the singular in describing practices, as if going from a generalization to the specific event that provided him the evidence of the former. The 1727 copy is better written, more grammatically sound, and spelling is more consistent. Since there is no page numbering in the 1718 *Relation du sieur De lamotte Cadillac*, and that added later is not consistent,

I have numbered each page of text, recto and verso, as in modern works. The pages of the 1727 edition are numbered, but due to the fact that it is part of a volume with numerous *mémoires*, and the pages are much larger (six or seven times as large), there is no concordance of content per page between the two copies. In the case of the Bégon and d'Aigremont *mémoires*, I have followed the numbering system added to the folio pages when they were bound into volumes in the French archives, and added the verso number missing in the archival volume. For each document, the page number is on the left side, and all text following that number is from that page.

The notes in the transcription are confined to those dealing with textual matters such as missing words. In the case of the *Relation du sieur De lamotte Cadillac*, notes also point to differences between the various versions of the *mémoire*. Where a note reads "two [etc.] words missing in Margry/1727 copy," the reference is to the given number of words preceding the note. Where a note reads "inserted here in Margry/1727 copy" the reference is to a space following the note.

Note on Translation

The translations offered here of these documents are new. These are based on the original documents in their entirety or, in the case of d'Aigremont's *mémoire*, of the entire section related to Michilimackinac. I have not sought to point to differences between my translation and those already existing for numerous reasons. Translation, to state the obvious, is a subjective process. There are rules of grammar, accepted word equivalents, and accepted goals in translation; but translation is not simply replacing a word in one language with that in another. One must try to determine what the author meant in any given sentence or combination of sentences and find the word(s) that best convey(s) that meaning, while keeping in mind that words have shades of meaning and a given word may be used in more than one context and with a different meaning in each. The word *faire*, for example, depending on how it is used, can be translated in a variety of ways, including make, do, take, build, cover, and travel. Translators, with different audiences and goals in mind, can legitimately arrive at different conclusions about how to approach a translation project. The differences are likely to be more pronounced when translations were made generations ago when accepted practices were quite different. And, other than trying to produce "accurate" translations based upon the "original document," one knows little about the editorial practices and choices that led to the first translations of the documents offered here. Nor, to be fair, can one dismiss every aspect of past translations. There are instances when there is simply only one correct way to render a word, phrase, or sentence and not every previous translator got things wrong. The value of the translations here, then, rests in offering fully edited and annotated translations of the various *mémoires*—something not done in past translations—which correct some errors, and which are based upon the original documents in all their known versions and in their entirety. In the case of the two copies of the *Relation du sieur De lamotte Cadillac*, I have used text from both copies in constructing a more complete document and translation.

As in the past, I have approached my translations as a historian rather than as a linguistic specialist. I do this in part because I am the former and not the latter, and because as a historian I think that a translation should be as close a "reproduction" of the original document as possible, however difficult that is—admittedly—to achieve. For example, the French word for circumference (*circuit*) existed decades before any of the *mémoires* offered here were written, yet one author used "around" (*au tour*) to convey that point. Translating the latter as circumference, which is what the author intended, would make for a more readable sentence, but would be, literally, putting words in the mouth of the writer by giving him a vocabulary he did not have or did not choose to use. The same is true in instances where the author used a word in one place (tormentors) and a less elegant or less concise phrasing elsewhere (those who made him suffer). To tidy up the French via translation in the second instance is to, again, alter the original too much. In other instances, words in French usage have ready equivalents in English but they may not be the norm today. For example, rather than write that men and women had sexual intercourse, the writer observed that they "had commerce" with one another. That would have been normal phrasing in the English of the period, and I have chosen to translate such words as they appear rather than risk introducing anachronistic notions into the document and, yet again, putting words in the author's mouth. In short, if there is ambiguity in the original language, it should remain in the translation; if something reads awkwardly in French, it can read awkwardly in English as well; and if the work does not read as it might if written today, that is fine—it was written over three hundred years ago, and the English documents of that period do not read like those written in the twenty-first century. The documents translated here are not literary works, and a historian's task is to let the actors of the past speak in their own voice as much as possible, even in translation. It is important to do all that is possible to leave the translation as close to the original document as possible, and leave the reader to formulate his or her interpretation and not create one via the translation process.

Paragraphing in the translation remains as in the original, as does use, or not, of chapter divisions and titles. Some changes, nonetheless, have been introduced via the translation. Articles such as *le*, *la*, and *des*, while needed in French, are most often superfluous in English: *le lac Erie*, literally "the Lake Erie," is both awkward and needless in English. In such instances the article has been omitted in the translation. Modern punctuation has been added, and in most cases it is simply putting in a period to end a sentence or thought. That, however, is not always a straightforward matter because it often reflects a translator's decision about what constitutes a complete thought or sentence. Such decisions have to be made in order to translate, and the reader needs to keep that in mind. Place names, group names, and proper names—where they were obvious—have been rendered as found in the *Dictionary of Canadian Biography* or the appropriate volume of the *Handbook of North American Indians*. Given that the original texts accompany the translations, it seemed better to do this than clutter the page with endless identification notes. If a name, personal or geographic, is not clear, the word remains as in the original document.

Some French words and terms have no ready English equivalent and remain in French with an accompanying note of explanation at their first appearance. Such words are rendered in italics each time they appear in the translation. Gallicisms—expressions that in French make sense, but that if translated literally make no sense in English—have been rendered as they are intended and the literal translation and explanation provided in the notes. The word *sauvage* presents its own challenge: it has a ready and recognizable English equivalent (savage), but it has long been argued that the French did not use the word as it has come to be understood in English and used barbarians (*barbares*) when they wanted to pass negative judgment on Indians.[1] As a result I have, in the past, translated *sauvage* as "Native" or "Indian." However, *sauvage*, as John DuVal and Kathleen DuVal have argued, was used in a variety of different ways to comment upon and judge people and manners, and to simply ignore that variety for a uniform usage of, for example, Indian, is problematic.[2] It is a compelling argument and I have chosen to leave the word in French and let the reader determine the author's intent when the word appears.

Notes in the translation serve to identify, where possible, places and people(s) mentioned in the manuscript and to provide background information that clarifies some matter raised in it—either in terms of historical content or related to language and its translation.

1. James Axtell, *After Columbus: Essays in the Ethnohistory of Colonial North America* (New York: Oxford University Press, 1988), 34–44.
2. John DuVal and Kathleen DuVal, "Are Sauvages Savages, Wild People, or Indians in a Colonial American Reader?," *Translation Review* 79 (Winter 2010): 1–17.

Introduction

The three *mémoires* transcribed and translated here have all been published in translation before, precisely because they lay out, in very clear terms, the reasons for French preoccupation with Michilimackinac, the *pays d'en haut* (upper country), and the Native peoples of the region, and they reveal French imperial strategies and economic ambitions at a time when the struggle with England for mastery of North America began in earnest. There are, however, numerous problems with all of the extant versions. Pierre Margry, who first brought the *Relation du sieur De lamotte Cadillac* to scholars' attention, altered a great deal in preparing the manuscript for publication, not the least of which was the name of its supposed author. The only published English translations of the *Relation du sieur De lamotte Cadillac* are based upon Margry's flawed transcription. The translations of Bégon's and d'Aigremont's *mémoires* are based upon abbreviated, and not indicated to be such, versions of the French documents and are of dubious accuracy. Before turning to the contexts of the three *mémoires*' creation, what the *mémoires* reveal about Michilimackinac, its

Native inhabitants, the place of both in French imperial policy, let us first consider each *mémoire* in turn and the limitations of the extant published versions.

The *Relation du sieur De lamotte Cadillac*

The *mémoire* attributed to Antoine Laumet, *dit*[1] de Lamothe Cadillac has the most interesting and complicated history of the three translated works. Its best-known version is that published by Pierre Margry in his *Découvertes et établissements des Français dans l'ouest et dans le sud de l'Amérique septentrionale.*[2] Margry based his published version on the then only known copy of a work since lost. That copy, titled *Relation du sieur De lamotte Cadillac* . . . . (Versailles au Parc au Cerf, 1718) is now held by the Newberry Library.[3] The *mémoire* offers one of the fullest treatments of the *pays d'en haut* centered on Michilimackinac, its place in the French empire, and of the Native peoples in the region. Portions of chapter 1 and chapter 5 of Margry's edition of the *Relation du sieur De lamotte Cadillac* were published in the Collections of the State Historical Society of Wisconsin.[4] The whole of the *Relation du sieur De lamotte Cadillac* was translated by Milo Milton Quaife in his *The Western Country in the 17th Century: The Memoirs of Lamothe Cadillac and Pierre Liette*,[5] and portions of Quaife's translation, with a few

1. This word means story or fable, but is used as if it meant "said." It should be read, then, as "said to be," "so-called," "known as," or even "better known as."

2. Pierre Margry, ed., *Découvertes et établissements des Français dans l'ouest et dans le sud de l'Amérique septentrionale, 1614–1754*, 6 vols. (Paris: D. Jouaust, 1876–1886), 5:75–132.

3. Ayer Manuscript Collection, Newberry Library, Ayer MS 130. It should be noted that when referring to sources, primary or otherwise, French names are spelled as they appear there. At all other times they are spelled according to the conventions adopted in George Brown et al., *Dictionary of Canadian Biography* (Toronto: University of Toronto Press, 1966–) (hereafter *DCB*).

4. Madison: State Historical Society of Wisconsin (hereafter WHC), 16:350–63. R. G. Thwaites, editor of the series and the 1902 volume, was a well-known and skilled translator, but in the foreword to the volume he thanked Emma Blair, also a skilled and published translator, for her extensive work on the 1902 volume (ibid., xvi). Either or both could have translated the published sections.

5. (Chicago: Lakeside Press, 1947), 3–83.

new editorial notes, were reprinted in Cornelius Jaenen, ed., *The French Regime in the Upper Country of Canada during the Seventeenth Century*.[6]

Quaife's published translation of the *mémoire* he attributed to Cadillac was based upon an unpublished one prepared by Edith Moodie for a Detroit businessman and local historian, Clarence M. Burton. Moodie apparently was commissioned by Burton to translate some documents, including "Cadillac's," based upon Margry's published versions. She, however, checked them against the "Paris originals, with a view to eliminating those errors which had gained entrance to Margry's published volumes."[7] Moodie, however, was either not able to consult the manuscript copy of the *Relation du sieur De lamotte Cadillac*, or not that careful with her transcribing or translating: all of Margry's major changes are found in Quaife's translation, which he claims he changed from Moodie's only to furnish "a less literal and more smoothly flowing English version."[8] Either that, or Quaife made more changes than he admitted, and based them upon the published Margry version of the document. Quaife indicated that he had "no access to the copy of the Memoir in the Ayer Collection."[9] Why that should have been the case is not explained. He was either denied access, which seems odd given the Newberry's role as a research library, or he did not have the time, or inclination, to visit the Newberry. Unfortunately for posterity, the transcription that Margry produced is filled with errors and deliberate and unacknowledged changes, and most scholars have invariably relied upon it, and not the manuscript *mémoire*, for their research. Others have turned to Quaife's translation, based as it was on the altered transcription. Despite Margry's discussion about the document's authorship, and his tampering with its content, the *mémoire* was not written by Cadillac, although it may

6. (Toronto: Champlain Society, 1996), 37–45.

7. Quaife, *The Western Country in the 17th Century* (Chicago: Lakeside Press, 1947), xxiii. Quaife, however, was aware of the partial WHC translation and wrote that "some of its phraseology has been substituted for Miss Moodie's translation" (ibid., xxiv).

8. Ibid., xxiv.

9. Ibid. Quaife's speculation that what Margry transcribed and printed "was *probably* a longhand copy" of the document confirms that he had not seen the little book at the Newberry, let alone consulted it (ibid., xxii, emphasis added).

be based upon his work; it was not first written in 1718; and it is not the only copy of the *Relation du sieur De lamotte Cadillac.*

The *mémoire* attributed to Cadillac is a small bound volume, in smooth brown leather covers, measuring 9.5 cm wide by 15.3 cm long. It has no title on either the spine or cover. On the inside of the front cover is glued a book plate indicating that the book is EX / BIBLIOTHECA / MICHAELIS / CHASLES / ACAD. SCIENTIAR. SOCII. This is followed, also centered in the book plate, by the initials MC superimposed on one another. The pages of the volume are stitched together and are glued to the cover boards by sheets of paper identical to those on which the text is found. On the facing page someone has drawn, in ink and using a ruler, a rectangular shape in which the horizontal line at the top of the page extends beyond the vertical one on the right hand side. Written in pencil, in English and clearly after the document was bound, is: "Book used by Margry on Cadillac, vol 5, page 73." The verso of this page is blank. Opposite that blank page is a more neatly drawn rectangle and the number "190."[10] This is followed by the title, the first three words of which are in red block letters: "*RELATION DU SIEUR De lamotte Cadillac capitaine en pied, aiant une compagnie dela Marine en Canada cy devant commandant De MissilimaKinaK et autres postes Eloignée ou il a eté pendant trois annees. ouvrage tres curieux, tiré sur L'orignal de Lauteur et non encore Imprimé Par D. . . . D. A Versailles au Parc au Cerf 1718.*"[11] The verso of this page is blank, and facing it is the first page of text as it appears—more or less—in Margry.

The pages of text are unnumbered, but some time after the volume's creation, and possibly at the Newberry, numbers were added in pencil

10. Possibly the first page with the rectangle was meant to be the title page but was not used because of the error in drawing the shape.

11. Translation: "Relation of the sieur De lamotte Cadillac, Captain *en pied*, having a Company of the Marine in Canada, the aforementioned [being the] Commandant of Michilimackinac and other distant posts where he was for three years. A very interesting work, based upon the author's original and not yet printed. By D . . . D., at Versailles at Parc au Cerf, 1718." All translations from French here, and in what follows, are my own. For the phrase *en pied*, see the discussion in the translation below. D . . . D, in what follows, is abbreviated as "DD."

at irregular intervals. Pages were counted, apparently, starting with the first page of text, but the first number appears only at page 10. According to these numbers, and in fact, there are 111 pages of text. Written on that last page, in ink and in the same hand as the rest of the text, is: *ce 21e Juillet 1718.*[12] On the inside of the back cover is written, in English, "Aug. 25, 1934." This may have been when the volume was accessioned at the Newberry as part of the preparation of the catalog of the Ayer Collection.[13] The pages are unlined and the handwriting is small, neat, and evenly spaced. It is evident from faint markings on the recto of each sheet of paper that some device, probably made of metal, was placed on the page to assist in spacing. The rectangular shape is evident, as are four small indentions (actual holes in some instances), at the four corners of the page—the latter presumably caused by some part of the device, and which served to secure it on the paper. On the verso, the writing is kept straight by writing in between the lines of text of the preceding page, which appear faintly through the paper. It was all written in the same hand and by the same person.

Pierre Margry, who worked at the French national archives as a "conservator," published the *mémoire* in his *Découvertes et établissements des Français dans l'ouest et dans le sud de l'Amérique septentrionale*. The problems with his edition are legion. He added words to, and deleted them from, the document as he saw fit. He reordered sentences, added punctuation and accents to modernize the text, and, at other times, changed words to make the text look older.[14] A comparison of any page of Margry's edition with the corrections made using Microsoft's "Track

12. Margry rendered the date as 31 *juillet* (Margry, *Découvertes et établissements des Français*, 5:679). Quaife did not put the date in his translation, but in his introduction to the document indicated that Margry dated the document to 31 January (Quaife, *The Western Country*, xxii).

13. See Ruth Butler, comp., *A Check List of Manuscripts in the Edward E. Ayer Collection* (Chicago: Newberry Library, 1937), 15.

14. In the case of making words look "older" it appears most often when the word is in the process of changing from an older spelling (e.g., from *estre*, meaning "to be," to *etre*) but has not yet attained its accepted modern form (*être*). In such cases Margry converted the word back to its older form. Why he bothered to do this when he added accents and modernized completely other words is anyone's guess.

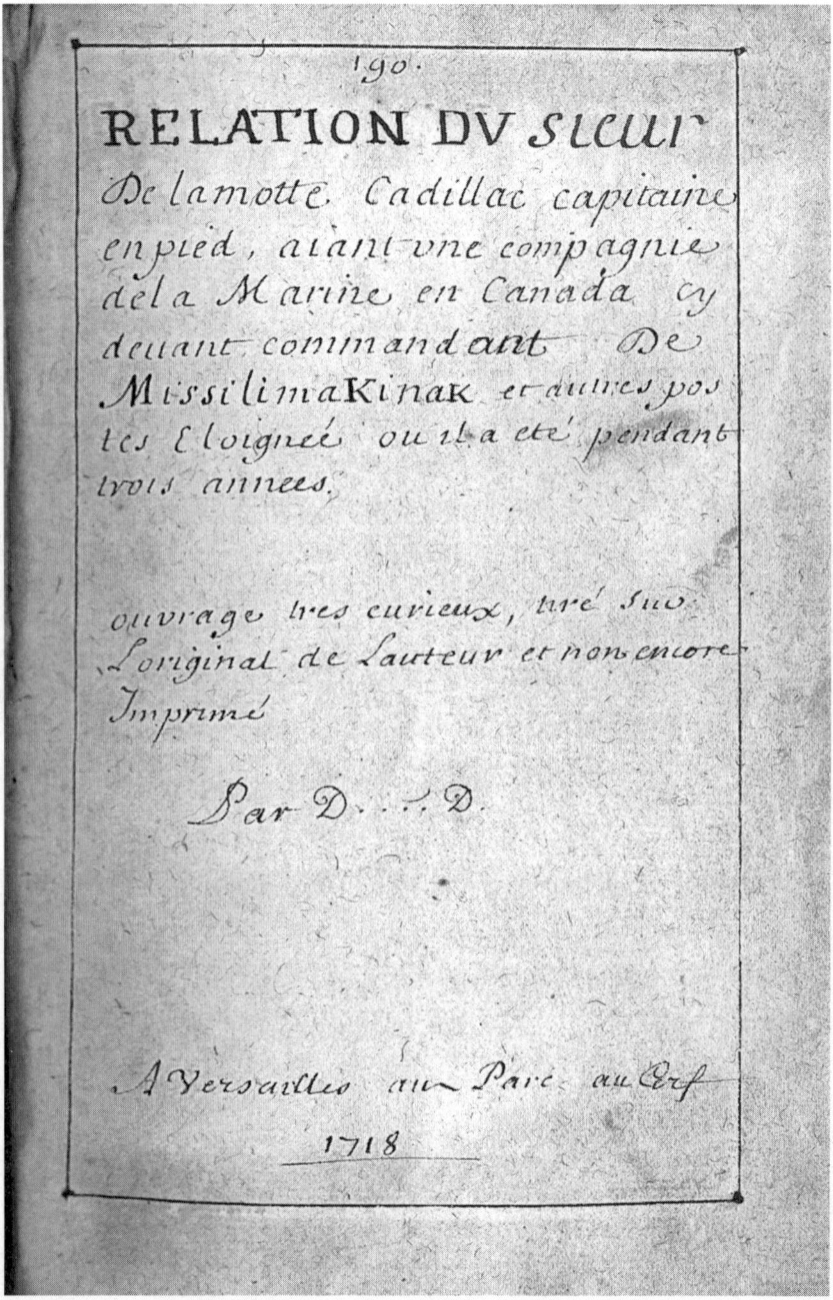

190.

RELATION DV sieur
De lamotte Cadillac capitaine
en pied, aiant une compagnie
dela Marine en Canada cy
deuant commandant De
MissilimaKinak et autres pos
tes Eloignée ou il a eté pendant
trois années.

ouvrage tres curieux, tiré sur
Loriginal de Lauteur et non encore
Imprimé

Par D. . . D.

A Versailles au Parc au Cerf
1718

1. Title page of the *Relation du sieur De lamotte Cadillac* from the 1718 copy of that document.

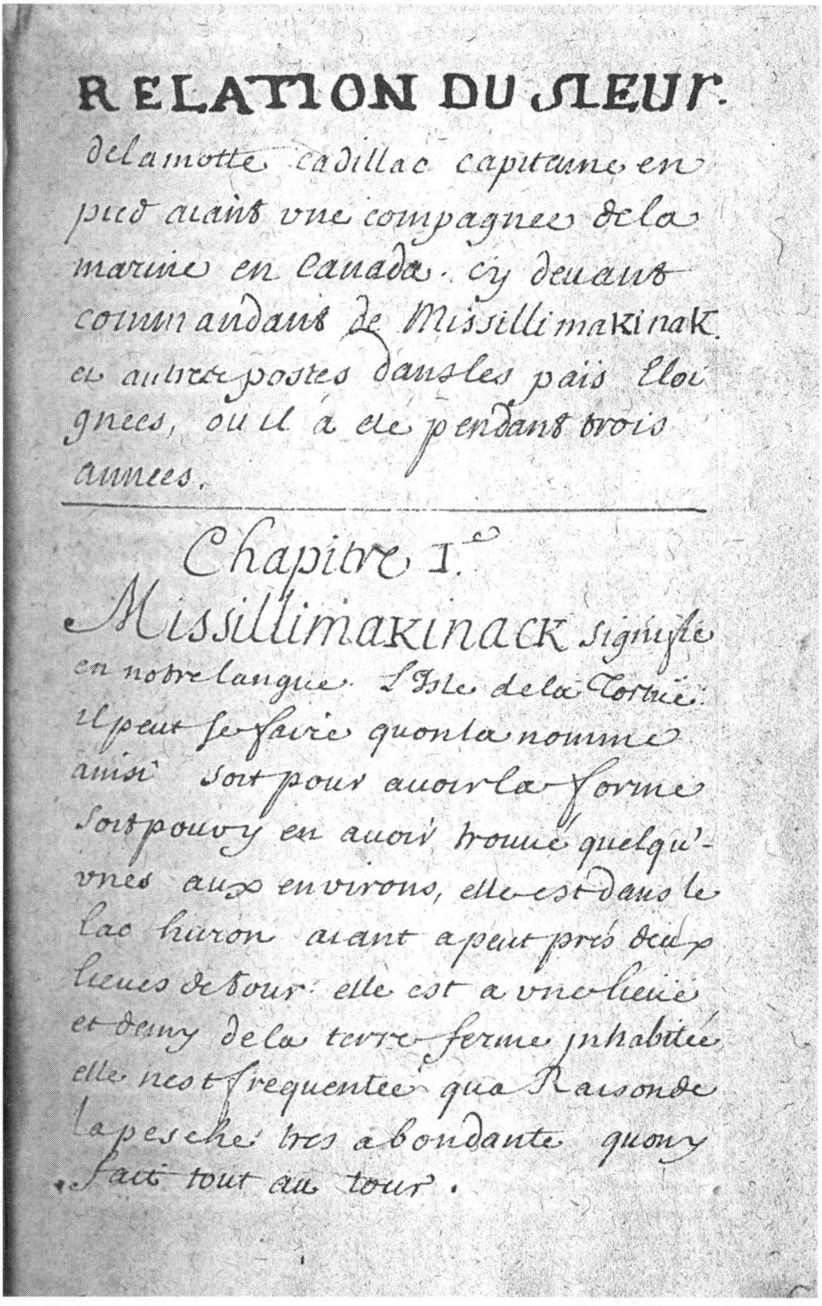

RELATION DU SIEUR.

delamotte cadillac capitaine en pied aiant vne compagnee dela marine en Canada. cy deuant commandant de Missillimakinak. et autres postes dansles pais Eloignees, ou il a ete pendant trois annees.

Chapitre I.er

Missillimakinack signifie en notre langue. L'Isle dela Tortue: il peut se faire quonla nomme ainsi soit pour auoirla forme soit pour y en auoir trouué quelqu'vnes aux environs, elle est dans le lac huron aiant a peut prés deux lieues de tour: elle est a vne lieue et demy dela terre ferme inhabitée, elle nest frequentée qua Raison de la pesche tres abondante quon y fait tout au tour.

The Newberry Library, Chicago.

2. First page of the *Relation du sieur De lamotte Cadillac* from the 1718 copy of that document.

Changes" feature reveals the extent of editorial interference—there are literally dozens of changes per paragraph.

Some of Margry's changes were likely introduced to make the manuscript more readable for his audience and, while annoying and representing a significant degree of unacknowledged editorial interference, do not alter the original author's meaning. Still, even by the admittedly "looser" standards of historical scholarship of the late nineteenth century, his degree of interference was not on a par with that found in the works of many scholars—including Ruben Gold Thwaites, whose transcriptions (and translations) of French documents date to the same period.[15] Moreover, given the specialized nature of the documents he published, Margry could reasonably assume that his readers would be mostly scholars who understood that documents in seventeenth- and eighteenth-century French would not look like those written hundreds of years later. At the very least, he should have revealed his rules of transcription.

At other times, however, Margry's changes alter the author's intent, and this is particularly problematic in descriptions of cultural practices. The changes Margry made are all indicated in the new transcription in this book, but a few examples here should suffice to make the case about the extent of his editorial interference. In one instance, for example, instead of a shaman having an "appearance horrible" to contemplate, as is written in the *mémoire,* he is said to have had a "humble" one. Margry's change in wording not only altered what the author wrote, it also makes nonsense of a description of a Native curing ritual that follows. In yet another instance the *mémoire*'s author wrote that a group of people often speak "metaphorically," and Margry rendered the word as "metaphysically." These are clearly not the same thing, and while there are one or two places in the manuscript

15. See for example Reuben Gold Thwaites, ed., *The Jesuit Relations and Allied Documents: Travels and Explorations of the Jesuit Missionaries in New France, 1610–1791,* 73 vols. (Cleveland: Burrows Brothers Co., 1886–1901) (hereafter *JR*). But even Thwaite's work has been found in need of revision. See Luca Codignola, "The Battle Is Over: Campeau's *Monumenta* vs. Thwaite's *Jesuit Relations,* 1602–1650," in *Missionaries, Native Americans, and Cultural Processes,* ed. Sylvia S. Kaspyrcki, special issue, *European Review of Native American Studies* 10, no. 2 (1996): 3–10.

where it is difficult to determine what word is meant, in neither of the above examples, and in others noted in the transcription, is that the case. Margry simply decided that his description of Indian actions, or word choice, was better than that of the manuscript's creator.

Nor did Margry limit himself to just switching a word in a sentence. He sometimes rewrote sentences, or portions of them. For example, the author of the *mémoire* wrote that Indians did not frequent Michilimackinac Island "except to fish," and Margry changed it to "except in fishing season." But there is a difference between saying that Indians visited to fish and saying they did so only during fishing season. The latter introduces a notion of a specific time and limited Indian presence on the island, while the former reflects an Indian reality in which fishing took place year round, including in winter, and a more durable presence on the island. In another instance, Margry eliminated a sentence that revealed an insight into the author's thinking and possibly his origins. The author wrote that "it should be observed that in that country, the word city is unknown *which makes one believe that the sauvages*[16] *are not descended from the Normans*, so that if they wished to speak of Paris, they would denote it by the word for 'great village.'" Margry removed the portion in italics, and thus the reader misses the opportunity to understand something about the document's creator and is left with one less piece of evidence to use to evaluate how much credence to attach to his observations, or to understand his biases.[17] It bears repeating that none of the changes, minor or otherwise, are ever indicated as such by Margry.[18]

But Margry's worst offenses are related to the *mémoire*'s history and authorship. He offered very few clues about its origins and actually provided misleading evidence regarding its provenance.[19] Margry did indicate that

16. On this word, see the discussion in my "Note on Editorial and Transcription Approach."

17. Margry may have removed this portion of the sentence because he was from Normandy and he thought the later description of Indian practices was insulting to Normans. Cadillac, the supposed author of the relation, was from Gascony.

18. It should be needless to add that translations based on such a flawed transcription only replicate the errors and misunderstandings.

19. Margry was well known to be secretive about his sources and often refused to share them. See John Spencer Basset, Explanatory Note to "Letters of Francis Parkman to Pierre Margry," in

the *mémoire* had belonged to Michel Chasles and that he had seen it at M. Dufossé's, whom he had identified elsewhere as a book dealer.[20] Margry also noted that a passage from the *mémoire* could be found in the "Considérations de Philippe Buache sur les *Nouvelles découvertes au nord de la mer du Sud*" (a 1753 publication for which he provides no bibliographic data and offers an incorrect title), and that he has "seen it cited elsewhere and always attributed to Cadillac."[21] Margry did not provide references to the other citations, but, as will be discussed below, that was not true of Buache, who did not identify the work with Cadillac.

Margry, however, was not content to let matters rest there, and he changed the document that he published to bolster his claim that it was produced by Antoine Laumet, *dit* Lamothe Cadillac. The latter had commanded at Michilimackinac, founded Detroit, and governed in Louisiana before he was put in the Bastille in 1717. Unfortunately for Margry, Cadillac signed his name La Mothe or Lamothe Cadillac and the *mémoire* has it written as De lamotte Cadillac.[22] Margry silently "corrected" this spelling "error" in two different places in his printed version of the document.[23] As well, the *mémoire* has only four chapters—two of which are numbered and have no title, one that has a title and number, and a fourth that has a title but not a number. Margry added a fifth and sixth chapter, and titles not in "DD's" copy of the *mémoire*. "Chapter V," according to Margry is "Nations inhabiting the area governed by de Lamothe Cadillac."[24] Making these changes allowed

Smith College Studies in History 7, nos. 3–4 (April–July 1923): 124. See also Ls-P. Cormier, ed., *Lettres à Pierre Margry de 1844 à 1886* (Quebec: Les presses de l'Université Laval, 1968), ix–x. Indeed, notes regarding the locations of the documents published in the first two volumes of Margry's *Découvertes et établissements des Français* only appear, and with some precision, in volume 3. After that, document attribution is part of each volume, but the source/location of the document is usually provided in general terms, and even if a particular collection is mentioned, volume numbers and pages are not.

20. Margry, *Découvertes et établissements des Français*, 5:674.

21. Ibid., 5:679.

22. See for example Lamothe Cadillac au ministre, 20 [octobre], 1697, Archives Nationales (France), Archives des Colonies, Ser. C11E, 14: ff. 26r–27r (hereafter AN *and series indication*). In extracts of his letters and documents where he is mentioned, Cadillac's name is variously spelled. His own signature, however, is consistent.

23. Margry, *Découvertes et établissements des Français*, 5:75, 678.

24. Ibid., 5:118.

Margry to strengthen the connection between the *mémoire* and Cadillac. In furtherance of this objective, and because the *mémoire* clearly was not in Cadillac's hand, Margry suggested it was written by the latter's scribe "d'Olivier." The handwriting in the *mémoire*, Margry noted, "has affinities" with those of the "old governor's" secretary.[25] Cadillac, Margry added, left the Bastille on February 6, 1718, months before the document's July creation date. Cadillac had been put there based upon accusations that his leadership had led to economic stagnation in Louisiana and that his repeated criticisms of the colony were undermining French interests there.[26]

In short, Margry would have his readers believe that a recently freed Cadillac supervised his secretary's writing of the *mémoire* in 1718 while stationed somewhere on the grounds of the palace of Versailles. Unexplained is how "d'Olivier"—whose first name seems to be unknown—fits the "D . . . D" name of the copyist, why he would hide his identity if he was working for Cadillac, and why he would not know how to spell his employer's name. Indeed, Margry seems to have added the "d" to Olivier's name in order to help it better fit that of the purported copyist. Cadillac's secretary appears to be known in the historical record only as Olivier or "*sieur* Olivier."[27] Moreover, given that Cadillac owed Olivier over 2,000 *livres* for his four years of service with Cadillac in Louisiana, of which only 200 had been paid, it seems unlikely that Olivier would have much interest in further work for Cadillac. Indeed, Olivier's petition asking the Council of the Marine to pay him from what Cadillac was to be given for his appointments as governor—essentially to garnish Cadillac's wages—would suggest a less than amicable employer-employee relationship.[28]

---

25. Ibid., 5:679.

26. Yves Zoltvany, "Antoine Laumet, dit Lamothe Cadillac," *DCB*, 2:351–56.

27. On Olivier's name, see Marcel Giraud, *A History of French Louisiana*, vol. 2 (Baton Rouge: Louisiana State University Press, 1993), 82, 125; and the petition of "Le Sr Olivier Secretaire de M de la Mothe Cadillac cy devant Gouverneur de la Louisiane, 29e 9bre, 1717" in AN, Archives de la Marine, série B 1, vol. 21: ff. 286v–87r. The name is rendered in the same way, with a slightly different title for the petition, in the index to the volume (ibid., f. 348v).

28. "Le Sr Olivier Secretaire de M de la Mothe Cadillac cy devant Gouverneur de la Louisiane, 29e 9b^{re}, 1717," AN, Archives de la Marine, B 1, 21: ff. 286v–87r. Olivier had already written to Cadillac and his son, to no avail. The Council of the Marine declined to take up the matter (ibid., f. 286v).

Also left unsaid by Margry is why Cadillac would write in 1718 about his first command at Michilimackinac when he had already discussed the post and surrounding area at length in letters to the Minister of the Marine and claimed, around 1695, that he was producing such a *mémoire*.[29] Having done that, and given that he was put in jail for his actions in Louisiana, it would make far more sense for Cadillac to write about the latter in order to tell his side of the story to salvage what he could of his reputation, or focus upon Detroit, which he had established and, if not without its problems, was growing in importance. And, in fact, after his release from prison, Cadillac was seeking the return of his property at Detroit and asking that he be granted the post and surrounding area as a seigneury, with all rights of justice, hunting, fishing, and trade, and, further, that the seigneury come with the right to the title of marquis.[30] Indeed, Cadillac was so focused on his claims to Detroit that in a petition to the Council of the Marine he listed his previous commands only as those of Detroit and Louisiana, and failed to mention Michilimackinac—a rather surprising omission if he was touting his role at the latter, and its importance, in the document he supposedly created in 1718.[31] Nor does Margry explain why anyone would bother to copy such a long account written in the first instance, supposedly, by someone in such disfavor with the Crown. Indeed, one must question if the title in "DD's" version of this *mémoire* existed in the original or was added by "DD." After all, if the *mémoire* "DD" copied was written by Cadillac, or someone associated with him, surely his name would be spelled correctly. Even in an age of flexible rules concerning spelling, one could rest assured that someone

29. In those early letters, however, Cadillac painted a far less flattering image of Michilimackinac than that offered in this *mémoire*. See for example Lamothe Cadillac au ministre, 3 aoust, 1695, AN, C11E, 14: ff. 10r–13v. Cadillac's claims about preparing a longer *mémoire* around this time will be taken up below.

30. "La Mothe Cadillac A son altesse serenissme Monseigneur Le comte de Toulouse admiral de france [1718]," AN, C11E, 15: f. 86r. On Cadillac's lengthy efforts, and those of his sons to realize these, and other, claims to Detroit, see Giraud, *A History of French Louisiana*, 2:83–84.

31. See Cadillac's petition Au Conseil de Marine, 1718, wherein he identifies himself as "La Mothe Cadillac, cy deuant Gouuerneur de La Louiziane et precedament Capitaine dune Compagnie, et Commadant du fort Ponchartrain de Detroit sur le lac Erie." AN, C11E, 15: f. 97r.

of Cadillac's ego would insist on his proper name and title—even if it was an invented one.

The question of the *mémoire*'s authorship and date of creation is complicated, but it is worth following all the evidence in the *mémoire*, and elsewhere, to get past the false leads Margry created. Parc au Cerfs (Deer Park), mentioned as the place where the original document was found and copied by "DD," refers to a section of the grounds at the palace of Versailles. In the later eighteenth century the name became associated with a house in which the king kept his concubines.[32] But in 1718 Louis XV was only eight years old. He did not come to occupy the palace until 1722, when he was twelve years old, and mistresses, presumably, were not yet on his mind.[33] In 1718, the reference was to a real park stocked with deer for the king's hunts. It was located to the left of Avenue de Sceaux as one traveled toward the Place d'Armes and the main palace buildings. Protruding into the park, separated from it by walls, but taking its name from the adjacent animal reserve, was a neighborhood that included, in time, hotels, guard houses, and, eventually, an Ursuline convent and chapel.[34] How "DD" and the *mémoire* both came to be at Parc au Cerfs remains a mystery. Given that Parc aux Cerfs housed visitors and soldiers, in addition to others, it is possible that some soldier or traveler who had been in New France brought back a *mémoire* that "DD" found fascinating. But who brought it, who "DD" was, and the chain of events that led to the *mémoire* being copied remain little more than a fascinating set of possibilities.[35]

It has proven impossible to determine "DD's" identity. It is likely that the letters represent the person's real name; otherwise why go to the trouble of masking it? But is it the first name, last name, or the complete name? Possibly

32. Jacques Levron, *La vie quotidienne a la cour de Versailles aux XVIIe et XVIIIe siècles* (Monaco: Librairie Hachette, 1965), 184–85.

33. Alfred and Jeanne Marie, *Versailles au temps de Louis XV, 1715–1745* (Paris: Imprimerie Nationale, 1984), 11, 21. It is properly called Parc aux Cerfs in period plans and drawings.

34. Ibid., 89–91. See especially the image at p. 90 dated to 1693. In 1719, the park shows up in essentially the same shape, number of streets, etc. See Guy Walton, *Louis XIV's Versailles* (Chicago: University of Chicago Press, 1986), image at p. 30.

35. One possible explanation is, however, attempted below.

the name is disguised because of Cadillac's uncertain status in 1718. Even with a complete name, however, it might not have been possible to determine "DD's" identity fully. Some estimates are that approximately 15,000 people lived at Versailles by the end of Louis XIV's reign. It held the royal household, much of Louis's administration, a massive support staff of cooks, guards, personal assistants, carpenters, stone masons, etc., and was almost a city in itself.[36] After Louis XIV's death, the palace was not home to the king until Louis XV returned to it in 1722. Still, it was occupied, and people worked and lived there in the interim.[37] Unfortunately the records of who lived where are scattered, scarce, and incomplete for all but the most illustrious of those who stayed, came, and went at Versailles. Moreover, it is not clear whether "DD" lived there or was passing through, where he stayed/lived, and how he came to find, and be curious about, the *mémoire* in question. Indeed, might "DD" be a female, and might the character of the *mémoire*, with its accounts of war and torture and "loose" sexual practices among Indians, account for the copyist's need for secrecy? It seems unlikely that these questions can ever be fully resolved.

It has proven easier to track down Philippe Buache and the work in which Margry noted that he had seen portions of the *mémoire* he attributed to Cadillac. Buache was a geographer and cartographer who lived from 1700 to 1773. He married the daughter of *Premier Géographe du Roi* (The Geographer Royal) Guillaume Delisle. Buache assumed his father-in-law's title in 1730, the same year he was also elected to the Académie des Sciences.[38] In 1750 Buache published a map, and in 1752 he presented his justifications for the

36. Gilette Ziegler, *The Court of Versailles in the Reign of Louis XIV* (London: George Allen & Unwin Ltd., 1966), 32–34, population estimate at 34; Walton, *Louis XIV's Versailles*, 13, 17, 38–39.

37. Marie, *Versailles au temps de Louis XV*, 26–29.

38. On Buache, Delisle, and their work, see R. V. Tooley, *French Mapping of the Americas: The De l'Isle, Buache, Dezaucher Succession (1700–1830)*, Map Collectors' Circle, no. 33 (London: Durrant House, 1967). On Philippe Buache and his contributions to French cartography, see M. Ludovic Drapeyron, *Les deux Buache et l'éducation géographique de trois rois de France* (Paris: Institut Géographique de Paris, Ch. Delagrave, 1888); and Numa Broc, "Deux géographes 'révolutionnaires': Philippe Buache et Jean Nicolas Buache de La Neuville," in *Cartes, Cartographes et Géographes: Actes du 114ᵉ Congrès National des Sociétés Savantes, 1989* (Paris: Editions du CTHS, 1990), 7–13.

map to the Académie in a series of papers that were later published as a book under the title *Considérations Géographiques et Physiques Sur les Nouvelles Découvertes au Nord de la Grande Mer, appellée vulgairement la Mer du Sud; Avec des Cartes qui y sont relatives*, Par Philippe Buache, Premier Géographe de Sa Majesté & de l'Académie Royale des Sciences.[39] There, in defense of his creating a *mer de l'Ouest* (Western Sea) on his 1750 map, Buache cited the *mémoire* that Margry came to attribute to Cadillac. In the latter half of the second decade of the eighteenth century, some French cartographers, among others, were convinced that a Western Sea existed in western North America and that it protruded into the continent, much as did Hudson's Bay in the north and the Gulf of Mexico in the south. This sea, moreover, was thought to connect to the fabled Northwest Passage across the top of North America. The believers all waxed poetic about the advantages to the French Crown of discovering and controlling this sea. But by the 1750s, few in France still believed in the Western Sea, and Buache was challenged to defend his placing a Western Sea on his map.[40]

In order to defend his 1750 map, and its depiction of the Western Sea, Buache reproduced the work of his respected and deceased father-in-law, Guillaume Delisle, former *Premier Géographe du Roi*. In February 1717,

39. (Paris: l'Académie Royale des Sciences, 1752).

40. On French exploration in North America in the eighteenth century, and the search for the Western Sea, see W. J. Eccles, "French Exploration in North America, 1700–1800," in *North American Exploration*, vol. 2, *A Continent Defined*, ed. John Logan Allen (Lincoln: University of Nebraska Press, 1997), 149–202. The search for the Western Sea was supported and encouraged by the Crown for both scientific reasons and those of national glory in France. In New France, profiting from newfound fur-bearing territories dominated the reasons for the continued search into the 1750s (William J. Eccles, "La Mer de l'Ouest: Outpost of Empire," in *Essays on New France* [Toronto: Oxford University Press, 1987], 96–109). Given that the Crown was willing to support such explorations as long as they did not add to the cost of running the colony, the focus on financial return should not be wondered at. This determination to limit expenses in New France, argues Eccles, was of a piece with the general policy of viewing New France as merely a bulwark against English expansion. Dated, but still useful, are Jean Delanglez's articles, "A Mirage: The Sea of the West," part 1, *Revue d'histoire de l'Amérique française* 1, no. 3 (December 1947): 346–81, and "A Mirage: The Sea of the West," part 2, ibid., 1, 4 (March 1948): 541–68. For a discussion of the search and its cartographic development, see Lucie Lagarde, "Le passage du Nord-Ouest et la Mer de l'Ouest dans la cartographie française du 18e siècle: Contribution à l'étude de l'oeuvre des Delisle et Buache," *Imago Mundi* 41 (1989): 19–43. On the challenge to Buache, see ibid. and Christine Marie Petto, *When France Was King of Cartography: The Patronage and Production of Maps in Early Modern France* (Lanham, MD: Lexington Books, 2007), 113–19.

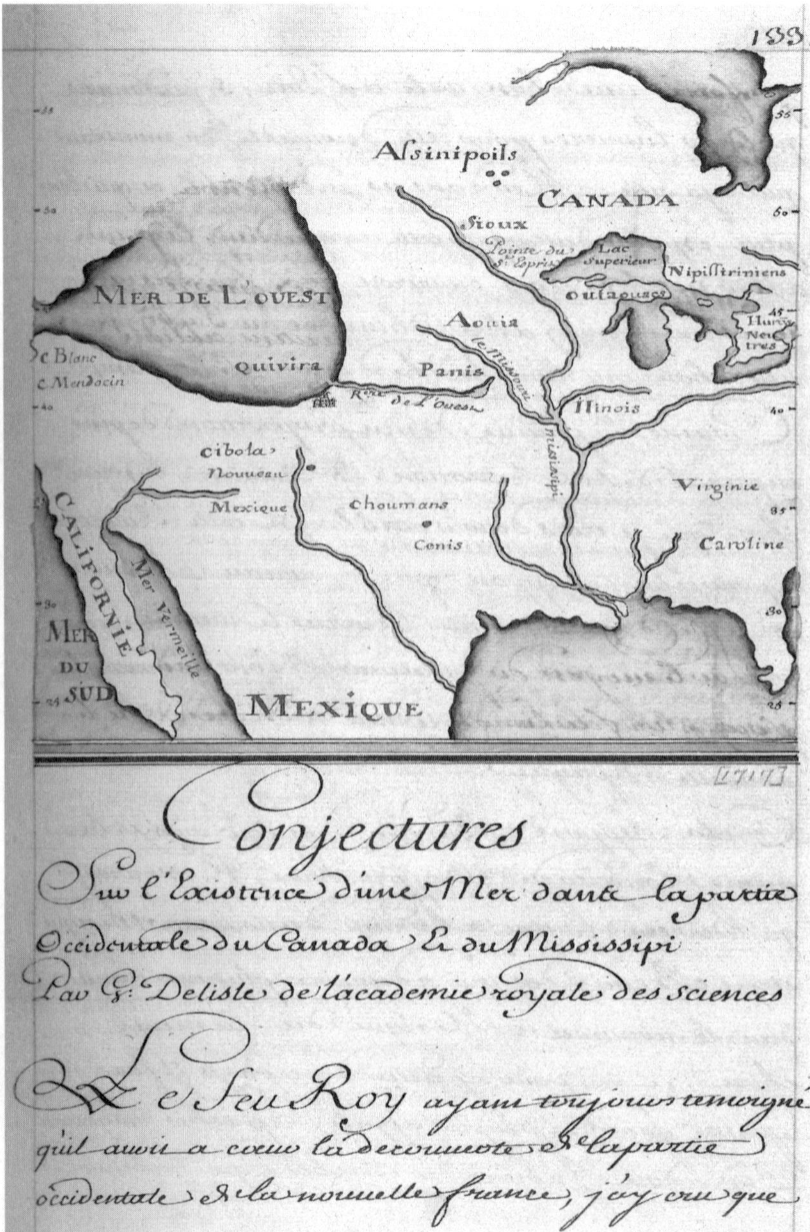

The Newberry Library, Chicago.

3. Guillaume Delisle's map of the Western Sea, which accompanied his 1717 presentation to the court about the Sea. This version is taken from Philippe Buache's 1753 book making a similar claim for the mythical Sea's existence.

Guillaume Delisle had made a presentation to the Court about the Western Sea and produced a *mémoire* titled *Conjectures sur l'existence d'une Mer dans la partie Occidentale de la Nouvelle France [& du Mississipi]*. It was an expansion of a *mémoire* that he had written in 1697 and it had included a map showing an approximate location for the Western Sea. The original map was lost, but someone had kept a copy and Buache reproduced it *exactement* in his *Considérations*.[41] Guillaume Delisle's *mémoire* is also reproduced there.[42] It is, in reality, a combination of his 1697 and 1717 reports, since, as Buache noted, the first one had included citations, including that to a manuscript map by Louis La Porte de Louvigny, who had commanded at Michilimackinac from 1690 to 1694.[43] Buache then carried on the case for a Western Sea by citing references to a possible Western Sea that his father-in-law had not used, and offered a passage from *Un grand Mémoire dressé en 1700 par un Officier du Fort de MichilimaKinaK (à l'entrée du Lac Michigan)* (a long report prepared in 1700 by an officer from Fort Michilimackinac [at the entrance of Lake Michigan]), which stated that

> chez les Nadouessis, il y a une Riviere connue dans la profondeur des Terres jusqu'à milles lieues, selon les Sauvages; que son courrant vient & descend du côté du Nord-Ouest, & qu'elle se joint à celle du Mississipi . . . Ma pensée (dit l'Auteur du Mémoire de 1700) est que par cette Riviere

41. Philippe Buache, *Considérations Géographiques et Physiques Sur les Nouvelles Découvertes au Nord de la Grande Mer, appellée vulgairement la Mer du Sud; Avec des Cartes qui y sont relatives* (Paris: l'Académie Royale des Sciences, 1752), 25. The map is to be found between pages 24 and 25.

42. Ibid., 26–33. Although Buache provided the correct title of Delisle's *mémoire* when referring to it, the version he offered in his book is merely titled "Memoire de Guillaume Delisle sur la mer de l'ouest." Delisle's *mémoire*, somewhat differently titled as *Conjectures Sur l'Existence d'une Mer dans la partie Occidentale du Canada et du Misissipi Par G. Delisle de l'academie royale des sciences*, and a color version of this map, can also be found in Ayer Manuscript Collection, Newberry Library, Ayer MS. 293, 2:133–49, map at 133.

43. Buache, *Considérations*, 25, 30. Delisle's reference to Louvigny's map is virtually the same in Buache and in the version in Ayer MS 293. "J'ai la Copie d'une Carte Manuscrite de M. de Louvigny qui commande en Canada depuis plusieurs années faite par lui sur ses propres connoissances & sur les Relations de plusieurs François . . . ." Delisle in Buache, *Considérations*, 30; "J'ay la copie d'une Carte manuscrit de M. du Louuigny qui a commandé en canada pendant plusieures annés, faitte par luy sur ses propres connaissances, et sur les relations de plusieurs françois . . . ." Delisle, *Conjectures*, Ayer MS 293, 2:142.

> qui passe chez les Sioux, on pourroit découvrir la Mer de l'Ouest; car l'expérience fait voir à ceux qui voyagent dans le Canada que toutes les Riviere prennent leur source de quelque lac situé sur une hauteur de Terres, qui a deux pentes: ce qui forme toujours deux ou plusieurs Rivieres.[44]

If one compares the above to what follows from the *mémoire* Margry attributed to Cadillac, there is no doubt that Buache is using the same document and had merely adjusted the text to modernize spelling and clarify what is evident in the original but not really clear in the part he has chosen to cite, namely, that the author was referring to the Sioux Indian nation:

> IL y a aussi chez cette nation vne riuière connuë dans la profondeur des terres jusqua millle lieues . . . , la riuiere coure et descend du costé de L'ouest et vient se joindre a celle du Missicipi qui va a la mer du sud, ma pensee est quon pourroit par cette riuiere, decouurir la mer de louest, car lexperience fait voir a ceux qui voyage dans ce pais la que toutes riuieres prennent leurs sources de quelque lac situé sur vne montagne, ou hauteur de terre en equilibre qui a deux pentes qui forment quasi toujours deux ou plusieurs riuieres.[45]

What is noteworthy, beyond the fact that Buache cited the *mémoire* as Margry claimed, is that Buache, despite what Margry wrote, did not attribute the *mémoire* to Cadillac, nor did he date it to 1718. Buache explicitly failed to name the officer whose work he was relying upon, and dated the document to 1700. Margry deliberately omitted these facts from his discussion in order to bolster his claim for Cadillac's authorship and a 1718 creation date for the original document.

44. Buache, *Considérations*, 38. This passage is left in French, as is that which follows, for purposes of comparison. To translate them might raise the question of whether the similarities are a function of the translation process. Moreover, even if one can't read French, one can compare words and determine whether or not there are similarities.

45. *Relation . . . De lamotte Cadillac*, 97–98.

From its appearance in Buache's work, the document seems to disappear from the historical record until its association with Michel Chasles, who came to own a copy of the *mémoire* and, in particular, the version at the Newberry. Chasles was a well-known and well-regarded mathematician in France. He was born in 1793 in Épernon and died in 1880 in Paris. Chasles published several seminal works and taught at a number of prestigious institutions during his career. He was also an avid collector of historical materials and late in his life became caught up in a scandal when he purchased a collection of documents purportedly written by famous historical figures, Galileo and Cleopatra among them. The documents (written in French!) were fraudulent, and he was called to testify at the trial of the criminal who produced them.[46]

How, when, and from whom Chasles acquired the *mémoire* that Margry came to publish remains unknown, but as the book plate in the little volume reveals, he did own it for a time. When he sold it is not clear, but it may have been some time before his death. A catalog of his vast library, which was auctioned off June 27 to July 18, 1881, made no mention of it.[47] Possibly Chasles sold some of his library during his life to raise money for the purchase of the fraudulent, it turns out, letters of famous historical figures. Possibly E. Dufossé, a Paris book dealer who specialized in colonial-era Americana and at whose shop Margry had seen the *mémoire*, had purchased the little volume from Chasles before 1881.[48] Dufossé opened his shop in 1876, and Margry came to publish the work he attributed to Cadillac in volume 5 of his *Découvertes et établissements des Français*, which was published in 1883. But as early as October 1882, Francis Parkman, the well-known American historian

46. J. J. O'Connor and E. F. Robertson, "Michel Chasles," http://www-history.mcs.st-andrews.ac.uk. The possibility that the *Relation . . . De lamotte Cadillac* is also a forgery sold to Chasles is vitiated by the fact that it existed, as Buache's reference to it shows, in the mid-eighteenth century.

47. *Catalogue de la Bibliothèque de feu M. Michel Chasles* (Paris: A. Claudin, 1881), 56–95.

48. Edward E. Ayer Papers, Newberry Library, Ayer Collection Correspondence, 1899, box 1, folder 4. An undated invoice from Charles Chadenat, but included in folder 4, has the following information (clearly, given the information that follows, the invoice has been misfiled): "LA LIBRAIRIE AMÉRICAINE ET COLONIALE DE E. DUFOSSÉ (FONDÉE EN 1876) a été annexée à ma Librairie en 1901." Charles Chadenat was Edward Ayer's main Paris-based supplier of rare books and manuscripts. His shop, Americana: Librairie Ch. Chadenat, was located at 17, Quai des Grands-Augustins, 17 Paris (ibid.).

to whom Margry sent proofs of the forthcoming volumes, commented on the "Cadillac" *mémoire*. Returning from a hunting trip in the Adirondacks, Parkman wrote to Margry that he had found "the proofs of the first pages of your 5th volume. I see again some items which are already well known to me with others wholly new, first of all the *Mémoire de La Mothe Cadillac* of which I await the rest with interest."[49] Unfortunately, a search of an admittedly incomplete series of Dufossé's catalogs, and of those of booksellers associated with him, for the period from 1877 to the late 1890s, reveals no mention of Cadillac, or any *mémoire* or relation associated with him that fits the description of the volume in question here.[50]

It is not clear how Chasles's copy of the *mémoire* came to Margry's attention. But he was a researcher with ambitions to publish documents, worked in the national archives, and was in contact with most major scholars in the United States and Canada who wrote about New France. Although he was quite secretive and often unwilling to share access to documents he found, he was often asked specifically about Cadillac by numerous correspondents.[51] This may have led him to look more widely than in the archives in which he worked in order to find something that would make his books more valuable. He had trouble getting interest from a publisher to print the documents he had copied, and sometimes taken, from the archives.[52] It was only with the assistance of Francis Parkman that he was

49. Francis Parkman to Pierre Margry, 17 October 1882, in Wilbur Jacobs, ed., *Letters of Francis Parkman*, 2 vols. (Norman: University of Oklahoma Press, 1960), 2:155 (hereafter *Parkman Letters*).

50. [E. Dufossé], *Americana: Bulletin du bouquiniste, américain et colonial, et de l'amateur de livres relatifs, à l'Asie, à l'Afrique, à l'Océanie, et au nord de l'Europe* (Paris: E. Dufossé, 1884); Anon., *Americana: Autographes, manuscrits, pièces et documents historiques*, 2 vols. (n.p.: Newberry Library, n.d.).

51. See for example Francis Parkman to Pierre Margry, 30 January 1870, *Parkman Letters*, 2:39–40. See also E. Faillon à Pierre Margry, 9 avril, 1853, in Ls-P. Cormier, ed., *Lettres à Pierre Margy de 1844 à 1886*, 83.

52. Wilbur Jacobs, editor of Parkman's *Letters*, remarked (vol. 1:117, note 7) that "one authority" who examined the large Margry Collection held by the French national archives "concludes that Margry tired of the laborious task of copying and filched originals from the archives under his care." Jacobs did not identify his source, but it is not a secret that Margry's papers, eventually acquired by the national library, held original documents as well as copies. See *Catalogue des manuscrits français de la Bibliothèque nationale: Nouvelles acquisitions françaises*, vol. 3, nos. 6501–10000 (Paris: Ernest Leroux, Éditeur, 1900), 276–321, items 9256–510.

able to publish the multivolume work in which the *Relation du sieur De lamotte Cadillac* appeared. Interestingly enough, it was again because Margry refused to share what he claimed were important sources with Parkman. As Parkman wrote to one correspondent, he had a good deal of material for his La Salle biography, "and but for M. Margry, should have still more."[53] To see the documents Margry refused to share, and which he claimed were original, Parkman pushed for their publication.[54] On the other hand, Margry published in the same volume as the *Relation du sieur De lamotte Cadillac* another document, which he indicated came to his attention via a Dufossé catalog for 1881.[55] Possibly he learned of the *mémoire* via the same means.

Nor is it clear how Chasles's copy of the *mémoire* ended up at the Newberry, apart from the fact that it was part of the collection that Edward E. Ayer donated to the library in 1911. How Ayer acquired it, and when, is uncertain. An avid and knowledgeable collector, Ayer may have recognized the uniqueness of the document published in Margry's 1883 work and tracked down Dufossé. Or it may have come to Ayer's attention before that as he checked catalogs for rare materials, or it may have been suggested to him, as were many works, by collectors eager to sell to Ayer. Indeed, it may have come to Ayer's attention when his usual contact for French materials, Charles Chadenat, acquired Dufossé's library in 1901. Unfortunately, a perusal of Ayer's personal papers reveals very little for the period before 1901, and after that to about 1913, while there is more material, there remains no mention of the *mémoire*. On the other hand, Ayer bought a good deal from Chadenat, and only two invoices from the latter appear in Ayer's papers.[56]

53. Francis Parkman to Abbé Henri-Raymond Casgrain, 13 February 1868, *Parkman Letters*, 2:22.

54. Parkman's efforts to get Margry's work published are chronicled in a series of letters from November 1872 to August 1873 (ibid., 2:62–71). Margry was not, apparently, all that grateful for Parkman's efforts. In response to a letter from Margry, Parkman wrote: "With regard to the amount of the appropriation, I would gladly have made it $20,000 instead of $10,000 but it was absolutely out of my power . . . The amount was determined at Washington, and I thought it very fortunate that any money at all was granted" (Francis Parkman to Pierre Margry, 1 August 1873, ibid., 2:71). Margry had amassed far more material than he ended up publishing (ibid., 2:117–18 n. 7). He probably wanted more money in order to publish more material.

55. Margry, *Découvertes et établissements des Français*, 5:674.

56. Edward E. Ayer Papers, Newberry Library, Ayer Collection Correspondence, 1899, box 1, folder 4, invoices from Charles Chadenat, one undated but post-1901, and the other from 1899. In

None of this helps determine, however, the *mémoire*'s authorship (although if one could determine who "DD" was, it might). For that and the time of its creation one needs to turn to the document itself and other sources. It is clear, despite the case that Margry sought to make for a 1718 date, that the original *mémoire* was written before then, and likely before 1701.[57] The spelling, use of accents, or lack thereof, in the *mémoire*, despite Margry's efforts to modernize them, clearly indicate a seventeenth-century creation date. And there are other signs pointing in that direction. For example, the author of the *mémoire* makes reference to the impudence of the Fox Indians (also known as Mesquakies) and suggests that they need to be humbled.[58] Yet in 1716 Louis La Porte de Louvigny, who had also commanded at Michilimackinac, from 1690 to 1694, had led an expedition against the Fox Indians from his base at Michilimackinac.[59] In addition, there are several references to war with the Iroquois Indians, who occupied what is now Upstate New York.[60] In 1701 a peace was concluded with the Iroquois and a wide array of French Indian allies. It was a significant occasion, with over a thousand Indians in attendance in Montreal. The pomp and pageantry drew the attention of numerous observers, and the correspondence of French officials for the year is filled with accounts of the event and the actual terms of the treaties worked out.[61] Finally, another example that suggests a pre-1701 date is the reference to Huron headman Sataresky as the main speaker at

---

the Edward E. Ayer Papers, Ayer Collection Correspondence, box 2, folder 39, is a *List of Early and Rare Books in the Library of Edward E. Ayer, Chicago, 1900*. This is actually a little bound volume with typewritten pages. There is nothing listed relating to Cadillac. Indeed, only published books appear to be listed. The standard published description of the Ayer Collection material, Ruth Butler, comp., *A Check List of Manuscripts in the Edward E. Ayer Collection*, 15, has no provenance information for MS 130, the *mémoire* in question here.

57. Although, as will be discussed below, the 1718 copy of the document may include portions added after its first creation, and not by its creator.

58. *Relation . . . De lamotte Cadillac*, 91.

59. R. David Edmunds and Joseph L. Peyser, *The Fox Wars: The Mesquakie Challenge to New France* (Norman: University of Oklahoma Press, 1993).

60. *Relation . . . De lamotte Cadillac*, 50, 91.

61. On the 1701 treaties, see J. A. Brandão and William A. Starna, "The Treaties of 1701: The Triumph of Iroquois Diplomacy," *Ethnohistory* 43, no. 2 (Spring 1996): 209–44; and Gilles Havard, *The Great Peace of Montreal of 1701: French-Native Diplomacy in the Seventeenth Century* (Montreal: McGill-Queen's University Press, 2001).

conferences of the Huron Indians.[62] Also known as Kondiaronk, and *Le Rat* in French sources, he died in Montreal during the 1701 peace negotiations.[63] It is too much to credit that anyone as knowledgeable as the author appears to be about Michilimackinac and its Indians could not have known all of the above. This evidence, and Buache's dating of the *mémoire* to 1700, lead one to conclude that the original *mémoire* was written sometime before 1701 and not during the summer in 1718.

Margry, however, did not fool every modern scholar interested in the *Relation du sieur De lamotte Cadillac.* Jesuit scholar Jean Delanglez, writing in 1945 and convinced that Cadillac was the author of the *mémoire*, concluded that it was written around 1696–1699. Delanglez cited as evidence the lack of references to Detroit, and letters from Cadillac to various officials announcing that he was creating a map of the Great Lakes region and a little book in which he would discuss what he has learned of Indians, and show their origins from the ancient Hebrews as, in fact, does the *Relation du sieur De lamotte Cadillac.* Quaife followed Delanglez on this matter.[64] However, as discussed below, Cadillac is not the only one said to have produced an account of Great Lakes Indians and a map in this period, and the notion of Indians as descendants of ancient peoples is a common theme in most French works on Indians.[65]

A comparison of the *mémoire* with documents and other works touching on Michilimackinac, and written in the first decades of the eighteenth century, seems to confirm that others knew of the *mémoire* Margry attributed to Cadillac well before Buache cited it in 1752. Unfortunately, the information

62. *Relation . . . De lamotte Cadillac*, 86.

63. William Fenton, "Satareski," *DCB*, 2:320–23.

64. Jean Delanglez, "Antoine Laumet, alias Cadillac, Commandant at Michilimackinac: 1694–97," *Mid-America: An Historical Review* 27 (1945): 110, 202, 212; Quaife, *The Western Country in the 17th Century*, xxi. The question of authorship seems not to have been in doubt after Margry's publication, and Delanglez's dating of it has also been accepted by scholars.

65. See for example Pierre-François-Xavier Charlevoix, *Histoire et description générale de la Nouvelle France avec le Journal Historique d'un Voyage fait par ordre du Roi dans l'Amérique Septentrionale*, 6 vols. (Paris: Chez Pierre-François Giffart, 1744), 6:72–73. Joseph François Lafitau devoted two volumes to the subject: *Moeurs des sauvages ameriquains comparée aux moeurs des premiers temps*, 2 vols. (Paris: Saugrain l'aîné, 1724).

gathered to date only further muddies the waters of authorship. Assuming a circa 1700 date for the original, the *mémoire* was compared to other published or manuscript works produced after 1700. The only one that appeared to have relied on the *Relation du sieur De lamotte Cadillac* was Antoine-Denis Raudot's *Relation par lettres de l'Amerique septentrionale.* Written shortly after 1710, but only published in 1904 and misattributed for many years to the Jesuit Antoine Silvy, Raudot's book is known to be based upon reports prepared by others who lived and worked in New France before he became the intendant there in 1705.[66] Of those sources, the only one that he ever mentioned is Louis La Porte de Louvigny, whose *mémoire* he used, and which has not been seen since. Writing in 1709 to Minister of the Marine Jérome Phélypeux de Pontchartain, Raudot explained that he was sending him a relation about Canada based upon, "as far as the Indians are concerned," a *mémoire* written by "*sieur* Louvigny," who "knows perfectly well the nations" of New France.[67]

Louvigny also produced, about 1697, a well-known and well-regarded map of the Great Lakes and Mississippi River, and, importantly, the author of the *mémoire* attributed to Cadillac noted that he had produced a map showing various geographic features and the locations of Indian nations.[68] Louvigny's map is titled *Carte du fleuue Mississipi auec les noms des peuples qui L'habitent et des Etablissments Espagnols et Anglois qui en sons proches[,]*

66. Camille de Rochemonteix, ed. (Paris: Letouzey et Ané, Éditeurs, 1904). On Raudot as the author, and some of the sources he used but did not credit, see Jean Delanglez, *Frontenac and the Jesuits* (Chicago: Institute of Jesuit History, 1939), 65, note 44; Vernon Kinietz, *Indians of the Great Lakes, 1615–1760* (Ann Arbor: University of Michigan Press, 1940), 336; José António Brandão, ed. and trans., *Nation Iroquoise: A Seventeenth-Century Ethnography of the Iroquois* (Lincoln: University of Nebraska Press, 2003), 21–27. Antoine-Denis Raudot served as intendant of New France from 1705 to 1710, a position he shared with his father, Jacques Raudot. See Donald J. Horton, "Antoine-Denis Raudot," *DCB*, 2:549–54, and "Jacques Raudot," ibid., 554–61.

67. [Marginal note], 24 septembre, 1709, "Correspondance Raudot-Pontchartrain," AN, C11G, 4: f. 242v.

68. *Relation . . . De lamotte Cadillac*, 87. Cadillac, in signed letters, had written that he produced a map of the Great Lakes region, which most scholars describe as "lost." See Delanglez, "Antoine Laumet, alias Cadillac," 202. If Cadillac, indeed, ever produced one, it was not mentioned in official records of the colony or cited by the cartographers of the period.

par de laporte de louvigny.[69] It was this map that Guillaume Delisle cited in support of his *Conjectures sur l'existence d'une Mer dans la partie Occidentale de la Nouvelle France [& du Mississipi].*[70] The map may have been produced in association with the *mémoire* Raudot used, or with Louvigny's plan to continue exploration to the west and southwest of Michilimackinac. In a *mémoire* dated October 14, 1697, Louvigny laid out for the Minister of the Marine his proposal for this planned exploration, and how to fund it.[71] Louvigny also mentioned that during his four-year stay in the "posts among the Indians," that is to say, at Michilimackinac, he worked to promote the king's interests, and that he and *sieur* de Manthet, who had commanded at Chicago, queried Indians for geographic information such as the locations of mines and routes to distant locales.[72] While Louvigny did not mention in his

69. Paris, Serv. Hyd. Bib. 4040 C 10; Ayer Collection, Newberry Library, Map Photo France AN, BN-BSH, box 8, folder SHB C4040–10.

70. See Buache, *Considérations*, 30; [Delisle], *Conjectures*, Ayer MS 293, 2:142. In 1703 Delisle produced a map of North America and a report indicating the sources upon which it was based. He once again listed, among his sources, the *carte m[anuscrit] de* M. de Louvigny. Delisle's 1703 report is reproduced, and discussed, in Jean Delanglez, "The Sources of the Delisle Map of North America, 1703," *Mid-America: An Historical Review* 25 (October 1943): 275–98, quote at 287.

71. "Mémoire pour continuer la découverte des Mines et Établissements des Espagnols dans le Mexique par le Mississipi," Margry, *Découvertes et établissements des Français*, 4:9–18. I have been unable to locate the original of this document in the Archives de la Marine where Margry wrote that it was to be found (ibid., 4:638). Margry rarely cited the particular collection, volume number, or pages from which he drew his documents, and a search through AN C11A, C11E, and F3, where most such Archives de la Marine documents ended up, turns up no such document. It may be that I have failed to look in the right place, or this is one of the documents that, according to Jacobs, Margry "filched." If so, it does not show up in the inventory of Margry's materials in the national library. (See *Catalogue des manuscrits français de la Bibliothèque nationale: Nouvelles acquisitions françaises*, vol. 3, nos. 6501–10000 (Paris: Ernest Leroux, Éditeur, 1900), 276–321, items 9256–9510.) On the other hand, while Louvigny's October 1697 "Mémoire pour continuer la découverte . . . ." is not specifically mentioned in the catalog, the descriptions of the specific items that the library acquired are usually very brief and cover an undefined number of documents comprising hundreds of pages of material, sometimes identified as "copie" and other times without indication of whether it is a copy or not. In the end, Margry's lack of precise attribution was in keeping with his secretive, and proprietary, approach to documents under his care at the Archives Nationales. Even when he agreed to copy documents for people, he did not always offer proper provenance. See for example the complaint of his friend Francis Parkman (Parkman to Margry, 29 December 1881, *Parkman Letters*, 2:148). It is hard to credit that such omissions were not deliberate. On the other hand, Margry was inattentive to details and often even failed to date his letters (Parkman to Margry, 17 January 1873, ibid., 67). Parkman called this an "exasperating habit" (Parkman to Margry, 27 October 1873, ibid., 72).

72. Margry, *Découvertes et établissements des Français*, 4:9, 11.

October 1697 *mémoire* producing a map, route information and the locations of Native nations and mines are plotted on the map attributed to him, and the handwriting on the map matches that of Louvigny in signed letters.[73]

A comparison of language in Raudot's *Relation* to that of the *Relation du sieur De lamotte Cadillac* suggests that Raudot drew information from the *mémoire* that "DD" copied in 1718. However, based on that alone, it is hard to arrive at a conclusive judgment. Raudot did not always copy things verbatim from the sources he consulted; rather, like any clever plagiarist, he often changed a few words here and there, and restructured sentences or paragraphs. As well, he could have borrowed from a large number of manuscripts dealing with Indians in the Great Lakes and not just those to which his work has already been traced.[74] Still, a few phrases that are specific to the *Relation du sieur De lamotte Cadillac* appear in Raudot's work, among them a reference to the Mesquakie Indians being adept at stealing with both their hands and feet.[75] Raudot's language about Indian belief in the immortality of the soul, as well as his description of Native courtship via the *allumette* ritual are not as fulsomely described in the other sources he is now known to have relied upon.[76] In the end, the strongest evidence that Raudot read and used at least some portions of the *Relation du sieur De lamotte Cadillac* is that it was he who gave Buache the copy from which the latter reproduced the passages from that document in his *Considérations*. The *mémoire dressé en 1700 par un Officier du Fort de MichilimaKinaK* (à l'entrée du Lac Michigan), wrote Buache, *m'a été donné par M. Raudot* (was

73. See for example Louvigny au ministre, 21 octobre, 1706, AN C11A, 25: f. 23r; Louvigny au minsitre, 6 [novem]bre, 1706, ibid., 27: f. 20r.

74. For a partial list of those possible sources, see Kinietz, *Indians of the Great Lakes*, 330–38.

75. *Relation . . . De lamotte Cadillac*, 92; Raudot, *Relation par lettres de l'Amerique septentrionale*, 134.

76. *Relation . . . De lamotte Cadillac*, 60, 63–64; Raudot, *Relation par lettres de l'Amerique septentrionale*, 80, 101–2. And, of course, Raudot may have relied on other sources as yet unidentified. Louis-Armand Lom D'Arce, Baron de Lahontan, published journals, in various editions, in which he refers to the "allumette" courtship process. See the second edition of his *Des voyages . . .*, titled *Memoirs de l'Amerique Septentrionale, ou la suite des voyages de Mr. de la Hontan: Qui contiennent la Description d'une grande étenduë de païs de ce Continent . . . .* (Amsterdam: Chez François l'Honoré, 1705), 132 and the plates following.

given to me by *Monsieur* Raudot), who managed New France under the direction of *M. le Comte de Pontchartain*.[77]

But does that mean Louvigny wrote the *mémoire*, or that it was based upon his work and not Cadillac's? Certainly that has to be considered a possibility. Raudot used the *mémoire* and acknowledged his debt to Louvigny's *mémoire* for information about the Indians in his own *Relation*, and Louvigny had commanded at Michilimackinac, had produced a map of the region, and was so well regarded for his knowledge of the Upper Country that in 1720 Louvigny was named *commandant des pays d'en haut* (Commander of the Upper Country), where Michilimackinac was located.[78] Cadillac's map, mentioned in his letters to the court, has never been found, and Louvigny produced one that was known of and used at about the same time as the *mémoire* attributed to Cadillac was originally composed.[79] However, efforts to compare the *mémoire* to Louvigny's map to see if a significant degree of concordance in place and Indian group names would confirm or exclude Louvigny as author of the *mémoire* proved inconclusive. There was, in fact, a good degree of concordance in names and locations of Native groups, etc., but the explicit discussion of the Western Sea found in the *mémoire*, and the central place of the Missouri River as the route to it, is not replicated on the map, although Louvigny places a river (left uppermost part of the map) that

77. Buache, *Considérations*, 38. The draft version of Raudot's relation can be found in AN, C11A, volume 122. Misleadingly titled *Sioux ou Nadouesis*, this version seems to have been planned as more of a history of the colony and less as a summary survey of New France's Native inhabitants. It also includes copies of some of the documents Raudot used to create his final work. Nothing matching the *mémoire* in question here is found there. Nor, among the various documents, emendations, corrections, etc., is there anything that matches the writing of either Cadillac or Louvigny.

78. Yves Zoltvany, "Louis La Porte de Louvigny," *DCB*, 2:345–47.

79. A quick perusal of AN Col. B, volume 19, 1696 and 1697, correspondence from the Court for the years after Cadillac wrote that he was producing his map and account of Indians, reveals no indication that Cadillac's map or *mémoire* were presented and/or received at court. Delisle, as noted above, did not indicate using either, and as the *Premier Géographe du Roi*, it is he who would most likely have been given a map made of New France, and the west, in this period. Delisle's unpublished sketch and research maps, all carefully labeled with their sources of information, reveal nothing by Cadillac (see Ayer Collection, Newberry Library, Map Photo, France AN, Delisle Sketches, vols. 1–7). A review of maps from various archives in France (Marine, Guerre, Hydrographie, etc.) fails to turn up one by Cadillac or an anonymous map that fits the description of what the map should look like (see ibid., Map Photo, BN through BSH, boxes 1–8). Louvigny's map can be found in ibid., box 8, folder SHB C4040-10.

is near the headwaters of the Missouri and is said to drain into the "sea of the west." Given the centrality of the discussion of the Western Sea in the *mémoire*, this can be viewed as a major counterargument against Louvigny as the author of both. Either that, or the section on the Western Sea was written after the map was produced, and possibly even added as late as 1718, when interest in the Western Sea was again stirred up.[80] Still, Louvigny was clearly in a position to have produced what, in 1718, came to be attributed to Cadillac. Indeed, Buache's failure to identify Cadillac, or anyone for that matter, as the author of the *mémoire* he cited, and which the above evidence establishes is that which has come to be attributed to Cadillac, suggests that it might not have had a title, that a title may have been added by "DD" in 1718, or that Raudot or Buache were concealing the *mémoire*'s authorship.

But if Louvigny was the author of a *mémoire* Raudot used and gave to Buache, then why did Raudot fail to identify Louvigny as the source of the *mémoire* he shared with Buache? Raudot, it has now been shown, relied on at least two other sources for the information in his *Relation par lettres de l'Amerique septentrionale*, among them trader and soldier Pierre de Liette for the Great Lakes groups, and captive René Cuillerier for that on the Iroquois.[81] He had literally lied to his superior, Minister of the Marine Jérôme Phélypeaux de Pontchartrain, to give credit to Louvigny for his information on Indians. It defies logic to understand why he would have failed to indicate to Buache that Louvigny was the officer from Michilimackinac who produced the *mémoire* he had shared with him. And if it was Buache who failed to identify the author, what could have been his reasons for doing so when he identified his other sources? Could it have been because his father-in-law had relied on Louvigny's map, said so in the report he wrote and that Buache reproduced, and Buache, to bolster his case, wanted to make it look as if he had found another, independent, source?

There are, unfortunately, no ready answers to the above questions, but there is suggestive evidence that Buache may have, indeed, been playing

80. The notion of the *mémoire* being written over time is discussed more fully below.

81. Kinietz, *Indians of the Great Lakes, 1615–1760*, 336; Brandão, *Nation Iroquoise*, 21–27.

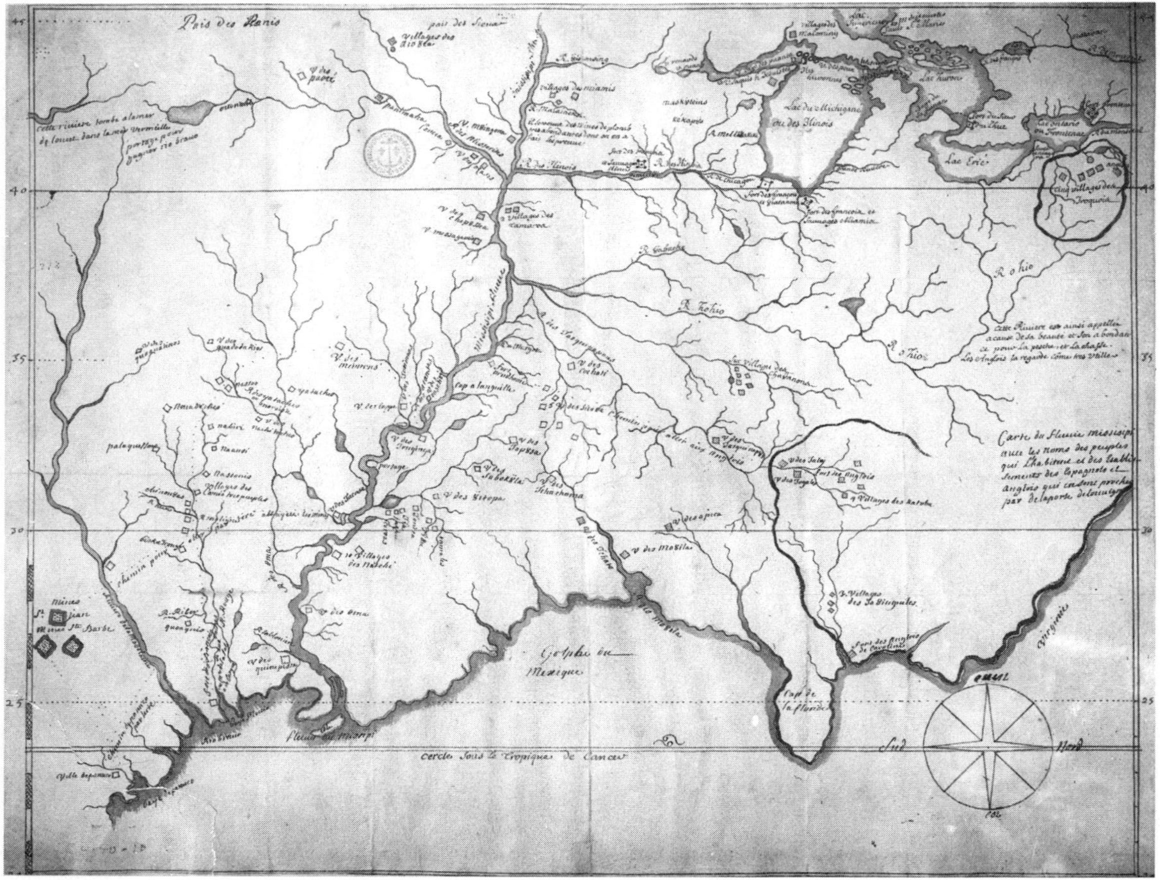

4. Louis La Porte de Louvigny's map showing the Great Lakes and the Mississippi River basins. Note the river at the uppermost left of the map that is said to drain into the "sea of the west."

The Newberry Library, Chicago.

a little loose with his sources. In the section of his *Considérations* where Buache quoted from the unnamed officer from Michilimackinac, he also reproduced a portion of a March 15, 1716, letter from a M. Bobé *Lazariste de Versailles*.[82] Abbé Jean Bobé (1654–1735) was a member of the Congregation of the Mission, also known as the Lazarists of Vincentian, founded in 1625 by Vincent de Paul. He served as chaplain at Versailles, where he had arrived in 1717.[83] The good cleric was quite taken up with the search for the Western Sea, and in his letter that Buache cited at length, Bobé specifically mentioned information on the Western Sea that is almost identical to that found in the 1718 *Relation du sieur De lamotte Cadillac*. Moreover, Bobé made it clear that he got his information from M. la Motte-Cadillac . . . *Gouverneur de MichilimakinaK*.[84] Based upon the information in Bobé's letter—which Buache reproduced in his book—and that which Buache cited from the unnamed Michilimackinac officer, it is hard to fathom how Buache could fail to see that he and Bobé were drawing upon the same work.

Buache's failure to recognize whose work he was citing is even more surprising when compared to the complete letter in question by Bobé.[85] In his lengthy 1718 letter, Abbé Bobé cited passages from a *mémoire* that he on four occasions identified as one produced by *M[onsieu]r de la Motte*.[86] The information in those passages is virtually identical to that which Buache cited as coming from the unnamed Michilimackinac officer and is also found in

82. Buache, *Considérations*, 38.

83. Nelson-Martin Dawson, *L'Atelier Delisle: L'Amerique du Nord sur la table à dessein* (Sillery: Les éditions du Septentrion, 2000), 109–11.

84. Ibid., 38–39.

85. Copies of Bobé's letter, but called a *mémoire* and dated to 1718, exist in several archives. The language from the 1716 letter Buache reproduced in his *Considérations* is too similar to that in the 1718 versions to think it is not the same letter, or a copy of the one Buache had. It is possible that Buache misdated the document he reproduced. See "Memoire pour la decouuerte a faire de la Mer de l'ouest dressé et presenté par M.r Bobé prestre de la Congregation de la Mission, 1718" [Memoirs concerning French Possessions], Newberry Library, Ayer MS 293, 3:109–226; "Memoire Pour La decouuerte de la mer de L'ouest dressé et presenté en Avril 1718 par Bobé prêtre de La Congregation de la mission," AN, C11E, 16: ff. 40r–50v. The supposed original is in the Bibliothèque Mazarine. Lagarde, "Le Passage du Nord-Ouest," 28. Lagarde has found a map by Bobé with the Western Sea depicted, but reduced to the size of a gulf (ibid., 28–29, map at 29).

86. "Memoire pour la découuerte a faire de la Mer de l'ouest dressé et presenté par M.r Bobé prestre de la Congregation de la Mission, 1718," Newberry Library, Ayer MS 293, 3:121–22.

the 1718 *Relation du sieur De lamotte Cadillac.* One can only conclude that Buache was dense, deliberately trying to create the illusion that he had more sources for his claims about the Western Sea than he, in fact, had; or he was convinced, for reasons that he did not share, that Bobé was completely mistaken about who had produced the *mémoire* they both used.

Abbé Bobé, however, appears to have had no doubt about his sources, and his comments and involvement with what has come to be known as the *Relation du sieur De lamotte Cadillac* appear to resolve a number of the questions raised earlier about the document's creation and history. The question of authorship seems to be resolved. Clearly Bobé was convinced he knew who had produced the *mémoire* he was citing. His evidence for a Western Sea came, he wrote, from *M[onsieu]r de la Motte dans le memoire qu'il a fait et presenté a la Cour Lors qu'il estoit commmandant de MissilimaKinaK, et dont j'ay vne Copie* (*sieur* de la Motte in the memoir that he made and presented to the court when he was commandant of Michilimackinac, and of which I have a copy).[87] Cadillac commanded at Michilimackinac from 1694 to 1697 and traveled to France at the end of 1697.[88] This, and the fact that Bobé came to reside at Versailles, may account for how the document got to Versailles and why it might have been copied. "DD" might simply have been a copyist, working in 1718 at the behest of Bobé or some Crown official interested in a memoir that had so much to say about the Western Sea that had captured the imagination of some at court in the second decade of the eighteenth century.

That, however, would be too neat a resolution to the story. In 1698, during his stay in France, Cadillac was pleading for the creation of Detroit as a new settlement—one that would be a gateway to the west, which could control Iroquois expansion; replace the forts, such as those at St. Joseph and Michilimackinac, that had been ordered closed by the king; and serve as the

87. Ibid., 3:121. See also "Memoire Pour La decouuerte de la mer de L'ouest dressé et presenté en Avril 1718 par Bobé prêtre de La Congregation de la mission," AN, C11E, 16: f. 43r, where that assertion is repeated verbatim: *Monsieur De lamotte dans le memoire qu'il a fait et presenté a la cour lors qu'il éstoit Commandant de Missilimakinac et dont jay une Copie* . . . .

88. Zoltvany, "Cadillac," *DCB*, 2:351–56.

heart of a new colony in the west of New France.[89] Why would he present to the court an account of Michilimackinac in which was made essentially the same argument for that location? One possible answer to this question is that by "presented to the court" Bobé did not mean present in person. Cadillac's *mémoire* could have arrived sometime before his 1697 trip to France. The other possibility is that scholars have been wrong about the purpose of Cadillac's trip to France. He may, indeed, have gone to France to try to save Michilimackinac, presented his *mémoire* on the place and its inhabitants, and only when his request was denied did he turn to the creation of Detroit as the means to return to command and add to his fortune in New France. Certainly as late as October 1697, he was still writing to the Minister of the Marine to reconsider the decision to close Michilimackinac.[90]

Nor can it be assumed that Bobé got the *mémoire* he attributed to Cadillac from Cadillac in the 1690s. Bobé served as chaplain at Versailles, but he only took up that position in 1717, and there is no indication that he knew Cadillac before then. Bobé was, after all, very interested in the Western Sea and connected with numerous important people at court, including Raudot. Thus, Bobé may have obtained the *mémoire* he attributed to Cadillac from Raudot, or found the one that "DD" later copied.[91] For one needs to consider that, if Buache's dating of Bobé's letter to 1716 is correct, the one in which Bobé explicitly mentioned Cadillac as his source, then Bobé had a copy of the *mémoire* he attributed to Cadillac before 1718. But, to make matters more complex, Louvigny had also gone to France after 1694, and he had as much reason as did Cadillac to play up the importance of Michilimackinac as a gateway to the west and southwest surrounded by an array of important Native allies and trading partners. That is evident from his 1697 plan for

89. Ibid.

90. Lamothe Cadillac [au ministre], 20 octobre, 1697, AN, C11E, 14: ff. 28r–29v. Cadillac, in any case, changed his mind and tactics quickly. By May 1699, Louis XIV was writing to leading officials in New France asking them to comment on Cadillac's plans for Detroit, a copy of which he included in his instructions to them. See "Memoire du Roy au Sieurs Callieres et Champigny," 27 mai, 1699, AN Col. B, 20: ff. 215r–215v.

91. Antoine-Denis Raudot died at Versailles in 1737 and certainly would have had opportunity to give both Buache and Bobé the *mémoire* in question.

continuing La Salle's explorations. It may have been on that occasion that Louvigny gave Guillaume Delisle his map. On the other hand, if Louvigny had a *mémoire* as well, why did he not give it to Delisle, and if he did give him one, why did the latter not cite that in support of his conjectures about the Western Sea?[92] To muddy the waters even more, Bobé knew and corresponded with both Raudot and Delisle, and it is hard to credit that he did not confirm with Cadillac, around 1718, that it was his *mémoire* even if he had obtained it through Raudot or, if Buache's dating is correct, simply found "DD's" version. Bobé apparently knew Cadillac and corresponded with him.[93] Cadillac, moreover, one can presume, might have been around Versailles after his release from the Bastille if for no other reason than to try to repair his reputation.[94]

None of this, however, resolves the questions raised in discussing Raudot's actions, those of Buache, and Margry in dealing with the *mémoire* in question. Margry's, indeed, may be the easiest to resolve: he was simply a careless or unprincipled editor and historian with too little respect for his sources and his readers, when he had a position to advance. However, why he would have a "position to advance" in the case of Cadillac is not clear. Certainly Margry was fixated on the idea of establishing before the world that the French, even if booted out of North America, had been among the first Europeans to "discover" and map most of it. That is evident from his published works and the sort of materials he gathered and that remained unpublished. But why would he care whether it was Cadillac or some other Frenchman who had written the document he came to publish? Certainly it would make no

92. Unless, again, the Western Sea section was not part of the *mémoire* before 1700.

93. See Bobé's comment, reproduced by Buache in his *Considérations* (39), that he pestered Raudot and Cadillac to look for the Western Sea. On knowing Cadillac, see Bobé's references to "M. La Motte" in a 1718 letter to Guillaume Delisle in Dawson, *L'Atelier Delisle*, 239. Raudot is mentioned in this same correspondence, in ibid., 233–37, 239, 241–44.

94. One is tempted to speculate that Cadillac himself might have given Bobé his mémoire for the latter to copy. Associating himself, and his work, with the renewed interest in the Western Sea might serve to rehabilitate Cadillac's image at court. Still, Bobé's language suggests that he got the *mémoire* indirectly. If he had obtained it from Cadillac, he surely would have made that known explicitly, and Cadillac would have made sure that his name was properly spelled on the document he gave to Bobé.

difference to his larger purpose. Possibly he was such a follower of the "great man" approach to history; Cadillac was considered such by those with whom Margry corresponded, and perhaps he was so insecure about his place in the pantheon of scholars of French "new" world studies that he felt compelled to be the one who produced a "new" Cadillac document. Margry had, it appears, plans to write a biography of Cadillac and had gathered materials to that end.[95] There appears to be even less of an answer to the question of why either Buache or Raudot failed to acknowledge who wrote the *mémoire* Buache cited and that Raudot had given him.

Lastly, it is worth noting that there is another version of the *Relation du sieur De lamotte Cadillac*, and perhaps not so surprisingly, it is also housed at the Newberry, part of the Ayer Collection, and its existence raises as many questions as it potentially answers about who wrote the *mémoire* attributed to Cadillac. The second version of the *Relation du sieur De lamotte Cadillac* is to be found in Ayer MS 293, volume 3, pages 362–449. It has the same title and much of the same text, although few of the internal chapter divisions, of "DD's" 1718 version. It follows a document dated 1721, precedes one from 1724, and is part of a volume dated to 1727 that is filled with *mémoires*. I have found no references in the historical literature to this version of the *Relation du sieur De lamotte Cadillac*.[96]

The group of volumes in which it is found has no single title but is listed in Newberry materials as "A collection of memoirs concerning French possessions, 1702–1750."[97] It is not clear from whence these dates derive since there are numerous documents that antedate 1702 and none post-1732. Nor do the dates match those on the respective volume covers. The volumes are

95. See *Catalogue des manuscrits français de la Bibliothèque nationale: Nouvelles acquisitions françaises*, vol. 3, Documents pour servir à la biographie d'Antoine de La Mothe-Cadillac . . . sa correspondance avec la cour . . . 201 feuillets," 283, item 9298.

96. I came across the reference to the second copy of the *mémoire* in the Newberry catalog while looking for other documents written about the same time as the 1718 version and which I hoped might have similar handwriting. What I found was, I thought, a published work, and only a conversation with Mr. John Aubrey, Ayer Collection librarian, pointed out my error—which point he made very graciously and for which I am thankful.

97. Butler, comp., *A Check List of Manuscripts in the Edward E. Ayer Collection*, 33–35.

not numbered but have been assigned numbers 1–4 by the Newberry. All are bound in the exact same material and style: brown leather, embossed/gilded writing on the spine and on the cover. The volumes vary in length, from over 850 pages of text in volume 2, to 393 in volume 4. They average 32 cm long and 21 cm wide. The writing is not the same across all the volumes but appears mostly the same within each volume, but that is not always the case. The writing in the fourth volume, in particular, is quite varied. Each volume has a different title on the spine and the same information on the front cover, all in block letters, *A LA SVBSTITVTION/ DV VALDEC / PROCHE SOLEVRE / EN SVISSE /*, followed by a date.[98] Each volume has a stamp on the inside of the front flyleaf indicating that it came from Ch. Chadenat's shop. Three of the volumes have a table of contents with no further title or information beyond that on the spine. The exception is the first volume, which indicates, at the table of contents, that the material was gathered to assist commissioners negotiating at Ryswick—presumably the Treaty of Ryswick concluded in 1697, although there are documents that postdate that year.[99] It is nonetheless possible that the documents were gathered for the purposes of negotiations between French officials and others. The materials in the volumes appear to be drawn from French archives, what later came to be the Colonial and Marine archives. The dates on the covers may represent those during which negotiations took place or when the documents were copied in preparation for negotiations. That would account for the post-1697 documents in volume 1. The material there may have been gathered, at first,

98. The information about the respective volumes is as follows: [Vol. 1] On the spine is written—all in block letters: *MEMOIRES / DE LA / MARINE / COMMERCE / & COLONIE*. On the front cover, all block letters: *A LA SVBSTITVTION / DV VALDEC / PROCHE SOLEVRE / EN SVISSE / MDCCXXV* [1725]. Title on table of contents page: *Memoires par rapport au Traitté general concernant les Colonies, la Navigaation et le Com[m]erce Mss[rs] Les Commissaires Plenipo[t]aires à Ryswick*. It has a table of contents. [Vol. 2] Spine: *MEMOIRES / DE LA LOVISIANA / ST. DOMINGUE / MARTINIQUE / CAIENNE GUINCE / DES ILLES DE BOURB / DE FRANCE & / DE PONDICHICRI*. On the front, same as above with the date MDCCXXVII [1727]. It has neither an additional title nor table of contents. [Vol. 3] Spine: *MEMOIRES / DE L'AMERI. / & OPINION / DE L'ORIGI / DE SES / HABITANS*. On the front, same as above with the date *MDCCXXVII* [1727]. It has neither an additional title nor a table of contents. [Vol. 4] Spine: *ETABLIS / DES / ILSES / FRANCOI / ET / CHRONOL / CHINOISE / TROUBL / DE CONST / APRILE 28 / [S]EPT 1730*. On the front, same as above with the date MDCCXXXII [1732].

99. See for example 74–118, a 1698 memoir on trade and commerce, and 28–73, which dates to 1708 and is signed by Raudot.

for negotiations at Ryswick, but then enhanced for whatever negotiations took place in 1725. However, the period covered by the dates on the volumes (1725 to 1732) was one of relative peace in France, with the exception of the War of Polish Succession, and seem to have included no major negotiations related to France's North American holdings.[100]

There is some information about these volumes in Newberry catalogs. Ruth Butler, *A Check List of Manuscripts in the Edward E. Ayer Collection* (33–35), indicates that they were acquired by Edward Ayer in 1899, but an invoice in Ayer's papers reveals that only one volume was purchased that year and that it was a companion volume to the "three others purchased last year."[101] Yet another volume, one made up of maps, seems to share the same binding, cover design, and title. The latter volume was taken apart, the maps cataloged individually, and they form the basis of the Newberry's *Cartes Marines* collection. The information about the latter collection makes reference to the four volumes of documents known as Ayer MS 293 and mentions that the map volume may have been compiled by, or for, the Besenval brothers. It is likely that all the volumes were prepared for Jean-Victor Besenval. He was born in 1671 at Soleure, Switzerland. He entered the service of France in 1689 as a cadet in the Swiss Guards, and in 1706 he was made a special envoy and minister plenipotentiary to negotiate a treaty with Sweden and Poland. In 1713 he was again sent as ambassador to Poland and remained there until he asked to be recalled in 1721. He died in Paris, December 11, 1736.[102] Valdec, or Waldeck, was the name of his ancestral estate. He may have just wanted copies of the materials that ended up in the

100. Emmanuel Le Roy Ladurie, *The Ancien Régime: A History of France, 1610–1774* (Oxford: Blackwell Publishers, 1998), 334, 341, 344–47; Gaston Zeller, *Histoire des relations internationales*, vol. 3, *Les temps modernes: De Louis XIV à 1789* (Paris: Librairie Hachette, 1955), 170–221.

101. Edward E. Ayer Papers, Ayer Collection Correspondence, 1899, box 1, folder 4, invoice for 17 V [May?] 1899. Purchased for 400 francs was *Manuscrit provenant de la 'Substitution du Valdec' et formant la compliment des trois autre achetés l'année dernier*. There is no indication as to which volume was purchased in 1899 and which others in 1898. Other volumes fitting the description of Ayer MS 293 apparently exist at, among other places, the Bibliothèque Nationale in France.

102. J. Balteau, M. Barroux, M. Prevost et al., eds., *Dictionnaire de biographie française*, 20 vols. to date (Paris-VI: Librairie Letouzey et Ané, 1932–), 6:308–9.

volumes in question for his estate library. This supposition is reinforced by the word "substitution" in the cover title. In the seventeenth century the word meant more than replacement. It also referred to a right attached to noble property that the owner could not sever from it.[103] Thus a translation of "A LA SVBSTITVTION DV VALDEC PROCHE SOLEVRE EN SVISSE" might be "For the estate at Valdec, near Solevre, in Switzerland."

The 1727 version of the *Relation du sieur De lamotte Cadillac*—for lack of a better identifier—may be based upon the 1718 version made by "DD," but at this point that cannot be concluded with certainty. It may just as easily have been based upon the original or another copy. The title of the 1727 version matches that of 1718, with the exception that Cadillac's name is spelled more in accordance with his own practice: *Relation du sieur de La Mothe Cadillac Capitaine en pied ayant vne Compagnie de La Marine en Canada, cy deuant Commandant de Misilimakinak et autres Postes dans Le pays Eloigné, ou il a esté pendant trois années.*[104] Still, a number of differences between the two copies are worth noting here. Some changes are relatively minor. For example, the number for chapter 1 is missing, and chapter 2 is marked. After that, chapter divisions no longer follow the 1718 "Parc au Cerf" version, and new titles become more frequent and more directly related to the topic that follows in the text. In some cases the titles are merely what, in the 1718 edition, were the enlarged first words of a paragraph—this is especially true when one comes to the section on Indian nations. At other times the titles are created anew.

More substantive differences include a change in description of a cultural practice. In the section on the treatment supposedly accorded adulterous Miami women, the copyist changed the number of young men involved in the gang rape punishment from the "2–300" in the 1718 edition to "two or three." The latter change makes more sense for a number of reasons, not the

103. "Substitution," in Émile Littré, *Dictionnaire de la langue française* (Colombes: Gallimard et Hachette, 1958).

104. This is the title found on the first page of the 1718 copy and not that on the title page. A line-by-line collation has been completed, and the differences are all noted in the transcription.

least of which is the absurdity of the number in "DD's" version and the fact that Miami groupings were rarely large enough to gather that many men. It is hard, however, to know whether that change represents a "logical" correction of the 1718 edition or reliance upon language in the "original" manuscript—that of the 1690s. Another notable change is in a section on geographic information. Whereas in the 1718 copy the coordinates for the source of the Mississippi River are provided, in the 1727 version that information is missing and it is written that the source of the Mississippi *est encore jnnconnuë* (is yet unknown). The missing information, and corresponding to that of the 1718 copy, is added as a note a page later. It is hard to imagine that a scribe would make a decision to delete something as central to the concerns of those searching for the Western Sea as the coordinates of the source of the Mississippi. Possibly the "yet unknown" wording was in the original version of the document, that dating to the 1690s, and the coordinates added in the 1718 version when the author had some confidence as to the Mississippi's source. If so, that would suggest that the 1727 version was not based entirely upon the 1718 "Parc au Cerf" copy.

The recovery of the second version of the *Relation du sieur De lamotte Cadillac* clears up none of the remaining questions about its history and adds one more question to the extant list. It is found in association with a number of documents by Abbé Jean Bobé. It follows, in volume 3 of Ayer MS 293, a lengthy treatise on the origins of America's peoples, and another on the Western Sea.[105] Is it possible that Besenval ordered a copy of Bobé's version of the *Relation du sieur De lamotte Cadillac* and which Bobé had used for his discussion of the Western Sea? Bobé seems to have assigned to himself the role of gatherer of sources for cartographer Guillaume Delisle, and it may

105. "Remarques Sur l'origine des Peuples de l'Amerique par Mr. Bobé prestre de la Mission," Ayer MS 293, 3:1–109. It is undated, but precedes one by the same author about the Western Sea dated 1718. It is clearly written in response to a question about the origins of people in the Americas. Regarding the Indians, Bobé summarized the debate in Europe (descendants of Adam and Eve? a species of human somewhere between humans and ape? a second Adam and Eve—one specific to the Americas?), and concluded that Indians are human, descendants of the one Adam and Eve and, like the rest of the world, the descendants of Noah (ibid., 1–3). Bobé then traced the way that may have happened and sought to link specific Indian tribes to specific nations: Sioux to Chinese (35), Ottawa to the Chananéns from Mesopotamia (36).

have been that process that led to the preservation of the *Relation du sieur De lamotte Cadillac*, whose name is spelled in the 1718 edition, perhaps not coincidentally, as Bobé most often wrote it.[106] Did he tell "DD" to add Cadillac's name to the *mémoire*, and by doing so strengthen the document's value as an "attributable" source and help rehabilitate Cadillac's image? Again, there are no answers to these questions, and one must simply consider that another copy of the *Relation du sieur De lamotte Cadillac* points to the document's continued life and importance among those in France interested in the *pays d'en haut* centered on Michilimackinac, and the region's original inhabitants.

Of course, all of this supposes that the 1718 "Parc au Cerf" document is a faithful copy of an original document, written by one person and all at one time. There remains, however, the possibility of forgery or compilation by others—at least for the 1718 and 1727 copies. For example, neither Louvigny nor Cadillac had visited the lower Mississippi region before 1700 and when the evidence indicates, as discussed above, the original document (or most of it) was written. Yet the *Relation du sieur De lamotte Cadillac* contains a good deal of information about the Natchez, a Native group located on the lower Mississippi River.[107] Some information in the *Relation du sieur De lamotte Cadillac* about Natchez cultural practices, such as sun worship, godlike leader, and human sacrifice, can also be found in the accounts by survivors of René-Robert Cavelier de La Salle's voyages to the mouth of the Mississippi.[108] Some of that same information is also found in the journals

---

106. See the Bobé-Delisle letters in Dawson, *L'Atelier Delisle*, 231–44.

107. See pages 104–10 of the transcription and translation below.

108. Nicolas de La Salle (no relation to Robert), "Relation dela découverte que Mr. dela Salle a faite dela Riviere de Mississipi en 1682, Et de son retour jusqu'a Quebec," Ayer MS 293, 3:229–64. A version of the "Relation de la descouverte que M. de La Salle a faite de la rivière Mississipi en 1682 et de son retour jusqu'à Québec," can also be found in Margry, *Decouvertes et établissements*, 1:547–70. See also *Relation écrite de Québec, le 14 novembre, par Henri de Tonty*, 1684, ibid., 573–614; Henri Joutel, *Journal historique du dernier voyage que feu M. de laSale fit dans le Golfe de Mexique, pour trouver l'embouchure, & le cours de la Riviere de Missicipi, nommé à present la Riviere de Saint Loüis, qui traverse la louisiane . . . Par Monsieur Joutel, l'un des Compagnons de ce Voyage, redigé & mis en ordre par Monsieur de Michel* (Paris: Chez Estienne Robinot, 1712). Joutel's "journal," which is actually a composite of writings, most by Joutel, has been recently translated. See William C. Foster, ed., and Johanna S. Warren, trans., *The La Salle Expedition to Texas: The Journal of Henri Joutel, 1684–1687* (Austin: Texas State Historical Association, 1998).

of French soldiers and missionaries to the region in the few years after 1700.[109] The information in these reports surely must have circulated in the St. Lawrence colony, and at least the account attributed to Henri Tonty, who accompanied La Salle on his first voyage and went looking for him after he failed to return from the second, was published by the late 1690s.[110] Tonty, who traveled regularly to Michilimackinac in the 1690s to exploit his license to trade in the Illinois region, would have had ample opportunity to discuss his southern travels, and those he encountered along the way, with both Louvigny and Cadillac, who commanded the post, each in their turn, from 1690 to 1697.

But of all the sources on the Natchez written by 1700, none mention the woman warrior and village leader Noema, who fascinated the author of the *Relation du sieur De lamotte Cadillac*. The account of such a figure, unnamed, appears only in an unpublished, at the time, account by the Jesuit missionary Jacques Gravier. The good father made a trip down the Mississippi in 1700 and wrote up his findings in February 1701. Not only does Father Gravier's account of Natchez practices most closely match that in the *Relation du sieur De lamotte Cadillac*, but it also notes the important role of women as coleaders among the group and recounts the story of a woman leader among the Houmas, a group that was culturally and politically allied to the Natchez. Gravier was shown, he wrote, "the bones of the woman Chief who died last year. That woman had so distinguished herself by the blows she had inflicted upon their enemies, having in person led several war-parties, that she was looked upon as an Amazon, and as the mistress of the whole village."[111]

This information raises some interesting issues. First, Father Gravier's

109. See, for example, "Journal D'un Voyage fait avec Mr. d'Iberville de la rade de Bilocehis dans le haut du Mississipi avec un detail de tous ce qui sest fait de puis ce temps jus quau depart des vaisseau par le R[évérend] P. Du Ru Jesuit," Ayer MS, 262. The former has been translated: Ruth Lapham Butler, ed. and trans., *Journal of Paul du Ru [February 1 to May 8, 1700] Missionary Priest to Louisiana* (Chicago: Printed for the Paxton Club, 1934).

110. The story of this publication will be discussed below.

111. "Relation or Journal of the voyage of Father Gravier, of the Society of Jesus, in 1700, from the Country of the Illinois to the Mouth of the Mississpi River . . . 16th of February, 1701," *JR* 65:101–79, quote at 147.

relation was sent to his superior in Quebec, Father Jacques de Lamberville. Even if it arrived the year it was penned, 1701, it is not clear how Cadillac would have gotten hold of it—certainly only after it had become more widely known in the colony, as he was on terrible terms with the Jesuits and they would be unlikely to simply pass along the information.[112] Louvigny may not have been on better terms with the Jesuits,[113] but his 1697 map locates both the Natchez and the Houmas, and that information is of a piece with his 1697 request for continued exploration of the Mississippi. Either way, this information on the woman leader suggests that the information was added after 1702 and after the original draft of the document was written. However, if either Cadillac or Louvigny added that information, why would they not, as well, have changed the references to pre-1700 events that, by 1702, they would have known to be out of date and incorrect?

Further suggestions that the 1690s *mémoire* may been have amended over time, if not reconstructed and by other than the original author, is Abbé Bobé's 1718 *mémoire*. In that document he revealed that the document he attributed to Cadillac, again called "la Motte," indicated that the source of the Mississippi *est encore jnconnuë* (is yet unknown).[114] In reality, however, the coordinates for the source of the Mississippi are found twice on page 100 of the 1718 "Parc au Cerf" copy. Bobé, then, was either ignoring evidence that would have helped make his case, or he was not using the 1718 "Parc au Cerf" copy of the *Relation du sieur De lamotte Cadillac*. The fact that, as noted above, the 1727 copy of the *Relation du sieur De lamotte Cadillac* also did not have those coordinates, and that they were later added as a note, suggests the

112. See, for example, Letter by Reverend Father Étienne de Carheil to Monsieur Louis Hector Callières, governor . . . 30th of august, 1702, ibid., 201, 247.

113. He certainly was not on better terms with at least Father Carheil, who, although he did not name him, seems to have lumped Louvigny in with Cadillac in his critique of the moral and ethical failings of Michilimackinac's commanders (ibid.). Father Carheil singled out only Olivier Morel de La Durantaye, who commanded at Michilimackinac from 1683 to 1690 as a good post commander (ibid., 237). Louvigny was not without fault, and two years after he was given command of the fort he was accused of charging an unauthorized one beaver pelt "tax" to all traders passing through the fort. Champigny au ministre, 10 novembre 1692, AN, C11A, 12: f. 91r.

114. "Memoire pour la découuerte a faire de la Mer de l'ouest dressé et presenté par M.r Bobé prestre de la Congregation de la Mission," 1718, Ayer MS 293, 3:122.

existence of more than one copy of *Relation du sieur De lamotte Cadillac* or that the 1690s document was altered over time. Nor is this practice unknown. Numerous scholars have pointed to the forgeries related to early travel narratives, and Henri Tonty's story is a particularly relevant example. His two letters to his patron in France, Abbé Eusèbe Renaudot, wound up altered and published under his name, and without his permission, during his lifetime. He disavowed the publication, for which he was chastised by other explorers for the embellishments to reality and which he claims he did not write. Still, the work was so popular that it appeared in English translation almost within a year of its French publication.[115] The little book titled *Dernières découvertes dans l'Amérique Septentrionale de M. de la Salle* was reprinted several times. In 1734 it appeared in a five volume set: *Recueil de Voyages au Nord, contenant Divers Memoires . . . .*[116] In the fifth volume is found, among other things, the *Relation de la Louisanne & du Fleuve Mississipi par le Chevalier de Tonty, Governeur du Fort Saint Louis aux Islinois.*[117] It includes, between pages 36 and 37, Delisles's 1718 map of Louisiana.

Interestingly, the notion of a copy of a work altered by someone other than its original author does help explain the misspelling of Cadillac's name, the hidden name of the copyist, and the inconsistency of the post-1700 information in the *Relation du sieur De lamotte Cadillac* without correcting

115. On "constructed" travel narratives, see Percy G. Adams, *Travelers and Travel Liars, 1660–1800* (New York: Dover Publications, 1980). For the situation in New France, see John R. Carpenter, *Histoire de la littérature française sur la Louisiane de 1673 jusqu'à 1766* (Paris: A.G. Nizet, 1966). Tonty's narrative was compiled from two letters he sent to Abbé Renaudot, one in 1684 and another in 1693 (ibid., 62, 63). Tonty repudiated that publication for its various errors and embellishments, which were not, in fact, found in his actual letters (ibid., 63). For the full story of all the machinations and constructed publications, see ibid., 89–120, 212–16. The English translation seems to have first appeared in 1698: Henri de Tonty, "An Account of Monsieur de La Salle's Last Expedition and Discoveries in North America Presented to the French King, and published by the Chevalier Tonty . . . Made English from the Paris Original. Reprinted from the London edition of 1698," in *Collections of the New York Historical Society*, vol. 2 (New York: Van Winkle and Wiley, 1814), 217–341. Tonty's 1684 letter can be found in Margry, *Découvertes et établissements des Français*, 1:573–614; and that of 1693 in Pierre Margry, ed., *Relations et mémoires inédits pour server a l'histoire de la France dans les pays d'outre-mer* (Paris: Challamel Aîné, Éditeur, 1867): 1–36. As with anything by Margry, the claim to unedited material should be taken with a grain of salt.

116. (Amsterdam: Chez Jean Frederic Bernard, 1734).

117. Ibid., 35–195.

that which suggests lack of knowledge about other post-1700 events. It also helps account for Buache's or Raudot's possible reluctance to name its author. After all, if the person preparing the 1718 "Parc au Cerf" copy was adding information, and possibly a title, to a document without the author's approval or knowledge—whether at someone's behest or to benefit personally in some way from making those changes—it would make sense to keep one's name hidden. That same "editor" might also not know enough to update the events, and information, that predate his involvement with the *mémoire,* nor Cadillac's preferred spelling of his name. Raudot or Buache, for their part, if they were working with a version other than the 1718 "Parc au Cerf" one, may have been using something without a title or, at least in the case of Raudot, one he knew had been edited by the time he gave it to Buache. This would be especially true if he had used, in his own work, information from the *mémoire dressé en 1700 par un Officier du Fort de MichilimaKinaK* (à l'entrée du Lac Michigan), and which he had attributed to Louvigny.

In the end, however, it appears that the questions surrounding the *Relation du sieur De lamotte Cadillac* cannot be fully resolved. It is not possible to conclude that the document is La Porte de Louvigny's lost *mémoire* or that it was not by Cadillac. Or, to be more precise, based upon something that Cadillac may have written about 1695 when he claimed that he had prepared a "summary of all the information he had discovered of the country" for the Minister, along "with a map of all the lakes and rivers he saw, and that he was informed of, as much by the Indians as the French."[118] The preponderance of evidence, independent of Margry's meddling, is in his favor. Cadillac's name is on the two known copies, and there is no irrefutable evidence that the title of the *Relation du sieur De lamotte Cadillac* was either erroneously or fraudulently added. And while there remain nagging questions about the document's history and changes over time, and intriguing questions about Louvigny's possible association with it, none can be resolved in a way that firmly removes Cadillac from the picture. Cadillac, however, appears to have

118. [Extract of a letter by] Le sr. de laMothe Cadillac, de sa lettre du 16 aoust, 1695, AN C11A, 13:261v.

had no hand in the version that was copied by "DD" in 1718 and reproduced by Margry in 1883, or that done in 1727. Both copies may have been made thanks to Abbé Jean Bobé, whose interest in the Western Sea around 1718 coincides with the two known copies of the *mémoire*. Louvigny's lost *mémoire* and Cadillac's lost map appear to remain that way.

The *Mémoires* of Bégon and d'Aigremont

The two documents that follow are far less problematic than the *Relation du sieur De lamotte Cadillac*. These much shorter *mémoires*, that of Daigremont au ministre, 14 novembre, 1708,[119] and Begon, *Memoire sur l'establissement de MichilimaKina*, 20 septembre, 1713,[120] are both dated and signed by the men who wrote them or, more likely, had them prepared for their signature. François Clairambault d'Aigremont was a naval commissary in New France. He served in the colony from 1701 and died at Quebec in 1728.[121] Michel Bégon de La Picardière was, among other things in a long career in the service of France, the intendant of New France from 1712 to 1723.[122]

Despite the fact that d'Aigremont's and Bégon's *mémoires* have been previously published, there is value in a new translation because there are numerous problems with the versions in print, not the least of which is the lack of scholarly apparatus and both the quality and completeness of the translations. In the case of d'Aigremont's document, for example, one "translation" is in reality a much abbreviated and modernized summary of the document. It is also written in the third person and not as d'Aigremont wrote it. First published in Electa M. Sheldon's *The Early History of Michigan: From the First Settlement to 1815*, the translation was based upon a transcript of the original ordered by Lewis Cass, who served, among other posts, as governor of Michigan Territory from 1813 to 1821. Cass had the *mémoire*

119. Archives Nationales de France, Archives des Colonies, Series C11A, 29: ff. 68r–77v.

120. Archives Nationales de France, Archives des Colonies, Series C11A, 34: ff. 128r–133v.

121. Étienne Taillemite, François Clairambault d'Aigremont, in *DCB*, 2:146–47.

122. Yves F. Zoltvany, "Michel Bégon de La Picardière," ibid., 3:57, 61–62. He was not, however, able to leave the colony and be officially relieved of his duties until 1726.

copied sometime between 1836 and 1842 when he served as United States ambassador to France.[123] This same translation appears, again without indication of its truncated nature, in the *Collections of the State Historical Society of Wisconsin*.[124] There the sections of the document that Sheldon had set apart in quotation marks, to indicate a direct translation from the French rather than a summary of it, are removed. A second translation of the document, more faithful to the original text, was published by the Michigan Pioneer and Historical Society in its historical *Collections*.[125] It is likely that this version of the document is not taken from Cass's transcription but is, rather, based upon a transcription of the original ordered by Clarence M. Burton. Burton, a businessman and avocational historian of Detroit, served as the president of the Michigan Pioneer and Historical Society for a number of years. Between 1874 and 1914 he collected, or had copied, French-language materials, with a special focus on Cadillac and the Detroit region, and which he later donated to the city of Detroit.[126] The documents in the two volumes of the *Michigan Pioneer and Historical Society Collections* (*MPHSC*) known as "The Cadillac Papers," amidst which is d'Aigremont's *mémoire*, were taken from among twenty-four manuscript volumes that "were collected, compiled, translated and edited from the Marine Archives of Paris, under C.M's [Clarence Burton's] direction."[127] According to Milton Milo Quaife, the

123. (New York: A. S. Barnes and Co., 1856), 280–94. The section dealing with Michilimackinac is at pp. 288–94. On Cass providing the copy of the document for Sheldon to translate, see ibid., 5.

124. WHC, 16:257–60. R. G. Thwaites, editor of the series and this volume, indicated that the translation is that of Sheldon (ibid., 251). It is not clear if Sheldon made all the changes to the document when she translated it, or if the changes were introduced when it was copied for Cass.

125. *Michigan Pioneer and Historical Society Collections* (Lansing, MI: Robert Smith Printing, 1904), 33:424–52, for the section on Michilimackinac (hereafter *MPHSC*). A further abridged version of this same translation is found in Timothy Kent, *Rendezvous at the Straits: Fur Trade and Military Activities at Fort de Buade and Fort Michilimackinac, 1669–1781*, 2 vols. (Ossineke, MI: Silver Fox Enterprises, 2004), 1:172–74.

126. Patricia Owens Burton, *Clarence Monroe Burton: Detroit's Historian* (Detroit: Burton Abstract and Title Co., 1953), 22, 42, 74. Burton sometimes copied materials himself and at times photographed documents (ibid., 22).

127. Ibid., 64; *MPHSC*, 33: iv–v. Interestingly Burton, who first had it translated, did not publish in these volumes the *mémoire* Margry attributed to Cadillac along with the latter's other papers. Possibly it would have taken up too much space in the Society's two volumes, which were already a departure from precedent in that they featured few, if any, papers by members. Nor

person who translated this wealth of material was "Miss Edith Moodie," who was a "long-time employee" of Burton's London bookseller, B. F. Stevens.[128] The *MPHSC* version of d'Aigremont's *mémoire*, unfortunately, also omits whole sections without indication of what, or how much, had been removed. Among the omitted sections is a paragraph critical of the colony's governor-general, Philippe de Rigaud de Vaudreuil, his conduct of the trade and Indian relations at Michilimackinac, as well as a folio page discussing the illegal trade, and those who conducted it, at the post.

There is only one translation of Bégon's *mémoire* and it is also, without indication of such, abridged.[129] Published in the *Collections of the State Historical Society of Wisconsin* in 1902, the translation was likely made, or reviewed, by R. G. Thwaites, the volume and series editor, and based upon a transcription of the document in the Paris archives.[130] Among the information left out of the first translated paragraph is the news about war against the Fox Indians. Given that the French wanted to reestablish the fort at Michilimackinac precisely to war against the Foxes, one can only wonder at the editorial decision to exclude that information.

The *Mémoires*, Michilimackinac, and the *Pays d'en Haut*

All three *mémoires*, prepared at different times for varying reasons, provide a window into Michilimackinac's centrality to the French imperial and trade network, and the place of Indians in French policy in this period. Furthermore, the information in them contributes to understanding trends, enduring and new, in the scholarship of French and Indians in the upper Great Lakes.

Despite the complicated history of the *Relation du sieur De lamotte Cadillac*, it seems clear that it was written, in the first instance, and whether

did Burton publish the *mémoire* at another time. The work's focus on Michilimackinac, rather than Detroit, may have made its publication less pressing to Burton.

128. Quaife, *The Western Country in the 17th Century*, xxiii.

129. WHC, 16, 295–98.

130. Ibid., xii.

by Cadillac or Louvigny, to make a case for the importance of the *pays d'en haut* centered on Michilimackinac. The 1690s marked a period of intense warfare with the Iroquois, who were based south of Lake Ontario and raided regularly into the St. Lawrence colony and attacked French Native allies far and wide.[131] Despite the difficulty of getting to Michilimackinac along the Ottawa River (period maps indicate anywhere from twenty to thirty-two portages along the route), it remained more viable before 1701 than any southern route. Until the Iroquois, who dominated the regions north and south of Lakes Ontario and Erie, made peace in that year, it was simply not safe to consider otherwise, and Michilimackinac remained relatively safe and economically and militarily important. Furthermore, however one got there, Michilimackinac's strategic location, as all three documents note, was its major asset: it was a gateway to the west and future riches and potential Indian allies, and in the center of a known universe of Native groups. The latter already served as vital trading partners and, if managed properly—the French believed—could assist in controlling less-willing trade partners, and as allies in wars. Moreover, the focus of French policy, at least within the colony, and as the preoccupation with the Western Sea indicates, was expansion westward, and Michilimackinac would continue to be a major entrepôt facilitating that movement of goods and people. The *Relation du sieur De lamotte Cadillac* thus stresses the linkages north and west from Michilimackinac, south to the Mississippi via Lake Michigan and its watersheds, and, later, to the mythical Western Sea. Another important feature of the document is the enumeration of Native groups and their potential fighting strengths and the roles they, and their lands, could play in French plans.[132] Underlying all the above is the discussion of the fur trade, its

131. José António Brandão, *"Your fyre shall burn no more": Iroquois Policy towards New France and Its Native Allies to 1701* (Lincoln: University of Nebraska Press, 1997).

132. In this regard, the document fits neatly into the "customs of the Indians" model outlined by Gordon M. Sayre in his *Les Sauvages Américains: Representations of Native Americans in French and English Colonial Literature* (Chapel Hill: University of North Carolina Press, 1997), especially pp. 79–143. Sayre points to the various ways Indians are represented and challenges historians to recognize the tropes and motifs of this sort of writing as a way to, among other things, distinguish between fact and invention. It remains the case that this *mémoire*, regardless of who wrote it, offers descriptions of Natives in the region and their locations beyond

importance in French political and economic aspirations, and the centrality of Michilimackinac to those plans.

The circumstances that led to the two other documents below, and their aims, are much clearer, but they both pick up the theme of Michilimackinac's importance and the role of Natives in French trade and imperial ambitions. The documents also stress the need for careful management of the trade with an eye to maintaining all important Native customers, suppliers, and allies. D'Aigremont's *mémoire* was the result of a commissioned voyage to the western posts to study what was going on there in terms of trade and which posts were most useful.[133] Louis XIV awaited d'Aigremont's report and instructed New France's leading officials, Governor-General Philippe de Rigaud de Vaudreuil and Intendant Jacques Raudot, to make sure it was sent to him when it was completed.[134] Vaudreuil and Raudot did not fail to send the report that "*sieur* d'Aigremont submitted to them in execution of his orders, [and] as he is a very honest man, they are persuaded that he will give himself the honor of sending you the truth in all things."[135] The king was pleased with what he read and informed Vaudreuil and Raudot that d'Aigremont "had provided an exact account of the voyage he had made by order of the King in the frontier posts in the colony of Canada," and that he "has resolved to follow his advice."[136]

What d'Aigremont recommended was closing Detroit and reestablishing the garrison at Michilimackinac headed by a commander who was respected by the Indians in the region. This was, he argued, important to show Great Lakes Native groups that the French had their interests at heart and could be relied upon to provide them with those goods they wanted. To do otherwise

those found in accounts by missionaries. And, if clouded by a particular agenda, the picture presented reflects familiarity with most of the groups, or information derived from those who had traveled and lived among them. That is, in the end, the same limitation for all the sources that deal with Natives from a perspective other than their own.

133. Le Roi à MM. de Vaudreuil et Raudot, 30 mai 1707, *Rapport de l'Archiviste de la Province de Québec, 1939–1940*, 359 (hereafter, *RAPQ*).

134. Memoire du Roi à MM. de Vaudreuil et Raudot, 6 juin, 1708, ibid., 408. As noted above, Jacques Raudot shared the position of intendant with his son Antoine-Denis.

135. MM. de Vaudreuil et Raudot au Ministre, 14 novembre, 1708, ibid., 450.

136. Memoire du Roi à MM. de Vaudreuil et Raudot, 6 juillet, 1709, *RAPQ, 1942–1943*, 409.

was to risk losing their trade to the English and, worse, Native allegiance. D'Aigremont also railed against Cadillac's conduct and establishment at Detroit as threats to all these things. These were the very concerns that Cadillac's detractors had expressed in opposing his plans for opening a post at Detroit.[137] D'Aigremont also advised tighter regulation of who could trade and increasing the prices paid for furs, again with the aim of protecting the fur trade and maintaining Native support. To regulate the trade, he recommended returning to the use of *congés*, fur trade licenses limited in number and to be given only to reputable traders.[138] Although both the governor and intendant of New France agreed with d'Aigremont, Jesuit opposition to more traders into the interior delayed the return of the *congés*, but Minister of the Marine Ponchartrain did scale back plans for Detroit and did approve the reopening of Michilimackinac.[139] But it would take another report and further deterioration of Indian-French relations before the *congés* would be approved and Michilimackinac actually garrisoned.

The period from 1712 to 1718, during which Michel Bégon de La Picardière was intendant, was a turbulent one in the history of the colony. Official policy concerning the western posts remained in flux, the economic fortunes of the colony continued tied to the fur trade, and if war with the English colonies was concluded by the Treaty of Utrecht (1713), troubles with the Fox Indians were only getting worse.[140] Bégon and Governor Vaudreuil, to make matters

137. Cadillac's machinations leading to the creation of Detroit, his claims for it, and the consequences his critics feared are discussed in Richard Weyhing, "'Gascon Exaggerations': The Rise of Antoine Laumet dit de Lamothe, Sieur de Cadillac, the Foundation of Colonial Detroit, and the Origins of the Fox Wars," in *French and Indians in the Heart of North America, 1630–1815*, ed. Robert Englebrecht and Guillaume Teasdale (East Lansing and Winnipeg: Michigan State University Press and University of Manitoba Press, 2013), 77–112. Weyhing argues that while Cadillac was undoubtedly a schemer, he was successful because he couched his plans in language that appealed to the Crown and its aims (ibid., especially pp. 97–101).

138. See W. J. Eccles, *The Canadian Frontier, 1534–1760* (Albuquerque: University of New Mexico Press, 1978), 113; Joseph L. Peyser and J. A. Brandão, eds. and trans., *Edge of Empire: Documents of Michilimackinac, 1671–1716* (East Lansing/Mackinac Island: Michigan State University Press/Mackinac State Historic Parks, 2008), xxvi–xxvii.

139. Yves Zoltvany, *Philippe de Rigaud de Vaudreuil: Governor of New France, 1703–1725* (Toronto: McClelland and Stewart, 1974), 116–19.

140. The classic exposition of French imperial policy in the 1700s remains William J. Eccles's "The Fur Trade and Eighteenth-Century Imperialism," *William and Mary Quarterly*, third series, 40, no. 3 (July 1983): 341–62. That view was recently questioned by one of Eccles's students

worse, did not share a vision about how to resolve the various problems New France faced. Not one to hide his views, Bégon determined, after only a year in the colony, to give the king his candid opinions concerning what should be done about Michilimackinac. In doing so he contradicted d'Aigremont's recommendations and put himself in opposition to Vaudreuil.[141]

Bégon's 1713 *mémoire* was an effort to weigh in on New France's western policy at a time of growing tension in the *pays d'en haut*. Using a rather simplistic cost-benefit analysis approach to the reopening of Michilimackinac, Bégon concluded that there was no pressing need to send Louvigny, the man chosen by Vaudreuil as early as 1709, to reestablish the fort to deal with the Foxes, and even less so without some form of revenue to maintain the post. Unlike Vaudreuil, Bégon was ambivalent about using *congés* to raise funds, but saw no other way other than funds from the Crown, which he was unwilling to spend without explicit orders from Ponchartrain. He was critical of Vaudreuil's support of trading to the posts, but conceded, as had d'Aigremont before him, that the illegal trading had served French aims by keeping the Indians from the *pays d'en haut* from taking their furs to the English and, thereby, potentially undermining their alliances with the French. Vaudreuil, upset at the delays such recommendations would entail, sent Louvigny to France to argue for the opening of the post.[142] In 1715, the *congés* were restored and Louvigny made preparations to return to Michilimackinac.[143]

(Dale Miquelon, "Ambiguous Concession: What Diplomatic Archives Reveal about Article 15 of the Treaty of Utrecht and France's North American Policy," *William and Mary Quarterly* 67, no. 3 (July 2010): 459–86). Miquelon challenges Eccles on the notion that after 1701, French policy was merely to contain the English and not to expand west. Using Article 15 of the Treaty of Utrecht as an entry point, Miquelon argues that it was of a piece with long-standing ambivalence to western expansion, as evinced by Colbert's earlier compact colony approach outlined by Eccles. The best history of the French in the *pays d'en haut* in this period is Gilles Havard's *Empire et métissages: Indiens et Français dans le Pays d'en Haut, 1660–1715* (Québec and Paris: Septentrion/Presses de l'Université Paris-Sorbonne, 2003). On the Fox Wars in particular, see R. David Edmunds and Joseph L. Peyser, *The Fox Wars: The Mesquakie Challenge to New France* (Norman: University of Oklahoma Press, 1993).

141. On Vaudreuil's policy and governorship, see Zoltvany, *Philippe de Rigaud de Vaudreuil: Governor of New France, 1703–1725*.

142. Zoltvany, *Philippe de Rigaud de Vaudreuil: Governor of New France, 1703–1725*, 134.

143. Ibid., 144–45. Louvigny, however, professed illness and did not leave for Michilimackinac until

In the end, even Bégon, newly arrived in New France and eager to start his administrative career there on a sound financial footing, had to concede the importance of the fur trade, Indians, and Michilimackinac in French colonial policy.

The importance of Indians has long been a staple of New France's history. It was inevitable for several reasons: not only is it a rare document from this period that fails to mention them, but scholars of New France have long focused on the fur trade and warfare, and Indians have been central to those stories—even if the focus has not always been on the *pays d'en haut*. In recent years the Upper Country and Michilimackinac have received particular attention, beginning with the much-lauded work of Richard White and the less-heralded but equally important work of Gilles Havard.[144] White's *The Middle Ground* has been criticized for, among other things, too much of a focus on the imperial aspect of Native-Euroamerican interaction, and given its similar nature, the like may be said of Havard's work.[145] Still, to be fair, one of White's goals in that work was to include the Indians in the *pays d'en haut* in the larger discussion of forming the early American republic.[146] Havard, for his part, sought to look at the *pays d'en haut* and the consequences of contact between Natives and French on both groups as a means to explore its place in the French empire. As a result, he puts greater emphasis on the tensions in Franco-Indian relations in the *pays d'en haut* and draws more attention to what the Indians wanted out of the relationship. Still, both White's and Havard's focus on Indians and the *pays d'en haut* reflect growing and long-due recognition of the place and its people. That Indian-centered focus on the *pays d'en haut* is continued in

1716. Louvigny au ministre, 3 octobre, 1715, AN, C11A, 35: f. 220r.

144. Richard White, *The Middle Ground: Indians, Empires and Republics in the Great Lakes Region, 1650–1815* (Cambridge: Cambridge University Press, 1991); Havard, *Empire et métissages.*

145. And, indeed, Michael McDonnell has made that observation; Michael McDonnell, *Masters of Empire: Great Lakes Indians and the Making of America* (New York: Hill and Wang, 2015), note 6, p. 333.

146. For a good scholarly evaluation of White's work, including his own assessment of it, see Susan Sleeper-Smith, Richard White et al., "Forum: The Middle Ground Revisited," *William and Mary Quarterly*, third series, 62, no. 1 (January 2006): 3–96.

recent works by Michael Witgen and Michael McDonnell.[147] As the subtitles to these works reveal, it was the Indians who shaped that new world and the America that followed it—Witgen making the case for the role of the Ojibwe, and McDonnell for that of the Odawa in that process.

The three *mémoires* offered here clearly reflect this trend toward more fully recognizing that the Indians really had the upper hand in their relations with the French. Despite what Richard White has written about a "middle ground" of accommodation in some matters, an equally (if not more) apt view of the period to 1718 in the Great Lakes is one of "shifting ground." (Although to be fair, the history of the region is too complex to be subject to a one-size-fits-all metaphor or catchy turn of phrase.) The Indians' world changed dramatically as a result of interactions with the French. In the period up to about 1690, due to war, disease, and dislocation, the ground shifted under their feet and they suffered a good deal of loss in terms of people and control over their socioeconomic and political aims. But in the period from 1690 to 1718, in the region centered around Michilimackinac, the ground shifted again—to belabor the metaphor—and they held the upper hand in their relations with the French. This is made clear in the *mémoires*, which reveal tensions about how to establish French security against some Native groups and English colonies, and promote economic growth. In either scenario, however, the Indians of the Great Lakes were vital to French plans. Indians eventually lost control of their world, but that process was not inevitable or consistent. In the Great Lakes in the period 1690 to 1718, they were in charge again.

The documents, their recommendations, and the contexts of their creation also reveal the tensions between longtime colonial administrators and those in France, or newly arrived from there, as in the case of Bégon. These tensions between metropole and frontier are readily evident in the careers

147. Michael Witgen, *An Infinity of Nations: How the Native New World Shaped Early North America* (Philadelphia: University of Pennsylvania Press, 2012); Michael McDonnell, *Masters of Empire: Great Lakes Indians and the Making of America*. The latter offers the most recent critique of White (ibid., notes 6 and 7, pp. 333–34).

of some of New France's leading, and sometimes controversial, figures. The careers and views of men like Louis de Buade, Count of Frontenac; Vaudreuil; and Cadillac reveal, along with their personal ambitions, their sense of what it takes to advance imperial policy in a context where the economic, political, and military well-being of the colony relied as much on Indians as it did on anything else.[148] While it can be difficult, and very often impossible, to distinguish policy initiatives that may have served personal aggrandizement from those in the best interests of the colony, New France endured because colonial officials such as those mentioned in the three documents, and those who responded to them, wanted the colony to succeed. If they made their fortunes along the way, all the better.

Lastly, all three *mémoires* also point to the importance of information, however suspect it may have turned out to be, as the basis of French policy decisions. The French may have been, as historian James Pritchard suggests, reluctant imperialists, but they seemed determined to govern well what they did have.[149] Scholars can be thankful for that quest for understanding about their colony, and those who lived in it long before the French arrived. The vast store of documents it has produced, including those translated here, shed light on the heart of Indian North America and the role its people and places played in shaping history and contributing to its development.

148. On Vaudreuil, see Zoltvany, *Philippe de Rigaud de Vaudreuil*, and for Cadillac, Richard Weyhing, "'Gascon Exaggerations': The Rise of Antoine Laumet dit de Lamothe, Sieur de Cadillac, the Foundation of Colonial Detroit, and the Origins of the Fox Wars," and the sources cited there. W. J. Eccles's 1959 biography of Frontenac remains the definitive study. W. J. Eccles, *Frontenac: The Courtier Governor*, intro. by Peter N. Moogk (Lincoln: University of Nebraska Press, 2003).

149. James Pritchard, *In Search of Empire: The French in the Americas, 1670–1730* (Cambridge: Cambridge University Press, 2004). The importance of information, and its timely arrival at the desks of decision makers, along with its accuracy, have drawn renewed scholarly attention. See Kenneth J. Banks, *Chasing Empire across the Sea: Communications and the State in the French Atlantic, 1713–1763* (Kingston, ON: McGill-Queen's University Press, 2002); Paul W. Mapp, *The Elusive West and the Contest for Empire, 1713–1763* (Chapel Hill: University of North Carolina Press, 2011). Mapp's work, with its focus on the impacts of England, Spain, and France's misunderstanding of the interior of North America, has particular resonance with the focus on the Western Sea in the *Relation . . . De lamotte Cadillac.*

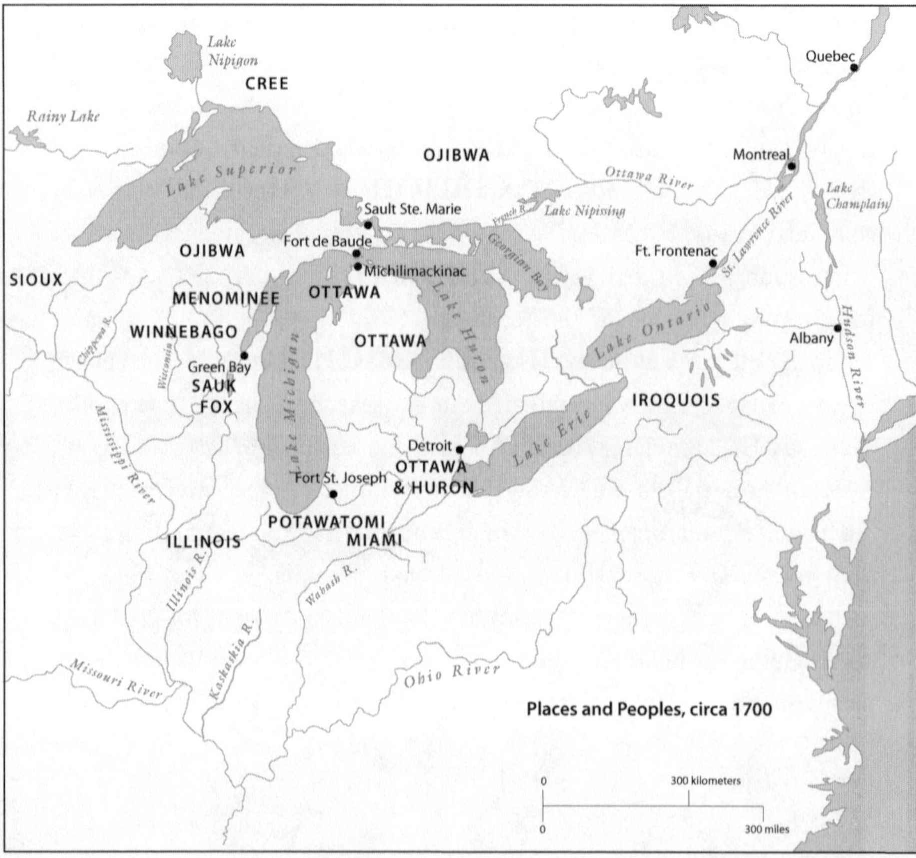
Lake Nipigon
CREE
Rainy Lake
Lake Superior
OJIBWA
Quebec
Montreal
Ottawa River
Lake Champlain
Sault Ste. Marie
French R.
Lake Nipissing
Fort de Baude
Michilimackinac
OJIBWA
SIOUX
MENOMINEE
OTTAWA
Georgian Bay
Lake Huron
Ft. Frontenac
St. Lawrence River
WINNEBAGO
Chippewa R.
Wisconsin
Green Bay
SAUK
FOX
OTTAWA
Lake Michigan
Lake Ontario
Albany
Hudson River
IROQUOIS
Mississippi River
Detroit
OTTAWA
& HURON
Lake Erie
Fort St. Joseph
POTAWATOMI
MIAMI
ILLINOIS
Illinois R.
Wabash R.
Kaskaskia R.
Missouri River
Ohio River
Places and Peoples, circa 1700
0
300 kilometers
0
300 miles
Ellen White

Relation
of the *sieur*
De lamotte Cadillac

[Title page]

190.[1]

RELATION DV SIEUR [in red ink]

De lamotte Cadillac capitaine
en pied, aiant vne compagnie
de la Marine en Canada cy
deuant commandant De
MissilimaKinaK et autres pos
tes Eloigneé ou il a eté pendant
trois annees.
ouvrage tres curieux, tiré sur
L'orignal de Lauteur et non encore
Imprimé
Par D. . . .D.[2]
A Versailles au Parc au Cerf
1718

1. The meaning of this number remains a mystery. Margry did not copy the number, or this title page, at the start of his transcription. He cited this title, and following information, at the end of volume 5. There he altered the spelling of Cadillac's name to Lamothe. (Margry, *Découvertes et établissements des Français dans l'ouest et dans le sud de l'Amérique septentrionale*, 5:678–79. Unless otherwise indicated, page references to Margry that follow are to this work.) The number 190, and a title page with indication that the work is a copy, etc., are missing from the 1727 version of the memoir found in Ayer MS 293, 3:362–449. References to "1727" copy are to this source.

2. See the introduction regarding the probability of identifying the copyist.

[Title Page]

Relation of the *sieur*
De lamotte Cadillac, Captain
en pied,[1] having a Company
of the Marine in Canada, the
aforementioned [being the] Commandant of
Michilimackinac and other
distant posts where he was for
three years.
A very interesting work, based upon
the author's original and not yet
printed. By D . . . D.,
at Versailles at Parc au Cerf,
1718.

1. The French phrase used here, *en pied*, is often translated as "of the foot" as a way to indicate an infantry captain, and *gens de pied* (literally foot people, but meaning foot soldiers) was one way to refer to infantry in this period (as was *infanterie*). But *en* is a preposition that can mean either "on" or "in." Thus, it reads "on his feet," which can be translated as "at the ready" and which suggests active duty status. The *Dictionnaire de l'Académie française* (1st ed., 1694) defines *officier en pied* as an officer in charge of a company of men, whether infantry or cavalry. My thanks to Joseph Gagné for the reference.

[1]

RELATION DU SIEUR delamotte[3] Cadillac capitaine en pied aiant vne compagnie dela marine en Canada. cy deuant commandant de MissillimaKinaK et autres postes dansles païs Eloignees, ou il a ete pendant trois annees.[4]

Chapitre Ie[5]

MissilmaKinacK[6] signifie en nostre langue L Isle de la Tortue il peut se faire quon la nomme ainsi soit pour auoir[7] la forme soit pour y en auoir trouué quelqu'vnes aux environs, elle est dans le lac huron, aiant a peu prés deux lieues de tour elle est a vne lieüe et demie de la terre ferme jnhabitée elle nest frequenteé qua Raison de la pesche tres abondante qu'on y fait tout autour.[8]

---

3. Margry (75) changed the name to "Lamothe." It is spelled "La Mothe" in the 1727 copy (362).
4. In addition to the changes in the words, Margry (75) rendered all of the title in block letters. Only the first three words are in block letters in the 1718 copy. There are no block letters in the 1727 copy.
5. Chapter designation missing in 1727 copy (362).
6. "MissilimaKinaK" in 1727 copy (362).
7. Margry (73) changed this to *parce qu'elle en a la forme*. It is *pour en auoit* in 1727 copy (362).
8. Margry (75) rendered this as *que dans la saison de la pesche*. The wording in the 1727 copy (363) is as that here.

[1]

Relation of the *sieur* delamotte Cadillac, Captain in charge, having a Company of the Marine in Canada, the aforementioned [being the] Commandant of Michilimackinac and other posts in distant lands where he was for three years.

1st Chapter

Michilimackinac means, in our language, "The Island of the Turtle." It could be that it was named thus either because it had that shape, or for some having been found thereabouts. It is in Lake Huron, being nearly two leagues around, and a league and a half from the inhabited mainland.[2] It is frequented for no reason other than the abundant fishing, which they do all around [there].

2. In this period the French league, as a unit of linear measurement, was roughly equivalent to 3 statute miles or 4 kilometers.

[2]

vis a vis de cette Isle il y a vne grande anse de sable sur le bord du lac, et cest dans son milieu que le fort des francois est situé ou ily a garnison, et ou le commandant ou chef de ce païs fait sa residence, aiant sous luy divers commandans dans de differens postes; mais les uns et les autres y sont par le choix du gouverneur general de la nouuelle France. ce poste est appelé le fort de Buade[9]

LE Couuent des Jesuistes, le village des francois, celui des hurons et houtauois[10] sont contigus les vns aux autres, et tous ensemble bordent, comblent et acheuent le font[11] de l ance.

Il est bon dobseruer que dans ce païs la, le nom de ville est jnconnu ce qui fait croire que les sauuages ne sont pas descendus des normans,[12] ensorte que si lon vouloit parler de paris on le destingueroit par Le mot de grand village

La situation de ce poste est tres auantageuse, parce quelle est tout proche du lac huron par ou toute les nations du Sud sont contraintes de Passer

9. Added here in 1727 copy (363): *parce qu'il a esté Basty par ordre de Mr. de frontenac, Comte de Buade.*

10. Margry regularly changed the spelling of place names and that of Indian groups, including that of the Ottawas noted here. The 1727 copy (363) has the same spelling as here for the Ottawas.

11. It is *fond* in 1727 copy (363).

12. Margry (76) deleted the portion of the sentence from *inconnu* to this point. The 1727 copy (363–64) has the sentence as is here.

[2]

Opposite this island there is a large sandy cove on the shore of the lake, and it is in its midst that the French fort is situated, where there is a garrison and where the commander or chief of the district makes his residence, having under him various commanders in the different posts; but they are all appointed by the governor-general of New France. This post is called Fort de Buade because it was ordered built by *Monsieur* de Frontenac, Count of Buade.[3]

The Jesuit[4] convent,[5] the village of the French, and those of the Huron and Ottawa[6] are adjacent to one another, and together they border and fill up the bottom of the cove.[7]

It should be observed that in that country, the word "city" is unknown,

3. Louis de Buade, Comte de Frontenac et Palluau, served two terms as governor-general of New France. A controversial figure, he was well connected at court and had profound impacts on the development of New France—both good and ill, depending on whether the assessment was provided by a friend or one of his many foes. He died at Quebec in 1698. See W. J. Eccles, "Buade de Frontenac," in *The Dictionary of Canadian Biography* ed. George W. Brown et al. (Toronto: University of Toronto Press, 1966–) (hereafter *DCB*), 1:133–42. Eccles's 1959 biography of Frontenac has been reissued and still stands up as a clear-eyed and critical assessment of Frontenac and his times: W. J. Eccles, *Frontenac: The Courtier Governor*, intro. by Peter Moogk (Lincoln: University of Nebraska Press, 2003).

4. Formally called the Society of Jesus, the Jesuits were the most active order of missionaries in New France working to convert Native peoples to Catholicism. See James Axtell, *The Invasion Within: The Contest of Cultures in Colonial North America* (New York: Oxford University Press, 1985), 23–127, 271–86. In her sweeping and masterful *Croire et faire croire: Les missions françaises au XVIIe siècle* (Paris: Fayard, 2003), Dominique Deslandres places Jesuit missionary efforts in New France in the broader context of overall French missionary efforts by numerous religious orders, including those of the Jesuits, in other parts of the world.

5. The word in French is clearly "convent." It is likely a reference to the group of structures that made up the Jesuit mission and enclosure there.

6. A few pages below, the author provides information about these groups, but see Conrad E. Heidenreich, "Huron," in *Handbook of North American Indians*, vol. 15, *The Northeast*, ed. William Sturtevant and Bruce G. Trigger (Washington, DC: Smithsonian Institution, 1978) (hereafter *Handbook*), 368–88, and Johanna E. Feest and Christian F. Feest, "Ottawa," ibid., 772–86. The Ottawa, also known as Odawa, had long lived in the region, while the Hurons had moved into the area (among others) from their home around Lake Simcoe in the aftermath of their wars with the Iroquois who lived south of Lake Ontario and had destroyed the Huron confederacy's home base by 1650. The Hurons, members of the Iroquoian language group, and the Ottawa, of the Algonquian language group, were also culturally distinct from one another.

7. See the 1717 Plan de Missilimakinak. The settlements were located around the western shoreline, which formed a "c" shape at that point.

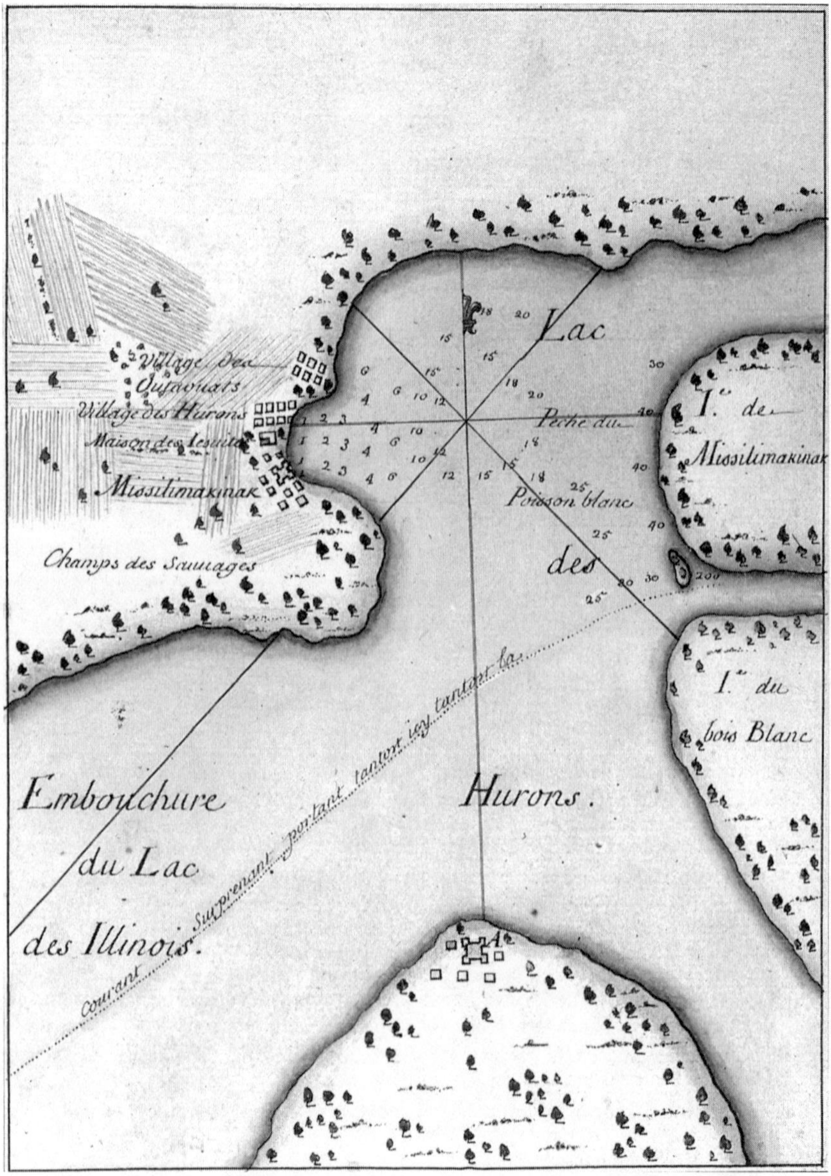

5. Close-up from an unsigned and undated map, but showing the St. Ignace area as it may have existed before 1700. Included are Fort Buade, the Jesuit mission, and Ottawa and Huron villages.

which makes one believe that the *sauvages*[8] are not descended from the Normans, so that if they wished to speak of Paris, they would denote it by the word for "great village."

The location of this post is most advantageous, because it is very close to Lake Huron, through which all the nations from the south are constrained to pass

8. On this word, see the discussion in the Note on Translation section.

[3]

Lors quelles descendent a Montreal ou lors quelles en reuiennent aussi bien que les francois qui veulent aller trafiquer dans les païs eloignees. n'y les vns ny les autres ne sauroient passer sans etre descouuerts, parce que l horison en est si beau que du fort auant[13] on peut voir les canots, d'aussi loin que la vuë la plus fine les peut joindre[14] en vn mot en vn mot[15] on peut dire que cet endroit la est comme le centre, de toute cette autres colonié, dou lon est lvne[16] porté et quasi dune egale distance, pour les autres postes establis, et parmy toutes les nations qui conversent[17] auec nous. je ne scai par quelle raison on a donné le nom de lac que de mer a[18] des abimes dleau dune si grande et si vastes etendue, Le premier lac est donc appellé le lac superieur le 2e Le Lac huron le 3e le lac michigan, ou illinois le 4e Le lac herié le 5e Le lac hontaris.

Je crois quil est important et meme necessaire pour la satisfaction des curieux

13. Word missing in Margry (76) and 1727 copy (364).

14. *peu porter* in 1727 copy (364).

15. The copyist repeated these three words here, but did not cross out the repetition.

16. This word makes little sense here. Margry (76) replaced it with *tout* and it was omitted entirely in the 1727 copy (364).

17. *Commercent* in 1727 copy (364).

18. Four words omitted by Margry (76). This is rendered as *donné plutôt le nom de Lac que de mer* in the 1727 copy (364).

[3]

when they go down to Montreal or when they come back, as well as the French who wish to go trade in the distant countries. None of them are able to pass without being discovered, for the horizon is so good that, from in front of the fort, one can see the canoes as far as the keenest sight can reach. In a word, one can say that this place is like the center of all those other colonies, from where one is carried, and almost at an equal distance to the other established posts, and among all the nations who traffic with us. I do not know for what reason the name "lake," rather than "sea," has been given to these watery deeps of such large and vast extent. The first lake is, then, called Lake Superior, the second Lake Huron, the third Lake Michigan or Illinois, the fourth Lake Erie, and the fifth Lake Ontario.

I think that it is important, and even necessary for the satisfaction of the curious,

[4]

dexpliquer les raisons quon a pu auoir de diuiser ce seul lac en 5 parties, je dis seul, et vn, puis quil est jncontestable que ce sont les memes eaux qui se communiquent et se joignent les vnes aux autres.

IL est neanmoins vrai qu au village des Sauteurs, ou saute[19] de Ste Marie ily a vn rapide en sorte que soit en montant, soit en descendans, toutes nauigations en barques ou navires y est jmpratiquable il faut par consequent y faire vn portage, cest a dire porter les effets par terre au dessus des rapides, on y peut pourtant passer en canots ou chaloupes.

Voila la raison principale pour laquelle on a diuisé le lac superieur qui a 500 lieuës de tour, d'auec le lac huron qui en a 600, or celuy cy nest point separé dauec le lac michigan, mais on pretend quil nest pas le meme a cause d'un detroit qui a deux lieues de large, et par ou les barques ou navires peuuent passer sans danger, ce detroit passé, ce lac selargit tout d'un coup et peut auoir trois cens lieues de tour

19. Margry (77) omitted the preceding two words. They are included in the 1727 copy (365).

[4]

to explain the reasons that one might have had for dividing this single lake into five parts. I call it one, and only, because it is indisputable that they are the same waters that communicate with, and join, one to the other.

It is, nonetheless, true that at the village of the Sauteurs,[9] or the Sainte-Marie rapids, there is a rapid such that, whether ascending or descending, any navigation by boat or ships is impracticable. It is, as a consequence, necessary to make a portage—that is to say, to carry the baggage by land over the rapids. You can, however, pass them in canoes or longboats.

That is the chief reason why they have divided Lake Superior, which is 500 leagues around, from Lake Huron, which is 600. Now, the latter is not separated from Lake Michigan, but it is claimed that it is not the same on account of a strait that is two leagues wide, and through which boats or ships can pass without danger. This strait passed, this lake suddenly broadens and could be 300 leagues around.

9. This is a reference to an Algonquian-speaking people who are identified imprecisely in the historical record and today are called, among other names, Saulteaux, Chippewa, and Ojibwa. The Ojibwa, who dominated the region around the north shores of Lakes Michigan and Superior, are, along with the Ottawa and Potawatomi, also known as the Anishinaabe—People of the Three Fires. See Robert A. Ritzenthaler, "Southwestern Chippewa," *Handbook*, 15:743–59; E. S. Rogers, "Southeastern Ojibwa," ibid., 760–71.

[5]

Le lac herié est aussi distingué du lac Huron par vn detroit par ou les navires peuuent aisement passer; il a deux cent lieuës de tour.

Ce dernier lac est separé d auec le premier, le lac hontario, qui a aussi deux cens lieues de tour a cause dvne chute jnvincible ou rien ne Sauvroit passer.

Si bien quil ny a rien de si aisé a concevoir, quon peut facilement naviguer autour de 1800 lieuës de païs dans le milieu des terres et dans leau douce, non seulement en canot, mais même en barques et gros navires, a cela prés que les vaisseaux qui seroient sur le lac huron, Michigan et sur le lac herié, ne pourroient passer sur le lac superieur ny sur le lac hontario, ou il faudroit faire des barques ou Navires.

On ne trouue point de font[20] au larges de ces lacs. non plus qu'en pleine mer et proche de la terre ily a quasi, partout 20 25 30 40 et 50 brasses dEau, Les Courrans surtout vers MissilimaKinack y sont aussi rapide[21] que la mer meme peut etre pourroit on en atribuer la cause aux vents qui y sont forts[22] frequens

20. *fond* in 1727 copy (367).

21. *Rudes* in 1727 copy (367).

22. Margry (78) omitted this word, but it is in 1727 copy (367).

[5]

Lake Erie is also distinguished from Lake Huron by a strait through which ships can easily pass. It is 200 leagues around.

This last lake is separated from the first, Lake Ontario, which is also 200 leagues around, due to an insurmountable waterfall where nothing could pass.[10]

Thus there is nothing easier to conceive than that one can readily navigate around 1,800 leagues of country, in the midst of land, and in fresh water, not only in canoes but even in boats and large ships, except that the ships that would be on Lake Huron, Michigan, and on Lake Erie could not pass onto Lake Superior or onto Lake Ontario, where it would be necessary to build boats or ships.

One cannot find the bottom out in these lakes, any more than on the high seas. And near the land, almost everywhere, there are 20, 25, 30, 40, and 50 fathoms of water. The currents, above all near Michilimackinac, are as rough as on the ocean itself. Perhaps this might be attributed to the winds, which are very frequent.

---

10. It is true that canoes and other forms of water transportation could not navigate through Niagara Falls, but there was a long-established portage around the falls.

[6]

Mais lexperience fait voir le contraire car les courrans portent toujours sans exception au vent, en sorte, si par exemple, il vente nort, le courant porte au nort, et sil vente sud le courant porte au sud, et ainsi du reste des vents et ce qui est encore de plus particulier, cest que pendant le calme, des courants portent du costé qu'il doit venter. cette obseruation est jnfaillible je laisse aux philosophes a Raisonner sur cette matiere les assurant que le temoignage que je rends est veritable, comme il est vray de dire quil est jour en plein midy.

Quand au lac de Michigan ily a maree, cest a dire flux et reflux que par 24 heures tout comme dans les mers du Sud et les marees haussent ou diminuënt suiuant le cours de la lune.

Il y a vn petit lac a dix lieues de celui cy dans la profondeur des terres; remarquable par son mouuement perpétuel il a environ deux lieues de long, et a chaque bout ily a divers Canots [Canaux][23] qui se diuisent en differents endroits, et quon prendroit pour des fossez faits par la main des hommes ors il arriue quon voit tantos vn bout

23. The copyist meant to write *canaux* here. Rather than cross out *Canots*, he indicated his error by putting a mark over *Canots* and putting *Canaux* by that same mark at the bottom of the page. It is *Canaux* in the 1727 copy (368).

[6]

But experience shows the opposite, for the currents run always, without exception, windward; such that, for example, if it is a north wind, the current carries towards the north, and if it is a south wind, the current carries towards the south, and so on with the other winds. And what is even more peculiar is that during a calm, currents carry from the direction from which the wind is about to blow. This observation is unfailing. I leave it to the philosophers to reason on this matter, assuring them that the testimony I give is true, as it is true to say that it is daytime at high noon.

As to Lake Michigan, there is a tide, that is to say, ebb and flow over twenty-four hours, just as in the seas of the south, and the tides rise and fall according to the course of the moon.

There is a small lake ten leagues from the latter, in the depths of the country, remarkable for its perpetual movement.[11] It is about two leagues long, and at each end there are various channels, dividing at different points, and which one might take for trenches made by the hands of men. Now it happens that one sometimes sees one end

11. It has not been possible to identify such a lake.

[7]

de ce petit lac a sec,[24] et tantos vn autre et les ruisseaux ou fossez qui sont contigus. sont tantos vuides et tantos comblees jusqua deborder par dessus en sorte que ces eaux sont en vne continuelle agitation, ne faisant que galoper dun bout[25] a L'autre, et comme on dit communement jouer aux barres, et on diroit que cest quelque lutin qui les ballotent de cette maniere la.

Puisque jay fait voir la situation du fort et du village des françois et de ceux des sauuages je vais faire remarquer comme ils sont fortifiez et batis, leurs forts sont de pieux, ceux du premier rang en dehors sont gros comme la cuisse, et ont environ 30 pieds de hauteur, le 2^e^ rang qui est en dedans est a vn grand pied du premier quy y courbe dessus et cest pour le soutenir et l'acoter le 3^e^ rang est a 4 pied du 2^e^ et ce sont des pieux de 3 pieds et Demy de Diamettre, aiant 15 ou 16 pieds hors de terre, ors en ce rang la ils ne laissent point de jour entre les pieux au contraire ils les serrent autant quils le peuuent faisant des meurtrieres de distance en distance a legard des deux premiers rangs

24. Rendered *tout a sec* in 1727 copy (368).

25. *Extremité* in 1727 copy (368).

[7]

of this little lake all dry and sometimes the other, and the streams or channels that are adjacent to one another are now empty and now full to overflowing, so that its waters are in continual agitation, doing nothing but rushing from one end to the other and, as is commonly said, playing prisoner's base.[12] And one would say it was some mischievous spirit that was tossing them about in that way.

As I have shown the position of the fort and village of the French, and those of the *sauvages*, I will comment on how they are fortified and built. Their forts are [made] of posts. Those of the first, outer row are as thick as a [man's] thigh and about 30 feet high. The second row, which is inside it, is a full foot from the first, which is bent over onto it, and is to support it and prop it up. The third row is four feet from the second, and these are posts of three and a half feet in diameter being 15 or 16 feet out of the ground.[13] Now, in that row they leave no space between the posts. On the contrary, they set them as close together as they can, making loopholes at intervals. Regarding the first two rows,

12. A children's game of chase wherein players run from one set place to another, presumably, without getting caught along the way.

13. Posts of this diameter have not been archaeologically associated with Great Lakes Indian villages. The description below of neatly organized village streets is also at odd with the archaeology of most villages. On the culture of the Great Lakes Indians, see the works cited above, and Charles Callender, "Great Lakes–Riverine Sociopolitical Organization," *Handbook*, 15:610–21.

[8]

Il y a vn jour entre les pieux denviron 6 pouces et par ce moyen le 1^{e} et le 2^{e} rang nempechent point que lennemy ne Soit a decouuert, mais il ny a ny courtines ny bastions, et ce nest proprement quvne triple[26] cloture.

Quand a leurs cabannes, elles sont en berceau, ils piquent en terre des perches grosses comme la jambe, et fort longues quils joignent les vnes aux autres en les faisant plier et obeïr par le haut bout, apres quoy ils les lient et serre auec des ecorces de bois blanc dont ils font le meme usage que nous faisons de notre fil et de nos cordages; ils entrelassent ensuite auec des lisses de la grosseur du bras. ces grandes perches qui couurent dun bout a lautre auec des Ecorces de sapin ou de cedre quils attachent aux perches et aux lisses, ils laisse au faistes vn jour denviron 2 pieds de large qui suit dun bout a lautre, il est certain que leurs cabanes sont bien[27] clauses et quil ny pleu point du tout, elles ont ordinaire 100 ou 130 pieds de longueur sur 24 de largeur

26. Margry (79) converted this word to *simple* and thereby introduced a subjective assessment of Indian village construction not present in the original author's description. The word is *triple* in the 1727 copy (370).

27. Word omitted by Margry (79) but found in 1727 copy (370).

[8]

there is a space between the posts of about 6 inches, and by this means the first and the second rows do not prevent the enemy from being discovered; but there are neither curtains nor bastions and this is not, in fact, but a triple enclosure.

As to their cabins,[14] they are as bowers.[15] They thrust into the ground poles as thick as a leg, and very long, that they join to one another by making them bend over at the top; after which they tie and fasten them one to another with white wood bark,[16] which they use in the same way we use string and rope. They then interlace, with pieces of wood as thick as an arm, these large poles, which run from one end to the other, with the bark of fir or cedar tree, which they fasten to the poles and the cross-branches. At the peak they leave a space about two feet in width, which runs from one end to the other. It is certain that their cabins are well closed and that no rain at all gets into them. They are generally 100 or 130 feet in length by 24 feet in width

14. *Cabannes*, then and now, is usually translated as "huts," but sometimes as "cabins." Both English words, generally referring to small, rough-hewn structures (such as animal or temporary human shelters, or cottages), convey accurately the sense of the French word, which was used to contrast Indian houses to more "polished" European forms of home construction—whether of stone or worked wood. It is worth noting, then, that in using *cabanne*, rather than *maison* (house), the author of the memoir is making a value judgment about Indian material culture, or revealing an ethnocentric blind spot about what constitutes a home and a house.

15. Literally, "they are cradles" or "like cradles," but used to reference the bowed understructure that supported a child's cradle. *Berceau*, in this period, was also used to mean bowers, a vaulted place created, naturally or otherwise, by trees or climbing vines.

16. Likely bass wood.

[9]

et 20 de hauteur ily a vn etage aux deux costez et chaque famille a son petit appartemens ily a aussi vne porte a chaque bout, leur ruës sont rangee comme nos villages.

Les maisons des françois sont de bois, de piece sur piece, mais elles sont couuertes auec des ecorces de cedre il ny a que celles des Jesuistes qui soient couuertes de planches.

on doit obseruer[28] que sous le nom d'vtaraz[29] quatre nations differentes y sont comprises, La première est celle des KisKaKous, cest a dire des queuës coupées et cest la plus nombreuse, la 2e est la nation du sable, ainsi appelee parce que leur ancienne demeure etoit dans vn païs sablonneux leur village estant situé sur vne anse de sable, mais ljroquois a chassé cette nation de ses terres la 3e cest le Sinago et la 4e est la NassaüaKuetoün,[30] cest a dire nation de la fourche, qui prend son etimologie du nom du chef, ou bien plus vraysemblablement de la riuiere dont ils sont originaire

28. Margry (80) replaced this word with *considérer*. It is as here in the 1727 copy (371).
29. This very garbled word should be some variant of *Outouas* in French. It is *d'outaouas* in the 1727 copy.
30. These group names are spelled identically in the 1727 copy (371).

[9]

and 20 in height. There is a platform on each side, and each family has its little apartment. There is also a door at each end.[17] Their streets are in rows like [in] our villages.

The houses of the French are [made] of wood, piece upon piece,[18] but they are covered with cedar bark, and only those of the Jesuits are covered with planks.

It should be noted that under the name Ottawa four different nations are included. The first is that of the Kiskakon, that is to say, the "Cut Tails," and it is the largest. The second is the Sable nation, so named because their ancient dwelling place was in a sandy area, their village being located in a sandy cove, but the Iroquois[19] chased this nation from its lands.[20] The third is the Sinago, and the fourth the Nassauakueton, that is to say the nation of the Fork, which takes its etymology from the name of the chief, or, much more probably, from the river where they originated,

---

17. This is the description of a typical seventeenth-century Iroquoian long house of the type likely used by Hurons in the region—although most period sources describe a covered opening, rather than an actual door—at each end of the house. Members of the Algonquian cultural and linguistic family, such as the Ottawas mentioned above, typically lived in smaller, rounded, single extended-family lodges. On Iroquoian culture, see William N. Fenton, "Northern Iroquoian Culture Patterns," *Handbook*, 15:296–321.

18. The expression refers to a construction style, most often of squared timbers and not unworked logs. See Peter Moogk, *Building a House in New France: An Account of the Perplexities of Client and Craftsmen in Early Canada* (Toronto: McClelland and Stewart, 1977), especially pp. 28–32.

19. The Iroquois refers, in this period, to five nations of the Iroquoian linguistic group who occupied territory south of Lake Ontario from about the Genesee River on the west to the Mohawk on the east. See Elisabeth Tooker, "The League of the Iroquois: Its History, Politics and Ritual," *Handbook*, 15:418–41; William Fenton and Elisabeth Tooker, "Mohawk," ibid., 466–80; Jack Campisi, "Oneida," ibid., 481–90; Harold Blau, Jack Campisi, and Elisabeth Tooker, "Onondaga," ibid., 491–99; Marian E. White, William E. Engelbrecht, and Elisabeth Tooker, "Cayuga," ibid., 500–504; Thomas S. Abler and Elisabeth Tooker, "Seneca," ibid., 505–17.

20. On the Iroquois wars against the Native groups in the Great Lakes, see B. G. Trigger, *The Children of Aataentsic*, 2 vols. (Montreal: McGill-Queens University Press, 1976); Lucien Campeau, SJ, *Catastrophe démographique sur les Grand Lacs* (Montreal: Éditions Bellarmin, 1983); Daniel K. Richter, *The Ordeal of the Longhouse: The Peoples of the Iroquois League in the Era of European Colonization* (Chapel Hill: University of North Carolina Press, 1992); José António Brandão, *"Your fyre shall burn no more": Iroquois Policy towards New France and Its Native Allies to 1701* (Lincoln: University of Nebraska Press, 1997). For a summary overview of French-Indian relations in the region during the period up to 1718, see the introduction to this work and the sources cited there.

[10]

qui fait vne espece de fourche en se diuisant en trois branches ces quatre nations sont alliées et bien vnies ensemble viuant en bonne jntelligence entre elles et ne parlent aujourd huy qu vne meme langue.

La Nation huronne ne fait point corps auec les 4 precedentes. aussi atelle son vilage separé de lautre, par vne pallissade, elle parle vne langue diferente en sorte que les uns et les autres ne sentendent que par les[31] interpretes. cetoit autre fois la nation la plus puissante la plus forte et meme la plus nombreuSe mais lJroquois la detruite et la chassée de ses terres en sorte qu'elle est a present reduite a vn fort petit nombre et il est bon pour nous quelle le soit ainsi, car ce sont des hommes malins intrigans, malintentionnes et capables de grandes entrepriSes, mais par bonheur leur epeé est trop courte, neanmoins ne pouuans agir en lyons, ils agissent en renards et metent tout en vsages pour brouiller les affaires entre nous et nos alliez

31. Changed to *par La voye des* in 1727 copy (372).

[10]

which forms a sort of fork in dividing into three branches. These four nations are allies and closely united, living in good understanding amongst themselves, and today speak just one language.

The Huron nation is not incorporated with the preceding four. Therefore, they have their village separated from the others by a palisade. They speak a different language, such that they do not understand each other except by means of interpreters. It was at one time the most powerful, the strongest, and even the largest nation, but the Iroquois destroyed it and chased them from their lands such that it is at present reduced to a very small number. And it is good for us that this is so, for these men are cunning, intriguing, ill-intentioned, and capable of great undertakings, but fortunately their sword has a short reach.[21] Nevertheless, being unable to act like lions, they act like foxes and use every possible means to stir things up between us and our allies.

21. Literally, their "sword is very short," but meaning that the Hurons lack the capacity to do what they might want or need to do.

[11]

pour ce qui est des terres chaque nation prend son cartier, et chaque famille marque son terrain et ses champs, ce sont les femmes qui ont soint de cultiuer et densemenser la terre, et cest en verité vn plaisir de les voir auec vn outil dun bois dur en forme de grat[32] par vn bout et plat par lautre, reduire la terre auec vne vigueur et vne diligence incroyable leur recolte consiste en bled djnde, pois, féves, citroüilles et melons dEau

LA pêche tres abondante et la comodite quily a pour la faire a donné occasion aux Sauuages de faire vn etablissement Sedentaire en ce lieue la, cest vne manne quotidienne et qui ne manque jamai, et il y a point de famille qui dans le cours de lannée ne fasse vne pêche Suffisante pour sa Subsistance, au reste il est impossible que lon puisse manger de meilleur poison aussi estil Baigné et nourry dans leau la plus belle et la plus claire la plus cristaline quon puisse jamais voir

32. *crot* in the 1727 copy (373).

[11]

As for land, each nation has its own quarter and each family marks its land and its fields. It is the women who have the task of cultivating and sowing the land. And it is, in truth, a pleasure to see them, with a tool of a hard wood in the shape of a *grat*[22] at one end and flat at the other, tilling the soil with incredible vigor and diligence. Their harvest consists of Indies' wheat,[23] peas, beans, pumpkins, and watermelons.[24]

The very abundant fishing, and the ease of doing it, has led the *sauvages* to make a settlement in that place. It is a daily manna and [one] that never fails, and there is no family that, in the course of the year, does not fish enough for its subsistence. Moreover, it is impossible that one could eat better fish, as it is bathed and nourished in water that is the most beautiful, the most clear, and most crystalline that one could ever see.

22. I have been unable to find a precise definition for this tool. It is seems to be some sort of rake or scraper based upon the word *gratter*, to scrape or scratch. A *gratte* is defined in one source as an adze-like tool used to scrape the sides of bread-dough troughs (Nicole Genêt, Luce Vermette, and Louise Décarie-Audet, *Les objets familiers de nos ancêtres* [Montreal: Les Éditions de l'Homme, 1974], 138, 143). If so, the tool is similar to a hoe, which in French is called a *houe*. The latter term, however, was not common in this period.

23. The French term here, *bled djnde*, is usually translated (as I have also done in the past) as Indian wheat and refers to corn or maize. Yet as early as 1512, there was a French word for corn (*maïs*), and *Inde* was not used to refer to North American Indians, but, rather, a way to indicate a place such as India or East or West Indies. Thus to write Indian wheat is misleading as it might suggest a reference to Indians in the Americas. I have, thus, chosen to translate the French as "Indies' wheat." India wheat is also possible, but as corn comes from the Americas, and the French word for it from the Taino Indian peoples of the Caribbean, Indies' wheat made most sense.

24. The latter were a recent introduction and not native to Indian horticulture in the Great Lakes region. The same is true of peas.

[12]

Je crois quil seroit Jnutile dexpliquer la maniere de pêcher puisque chaque païs a sa methode, mais ce que je crois endeuoir dire, cest de leuer en vn fillet jusqua cent poissons blanc, cest le plus delicat du lac, ils sont gros comme des aloSes en France, on prend aussi quantité de truites qui pezent jusqua 50#[livres][33]; cest asSurement vn tres bon manger, enfin lesturgeon, le brochet, la carpe, le harang, le poisson doré et cent sortes de différents abondent en cet endroit du lac, on sera peut etre bien aise[34] aussy de quoy et de quelle maniere, les Francois et les Sauvages Se nourrissent voicy ce quon fait

on sciè vn gros arbre et on fait vne bille denviron trois pieds de long on la creuse d'environ deux pieds, a peut prets, comme vn mortiér, on fait ensuite auec du bois dur vn pillon de 5 pieds de long on met apres cela du bled djnde dans cette pille, et on lecrase a force de Coups des pillons apres quil est suffisamment pillé, on les vanne, et le son en est

33. Here the copyist used the symbol for *livres*, not the word. It approximates in appearance the pound symbol used here.

34. A word is needed here. Margry (81) added *connoistre* and *sçauuoir* was inserted in the 1727 copy (374).

[12]

I think it would be useless to explain the manner of fishing, since each area has its own method, but what I think I should say [is that they] bring up, in one net, up to a hundred whitefish. This is the most delicate from the lake. They are large like shads in France. They also take a great many trout, which weigh up to 50 pounds; they are certainly very good eating. Finally, the sturgeon, pike, carp, herring, golden fish,[25] and a hundred different fish, abound in this part of the lake. One might also be interested to know on what, and in what manner, the French and the Indians sustain themselves. This is what is done.

They saw a large tree and make a block about three feet long. They hollow it out for about two feet, or thereabouts, like a mortar. They then make, of hardwood, a pestle about five feet long; after this they put corn into the [hollowed-out] block and crush it with blows from the pestle. After it is sufficiently pounded, they winnow it and the bran is

25. *Poisson doré* (golden fish) is known as dory in the United States and as walleyed pike in Canada.

[13]

Separé, si bien quil ne reste que le grû[35] que lon sasse pour en oter la farine, cela fait ce gru deuient tout pur, net et blanc comme du Ris, on le met bouillir dans vne marmitte, ou chaudiere auec de leau, et en meme temps on fait cuire du poisson blanc dans vne autre chaudiere et lors quon voit que le gru est a demy cuit, on ote le poisson et on le delaye auec le boüillon du gru qui se reduit en eau blanche, comme du lait on le jette ensuite dans la marmitte, et auec vne mouuette on le remuë comme on fait le ris jusqu'a ce qu'il soit entierement cuit, et comme la coutume du pais est d'avoir chacun son plat chacun emplit le sien de cette soupe, que les Sauuages appellent sagamité cest a dire diverses choses mellees ensemble pour les manger.

Cette nourriture n'est point friande mais elle est assurement tres seine car elle tient toujours le ventre libre, et elle est tres aperitiue, car on vrine jus qu'a 50 fois par jour, et si jamais on ne mangeoit autre choSe on ne Seroit jamais

35. *grüon* in 1727 copy (375).

[13]

separated, so that only the meal is left. It is sifted in order to remove the [corn] flour. That done, the flour comes [out] pure, clean, and white like rice. They put it to boil in a large cooking pot or kettle[26] with water, and at the same time they cook some whitefish in another kettle. And when they see that the [corn] meal is half cooked, they take out the fish and mix it with the meal broth, which is reduced to a white liquid like milk. They then throw it into the large cooking pot and, with a wooden spoon, stir it as one does rice until it is thoroughly cooked. And as the custom of the country is for each to have his dish, each fills their own with this soup, which the *sauvages* call *sagamité*, that is to say, different things mixed together to be eaten.

This food is not dainty, but it is most certainly very wholesome, for it always keeps the bowels open, and it is very aperitive,[27] for one urinates up to fifty times a day. And if one never ate any other food one would never

26. The author seems to be distinguishing here, and below, between types of cooking vessels, with a *marmitte* being larger than a *chaudiere*, but both came in varying sizes. See Nicole Genêt et al., *Les objets familiers de nos ancêtres*, 81–82, 161.

27. The word is used here in its older sense of "opening pores" to release liquids. Thus, the meaning is that *sagamite* acts as a diuretic.

[14]

alteré comme[36] il est arrivé a plusieurs qui ont passé des mois entiers sans y penser[37] a boire, je puis assurer que j'ay eté vingt jours sans sentir la moindre alteration, ce qui me donne lieu de croire que se Seroit vne[38] bonne nourriture a ceux qui sont attaquez de la grauelle, le soir on mange du poisson a toutes Sauces, frit, roti, boüilly, boucané, ou en ragout, on n'a ny huile ne beurre, mais on a de la graisse ou mouelle d'orignal, de cerf, ou de boeuf sauuage quon a porte a MassilimaKinaK des illinois, ou chicagou et dans le fond je crois que cette sausse est aussi bonne que celle des chartreux, ou des minimes.

on fait du pain auec de la farine de bled d'jnde, quon fait cuire sous la cendre, ou dans le sable brulant il est bon quand on a bon appetit, et il engraisse a merueille, en tout temps on y possede vne bonne santé,[39] on on[40] peut lattribuer a la bonté de l'air ou de la nourriture, mais il est

36. Changed to *ainsi* in Margry and as here in 1727 copy (376).

37. *songer* in 1727 copy (376).

38. Inserted here in 1727 copy (376): *tres*.

39. Margry (83) added the word Michilimackinac here.

40. The copyist repeated the word *on*.

[14]

be thirsty, as has happened to many who have gone whole months without thinking of drinking. I can affirm that I went twenty days without feeling the least thirst, which led me to believe that this would be very good food for those who suffer from gravel.[28] In the evening they eat fish in all sorts of ways[29]—fried, roasted, boiled, smoked, or stewed. They have neither oil nor butter, but they have grease[30] or marrow from the moose, deer, or wild oxen,[31] which is brought to Michilimackinac from the Illinois or Chicago,[32] and in the end, I think that this sauce is as good as that of the Carthusians or the Minims.[33]

Bread is made with corn flour, which one bakes under the ashes or in burning [hot] sand. It is good when one is hungry, and it is wonderfully fattening. One is always in good health; this may be attributed to the goodness of the air or of the food, but it is

28. A medical condition caused by formation, and accumulation, of crystals in the urinary tract.

29. Literally, "in all sauces," but meaning "in all sorts of ways" as what is described are cooking methods and not sauces in the traditional sense. *Sauce* is used metaphorically and euphemistically in French, e.g., *mettre toute la sauce* can mean "step on the gas pedal" or "give it all you have."

30. The French word here (*graisse*) can mean both grease and fat. Either of the latter is a reasonable translation, but grease is used in order to make clear that what is most likely being referenced here is rendered fat (which looks more like grease or lard), and not actual slabs of animal fat.

31. Likely a reference to bison.

32. French writers in this period used "Illinois" to refer to both a region and the Indian peoples they called the Illinois, who were part of the Algonquian language family. Illinois was an umbrella term used to refer to a group of as many as twelve different peoples—depending on the time frame under consideration. See Charles Callender, "Illinois," *Handbook*, 15:673–80. The author returns to the subject of the people at page 103 of the manuscript and there mentions some of the specific subgroups of the Illinois. The region is that associated with these groups and is centered along the river of the same name, from about the region where the Fox and Illinois Rivers meet, to an area north of the confluence of the Illinois and Ohio Rivers. Chicago was a French fort, established in 1680 at about the site of the modern-day city of the same name.

33. Sauce here seems be a reference to the grease and marrow just mentioned. The latter are being compared to good food, or actual sauces, associated by the author with the religious orders mentioned here. The latter were established by, respectively, St. Bruno and St. Francis of Paola. The Carthusians had a monastery in Chartreux.

[15]

encore mieux de lattribuer a lune et a lautre vne preuue certaine de la bonté de ce climat, cest dy uoir des vieillards dont les petits fils grisonnent et on diroit que la mort na pas la force dassommer, cest spectres qui ont neanmoins l'ouye bonne, et la vuë aussy, mais leur memoire fait souuent des incartades, car ils soutiennent quelque fois etre agez de 150 et de 200 ans, ils disent des comptes et des histoires quils soutiennent etre arriuée de ce temps la ce qui n'est point croyable, mais ils ont cet auantage quil ne se trouue personne qui puisse les contredire ou les dementir que par Jnduction.

Le castor et tres rare aux environs de missilliKinacK et les sauuages de ce poste les vont chasser jusqua 200 lieuës et vn bon chasser nen tuë ordinairement depuis le mois doctobre jusquau mois de may que 50 ou 60. quelquefois plus quelquefois moins ils changent et troquent leurs peaux de Castor auec nos marchandiSes

[15]

even better to attribute it to both.[34] A certain proof of the goodness of the climate is to see the old men there, whose grandsons are growing gray, and one would say that death had no power to carry off these specters, who nevertheless have good hearing, and good sight also. But their memory often plays tricks on them, for they sometimes claim to be 150 or 200 years old. They tell tales and stories that they claim happened at that time, which is not credible. But they have this advantage: that no one can be found who can contradict them or call them liars except by induction.

Beaver is very scarce around Michilimackinac, and the *sauvages* from that post go up to 200 leagues to hunt for them. And from the month of October until the month of May, a good hunter does not usually kill but 50 or 60, sometimes more and sometimes less. They exchange and barter their beaver skins for our goods,

34. Compare what follows with the very negative portrayal of the region in Cadillac's August 3, 1695, letter to the Minister, in Joseph L. Peyser and J. A. Brandão, eds. and trans., *Edge of Empire: Documents of Michilimackinac, 1671–1716* (East Lansing/Mackinac Island, MI: Michigan State University Press/Mackinac State Historic Parks, 2008), 103–4. If this memoir was, indeed, written by Cadillac, he changed his tune—possibly because of his intended audience and plans.

[16]

et cest ce quon appelle traiter, ou faire la traite, Nous leur fournissons de la poudre, des balles, des armes, de l'Etoffe du tabac et de tout ce qui est en vsage parmy nous.

Si on pouuoit comprendre quelle fatiguent[41] ily a pour trouuer du Castor on ne mepriseroit pas tant cette MarchandiSe, car il faict[42] scauoir que le convoy des francois par ordinairem[en]t du mont Real au commancement du printemps, ou bien vers le quinze de septembre si bien que dans ce païs la les deux saisons sont facheuses lun parce que cest a la fonte des glaces et des neiges qui rendent leau viue et tres froide lautre parce que c'en est le commancement, ors comme[43] il y a quantité de rapides en chemin presque[44] tousjours invincibles a la pesche, les canadiens sont ordinairement en chemises, nuds pieds et nuds jambes, en sorte que lors que[45] leurs canots ne peuuent tenir contre la rapidité des eaux, ils sy jettent dedans hardiment a force de bras. Sentre aidant les uns

41. *fatigue* in 1727 copy (378).

42. *faut* in 1727 copy (378).

43. Word omitted by Margry (84) and found in 1727 copy (378).

44. *quaSi* in 1727 edition (378).

45. Margry (84) reduced these four words to *lorsque*. It is written as here in the 1727 copy (378–79).

[16]

and this is what is called trading or doing trade. We furnish them with powder, [musket] balls, arms, cloth, tobacco, and all that is in use among us.

If it could be understood how fatiguing it is to find beavers, this commodity would not be so disdained, for it should be known that the convoy of French generally leaves Montreal at the beginning of spring, or else about the 15th of September, such that, in that country the two seasons are troublesome—the one because it is when the melting of the ice and snow make the water lively and very cold, the other because it is the start [of the ice and snow]. Now, as there are many rapids along the route, almost always insuperable for fishing,[35] the Canadians are usually in shirts, barefooted and barelegged such that when their canoes cannot make headway against the swiftness of the water, they boldly throw themselves into the water by sheer strength. By helping one

35. The French word here, *pesche* (fishing), should be *poisson* (fish) as it makes little sense, in the context of the sentence, to say that the rapids are unconquerable or insuperable even for fishing. Still, that is the word found in both the 1718 and 1727 versions of the document.

[17]

les autres, ils en viennent a bout mais non pas sans auoir leurs pieds et leurs jambes souuent ecorcheé, les roches etant si froide quelles se collent fort bien a leur peau, et ne sendetache point sen Enleuer la pièce si cela n'arriuoit quvne fois le[46] jour ce seroit peu de chose, mais ils sont contraire,[47] ce manege la dans tout le cours de leur voyage.

Ce nest pas tout, on trouue en chemin tres frequemment des chutes deau ou cascades par ou on ne peut monter ny descendre si bien quil faut debarquer aux pieds des cascades et porter son canot sur ces epaules par dedans le bois, et toutes les marchandiSes ou castors jusquau[48] dessus des chutes, et lon se rembarque. ces ce que lon appelle faire vn portage, il y en a qui sont de deux Cens[49] lieues.

ILs faut donc que les Canadiens fassent 300 lieues dans ce mouuement perpetuel et penible auant darriuer a MissillimaKinacK, ce qui fait voir leur forces leurs vigueur et leur endurcis

---

46. Margry (84) inserted *par* in place of this article, and it remains as here in the 1727 copy (379).

47. Changed to *mais ils sont contrains de faire ce manége* in 1727 copy (379).

48. Margry (84) replaced this with *par*. The 1727 copy has the word as here (379).

49. This number is reduced to *2 Lieuës* in the 1727 copy (379). This number makes more sense as there are no 200 league portages on the way to Michilimackinac from Montreal. Quaife (17 n. 7) considered the larger number a copyist error.

[17]

another, they attain the [desired] end, but often not without getting their feet and legs skinned, the rocks being so cold that they stick to their skin and cannot be freed without leaving a piece [of skin]. If this happened but once a day, it would be a small matter, but they are constrained to do that maneuver throughout the course of their voyage.

That is not all. Very frequently one finds, en route, waterfalls or rapids by which one can neither ascend nor descend, such that it is necessary to disembark at the foot of the rapids and carry one's canoe on one's shoulders through the woods, and all the merchandise or beaver, up to the top of the falls, and then reembark. This is what they call making a *portage*, [and] some are two leagues [long].

Thus it is that the Canadians make [a journey of] 300 leagues, in this perpetual and laborious movement, before reaching Michilimackinac, which shows their strength, their vigor, and how

[18]

sement a la fatigue et il semble incroyable que le corps humain puisse resister a vn froid si extraordinaire.

Lors quils sont donc arrivee la, au lieu de Songer a Se refaire vn peu de leurs fatigues, ils se depechent au contraire[50] auplustos pour prendre leur parti ailleurs, et passer outre, ils se requipent ordinairement de Canots, et de vivres apres quoi les uns gagnent le Nort du lac superieur, et les autres le Sud, et senfoncent par des riuieres dans la profondeur des terres jusqua 2 ou 300 lieues ils y en a qui suiuant le lac du michigan allant[51] par le sud jusqu'aux nations les plus eloigneés, et tout ensemble nont en vuë que de faire des peaux des Castor.

Lors que les voyageurs ont debité leurs marchandiSes ils sen reuiennent a Missillimakinak et se rendent ordinairement au commancement de Juillet ou ils se requipent de nouueau pour descendre en convoit, Si le commandant du pais le juge apropos, il est donc

50. Word omitted by Margry (85) but found in 1727 copy (380).

51. Margry (85) substituted *vont* here while the 1727 copy (380) has *allant*.

[18]

hardened they are to fatigue. And it seems incredible that the human body can stand up to such extraordinary cold.

When they arrive there, then, instead of dreaming to recover themselves a little from their fatigue, they hasten rather, on the contrary, to take their party elsewhere and pass through. They generally reequip themselves with canoes and provisions, after which some head to the north of Lake Superior and the others to the south, and disappear, via the rivers, into the interior of the country up to 200 or 300 leagues. There are those who follow Lake Michigan, going south as far as the most distant nations. And all of them alike have nothing in sight but to get beaver skins.

When the *voyageurs*[36] have sold their merchandise, they come back to Michilimackinac, and generally return at the beginning of July where they reequip themselves anew to go down in a convoy [to Montreal], if the commandant of the country judges it appropriate. It is then

36. This is a generic term used to describe men who worked as traders, making "voyages" to distant parts to gather furs from Natives in exchange for goods of European manufacture. Those who did so illegally were called *coureurs des bois* (runners of the woods), while those under legal contractual work agreements were known as *engagés*.

[19]

clair et tres jntelligible que ceux qui commercent et font trafic des peaux de castor sont obligez de faire pour le moins mille lieues, auant destre de retour a montreal; mais outre cela on ne peut conceuoir les perils ou ils sexposent en sautant et passant par des bouillons deau, des chutes et des Cascades qui font dresser les cheueux a la teste lors quon y fait reflexion.

Ce nest pas tout il faut risquer de perdre la vie par la main des jroquois qui dressent des embuches[52] dans les defilez et si lon est pris en vie, il faut se resoudre detre grillé a petit feu, il est vray quon prend toutes les precautions necessaires pour Euiter ce malheur et quil est rarem[en]t arrivé que nos convois ayent eté battus

52. *Embuscades* in 1727 copy (381).

[19]

clear and very understandable that those who trade and traffic beaver skins are obliged to travel at least a thousand leagues before being back in Montreal. But, aside from this, one cannot conceive of the dangers to which they are exposed in jumping and passing through whirlpools, falls, and rapids, which makes one's hair stand on end when one reflects on it.

This is not all. One must risk losing one's life at the hands of the Iroquois, who prepare ambushes in narrow passes, and, if taken alive, one must be prepared to be burned by *petit feu*.[37] It is true that all necessary precautions are taken to avoid this misfortune, and that it rarely happens that our convoys are defeated.

37. This term, literally "little fire," reflects an attempt by French writers to capture the sense of torture by fire described a few pages below and which stands in distinction to being burned alive at the stake in a bonfire. The latter is how most readers in France might have understood things if the author had simply written burned by fire, or burned alive.

[20]

Chapitre 2e[53]

Tous les sauuages en general son bien decouplez de belle tailles extremement nerueux vigoureux et fort, de grande fatigue ils on tous[54] les yeux noirs, la prunelle forte la vuë fine et aiguë et perşante[55] leurs cheueux sont gros et noirs, leurs dents sont tres blanches, petites et bien rangeés ils on le col long le ventre plat, le pied grand et les jambes longues ils nont point de poil au visage, ny en aucune partie du corps et rarement voit on parmy eux quleque boiteux ou bossu.

On peut dire sans façon que tous les sauuages onts naturellement de lEsprit, mais comme il nest point cultiué et quils n'agissent en Rien que par leur propre mouuement ils sont retrains a scauoir simplement[56] ce qui Se passe. dans leur village et chez leur plus proches voisins tellement quils regardent ce que les europens leur racomptent comme autant de Chimieres, dont ljmagination

53. Margry (86) added the title *Portrait des Sauvages* to this chapter. The chapter number, without a title, is included in the 1727 copy (382).

54. Word omitted by Margry (86) but found in 1727 copy (382).

55. This word is spelled with a "ç" in the 1727 copy (382).

56. In the 1727 copy (382) this is changed to: *Ils S'attachent Simplement a sçauoir.*

[20]

2nd Chapter

All the *sauvages*, in general, are well-built, of fine stature, extremely wiry, vigorous, and strong, [and] of great endurance. They all have black eyes, large pupils, good sight, and keen and piercing. Their hair is thick and black, their teeth are very white, small, and regular. They have a long neck, a flat stomach, large feet, and long legs. They do not have hair on the face nor on any part of the body, and one rarely sees among them any lame or humpbacked.

One may say, without ceremony, that all the *sauvages* are naturally intelligent, but as it is not cultivated, and as they are concerned only about themselves,[38] they are limited to knowing simply what takes place in their own village and among their nearest neighbors so that they regard what Europeans tell them as so many idle fancies that the imagination

38. More literally: "and they act in nothing but for their own inclinations."

[21]

aime a se repaitre et a sentretenir il est aise de remarquer quils ont vne jdee charmante, et vne tres grande facilité[57] pour le dessein pour la peinture et Sculpture, et comme ils n'ont aucun vsage de lettres ny dEscriture Dieu leur a donné aussy en partage vne tres heureuSe memoire.

Deux articles font la distinction des veritables hommes le premier cest la guerre, le 2e cest la chasse, en sort que[58] les meilleurs guerriers et les meilleurs Chasseurs, sont les plus estimez et les plus considerez et les plus recommandables parmy eux, si bien que celuy qui possede cest deux qualitez semble etre declaré et publié pour un chef parmy sa nation, si le chasseur va de paire auec le guerier, il ne faut point en etre surpris, car il faut sauoir que tous les sauuages, vivent sentretiennent, et font subsister leur[59] famille au bout de leur fusil ou pour mieux dire de leur jndustrie ruse et adresse

57. *Attitude* in 1727 copy (383). Aptitude makes sense, but not this word. Facility also works here.

58. Preceding three words omitted by Margry (86), but found in 1727 copy (383).

59. Margry (87) changed this to *une*, but *leur* is found in 1727 copy (383).

[21]

loves to revel in and talk about. It is easy to see that they have a charming imagination and very great facility for drawing, painting, and sculpture; and as they have no familiarity with letters or writing, God has given them as well, in place of this, a very felicitous memory.

Two articles mark true men: the first is war and the second hunting, so that the best warriors and the best hunters are the most esteemed, and the most highly considered, and the most worthy of recommendation among them; such that he who possesses these two qualities seems to be declared and announced as a chief among his nation. If the hunter is on a par with the warrior, there is no need to be surprised, for it should be known that all the *sauvages* live, sustain themselves, and maintain their family on the basis of their guns or, more properly speaking, by their industry, wiles, and skill

[22]

a faire tomber les bêtes dans les pieges quils leur tendent, or pour y bien reussir il faut auoir il faut auoir[60] Ce pratique des lieux de chasse, connoitre les passages les retraites ljnstint des bêtes etre patient, penible,[61] heureux, ardent, vif, hardy, bon coureur; il faut auoir loeil bon et bonne haleine ils chassent lorignal, le cerf, la biche, lours, le Chevreil, le Caribou, le Castor et le boeuf sauuage il faut tuer ces animaux dans les bois, ou dans les prairies a la surpriSe ou a force de jambes qu on en pense ce quon voudra, mais je scai bien quil faut auoir le jaret souple pour continuee cet Exercice, cependant vn bon chasseur tue quelques fois jusqua douze bestes dans vn jour, et cest vn plaisir de voir de temps en temps les miamis amener dans leur village des ours monstreux domptez a la course et quils conduissent deuant eux a coups de houssine, comme des moutons quon menne

60. The copyist repeated these three words.

61. Margry (87) rewrote this portion as: *sçavoir supporter la peine, estre patient*. This addition by Margry also serves as an example of his making words "appear" older. Having changed the sentence and added the modern spelling of *sçavoir*, he inexplicably chooses to use an older spelling of *être* in place of its modern form. In the 1727 copy (384) this passage is also changed to *estre patient dans la peine*, and the characteristic that follows here, *heureux*, is omitted.

[22]

in catching animals in the traps that they set for them. Now, to be very successful, he must be familiar with the hunting grounds, know the trails, the lairs, [and] the instincts of the animals; be patient, bear pain, be lucky, eager, energetic, hardy, [and] a good runner. One must have a keen eye and good lung capacity.[39] They hunt moose, stags, does, bears, roe deer, caribou, beaver, and wild oxen. One has to kill these animals in the woods, or on the prairies, by surprise or by swiftness of foot. Think what one will, but I well know that they must have good legs to continue in this activity. Nevertheless, a good hunter sometimes kills up to a dozen animals in a day, and it is a pleasure to see, from time to time, the Miami bringing into their village monstrous-sized bears, broken along the way, and which they drive before them with blows from switches, like sheep one

39. Literally, "good breathing."

[23]

quon mene[62] a la boucherie et ces dans ces occasions que les bons chasseurs font voir leurs proueSSes, et comme il est vray que par tout païs ceux qui sont passionnez pour la chasse si occupent plustos pour leurs plaisires particulier et pour leur propres satisfaction, ou pour acquerir cette reputation,[63] que pour le gain, le lucre, ou la friandiSe, de meme parmy les sauuages les bons chasseurs sont ceux qui profitent le moins de leur chasse ils festinent Souuent leurs amis, ou leurs parens, ou bien ils distribuent les bestes quil ont tueé par Cabannes ou par familles, vne preuue de la liberalité ou de la vanité quils tirent de cette profession, cest quen debarquant a leur vilage il est permis a ceux qui se trouue a leur debarquement de prendre, ou denleuer toute la viande qui est dans le Canot de celuy qui la tuée, et il ne fait quen rire, ce que fait croire sufisamment quils

62. Another error of repetition by the copyist.

63. Margry (87) omitted the preceding five words. They are found, as here, in the 1727 copy (385).

[23]

takes to the slaughter. And it is on such occasions that the good hunters show their prowess. And, as it is true that throughout every country those who are passionate about hunting do it more for their own pleasure and self-satisfaction, or to acquire that reputation, than for gain, profit, or love of food, so too among the *sauvages* the good hunters are those who profit the least from their hunting. They often feast their friends or their relatives, or they distribute the animals they have killed among cabins or among families. One proof of the liberality, or the vainglory, that they derive from this occupation is that when disembarking at their village, those who find themselves at their landing are permitted to take, or cart off, all the meat that is in the canoe of he who has killed it, and he does nothing but laugh; which is sufficient to make one believe that

[24]

ne songent qu a nourrir le public, or toute la nation se Sentent de semblables bien faits elle se trouue jnteressée daplaudir, a vn si noble exercice, et dautant plus quil arriue souuens qu vn seul chasseur fait subsister plusieurs familles ensemble qui sans son secours, en certain temps et en certain lieux, mourroient de faim ou[64] de misere, il ne faut donc point trouuer tout a fait etrange sils font aussy grand Cas dun chasseur que dun guerrier, la seule difference que jy trouue, cest que l'un est plus craint et plus redouté et lautre plus aimé et plus chery.

Pour ce qui est[65] dela guerre tous les sauuages ont la meme maxime, meme pratique, meme mode et memes facon de Combattre, leurs partis, ou compagnies se forment en cette maniere vn chef de guerre sabstient de manger et de boire et juene quel

64. Margry (88) changed this word to *et*. It is as here in the 1727 copy (386).

65. *concerne La Guerre* in the 1727 copy (386).

[24]

they think but of feeding the public. Now, with the whole nation similarly feeling itself well done by, it finds itself interested in applauding such a noble exercise, and even more so as it often happens that a single hunter provides subsistence for many families altogether who, without his aid at certain times and places, would perish of hunger or want. One should not, then, find it altogether strange that they make as much of an account of a hunter as of a warrior. The only difference I have found is that one is more feared and dreaded, and the other is more loved and more cherished.

As regards war, all the *sauvages* have the same maxim, the same method, and the same mode and manner of fighting. Their parties or companies are formed in this manner. A war chief abstains from eating and drinking, and fasts

[25]

que fois huit jours durant ils[66] se mattachent et se barbouille tout le visage en noir, il parle peu, il songe et reue nuit et jour, priant[67] lesprit quil a choisi pour son protecteur ou patron de luy donner des hommes cet esprit en qui il a Confiance, est quelque fois vn corbeau vn aigle, vne loutre, vn ours, vn renard, et ainsi des autres animaux, mais chacun a le sien en recommandation, qui est toujours celuy qui sest presenté a eux dans leurs songes, et dans leurs reues[68] si bien que Sils ont pendant leur Someil quelques visions de leurs ennemis, en certains lieux et en certains temps et quenfin leur reue[69] soit fauorable pendant[70] leur jeune, ils en tirent vn bon augure et concluent quils feront coup sur leurs ennemis ce terme de reuer etant vne fois fini ils se debarbouillent le visage, et le peinture de rouge, de noir de blanc, mais pour lordinaire cest de rouge seulement ils rafraichissent leurs cheveux, ils

66. *Il* in 1727 copy (386).

67. Word omitted then added above the line of text at this point.

68. Margry (88) changed the word here to *veües*, as did the copyist in the 1727 copy (387).

69. Margry (89) has *veüe* again, while the 1727 copy (389) has *Rêue*.

70. The 1727 copy (389) has inserted here: *Le Cours de*.

[25]

sometimes for eight days at a time. He *mattache[nt]*[40] himself and smears his whole face black; he says little; he dreams and reflects night and day, praying to the spirit he has chosen as his guardian or patron to give him men. This spirit in whom he has confidence is sometimes a crow, an eagle, an otter, a bear, a fox, and sometimes other animals, but each one has his own recommended to him, which is always the one that has presented itself to them in their visions and in their dreams; so that if during their sleep they have some visions of their enemies, and in certain places and at certain times, and finally the vision is favorable during their fast, they take it as a good omen and conclude that they will strike a blow upon their enemies. Once the period of dreaming is over, they wipe their faces and paint them red, black, white, but generally red only. They *refraichir*[41] their hair, they

40. The French word used here, *mattachent*, today *matassiner*, refers to a type of dance performed by a clown or jester. In modern usage it refers to a comical imitation of a warrior's dance. Quaife ignores the word here and later renders it as "put on your war paint" (Milo Milton Quaife, ed. and trans., *The Western Country in the 17th Century: The Memoirs of Lamothe Cadillac and Pierre Liette* [Chicago: Lakeside Press, 1947], 22, 23). The author of the relation explains below that to *mattacher* is to dress up in finery or adorn oneself. I have not been able to find a definition of the word that matches this description, but, based on the information the author has provided, one rendering of this passage might be: "adorns himself and smears his whole face black."

41. *Refraichir* means "refresh" and was often used in this period to mean "trim hair." But the instructions being given are for men to prepare their hair, and themselves, for war. As most Indian men had their own hairstyle for such occasions, "refresh," in the sense of touch up or make one's hair ready for war—style it—may be a better word choice than "trim." The author explains a few lines later that this action means to cease mourning, but that is not inconsistent with the preceding explanation. During the mourning period, family members do not look after their appearance in matters of clothing or hair.

[26]

les huilent, et ce mettent enfin sur leur propre ils festinent ensuite la Jeunesse et quelques vieillards mais auant que de commancer a manger le chef fait sa harangue a peu pres en ces termes.

Mes freres, Il est vray que je ne suis point vn homme, vous scauez neanmoins que jay quelque fois[71] veu lEnnemy, nous auons eté tuez il y a long temps que les os dun tel, notre frere, reposent en tel lieu, jl est temps que nous les allions voir, maintenant vous scauez que cestoit vn braue homme, il merite detre vengé, nous auons demeuré paisiblement sur nottre natte, je me leue aujourdhuy; parce que lesprit qui me gouuerne ma promis du bouillon et de la viande fraiche, prenez courage Jeunesse rafraichiSSez vos cheuelures

71. Margry (89) changed this to *j'ay déjà veu*. In the 1727 copy (389) the word order is changed to *veu quelque Fois L'ennemy*. The rest of the sentence is also changed: *Nous sçauons a nostre Regret, il y a longtems.*

[26]

oil it and, in the end, clean themselves up. They then feast the youths[42] and a few old men, but before beginning to eat, the chief makes his harangue in about these terms:

> My brothers, it is true that I am not a man; yet you know that I have sometimes seen the enemy.[43] We were killed. We know, to our regret, that it has been a long time that the bones of so-and-so, our brother, have rested in such and such a place. It is time that we go see them. Now you know that he was a brave man. He deserves to be avenged. We have remained peacefully on our mat. Today I arise, for the spirit who governs me has promised me broth and fresh meat. Take courage, young men, refresh your hair,

42. *Jeunesse*, meaning youths, is often translated as young men, especially in the context of describing warfare that, among the groups in question here, was undertaken—according to numerous observers—by men. Still, there are ways to say young men, and old men, and the author does make such distinctions in other places. It is not clear why he does not make things clear here or a few pages later when the author writes about "young people" (*jeunes gens*) going to war. He may assume that it is understood that young men is meant, but that is not what he has written and I make no such assumption.

43. "Faced" or "encountered" the enemy makes more sense, but the French word here, *veu*, means seen. This may be another of those awkward phrasings that reflect a relatively literal translation from an Indian phrasing to French by the author.

[27]

mattachez vous armez vos carquois, desennuyons nos morts, faisons retentir des chansons de guerre par tout le vilage reueillons notre frere qui a eté tué, il sera contant lors quil sera vangé

Il faut obseruer que les sauuages se traitent toujours en frere ou compagnons, et que dans vne harangue ce terme de bouillon, ou de viande fraiche, signifie tuer des hommes et faire des prisonniers, se rafraichir les cheveux, veut dire quitter le dëuil, ce mattacher, cest se parer et s'orner;[72] rester sur la natte cest se reposer Et viure en paix, ils ne parlent jamais de ceux quils ont tuez, ils ne parlent que de leurs morts

Le Chef aiant fini sa haran

72. *s'armer* in 1727 copy (388).

[27]

mattachez yourselves, fill your quivers, let us console our dead. Let our war songs ring through the whole village, awakening our brother who was killed. He will be content when he has been avenged.

It should be observed that the *sauvages* always refer to one another as brother or companions, and that in a harangue this term "broth," or "fresh meat," signifies killing men and taking prisoners; "refreshing the hair" means to cease mourning; to *mattacher* is to prepare themselves and adorn themselves; to "remain on the mat" is to rest and live in peace. They never speak of those whom they have killed. They speak but of their own dead.

The chief having finished his harangue,

[28]

gue, on luy repond par vn grand cri confus, pour marquer quon aplaudit et quon aprouue son dessein, apres quoy ce capitaine ou quelque autres, par lui attitré, se leue dans la place aiant le carquois en main, et chante en guerrier, sa chanson nest pour lordinaire quvne repetition de ce qui a eté harangué ils chantent ainsi les vns apres les autres, surtout ceux qui ont envie detre du party de la guerre, on mange ce qui a eté preparé il ny a que celuy qui festine qui ne goutte a rien se contentant seulement de fumer quelques pipes de tabac des que le repas est fini ils battent la Caisse continuellem[en]t jusqua ce que le party soit entierement formé.

Le Jour du depart les guerriers sajustent de leur mieux, ils rougissent leurs cheueux ils peintures leurs

[28]

they answer him by a loud, muddled cry, to show that they applaud him and approve his plan. After which, this chief, or some others nominated by him, stands up in place with quiver in hand, and sings a war song. His song is usually but a repetition of what was said in the harangue. They chant thus, one after another, especially those who want to be in the war party. They eat what has been prepared, [and] only the man who is giving the feast finds nothing to his taste, contenting himself with smoking a few pipes of tobacco. Once the meal is finished they beat the drum continually until the war party is completely formed.

On the day of departure the warriors fit themselves out in their best. They redden their hair, they paint their

[29]

visages de rouge, et de noir auec beaucoup d'art et de gentillesse, aussi bien que tout leur corps, les uns ont des tours de teste auec des queües[73] daigles ou autres oyseaux les autres en ont auec des dents de bestes feroces, comme loups et tigres, plusieurs au lieu dun chapeau arment leurs testes de casque auec des cornes de cerf de chevreuil ou de boeuf, ils ont autour deux[74] leurs arcs, leur carquois et leurs fleches leurs canots son enjoliuées, et parroissent de diuerses couleurs et figures ou des armes du Capitaine, sur le deuant du Canot on y uoit la natte de guerre, le corbeau lours ou quelque autre animal, comme je l'ay deja dit etant lesprit qui doit Conduire cette entreprise,

Des quils sont embarquez ils poussent leurs Canots au large environ 15 ou 20 pas, et se rangent en ligne etant fort serrez le bout de lun N'auançant

73. *plumes* in the 1727 copy (389) although *queües* as used here probably meant "tail feathers."

74. Two words missing in 1727 copy (390).

[29]

faces in red and in black, with a good deal of artistry and grace, as well as their entire body. Some have headpieces with the tail feathers of eagles or other birds. Others have them with the teeth of fierce animals, such as wolves and tigers.[44] Some, in place of a hat, fit their heads with a cap with the horns of a stag, roebuck, or ox. They gird themselves with their bows, quivers, and arrows. Their canoes are embellished and adorned with different colors and figures, or with the arms of the captain. On the front of the canoe you see the war mat, the crow, the bear, or some other animal such as I have already mentioned—being the guardian spirit that is to guide this enterprise.

Once they are embarked, they push their canoes fifteen or twenty paces[45] out and range themselves in line, very tightly, the end of one not projecting

44. Tigers are not native to North America. The author may have meant lynx, or some other wild cat, and, without knowing its proper name in French, written tiger instead.

45. In this period the measurement for a pace varied, but was roughly equivalent to the modern-day yard—three feet or so.

[30]

pas plus que l'autre, a quoi ils sont fort exats, le chef du party se leue ensuite tout debout dans le milieu du canot aiant vne gourde en sa main dans laquelle il y a de petites roches dedans il la Secouë il chant en jnvoquant son esprit protecteur afin quil fasse vn bon voyage, les gueriers repondent a son chant par un double Ché[75] en aspirant, et les autres chef qui sont a terre harangue en meme temps animent les jeunes gens a Se bien battre, a bien regarder dans la route deuant et derrière eux a faire bonne decouuerte, et a ne point ce laisser surprendre

Le chef de guerre qui pendant ce temps la, chante sans cesse dans son canot, prie tout le village de ne point les oublier sils sont tuees et de se souuenir de les venger; cela fait ils font tous ensemble vn grand cry, et nageant au meme jnstant vers la routte quils doivent tenir comme sils voyoient

75. Changed to *cris* in 1727 copy (390).

[30]

more than another, about which they are very particular. The chief of the party then stands all the way up in the middle of his canoe, having in his hand a gourd in which there are little stones inside. He shakes it. He chants in invoking his guardian spirit so that he will have a good journey. The warriors respond to his chant by a [sharp] intake of breath, with a double "*Che*," and the other chiefs, who are on land, harangue at the same time, exhorting the young people to fight well, to watch well along the route, in front of and behind them, to scout well, and to not let themselves be surprised.

The war chief, who during that time chants without letup in his canoe, implores all the village not to forget them if they are killed, and to remember to avenge them. That done, they give a great cry all together and, at the same time, row out towards the route they must take, as if they have seen

[31]

Lennemy, et lon peut dire que leurs canots vont comme des traits

Quoi quil en soit cet equipage de guerre ne laisse pas que destre afreuse, a ceux qui ny sont point accoutumez, ou qui n'en ont jamais vû

Lors quils sont arrиueé dans le pais ennemy ils marchent doucement ils obseruent le Silence on l'oeil a tout et ne tirent point auec des armes a feu sils tombent sur la piste et les traces de quelquuns, ils demellent aisement sil elles sont fraiches ou vieilles, ils connoissent le nombre de ceux qui ont passé et combien il y a de jours que leur chemin est fait, si bien que suiuant[76] le temps que leur ennemy a passé ils sauent a peu prés ou ils peut etre, et pour lors ils se determinent a le poursuivre ou a en chercher d'autres.

On diroit que ces gens la se conduisent plutos par jnstinct que par science ou par raison, car si vn homme ou plusieurs sont vne fois[77] decouuerts leur pertes est quasi toujours aSSurez et jnfaillible

76. Margry (91) changed this to *saçhant*. It is as here in the 1727 copy (392).

77. Preceding two words omitted by Margry (92) but found in 1727 copy (392).

[31]

the enemy. And one could say that their canoes go like darts.

In any event, these trappings of war cannot but be frightening to those who are not accustomed to them or who have never seen them before.

Once they have arrived in the country of the enemy, they march quietly. They observe silence, have an eye out for everything, and never shoot with their firearms. If they fall upon the trail and footprints of anyone, they easily discern whether they are fresh or old. They know the number of those who have passed by and how many days ago their journey was made, such that following the time when their enemy went by, they know about where they could be, and from this they determine to pursue them or to go in search of others.

One might say that those people conduct themselves more by instinct than by science or reason, for if one man, or a number [of them], are once discovered, their ruin is almost always assured and unfailing.

[32]

on a beau faire pour sechaper quon marche sur la mousse sur les feuilles dans les marets sur les rochers memes toute les precautions quon prend pour Sauuer sa routte sont fort jnutiles par ce que ceux qui poursuiuent tombent rarement en defaut ce qui cest de plus particulier cest quils connoissent par ljmpression ou la tournure du pied de quelle nation sont ceux qui marchent deuant eux lors quils jnferent quils sont aSSez proches de leurs ennemis, ils detachent les meilleurs coureurs, et les plus legers de leur troupe pour aller obseruer leur Campement, cest a dire la ou ils doiuent coucher, comme aussy quelles sont leurs armes, et la situation du lieu il est necessaires que les decouureurs aient de la ruse, de la pratique et de la fermeté car il faut scauoir que tous les partis de guerre pendant leur campagne font faire ainsi la decouuerte a trois ou quatre lieues aux environs du lieux, ou ils veulent camper et coucher, cest pourquoy ce sont le malheureux, cest a dire pour eux qui

[32]

Despite what they do to escape, be it walking on moss, on leaves, through marshes—even over rocks—all the precautions they take to safeguard their route are quite useless, for those who pursue them rarely fall into error. What is very peculiar is that they know by the impress of the foot, or its shape, to which nation those marching in front of them belong. Once they conclude that they are fairly near their enemies, they dispatch the best runners, and the quickest, of their troop to go observe their camp—that is to say, where they are to pass the night—as well as to see what weapons they have, and the situation of the place. The scouts must have cunning, experience, and boldness, for it should be understood that all war parties, during their campaign, scout in this manner for three or four leagues round the place where they wish to encamp and sleep. Which is why they are unfortunate, that is to say, for those who

[33]

son decouuerts, parce que[78] les decouureurs etant de retour dans leur campement, ceux qui n'ont rien vû en font leur raport, et tous les autres, sen remettant a eux, reposent et dorment tranquilement toute la nuit, leur coutume n'estant point de faire ny garde ny faction

Ceux au contraire qui ont decouuert lEnnemy, apres auoir bein tout[79] obSerué se rendent au gros ou rendez vous qui leur est marqué, et sur leur raport on tient Conseil, apres quoy sils se jugent assez forts pour attaquer ils marchent jncontinent, et ordinairement de Nuit, aiant les decouureurs a leurs testes[80] qui ne perdent point jdeé du chemin quils ont fait, ny du Cabanage de leurs ennemis, lors quils les ont approcheé a vne distance, ils se jettent sur le ventre aiant toujours loeil et loreille au guet, et des decouureurs deuant et derriere et sur les ailes en cet etat ils attendent la pointe du jour, comme etant lheure

78. Margry (92) omitted the preceding from *coucher* to this point. The same is true in the 1727 copy in which the next two words are also omitted (393).

79. Changed to *beaucoup* by Margry (92), and as here in 1727 copy (393).

80. Changed to *costez* in 1727 copy (393).

[33]

are discovered; for once the scouts have returned to their encampment, those who saw nothing make their report, and all the others, relying on them, rest and sleep tranquilly all night, it not being their custom to post any guard or sentry.

Those, on the contrary, who have discovered the enemy, after having observed everything well, return to the main body or their appointed rendezvous and, on their report, a council is held. After which, if they judge themselves strong enough to attack, they march off at once, and generally by night, with the scouts at their head,[46] who never lose their impression of the road they took or of the enemy's *cabannage*.[47] Once they have approached them at a distance, they throw themselves on their stomachs, always having eyes and ears alert, and scouts in front and rear and on the flanks. In this state they wait until break of day, as that is the hour

46. As noted at this point in the transcription, this word is changed to *costez* (side or flank) in the 1727 copy. The two words represent a significant difference in how a group carried out warfare, but without a clear reason to deviate from the 1718 text (there is no ambiguity in how the word is written), it bears pointing out but not changing.

47. The French word here, *cabanage*, refers to the process of making *cabanes*—huts or shanties—or a place where some of them are located. It is being used as a way to refer to the enemy's temporary camp as is common in other documents from this period. The author has used the word for camp, or encampment, above and chose, for some reason, to use this term here to make the same point.

[34]

ou lhomme est plus apesanti par lenvie et la demangeaison quil a de dormir, et pour mieux voir aussi a faire leur coup, et pouuoir profiter du reste de la journée a faire leur retraite, leurs maniere est de se trainer a quatre pattes comme des Chats, et faire leurs approches a la porteé du pistolet, ils se leuent ensuite tout debout auant de faire leur decharge, le chef du party fait son signal par vn petit cri; le reste fait en meme temps vne grande hueé et sils ont des fusils ils font feu tout dun coup sur lennemy, sinon ils decochent leurs fleches, leur première decharge faite, sils voient lennemy troublé et en deroute ils fonce dessus la hache ou le casse teste en main, sils sont victorieux ils leuent la cheuelure a ceux qui ont eté tuez sils ont fait des prisonniers Ils les lient et garottent si bien que les liens enfoncent[81] dans la chair, ils marchent apres cela nuit et jour

81. Inserted here, in the 1727 copy (395), are the words *vn pouce*.

[34]

when a man is most weighed down by the desire and longing he has to sleep, and also to better see to strike their blow and be able to take advantage of the rest of the day to make their retreat. Their custom is to crawl on all fours like cats, and make their approaches within pistol shot; they then stand up just before discharging [their weapons]. The head of the party gives his signal by a little cry. At the same time, the rest give a loud shout. And, if they have guns, they fire all at once upon the enemy; if not, they let fly their arrows. Their first discharge made, if they see the enemy is disordered and routed, they rush upon them, hatchet or war club[48] in hand. If they are victorious, they take the scalps of those who have been killed. If they take prisoners, they bind and pinion them so tightly that the bonds cut an inch into their flesh. They march, after that, night and day

48. The French term here, *casse teste*—literally, "head breaker"—is usually translated as "war club" or "tomahawk." The latter were different implements of war, and the tomahawk was developed and in wide use much later than the period in question here. For examples of war clubs used by nations in the Great Lakes regions, see *Handbook*, 15:307, figure 11; 433, figure 8; 739, figure 14.

[35]

jusqua ce quils soient hors de danger et a couuert de leurs ennemis, lors quils sont proches de leur village jls detachent du monde pour donner auis de tout ce qui S'est passé dans leurs campagne, apres quoy on se prepare a receuoir les guerriers, et a les haranguer auant dentrer dans le lieu mais en meme temps lon se dispoSe a faire lentreé des prisonniers qui commance toujours par vne salue de 3 ou 400 cens coups de batons qui leur fait donner cent fois du nez a terre, auant dentrer dans la Cabane du triomphe quon leur prepare et qui leur est destinez, des quils sont la, on leur dit de dancer et de chanter leur chanson de mort, leur chant est fier et lugubre, tout ensemble ils racomptent pour lors ce quils ont fait pendant leur vie, principalement le nombre de personnes quils on defait leurs noms et de quelles nations, l'endroit et comment, jls ont fait leur coup, tantos on les fait asseoir et

[35]

until they are out of danger and sheltered from their enemies. Once they are near their village, they send ahead [someone] from the group to give the news of all that has happened during their campaign; after which the villagers prepare to receive the warriors and harangue them before they enter the place. But, at the same time, they arrange for the entrance of the prisoners, which always begins with a greeting[49] of three to four hundred blows with sticks, which makes them fall to the ground, face first,[50] a hundred times before they enter the cabin of triumph that they have prepared for them and to which they are destined. As soon as they are there, they are told to dance and chant their death song. Their chant is both proud and mournful. All together, they recount, then, what they have done during their life, especially the number of persons they have defeated, their names and from which nations, the place, and how they struck the blow.

Sometimes they are made to sit and

49. It is not clear if the French word here, *salue*, is used to convey irony, sarcasm, or reflects the author's translating an Indian term for this part of the process. Its use is, however, common to descriptions of this part of prisoner treatment left by other French observers.

50. Literally, fall "nose to the ground."

[36]

tantos leuer, et toujours chanter surtout quand quelque considerable vient dans la cabanne pour les uoir; mais pendant quils chantent de la sorte l'un leur arrache vn ongle, l'autre leur fume vn doigt, dans vne pipe, on leur applique par intervale vn tison de feu sur la chair qu'on fait bruler jusqua l'os, quelquuns luy enleuent des lopuis[82] quils font cuire, et les mangent jncontinent, et sans[83] succent les doigts comme dun manger tres exquis, ils se divertissent et passent ainsi le temps deux ou trois jours durant, apres quoi les anciens, les chefs de guerre et tous[84] les principaux du village sassemble pour deliberer de la uie ou de la mort de ces malheureuse, leurs pertes ou leur conseruation depend ordinairement des femmes, et voicy pourquoy cest quil y en a qui ont perdu leurs marys ou leurs enfans dans la guerre, et[85] sils sen trouue qui

82. *lopins* in 1727 copy (396).

83. Margry (94) has *s'en*, which is also what is found in the 1727 copy (396), which makes more sense, but *sans* is clearly the word here, the "a" being written as it is elsewhere on the page.

84. Word missing in Margry (94), but as here in 1727 copy (396).

85. Word omitted in 1727 copy (396).

[36]

sometimes get up, and always to chant, above all when someone important comes into the cabin to see them. But while they are singing in this way, someone pulls out one of their fingernails, another smokes one of their fingers in a pipe.[51] At intervals, they apply a firebrand to their flesh, which they burn down to the bone. Some cut off pieces [of flesh], which they cook and eat forthwith, and suck their fingers as if having eaten a delicacy. They divert themselves, and pass the time thus, for two or three days, after which the elders,[52] the war chiefs, and all the principals of the village assemble to deliberate about the life or death of these unfortunates. Their ruin or preservation generally depends upon the women, and this is why: it is that there are those who have lost a husband or their children in the war, and if some [women] seeing

51. By this expression is meant the practice of putting a finger, still attached to the hand, in the bowl of the pipe. It does not mean that a cut-off finger, or part of one, is used in the place of tobacco in a pipe. If part of the finger has been first cut off, placing the stub on the burning tobacco embers in the pipe will, in addition to causing a great deal of pain, help cauterize small blood vessels in the finger. The latter prevents excessive bleeding, earlier than wanted death due to blood loss, and prolongs the victim's life and torture. The author explains this practice, but not its purpose, a few pages below.

52. Women get lost in Quaife's translation of this and some subsequent passages (29–31). He inserts gender, inevitably male, when the French does not make it clear and when it is not required in English. At other times, he deletes clear references to women. Here he has translated *anciens* (the ancient ones or elders) as "old men," rendered *principaux* (the principal people or leaders) as "principal men," and decided that despite the French clearly stating that women lost their *enfants* (children) to war, *enfants* should be translated as "sons." A few paragraphs later *jeunesse* (youths) becomes "young men." In the process he has taken some serious liberties with a discussion of cultural practices.

[37]

voyant des prisonniers bien faits ou plustos par boutade, ou par caprice les demandent pour remplacer les morts, en ce cas le conseil ne les leur refuSent jamais, d'abord quils sont declarez absous, on les delies, et les femmes ou filles qui les ont sauuez les amenent dans leurs cabanes, elles leur lauent leurs playe les huilent, et les enjoliuent le mieux quils peuuent, et a quelques jour de la on fait vn festin dans cette cabane et les etrangers sont adoptees pour enfans de la maison pour freres, gendres ou autres parens, apres quoy ils sont traitez honnestem[en]t, sans quon les jnsulte d'auantage et ce quil y a de surprenant, cest que ce sont les premiers qui vont en guerre contre leur propre nation et qui tuent ou ammenent prisonniers leurs peres, leurs oncles, ou autres parens jndifferenment comme sils

[37]

attractive prisoners, or rather on a whim or by caprice, ask for them to replace the dead, in that case, the council never refuses them. As soon as they are pardoned, they are unbound and the women or girls who have saved them take them into their cabins. They wash their wounds, oil them, and make them look as good as they can. And, a few days later a feast is held in this cabin and the strangers are adopted as children of the house, as brothers, sons-in-law, or other relatives. After which, they are treated kindly without their being insulted further. And what is surprising is that they are the first who go to war against their own nation, and kill or take as prisoners their fathers, their uncles, or other relatives indifferently, as if they

[38]

ne leur etoient rien du tout faisant plus de cas dela seconde vie qu'on leur a donneé que de celle quils ont recuë de leurs peres et de leurs meres, quils voyent[86] souuent bruler et dechirer, par morceaux pour auoir la dureté de ne point leur rendre la liberté apres les auoir pris, car comme jay desja dit la vie ou la mort des Esclaues depend, ou du conseil, ou des femmes le conseil en distribue quelqu'vns au commandant des françois, et dautres a diuerses,[87] et differentes nations, ce qui confirme et ratifie les alliances, des quils sont livrez ils nen sont plus les maitres mais leurs vies et leurs morts depend de ceux, ou de la nation a qui ils sont donnez le commun vsage est de les[88] faire mourir en la maniere quon vera bientôt, mais comme on a vù que le conseil des anciens accorde la vie aux Esclaves qui[89]

86. Word omitted in 1727 copy (397), which changes the description markedly from seeing relatives burned to carrying out the torture.

87. Word omitted by Margry (95) but found in 1727 copy (398).

88. In the 1727 copy (398) the word *BientoSt* is added here and deleted near the end of this line.

89. The following is inserted here in the 1727 copy: *les femmes Leur demandent.*

[38]

were nothing at all to them, making more cause of the second life that they had been given than that which they had received from their fathers and mothers, whom they often see burned and torn in pieces because they had the hardheartedness not to set them at liberty after capturing them; for, as I have already said, the life or death of the slaves depends either on the council or the women. The council distributes some to the French commandant, and others to various and different nations, which confirms and ratifies their alliances. Once they are delivered up, they are no longer their masters, but [rather,] their lives and their deaths depend upon those, or the nation, to whom they are given. The common practice is to put them to death, in the manner we shall presently see, but as we have seen that the council of the elders grants life to slaves that

[39]

de[90] meme si elles en disirent la mort leur demande ne leurs est jamais refuseé, et parce que la nature trouue mieux son compte, et se trouue plus contente et plus satisfaite principalement dans le sexe par la voye de la vengeance[91] que du pardon, le sort en est quasi toujours malheureux, et sil vit quelque fois il semble que ce nest que par vn miracle de la predestination car comme on a deja vû quils se trouue quelque femmes qui aiant perdu leurs maris, enfans ou parens, songent a remplacer vn mort, il sen rencontre aussy le plus grand nombre des femmes qui aiment a les venger ce quelles pretendent faire en faisant mourir ceux que le sort des armes à mis en leur pouuoir, et a leur diretion,[92] enfin, dés que ces pauures malheureux francois, ou barbares sont destinées a la mort voicy de

90. Margry (95) rewrote much of the rest of this paragraph. The most significant change is that whereas the original reads that some women sought to spare captives and a great many sought revenge, Margry omitted the part about some women seeking to spare prisoners. Several words are also changed in the 1727 copy, but the passage is not rewritten.

91. Word changed to *punition* in 1727 copy (398).

92. The word is *discrétion* in Margry (95) and *discretion* in the 1727 copy (399).

[39]

the women ask of them, so also, if they[53] wish them to die their request is never refused them. And because human nature finds what best serves it, and is happier and more satisfied by means of vengeance than by pardon, especially in the [female] sex,[54] the fate [of the slave] is almost always unhappy, and if he sometimes lives, it seems that it is by nothing but a miracle of predestination. For, as we have seen, some women can be found who, having lost their husbands, children, or relatives, wish to replace the deceased; one also finds the greatest number of women who love to avenge them, which they claim to do in putting to death those whom the fortune of war has placed in their power and at their discretion. Finally, when these poor unfortunates, whether Frenchmen or barbarians, are destined for death, here is

53. That is, the women.

54. The French word here, *sexe,* is gender neutral, as is the article before the word. Given the context of the discussion, and that the gender needs to be identified, female seems to be the logical word to add.

[40]

quelle etrange et funeste maniere Ils y sont conduits

Ces megeres remplies du souvenir et du ressentiment de la mort de leurs parens a qui on a[93] desja fait le meme Sausse,[94] se saisissens de ces patiens, elles les Caresses dabord les amement chez elle, elles les huillés et leur donne a manger et les excite a le Si bien remplir le ventre par ce quelles pretendent quayant a faire vn grand voyage, ils doiuent faire vn bon repas, ou bien prendre des forces pour soufrir plus long temps et auec plus de courage, a les voir faire on diroit quelles en vsent ainsi par amitié, ou[95] par Compassion mais ceux qui sauent la Coutume,[96] ne se rejouissent point de ses sortes de gentillesses, car ils scauent bien que ce quils mangent leur sera de dure digestion, pendant quon recoit toutes ces mignardiSes de la part de

93. The rest of this sentence, ending in *saisissens*, is deleted and replaced with the following in the 1727 copy (399): *fait ordinairement la méme cruauté et Le méme Suplice, se.*

94. *Sort*, in Margry (95).

95. Word omitted then added above the line of text at this point.

96. Margry (96) replaced this with *le contraire*. It is *Coutume* in the 1727 copy (399).

[40]

the strange and lamentable manner by which they are conducted.[55]

These furies, filled with the memory of, and resentment for, the death of their relatives, to whom ordinarily the same cruelties and same suffering have already been inflicted,[56] seize their patients.[57] The women caress them, then take them home with them. They oil them and feed them and urge them to fill their stomachs well, for they claim that, having a long journey to make, they should eat a good meal, or conserve strength to suffer longer and with more courage. To see them doing [this] one would say that they were acting thus out of friendship or compassion, but those who know the custom do not rejoice at these sort of niceties, for they know well that what they eat will be hard to digest. While they are receiving all of these affected niceties from

55. The French here suggests that what follows is a description of the process by which prisoners are tortured to death and not how the prisoners are led, or marched, to their death.

56. As noted at this point in the transcription, both Margry and the 1727 copyist replaced the more colloquial and euphemistic use of *meme Sausse* in the 1718 manuscript. I have used the 1727 text here as it clarifies the meaning of the colloquial expression.

57. Given the range of meanings of the French word here, *patiens*, it is not clear if it is being used to convey irony or sarcasm. The use of "ladies" later in this paragraph seems more clearly meant to mock, as the author does not otherwise use the term "ladies" to describe Indian women even when, in subsequent sections of the manuscript, he praises certain of their qualities.

[41]

ces dames, la jeunesse plante des poteaux, ou ses jnfortunez doiuent etre attachez, et dispose le feux les outils les ferremens, et tous les jnstrumens quils peuuent jnventer pour aSSoupir et rassaSier leur rage et leur f[97]

Tout cet appareil etant prest et acheué, on le fait scauoir a celles qui dorlottes ces pauures victimes, tout d'un coup on voit changer cette douceurs feminine en deespoir et en rage diabolique, et voicy de quelle maniere celle qui a demandé la mort dun prisonnier luy signifie le desastre qui lattend, elle apelle lesprit ou lombre de son mary, ou de son fils ou de tel autre de ces parens qui a eté tué ou brulé et voicy les termes dont elle se sert[98]

Aproche toy mon fils prens courage je te fais aujourdhuy festin de

97. The rest of this word is missing. Margry (96) completed the word as *férocité*, while the 1727 copy (400) has *fureur*. Either word makes sense in this context.

98. Margry (96) rewrote the sentence, to no particular advantage, as: *et elle se sert de ces termes*. It is as here in the 1727 copy (400).

[41]

these ladies, the youth drive posts [into the ground] where these unfortunates are to be tied, and prepare the fires, the tools, the irons, and all the instruments they can invent to appease and satisfy their rage and fury.

All of that preparation being done and ready, they make it known to those women who are coddling the poor victims. All of a sudden one sees this feminine sweetness change into despair and diabolical rage. And this is the manner by which she who has demanded a prisoner's death informs him of the disaster that awaits him. She calls upon the spirit or shade of her husband or son, or whichever other of her relatives has been killed or burned, and here are the terms she uses:

> Come hither, my son. Take courage. Today I will hold today a feast for you

[42]

viande fraiche, boy de ce bouillon, agreé le sacrifice que je te fais de ce guerrier; rejouis toy donc mon cher fils, il sera grillé, brule,[99] on luy arrachera tous les ongles, on grillera cette viande, on en mettra a la Chaudiere, on luy appliquera des colliers de haches rougiee dans le feu, on luy fumera paisiblement les doigts,[100] on luy arrachera les parties, on boira dans son Crâne, on luy leuera la cheuelure soy content mon fils, repose toy maintenant, tu seras vangé,

Dans[101] ces entrefaites vn des guerriers entre dans la Cabanne et dit aceluy qui est deja assez[102] Jnstruit de son sort, prend Courage, mon frere, on te va bruler; lautre luy respond, voila qui va[103] bien je te remercie de la nouuelle que tu m'apporte a meme Jnstant il se fait vn cri

99. These two words are in reverse order in the 1727 copy (401).
100. Inserted here in the 1727 copy (401): *comme on fait Le Tabac.*
101. *Sur* in Margry (97) and as here in the 1727 copy (401).
102. Word omitted in Margry (97) and found in 1727 copy (401).
103. Three words omitted in Margry (97) and found in 1727 copy (401).

[42]

> of fresh meat. Drink of this broth. Accept the sacrifice I make for you of this warrior. Be glad, then, my dear son. He will be roasted, burned; all his nails will be torn off. This meat will be roasted, it will be put in the pot, he will have necklaces of hatchets heated in the fire laid upon him. His fingers will be peacefully smoked as one does tobacco. His [private] parts will be torn out. We will drink from his skull. We will tear off his scalp. Be content, my son. Rest now; you will be avenged.

While this is going on, one of the warriors enters the cabin and says to the one who has already been informed of his fate, "Take courage, my brother, they are going to burn you." The other replies, "That is fine. I thank you for the news you bring me." At the same moment a horrible

[43]

horrible dans tout le village, ce cri Sappelle vn SaKaKüa,[104] on prend, on amene, on lattache au poteau par les pieds par les mains et par le milieu du Corps celuy qui va representer la scene la plus tragique que lhom[m]e[105] puisse jamais conceuoir, car enfin la vieille sacrificatrice na predit quvne partie des douleurs et des tourmens quon doit faire souffrir a sa victime en lhonneur de celui en lhonneur de celui[106] a qui elle est sacrifée ce funeste appareille, qui devroit faire fremir celui pour qui il est preparé, je parle des sauuages; ne lui est cependant quon sujet de mepris pour Ses tirans car[107] il n'est pas plustos serré au poteau quil chante d'un ton ferme et assuré Sa chanson de mort repettant toutes les actions guerriere quil a faite pend[an]t[108] sa vie, et de quelle maniere il a fait bruler

104. Five words missing in 1727 copy (401).

105. This word is spelled here with only one "m." However, in a practice that copyists often use, there is dash over the "m" to indicate that it is a double consonant. This is the first time the copyist has used this technique. In future, as here, the missing letter will be added in square brackets [ ].

106. Four words repeated by copyist.

107. Word omitted by Margry (97) and in 1727 copy (402).

108. Here the copyist used a short flourish/abbreviation to mean something like "read here the usual ending to this word." It is used several times in the manuscript, usually when the word cannot be finished on the line in question. At other times the copyist simply splits the word and completes it on the next line. Where the copyist has adopted this flourish/abbreviation, the missing letters are added in square brackets [ ].

[43]

cry arises throughout the village. This cry is called a *Sakaküa*. They seize [him], take [him] away, fasten him to the post by his feet, his hands, and the middle of his body. He who goes[58] represents the most tragic scene that man can ever conceive of, for in the end, the old-woman sacrificer did not predict but a part of the pain and the torments that they will make her victim suffer in honor of the one to whom he is being sacrificed. This baleful preparation, which should make the one for whom it is intended shudder (I speak of the *sauvages*), is not for him, however, but a subject of scorn for his tyrants,[59] for he is no sooner bound to the post than he chants, in a firm and assured voice, his death song; repeating all of the warlike deeds he has done during his life and in what manner he has burned

58. That is, the prisoner.

59. This should be read that the preparations offer a means by which the victim can show scorn for the efforts of his tormentors.

[44]

ses prisonniers, animant ceux qui sont autour de lui de[109] ne le point epargner, et de le faire mourir en homme de guerre je pense bien que tous ces discours ne partent point du font du coeur, mais[110] il est pourtant Certain que son ame n'en paroit point troubleé ce qui sobseruent en ce que le regardee en est assuré et la contenance egale.

Mais il est temps de commancer le bal, et de voir de quelle maniere on fait dancer le personnage.[111] le 1er pas quon luy[112] fait faire, est de lui arracher auec les dents les ongles des mains les uns apres les autres, leurs pipes et calumets sont faits dune pierre qui se creuse aisement et qui nest point cassante ils les emplissent de tabac, et mettent le doigt du patient dans le trou du calumet quils fument ainsi les dix doigts lun apres lautre[113] a

109. Margry (97) replaced this word here, and a few words later, with *à*. It remains *de* in the 1727 copy (402).

110. Word omitted in Margry (97) and 1727 copy (402).

111. Margry (97) made this plural: *les personnages*. It is as here in 1727 copy (403).

112. Word omitted by Margry (97) and in 1727 copy (403).

113. Margry (97–98) rewrote this sentence: *ils les emplissent de tabac et mettent le doigt du patient dans le trou du calumet, qu'ils fument ainsi les dix doigts l'un après l'autre*. The copyist of the 1727 version (403) also thought he could better convey this scene and wrote that they *mettant Le doight du patiens dans le Calumet qu'ils fûment ainSi doucement d'un bout a l'autre, tous les dix doight ont la méme avanture.*

[44]

his prisoners, urging those around him not to spare him, and to make him die like a man of war. I do think that all this talk is not heartfelt;[60] but it is certain, however, that his mind does not appear to be troubled, which can be seen in the sureness of his gaze and equanimity of his countenance.

But it is time to begin the ball and to see in what manner the character is made to dance.[61] The first step they have him do is, with their teeth, tear out the fingernails from his hands, one after another. Their pipes and calumets are made of a stone that is easily hollowed out and not brittle. They fill them with tobacco and put the fingers of the patient in the bowl of the pipe, which they smoke thus, the ten fingers, one after another.

60. Literally, "from the bottom of the heart."

61. The glibness that marks the preceding few pages reaches its peak in the effort here to compare torture to a theatrical performance.

[45]

près ce petit regal 5 ou 6 ouuriers s'arment d'un tison ardent, les uns les appliquent sur la cheuille du pied, sur les poignets et sur les tempes, ils ne les otent point que les nerfs et la chair nen soit bruleé jusqu'a l'os, cest la le second pas du menuet, le 3e est vn colier de haches ardentes et rougies au feu quon lui met au cou,[114] et qui tombent sur les epaules, et sur le stomach. on ne les en otes que lors quelles sont froides et sans chaleur, et parce que ceux qui font cet exercice sont des gens de bon appetis, chacun auec son couteau leve vn lopin des fesses,[115] dont ils font vne grillade quils mangent sur le champs sans aucun assaisonnemens, et pour lauer[116] les playes et le sang qui en decoule les femmes ont des chaudieres[117] prestes, remplies dEau boüillante quelles renversent dessus, on lui perce de temps en temps le col, et les aiselles,[118] et auec des ferremens

114. Margry (98) deleted the preceding five words, which provide important details about how and where the hatchets are placed. This passage, with *col* in place of *cou*, is found in the 1727 copy (403).

115. *de chaire* in 1727 copy (403).

116. Word missing in 1727 copy (404). The sentence is then rewritten: *Et pour Les playes ou le sang.*

117. Inserted here in 1727 copy (404): *toutes.*

118. *esselles* in 1727 copy (404).

[45]

After this little treat, five or six workers arm themselves with burning firebrands; some apply them to his ankles, wrists, and temples, and do not take them away until the nerves and flesh are burned to the bone. This is the second step of the minuet. The third is a necklace of burning hatchets, heated red hot in the fire, which they put around his neck and which falls over the shoulders and onto the stomach. They do not remove them until they are cold and without heat. And because those who do this work are people with good appetites, each with his knife takes a piece of the buttocks, which they grill and which they eat on the spot without any seasoning. And to wash the wounds and the blood that flows [out], the women have kettles ready, filled with boiling water, which they pour upon them. They pierce him from time to time in the neck and the armpits, and [that] with hot irons

[46]

chauds et rougis dans le feu, on lui brule les parties avec vne ecorce de boulleau qui fait vne flâme tres ardente, et tres penetrante, et pour finir vn si jndigne detail il sufit de dire quon ne lui laisse ny nerfs ny arteres[119] qui ne soit eprouue par le feu, ou par le fer on lui leue en dernier ressort la chevelure, cest a dire la peau ou les cheueux tiennent et cela se fait auec tant dart et dadresse qu'on loste tout dune pièce, et on diroit que cest vne perruque cela fait on jette sur cette chair viue et sanglante, des poignes de cendre chaude et de sable brulant, et lors quils voient que la chair est mortifiée,[120] ils luy donnent le coup de Grace, cest a dire le coup de hache sur la teste ou bien deux ou trois coups de couteau dans le coeur, on luy coupe la teste en meme temps quon fait

119. Added here in 1727 copy (404): *n'y acunes parties de son corps.*

120. Margry (98) transcribed this as *momifiée.* The latter word choice makes little sense in this context. It is as here in 1727 copy (404).

[46]

heated in the fire. They burn his [private] parts with a [piece of] birch bark, which makes a very hot and very penetrating flame. And to end such a shameful description, it suffices to say that they do not leave him either nerves or arteries, nor any part of his body that has not been tested by fire or by iron. Finally, they take off his scalp; that is to say, the skin that holds the hair. And that is done with such art and skill that they remove it all in one piece, and one might say it is a wig. That done, they throw handfuls of hot ashes and burning sand upon this raw and bleeding flesh. And when they see that it is mortified,[62] they give him the *coup de grace*,[63] that is to say, the hatchet blow on the head, or even stab him in the heart two or three times with a knife. They cut off his head while they

62. *Mortifée*, like its English equivalent, refers to flesh that either has gangrene or necrosis. It is not clear which the author meant.

63. Literally, the "favorable blow," which references a final blow to put a living thing out of its misery. It can be translated as "death blow," but the French expression is also used in English.

[47]

voler[121] par tout le village auec des grands cris de joye et de rejouissance comme sils auoient remporté quelques grande victoires

Ceux qui verront ce petit detail auront peut etre de la peine a le croire, et a se persuader qu'un mortel puisse tant souffrir et resister au feu, sans mourir, mais on en doit etre tres convaincu, et cest surtout la malice de la nation jroquoise qui fait bruler ses Esclaves a petit feu pendant 5 ou 6 jours consecutifs.

on pourroit encore sjmaginer quvn personnage ainsi maltraité doit quelque fois verser des larmes ou dans la force de ses tourmens faire des cris dignes de compassion, il s'en trouuent a la verité quelquvns qui ne peuuent s'en deffendre, mais la pluspart semble jgnorer leur douleurs et faire semblant De ne Rien scauoir

121. Margry (98) deleted this word and inserted *entendre*. It is as here in 1727 copy (405).

[47]

fly throughout the village with shouts of joy and delight, as if they had carried off some great victories.

Those who see this little account may perhaps have difficulty believing it, and persuading themselves that a [mere] mortal can suffer so much and withstand burning without dying. But they should be very convinced, and above all [of] the malice of the Iroquois that has its slaves burned by *petit feu* for five or six consecutive days.

One might also imagine that a person thus maltreated must sometimes shed tears or, in the extremity of his torment, utter cries worthy of compassion. In reality, some can be found who cannot help themselves [from doing so], but most seem to ignore their pain and pretend to know nothing

[48]

de ce qui se passent chez eux, car au lieu de demander quartier, Ils reprochent a ceux qui les martyrisent de sorte, que se sont des laches et des Femmes qui n'ont pas le Coeur de les depiecer par le menu, et sils ont sur eux quelque partie exempte Du feu, ils ljndiquent eux mêmes, et ils prient de ne les point epargner essuyant depuis le commancement jusqua la fin toute cette commuauté,[122] sans en faire la grimace, ils demandant seulement a fumer ou a boire de leau ce quon ne leur refuse jamais, et cela com[me] pour reprendre de nouuelles forces afin de donner moyen a leur ennemis dexercer sur eux plus longtemps leur cruauté, et ils leurs parlent en ces termes, prenez courage mes freres diuertissez vous aujourdhuy, et si vous etes jamais pris par ma Nation, et que vous soyez brulee dans

122. Margry (99) rendered this as *ces cruautés*. The 1727 copyist (406) also altered this part and wrote *cette cruautés de peine*.

[48]

of what is happening to them, for instead of asking for quarter, they reproach those who martyr them, in this way: that they are cowards and women who lack the heart to cut them up into bits. And if any part of them has been exempted from the fire, they point it out themselves and beg not to be spared, enduring all these cruelties from beginning to end without grimacing. They ask only to smoke or to drink water, which is never refused them, and [do] that as if to gain new strength in order to enable their enemies to exercise their cruelty upon them longer. And they speak to them in these terms:

> Take courage, my brothers. Amuse yourselves today and, if you are ever taken prisoner by my nation and if you be burned in

[49]

mon village, ne pleurer point, ne crié pas, fumez paisiblement com[m]e moy, il nest permis quaux femmes de verser des larmes vn vray guerrier doit mourir comme je fais.

La vanité[123] destre reputez pour braues est la source et luniqe motif qui produit ljndiference quils ont pour le supplice, et pour les tourmens, et la forme maniere et pratique de la punition et du chatim[en]t, nest quvn pensé y bien, et pour jntimider ceux qui embrassent lart militaire. cest lusage de suplicier ainsi, etoit autrefois en horreur aux françois, mais comme on sest apercus que lhumanité quon exerçoit envers ces barbares[124] etoit regardez parmy eux comme vne lacheté, et que cela leur donnoit lieu de venir plus souuent les attaquer ne risquant tout au plus que destre pris ou tuée, ils les

123. The word order is changed in the 1727 copy (406), and the words *L'unique motif* are moved from near the end of the sentence to here.

124. In the 1727 copy (407), the rest of this thought—indeed, the rest of the paragraph—is deleted. This thought is completed as follows: *ne les touchoit point, il falu ler jmiter*. There is then a gap in writing of about 7.5 cm, which seems to be a deliberate indication that text was left out. The 1727 copy then picks up the text at the first full paragraph on page 57 of the 1718 copy. In all, about seven pages of text are omitted.

[49]

> my village, do not weep, do not cry out. Smoke peacefully like me. It is only women who are permitted to shed tears. A true warrior should die as I do.

The vainglory of being reputed to be brave is the sole source and motive that produces the indifference they have for punishment and torture. And the form, manner, and practice of the punishment are only so that one thinks well of them and to intimidate those who embrace the art of war.[64] This practice of torture was formerly held in horror by the French, but as it was realized that the humanity exercised towards these barbarians[65] was regarded among them as cowardice, and that it led them to attack them [the French] more frequently, risking nothing more than being captured or killed, they

64. For a discussion of the role of torture among Great Lakes groups, see Adam Stueck, "A Place under Heaven: Amerindian Torture and Cultural Violence in Colonial New France, 1609–1729" (PhD diss., Marquette University, 2012); Brandão, "*Your fyre shall burn no more*," 39–41.

65. The use of "barbarians" (*barbares*) here, as a means to make a critical, and negative, value judgment about an Indian practice, adds support to the notion that the use elsewhere of *sauvage*, while serving to differentiate Indian peoples from those of France, has little of the modern pejorative connotation of that word.

[50]

sont a la fin mis sur le pied de les bruler, auec toutes sortes de cruautez tant il est vray qu auec les loups on aprend a heurler, et certainment[125] on ne sest que trop tard auise den user de la sorte; car on saperçoit bien maintenant, que leurs jncursions sont moins frequentes et leurs entreprises moins hardies en vn mot ce sont des hommes qui font autant dEtat de leurs vies que les autres, et sils ont de la bravoure, ou la malice de faire paroitre vne si grande fermeté, et si grand mespris pour la mort, lors quils sont entre les mains ou a la discretion de leurs ennemis, on peut dire aussi quils prennent toutes les precautions possibles pour Euiter nonseulment destre tuez[126] dans le combat, mais meme quils se sont fait vne jdee terrible et effroyable detre pris viuans pour etre ensuite exposé a la rigu[eur] des tourmens cest pourquoy tous les coups quils font sont a la surprise et ceux qui sont surpris sont toujours batus.

125. Preceding two words omitted by Margry (100).

126. Margry (100) made numerous additions and deletions in this section. The most significant was replacing this word with *priz*. Being killed and being taken captive are clearly not the same thing.

[50]

[the French] finally set them up to burn them with all sorts of cruelty—so true it is that among wolves one learns to howl.[66] And certainly it was only too late decided to resort to the like, for it is now very noticeable that their raids are less frequent and their attacks less bold.[67] In a word, they are men who make as much of an account of their lives as do others. And if they have the bravery, or the malice, to show such a great fortitude and such scorn for death when they are in the hands, or at the discretion, of their enemies, one can also say that they take every possible precaution to not only avoid being killed in combat, but also [one may say] that the idea of being taken alive to be afterwards exposed to the severities of torture is terrible and frightful to them. This is why all the blows they strike are by surprise, and those who are surprised are always beaten.

66. The author, like many other European observers who commented on Indian torture, speaks of the "barbarity" of the practice. Why this should be the case is unclear when in France, for example, torture was an accepted part of the questioning of criminals, some executions of criminals were public, and witch trials often ended in public burnings. The "horror" expressed here, feigned or real, may have simply been a device to indicate cultural superiority of the French over those that they sought to colonize and convert, or to justify French adoption of Native torture practices in their own warfare. It may also reflect surprise at both the more public nature of torture and participation in it by other than judicial or clerical authorities.

67. Likely a reference to raids against the French by the Iroquois, as before the early 1700s, the French were not at war with Upper Great Lakes groups. Needless to say, changes in Iroquois strategies had little or nothing to do with French adoption of torture practices, and this seems, again, a rationalization of the latter. On Iroquois policy towards New France and its allies, see Brandão, *"Your fyre shall burn no more."*

[51]

Cependans dans cette conjoncture ils ont recours a leurs jambes, et ils sen sauue souuent quelqu vns mais sils se trouuent tellemens serrez quils ne puissent point sen dedire, et quils soient contrains de combatre quoique leurs forces ne soyent pas egales ils agissent pour lors en deesstereés, et certainement ils vendent chairem[en]t leur peau, voila a peu pres ce que toutes ces nations pratiquent en ce qui concerne les guerres et la chasse.

Chapitre 3
De Leurs Guerres et chasse[127]

On va voir maintenant diuers autres coutumes qui leurs sont communes, comme depouser, ou associer autant de femmes quil leurs plait et quils en peuuent nourrir et entretenir alors quils en sont las ou ennuyez, ils rejettent celles que bon leur Semble, et les remplassent de quelques autre si cest leur fantaisie, et si les femmes

127. Margry (101) deleted this title and replaced it with *Usages des Sauvages*. He was correct that the original title was inappropriate to what follows, which deals not with war and hunting, but rather with other cultural practices. The original title best describes the content of chapter 2 just concluded.

[51]

However, in these predicaments they have recourse to their legs, and often some of them escape. But if they find themselves closed-in in such a way that they must honor their commitment and are constrained to fight, even if their forces are not equal [to their enemy's], they act out of desperation and certainly sell their lives dearly.[68] And that, more or less, is what all these nations practice with regard to war and hunting.

Chapter 3
Of Their Wars and Hunting[69]

We shall now see various other customs that they have in common, such as marrying or consorting with as many women as they please, and as they can feed and support. When they are bored with them, or find them tiresome, they cast off those they want [no more] and replace them by others if that is their wish. And if the women,

68. Literally, "sell their skins dearly."

69. As noted at this point in the transcription, this title better fits the content of the preceding chapter. What follows deals with other aspects of Native cultures.

[52]

pareillement ne sont pas contente de leurs maris, elles les plantent la et sassocie auec vn autre quelles trouuent a leur gré, si bien que par ce moyen il ny a jamais rien de perdu car lun prend ce que lautre quitte et par ces vsages fort naturels et tres comode ils banissent et etvuFFent[128] entre eux toute rancune et[129] antipatie qui trouble la vie et letat des familles on voit neanmoins rarement que les maris rejette sa femme ny que la femme quitte son mary sils ont des enfans, mais si cela arriue toute la progeniture garcons et filles appartiesment a la mere sans quil soit permis au mary den retenir aucun malgre elle, parce que la mere est fondeé sur le droit naturel personne ne luy pouuant disputer quelle ne Soit la mere des enfans quelle a mis au monde, au lieu que le pere en est toujours jncertain et souuent Jnconnu, et cest pour cette raison

128. Two words omitted in Margry (101). The word likely intended here is *etouffant*.

129. Margry (101) changed this to *ou*.

[52]

similarly, are not content with their husbands, they abandon them and consort with another more to their liking.[70] Thus, by this means nothing is ever lost, for one takes what the other gives up and, by these very natural and very convenient customs, they banish and stifle among them all the rancor and antipathy that trouble family life. However, one rarely sees that a husband casts off his wife, or a wife leaves her husband, if they have children. But if that happens, all the offspring, boys and girls, belong to the mother with the husband not being allowed to retain any of them against her will. Because the mother['s title] is based upon natural law, no one can dispute that she is not the mother of the children whom she has put into the world, whereas that of the father is always uncertain, and often unknown, and it is for that reason

70. Polygamy was practiced among Algonquian groups, but monogamy was the rule among the Iroquoians. Divorce, as it is commonly understood today, was an acceptable practice among both culture groups.

[53]

la que les sauuages font leur genealogie, par les femmes, lors quils veulent faire preuue de leur pretenduë noblesse, ors, parmy eux le nombre des enfans nest jamais acharger a la mere, au contraire elle en est plus respectée, plus honoree, estimee, et plus riche, cest pourquoy elle trouue plus facilem[en]t et plus promptement a se remarier, parce que celuy qui lepouse prenant le nom de mary, prend celui de pere et de chef de toute la famille et par ce moyen il en est plus acredité car si les enfans sont grands ils soutienne la cabane cest a dire la maison soit par leurs actions guerrieres soit par la chasse ou bien ou bien,[130] par les alliances quils font en prenant dautres femmes et sils sont encore petits le beau pere pretend et Espere, que si on lui fait jnjure ou quelque tort en sa personne il sera vengé lors que ses beaux fils qui le regardent pour leur propre pere seront paruenus a vn age com

130. Two words repeated by the copyist.

[53]

that the *sauvages* trace their genealogy through the women, when they want to prove their alleged nobility.[71] Now, among them the number of children is never a burden to the mother. On the contrary, she is more respected, more honored, more esteemed, and richer [for them]. That is why she is able to remarry more easily, because the one who marries her, in taking the name of husband, takes also that of father and head of the whole family. And, by this means, he is more accredited, for if the children are grown up they support the cabin—that is to say the household—either by their deeds as warriors or by hunting, or even by the alliances they make in taking wives of their own. And if they are still young, the stepfather claims and trusts that if he is done any personal wrong or injury he will be avenged when his stepsons, who regard him as their own father, reach an age of

71. Algonquians were patrilineal societies while Iroquoians were matrilineal.

[54]

ptans, cela arriue aussy car le sauuage n'a rien tant au Coeur que la vengeance, et ces pour ces raisons que les veuues ayant des Enfans trouue commodement vn mary.

Mais si vn homme tombe en veuuage et que sa femme luy laisse des enfans de son mariage, pour lors la parenté luy cherche vne epouse sortable a son etat quon propose et quon amene ensuite dans la Cabanne du veuf, et, si la refuse, et que par succession du temps il en prenne vne autre a sa fantaisie, il est permis a celle qui recoit cet afront de chanter pouille et de dire toutes les jnjures qui luy plait a celuy qui la refusée, et renvoyée apres quoy, elle casse romp et briSe toute ce quelle trouue[131] dans la cabane pille, prend et enleue tout ce quil y a de plus beau et de meilleur et lemporte chez elle, sans que le veuf remarié ny sa femme qui est repu[t]ée pour concubine y apporte aucun empechement ny sans dire aucune

131. Margry (102) changed this to *qu'il y a*.

[54]

maturity. This happens also, for the *sauvage* holds nothing more to heart than revenge, and it is for these reasons that widows who have children easily find a husband.

But if a man falls into widowerhood, and his wife leaves him children from their marriage, then the relatives look for a wife for him, suitable to his circumstances, whom they propose to him and afterwards take to the widower's cabin. And, if he refuses her and in the course of time takes another [more] to his liking, it is permitted to the woman who has received this affront to insult[72] and castigate, as much as she wants, the one who refused her. And after being dismissed, she smashes and breaks up everything that she finds in the cabin, plunders it, [and] carries off all that is finest and best in it, and takes it to her own home, without the remarried widower nor his wife, who is considered as a concubine, seeking to stop her, nor say a

72. The two French words here (sing and louse/flea) form a colloquial phrase that means to hurl insults at a person. Insult (*insulte*) also existed in this period.

[55]

parole lune et lautre ne font que baisser le nezs, et semble receuoir en cela quelque confusion, quoi que dans le font ils ne fasse quen rire si bien quapres que cette femme sest ainSy vengez elle est contente et satisfaite et ne parle plus de cette afaire la

Si vn homme marié decede sans lignee, et quil ait vn ou plusieurs freres morts,[132] vn dentre eux espouse la veuue, comme pour Susciter des enfans a son frere mort, ils arriuent aussy quils epouse souuent les deux soeurs et il nont point de degré de parenté du Costé des femmes qui leur servient[133] dobstacle a loccasion du mariage, ils se Servent des memes termes et prennent les memes qualitez qui sont en vsage parmy nous comme de grandpere, grand mere, gendre, oncle, neueu, et le reste

Les peres Et meres aiment tendrem[en]t leurs enfans et leur laissent la liberté de disposer de tout ce qui est dans

132. This appears to be an error and makes little sense given what follows. Margry (103) changed this to *vivans*.

133. Margry (103) changed this to *fasse*.

[55]

word. They[73] only hang their heads[74] and appear to be troubled by [all] that, however they really are only laughing, so that after the woman is thus avenged, she is happy and satisfied, and talks no more about the matter.

If a married man dies without issue, and has one or more brothers who have died,[75] one from among them marries the widow, as if to assure children for his dead brother. And it also often happens that they marry two sisters, and they have no degree of kinship on the women's side that serves as an obstacle on the occasion of marriage.[76] They use the same terms, and attach the same meanings, as those in use among us, such as grandfather, grandmother, son-in-law, uncle, nephew, and the rest.

Fathers and mothers love their children tenderly and give them liberty to make use of everything that is in

73. That is, the new couple.

74. Literally, "lower their noses."

75. As noted at this point in the transcription, the word here, *morts* (dead/died), makes little sense given what follows about "one among them" marrying the widow. Still, that is what is written. Logic suggests the use of *morts* here was a scribe's error and the sentence should read: "If a married man dies without issue, and has one or more brothers who are alive, one of them marries the widow to raise up children to assure that the brother's line continues." This is how that practice is described at page [76] below.

76. Both Algonquian and Iroquoian societies were governed by complex clan systems, which regulated all manner of social interactions, among other things. Clans were exogamous and people had to marry outside of their particular clan. By definition, then, clan rules regulated kinship relations.

[56]

la Cabanne, et de deliberer de affaires de leurs[134] familles de lavient que les soeurs ont plus de respects pour leurs freres que pour leurs pere et mere, de sorte que lors quvn frere desire et Souhaite quelque choSe dhonneste de Sa soeur, elle ne lon desdit jamais, et ne lui refuse point ce quil luy demande, et lors quils sont ensemble si quelquvn dit quelque parole [135]contre la bienseances, la pudeur leurs en vient au visage, ils baissent les yeux et en sont Confus, ce qui prouue le grand respect quils ont lun pour lautre, lors quune femme est accoucheé elle fait lit apart et demeure pendant 40 jours separee le 41e elle entre dans sa Cabane sa Cabanne,[136] ou elle bat du feu nouueau auec vne pierre à fusil du tondre et batte feu, apres quoi elle est purifiée, et lors que les fe[mmes] ou filles ont leurs Fleurs elles se bannissent de leur Cabannes et chacune fait vne petite[137] loge a lecart, les autres leur aportent a manger

134. Changed to *la* in Margry (103).

135. *chose* in Margry (103).

136. Words repeated by the copyist.

137. Word missing in Margry (104).

[56]

the cabin and to deliberate on the affairs of their families. From this it arises that sisters have more respect for their brothers than for their father or mother, such that when a brother desires and wishes something honest of his sister, she never says no and never refuses him what he asks. And if they are together, if someone says an unseemly word, they blush,[77] they lower their eyes and are troubled, which proves the great respect they have for one another. When a woman is confined, she makes her bed apart and remains separated from her husband for forty days. On the forty-first day she enters into her cabin, where she strikes a new fire with a flint stone, some *tondre*,[78] and a strike-a-light. After that she is purified. And when the women or girls have their flowering [of womanhood], they leave their cabins and each one makes a small lodge apart. The others bring them food

77. Literally, "their sense of modesty comes over their face."

78. This word, then and now, means to shear or crop. The Jesuit priest Paul Le Jeune (*Relation* of 1634, *JR*, 6:216) uses this word (*petit morceau du tondre*) and explains that it is a "dry, rotten wood which burns easily." (Ibid, 217) *Tondre*, at least as it was used in New France, seems to mean some sort of tinder or kindling.

[57]

dans vn plat, quelles laissent a leur porte, sans les vouloir aprocher, ny entrer chez elles, des quelles sont deliuree de cette jncomodité elles reuiennent dans leurs Cabans. [138]

Lors que Les femmes sont enceintes et[139] nourrices leurs maris sabtienne de coucher auec elles parce qu'ils estim[ent] et pretendent que laccouplement[140] charnel ruine la substance que lenfant recoit dans le ventre de sa mere le fait deperir, le peut deplacer, et lexpose a la mort,

Et quand aux nourrices, ils disent que ce meme commerce corompt leur lait et que si elles deuiennent enceintes, on ne peut echaper le nourrisson vû quils nont point dautres nourriture a leur donner; mais ils sont souuent les dupes de cette affaire la, car leurs femmes ne se payent point de ces sortes de Raisons, sallant pouruoir secretement ailleurs sembarrassant fort peu de ce regime

138. The 1727 copy (407) picks up the narrative, as per the 1718 copy, after this point.

139. It is *ou* in the 1727 copy (407).

140. Margry transcribed this as *accouchement*. It is as here in the 1727 copy (407).

[57]

in a dish, which they leave at their door, not wanting to approach them or enter among them. As soon as they are delivered from this inconvenience, they return to their cabins.

When the women are with child, or wet nursing,[79] their husbands abstain from sleeping with them, for they reckon and claim that coupling of the flesh ruins the substance that the child receives in the womb of its mother, weakens it, causes it to be displaced [from the womb], and exposes it to death.

As for nursing, they say that this same commerce spoils their milk and that if they become with child they could not avoid nursing, seeing as they have no other food to give it. But they[80] are often dupes in that matter, for their wives, paying no heed to such reasons, go off to provide for themselves secretly elsewhere, encumbering themselves very little with that way

79. The French word here (*nourrice*) refers, then and now, to a wet nurse. The word seems to be used here in the sense of *nourrir* (to nourish or feed), rather than as a reference to a wet nurse, but given the sentence structure, either is possible. In the next paragraph the word seems clearly to be used to mean nursing.

80. That is, the husbands.

[58]

de vie. Il est cependant vray quil y en a beaucoup qui obseruent cette coutume par la tendresse quelles ont pour leur fruit.

Voicy[141] de quelle manieres illes font leurs[142] festes pour les morts; ils dressent vne cabanne qui a environ six vingt pied de long, les Ecorces en sont neuues et nont servi a aucun vsage, ils plantent vn may a chaque bout et vn autre dans le milieu qui les surpasse en hauteur, ces mays sont huilez graissez et peints il y a a la cime de chacun vn prix, qui appartient a celuy qui le peut joindre le premier, et l'atteindre auec la main, ils entre ensuite dans cette Cabanne, neuue, ou il y a diuers etages. ils apportent les ossemens de leurs parens qui sont dans de petits Sacs, ou enveloppés fort proprement dans des Ecorces, ils les[143] rangent dun bout a l'autre et les enrichissent de tout ce quils ont

141. In the 1727 copy (408) this paragraph, and following section, is preceded by a title in large letters: *Festes pour les morts.*

142. *Les* in 1727 copy (408).

143. Word omitted and added above the line of text at this point.

[58]

of life. It is, however, true that there are many who do observe this custom because of affection they have for their offspring.

Here is the manner by which they hold their feasts for the dead. They erect a cabin that is about 120 feet long. The bark [coverings] are new and have never been used before. They plant a maypole at each end and one in the middle that surpasses them in height. These maypoles are oiled, greased, and painted. There is, at the top of each one, a prize that belongs to the one who can climb [the pole] first and reach it with his hand. Then they enter this new cabin, where there are several platforms. They bring the bones of their relatives, which are in small bags or wrapped very neatly in bark. They arrange them from one end to the other [of the cabin], enriching them with all they have

[59]

de plus beau et de meilleur et ordinairement de ce quils ont amassé[144] pendant trois anneés, cependant les chaudieres sont toujours sur le feu, remplies de viande, et en mange qui veut ils font un bruit continuel nuit et jour auec des tambours ou bien en frappant sur les chaudieres ou sur des ecorces auec des bâtons ils sortent de temps en temps, et entourent la cabanne, tirant des coups de fusils, faisant des Cris et des[145] heurlements que tout en tremble, ils rentrent apres cela mattachez de noir enfin, ce mesme fracas continuë pendant trois jours et trois nuits, mais, auant que le terme nen soit tout a fait expiré, ils font present a ceux qui sont jnuitez a la feste de tout ce qui appartient aux morts, cest a dire de tout le butin dont les os sont couuerts, lors que la distribution en est faite, ils sortent pour la derniere fois et environnent la Cabane en faisant de

144. *ramaSsez* in 1727 copy (409).

145. Three words omitted by Margry (105) and found in 1727 copy (409).

[59]

that is finest and best, and usually it is what they have amassed over three years. Meanwhile, the kettles are constantly on the fire, full of meat, and those who want, eat. They make a continual clamor, night and day, with drums or by striking on the kettles or on the bark [coverings] with sticks. They leave from time to time and surround the cabin, shooting guns and crying out and yelling until everything trembles. They reenter, after that, *mattachez* with black. Finally, this same din continues for three days and three nights, but before the time has quite expired, they make presents to those who are invited to the feast of everything that belongs to the dead—that is to say, all the booty with which the bones are covered. When the distribution is done, they go out for the last time and surround the cabin.

[60]

grands heurlemens, ils foncent dessus a grands Coups de bâtons et a coups de perches, faisant vn tintamarre enragé,[146] brisent et mettent en pieces toutes les ecorces, cela acheué les Femmes sont la toutes pretes auec des fagots de sapin, et en font vn lit[147] sur la terre dun bout a ıautre ou la cabanne etoit située, en meme temps ils tuent grande quantité de chiens qui sont leurs moutons et qui sont estimez parmy eux plus que toute autre animal, ils en font vn festin, mais auant de manger ils plantent deux grandes perches et y attachent au bout den haut vn chien quils sacrifient au soleil, et a la lune, les priant d'avoir pitié et prendre soin des ames de leurs parens de les Eclairer dans leurs voyage, et de les conduire dans la demeure de leurs anciens cette jdee prouue ljmmortalité de l'ame. cette festes etant ainsi acheuée chacun prens les ossemens de ses parens, ils portent tous de la main, et les apportent dans Des Lieux pierreux, creusez raboteux

146. Four words omitted in 1727 copy (409) and replaced with *frappant comme des enragez.*
147. *feu* in 1727 copy (410).

[60]

Yelling loudly, they fall upon it with heavy blows from cudgels and blows from big rods, making a maddening racket, shattering and breaking all the bark into pieces. That done, the women are there, all ready with pine faggots, and make a fire[81] on the ground from one end to the other of where the cabin was situated. At the same time they kill a large quantity of dogs, which are their sheep,[82] and which are more esteemed among them than any other animal, [and] they make a feast. But before eating they set up two tall, thin poles and attach to the top end [of each] a dog that they sacrifice to the sun and the moon, praying to them to have pity and to take care of the souls of their relatives, to light [the way for] them in their journeys, and to guide them to the dwelling place of their ancestors. This idea proves the immortality of the soul.[83] This feast being thus concluded, each one takes the bones of their relatives (they carry all by hand) and carries them to some stony place, hollow, rugged,

---

81. As noted at this point in the transcription, the 1718 version has *lit* (bed) here, and *feu* (fire) is found in the 1727 version. Given what follows about roasting dogs for a feast, and that beds generally were not made of sticks, fire makes more sense than bed.

82. That is to say, are to Indians what sheep are to the French.

83. That is, this proves that Indians believe in the immortality of souls.

[61]

et peu frequentez, ils les laissent la et cest la fin de la ceremonie et il nest plus parlé des morts, dont on a fait la feste en aucune maniere, et ils demeure dans vn perpetuel oubly.[148]

Leur oppinion est que les ames separeé des corps samusent et restent dans le village errans ça et la, dedans et autour de leur cabanes par vn allechement naturel, et a cause de lamitié quelles onts pour leurs parens et amis ils disent aussi quelles font peur aux petis enfans, aux jeunes gens et a eux memes principalement la nuit, et ils sjmaginent que ce grand bruit confus, ce tintamare et ce brisement decorces chagrine ces ames qui se Sont assembleés dans cette cabane, et leur faitt prendre la resolution et le dessein daller joindre celles de leurs peres, quils croyent etre dans vn tres bon pais, et dont le sejour est tres[149] agreable, et parce que dans le leur il y a[150] quantité de fraises et de framboiSes ils simaginent que dans ces contrees ou les ames reSident il y en a qui sont grandes et grosses comme la

148. Margry (106) rewrote the sentence, from "ceremonie" forward as: *Ensuite il n'est plus parlé, en aucune manière, des morts, dont on a fait la feste et ils demeurent dans un perpétuel oubly.* In the 1727 copy (410) the text is changed beginning at "la": *apres que tout cela est fait il n'est plus parlé des morts dont on a fait La feste en aucune maniere, ils demeurent dans un perpetuelle oubly.*

149. *fort* in 1727 copy (411).

150. Inserted here in 1727 copy (411): *une grande.*

[61]

and unfrequented. They leave them there, and that is the end of the ceremony. And after all that is done, the dead, whose feast they have held, are never spoken of again in any way: they remain in perpetual oblivion.

Their view is that the souls, separated from the body, amuse themselves and remain in the village, wandering hither and thither in and around their cabins by a natural enticement, and [do that] on account of the affection they have for their relatives and friends. They also say that they[84] frighten little children, young people, and themselves, especially at night. And they imagine that the great racket, the hammering and smashing to bits of the bark[85] vexes the souls that are assembled in this cabin, and causes them to resolve and plan to go and join those of their fathers—which they believe are in a very fine country, and where the stay is most pleasant. And, because in theirs[86] there are large quantities of strawberries and raspberries, they imagine that in those countries where the souls dwell there are some that are big and fat as a

84. That is, the souls.

85. That is, the bark-covered structure described above in which the feast was held.

86. That is, their own land.

[62]

teste, ils estiment que cette region est vers l'orient que lair en est doux et bien temperé, quil ny a ny pluye ny neige, ny vent ny pierre ny montagnes, que tous les chemins sont pauees de robbes de loustres de martres et de castors, en vn mot que cest vn païs de recreation, et ou l'on nendure jamais ny soif ny faim,[151] que tous y seront egalement heureux, et ils nyent entierement vn lieux ou les ames soient tourmenteés, rejetant loppinion de la resurrection des corps

Et comme, parmi les Europeens les filles sont a charges et quon est quasi toujours contraints de les dotter pour les marier, parmy les Sauuages au contraire elles sont la Richesse de leurs parens car celui qui en veut auoir en mariage n'en a que pour de largent, et les achetent par vn present considerable quil fait a son beau pere pretendu, ou sil est mort ou absent, auplus proche de la parentéil faut neanmoins qu'auparauant il ait le consentement de sa maitresse, il faut scauoir que les amans gallantisent la comme ailleurs

151. Two words missing in 1727 copy (411).

[62]

[person's] head. They reckon that this region is towards the east, that the air is mild and temperate, that there is neither rain nor snow nor wind, nor rocks nor mountains; that all the paths are paved with robes of otter, martens, and beaver; in a word, that it is a land of recreation, and where one endures neither thirst nor hunger, that all are equally happy, and they deny entirely [the notion of] a place where souls are tormented, rejecting the idea of a resurrection of the body.

And as among Europeans daughters are a burden and one is almost always compelled to give them a dowry in order to marry them [off], among the *sauvages*, on the contrary, they are the wealth of their parents, for the one who wants to have them in marriage cannot do so without money, and they buy them by a large present that he makes to his intended father-in-law or, if he is dead or absent, to the nearest relative. He must, however, first have the consent of his mistress. One should know that lovers court there, as elsewhere,

[63]

debittent la fleurette, et se donnent reciproquement des marques de respets et de tendresse, les filles ont cet auantage quil leur est permis de se diuertir et de faire le nouiciat du mariage autant de temps[152] quil leur plait, et auec autant de garçons que bon leur semble sans quon y trouue a redire, et sans que cela les empechent de trouuer vn mary lors que la fantaisie leur en prends et voicy comment ils se conduisent en leurs amours les jeunes gens ont des ecorces qui se roulent en forme de flambeau ils les allument la nuit par vn bout et courent ainsi toutes les cabanes, si tel est leur plaisir, les filles sont coucheés sur le bord de lalleé, et lors que leur bien aimé passent elles l'arretent par vn coin de sa robbe en meme temps que le gallant sent ce signal ils ce baisse, et pour lors sa maitresse prend son ecorce et leteint, et fait coucher le jeune homme aupres d'elle[153] qui lui compte sa passion, et au milieu de cette priuauté, et[154] liberté entiere il ne sy passe souuent rien que de

152. Seven words omitted in 1727 copy (412).

153. Margry (107) reordered this portion of the sentence: *et fait coucher auprès d'elle le jeune homme.* It is as here in the 1727 copy (413).

154. Two words omitted in the 1727 copy (413).

[63]

utter sweet nothings, and give one another tokens of respect and of affection. The girls have this advantage, that they are allowed to amuse themselves and try apprenticeship marriage as many times as it pleases them, and with as many boys as they think best, without reproach, and without that preventing them from finding a husband when the fancy takes them. And this is how they conduct themselves in their lovemaking. The young people[87] have [pieces of] bark that are rolled up in the form of a torch. They light them at night at one end, and wander thus [through] all the cabins, if that is their desire. The girls are lying down on the side of the passageway, and when their beloved passes they stop him by seizing a corner of his garment. At the same time the gallant feels this signal, he stoops down, and then his mistress takes his torch and puts it out, and makes the young man lie down beside her, for him to tell her [of] his love. And in the midst of this privacy and complete freedom, often nothing takes place but what

87. The French words here (*jeunes gens*) means young people and is usually rendered as young men. Given what follows, that seems to be what is meant. Still, this is a description of a cultural practice and nothing indicates that young women cannot, in other instances, do likewise.

[64]

fort honnete, et fort respectueux, tant il est vray qu'on fait moins de cas de ce qui est permis que de ce qui est deffendu, car il est constant que dans cette occasion, il ne depend que des deux amoureux de ce satisfaire et neanmoins la plus grande partie nen font rien, surtout sils ont dessein de ce marier ensemble, enfin, quand la belle Sennuye, et veut dormir, elle auertit son amant quils se retirent[155] aussitôt quelle le luy ordonne cela sapelle parmy eux courir l'allumette quand aux femmes mariees elles sont obligees de prendre dautres mesures, car elles sont rudement chastieé parmy quelques nations et non en toutes, si elles sont convaincuë de libertinage ainsi que je le marqueray dans vn autre endroit

Tous[156] les nations ont leurs mediciens chirurgiens et appotiquaires qui sont applez jongleurs lors quil y a donc quelque malade, on les fait venir tous les trois, le medecin examine lEtat de la maladie apres auoir

155. Changed to *qui se retire* in 1727 copy (413).

156. In the 1727 copy (414) a title, in large letters, precedes this paragraph: *Leurs Medicins.*

[64]

is very honest and very respectful. For it is true that people make less cause of what is permitted than of what is forbidden, for it is [a] constant that on those occasions nothing prevents the two lovers from satisfying themselves, and yet most of them do nothing, above all if they plan to get married. At last, when the *belle*[88] is tired and wants to sleep, she informs her lover, who retires as soon as she orders him [to]. That is called among them "roaming [with] the matchstick."[89] As to married women, they are obliged to make other arrangements, for they are roughly chastised among some nations, and not in all, if they are convicted of licentiousness, [as] I will so show in another place.

All the nations have their doctors, surgeons, and apothecaries, who are called jugglers.[90] When, then, someone is sick, they send for all three of them, [and] the doctor examines the state of illness. After having

88. This word in French and English means "pretty girl" or "pretty woman." Given the context of the passage, the former seems to be intended.

89. A few lines above, the light source was called a torch, but *allumette*—the word used here, then and now, means matchstick.

90. This should be read as "who are called jugglers by the French." The former have a long history in France, but by this period the term *jongleurs* had come to carry a connotation of deceit. (See José António Brandão, ed. and trans., *Nation Iroquoise: A Seventeenth-Century Ethnography of the Iroquois* (Lincoln: University of Nebraska Press, 2003), 134 n. 38.) Indians had other names for what are called in English today shamans or medicine men. The author is relatively unique in describing the various roles of a shaman as belonging to different individuals. Most early observers who describe the activities of shamans do not remark about specialization. (See, for example, René Cuillerier's account in ibid., 93–95.) It should also be noted that efforts such as these described here were undertaken most often when the immediate cause of an illness was not evident. Little of the process described here was needed to mend a broken bone or cut. Such matters, as the author notes below, were readily handled by most individuals.

[65]

longtemps[157] jonglé cest a dire revé ils ordonnent ordinairement de tuer plusieurs chiens parce que cest pour eux la viande la plus exquiSe, et pour mieux couurir la charlatanerie, il faut quil y en ait deux blancs deux noirs et deux d'une autre couleur, ils en fait[158] offrir vn ou deux en sacrifice au soleil et a la lune,[159] afin quils prennent pitié du malade, cette ordonnance ne Se fait qu apres vne penible contemplation, parce que le jongleur ou charlatan nattribue jamais la cause du mal aux jnfirmitez ou accidens[160] qui arriuent au corps humain, mais ils pretendent que cest vn sort qui lon a jetté sur le malade par la malice et la mechanceté de quelque ennemis ov ils font entendre que cest vn esprit protecter cest a dire le Dieu quils se Sont forgez dans leur jmagination qui leur reuele et leur fait connoitre comment et de quelle maniere le poison et le sort a eté jetté sur celui qui est jnfirme cest pourquoy il acheue son ordonnance indiquant a apoticaireé, les simples et

157. In the 1727 copy (414) this word is omitted here and added after *dire*.

158. *font* in Margry (108) and in 1727 copy (414).

159. Inserted here in the 1727 copy (414) is: *Et a quelques ESpirits en qui ils ont de la confiance.*

160. Here again in the 1727 copy (415) a large section of text is omitted—this time without indication. The copyist leaves out material from page 65 to the end of page 69 in the 1718 copy. He concludes this section as follows: *ou accidens a qui les autres hommes L'attribuent, Et qu'il y a des trompeurs et des charlatans Sur tout dans L'Ecole de Galien e d'hypocrates*. The latter part of this sentence is found at page 69 of the 1718 copy.

[65]

juggled[91] for a long time, that is to say dreamed, they usually order several dogs slaughtered, because for them this is the most exquisite meat. And to better cover up the quackery, there have to be two white, two black, and two of another color. They offer one or two in sacrifice to the sun or the moon,[92] so that they will take pity on the invalid. This prescription is not made until after a laborious contemplation, because the juggler or charlatan never attributes the cause of the illness to ailments or accidents that come upon the human body, but they claim that it is a spell that has been cast on the invalid by the malice or ill will of some enemy. Now[93] they lead [them to] understand that it is a guardian spirit, that is to say, the god whom they have invented in their imagination, who has revealed to them and made them understand how, and in what way, the poison and the spell were cast upon the one who is sick. This is why he completes his prescription [by] indicating to the apothecary the [medicinal] herbs

91. This should be read as something akin to "after having performed his role as a juggler [shaman]."

92. At this point in the 1727 copy is added: "and to some spirits in which they have confidence." While language from the 1727 copy is included in the translation when it helps advance clarity (see "Note on Translation" above), this partial sentence seems to introduce an entirely new concept into a description of a cultural practice. Without any clear reason as to why this was done, it seems worth noting here, but not adding to the translation.

93. In the sense of "sometimes they."

[66]

raciner ou animaux quil faut auoir pour composer et faire des contre poisons ou breuuages pour expulser et faire vomir ceux qui trauaillent le corps et lesprit du malade, lapoticaire execute Lordonnance du medecin cherche les simples ou animaux specifiée mais tous les deux jöuent fort bien leur rôle Car tout cela ne Se trouue jamais a leur dire qu auec beaucoup de peine, le chirurgien est le plus grand charlatan de tous, et le plus jnsigne jongleurs, le personnage quil fait est asseurement horrible[161] a voir, et ceux qui le regard[ent] faire ne peuuent sjmaginer autre choSe si ce nest quil est possedé du demon pendant quils fait sa jonglerie, ceux qui sont autour battent des tambours frappent auec des buchettere sur des chaudieres et des Ecorces ce qui continuë pendant le cours de la maladie pour donner le bal au malade, il nest pas convenable comment vn si grand bruit ne fait tourner la teste a Ses pauvres gens, cependant dans ces jnterualles

161. Margry (109) transcribed this word as *humble,* which makes no sense in the context of this passage.

[66]

and roots or animals he needs to have to compound and make the antidotes or beverages that will expel and cause to vomit out the [poisons] that are tormenting the body and mind of the sick person. The apothecary executes the doctor's prescription [and] seeks the [medicinal] herbs or animals specified, but both of them play their parts very well, for all that cannot be found, according to them, but with great difficulty. The surgeon is the greatest charlatan of all, and the most remarkable juggler. The part he plays is certainly horrible to see, and those who see him play it cannot but imagine anything other than that he is possessed by a demon while he is doing his juggling. Those who are around [him] beat drums, and strike kettles and bark with sticks, and this continues during the course of the illness, in order to hold a ball for the invalid.[94] It is inconceivable how such an uproar does not make these poor people's heads spin. Meanwhile, in these intervals,

94. Whether the author intends this phrasing as sarcasm, or to say this is to entertain or distract the invalid, is not clear.

[67]

le chirurgien dance, chante, fait des contorsions effroyables, tourne et renverse ses yeux, se rebiffe le nez, enfonce ses machoires, se disloque le menton son col tantos salonge et tantos Se racourcit, ses poulmons se gonflent, et son estomac senfle, ses doigts, ses mains ses bras setendent et Se retirent, il crache le sang par la bouche, il en fait sortir par le Nez et par les oreilles, et se dechire et inciSe la peau, et comme jay deja dit tout cecy et plusieurs autres choSes se font en chantant et dançans, enfin apres toutes ces meneés, celui decouure lendroit ou le sortilege est placé en telle sorte, que sil uoit que le malade a de la peine a cracher, ou a respirer il fait croire que le sort quon luy a jetté est vn os qui sest mis en trauer du gosier, il sapproche du malade en faisant des grimaces; il luy prend le gosier auec ses dents, mais tout bellement faisant semblant de chercher cet os quil trouue toujours parce quil la dans sa bouche ainsi apres auoir bien fait des facons

[67]

the surgeon dances, sings, makes frightful contortions, rolls his eyes, wrinkles up his nose, sinks his jaw in, contorts his chin; his neck now stretches and now shortens; his lungs expand and his stomach swells; his fingers, his hands, his arms stretch out and draw back in; he spits blood from his mouth; he makes it issue from his nose and ears, and he tears and cuts his flesh. And, as I have already said, these and many other things are done while chanting and dancing. Finally, after all of these maneuvers, he discovers the spot where the spell has been placed, such that if he sees that the invalid has difficulty spitting, or breathing, he make-believes that the spell that has been cast upon him is a bone that is in his[95] throat. He approaches the invalid, grimacing; he takes hold of his[96] throat with his teeth, but very gently, pretending to look for that bone, which he always finds because he has it in his mouth. So, after making much fuss

95. That is, the patient's.

96. That is, the invalid's.

[68]

en cette recherche, il se leue en sursaut et fait vn grand cri de joye pour marquer que le Sort est leué et crache cet os sur quelque chose, pour lors tous les assistant admirent son art et sa capacité, et le malade commance a se croire guery en vn mot toute la science consiste a sauoir la partie malade qui luy est declaré par celuy qui soufre, et pour lors il dit quil y a dans la partie affligée ou vn os, vne visse de fusil, vne Epine, ou vne areste, ou du poil ou autre chose Semblable, mais si le malade ne guerit point, et que son mal continuë et augmente le chirurgien continuë aussi de jongler il luy arrache toujours quelque piece ensorceleé et lappoticaire de son costé opere auec ses médicamens, et lors que le malade meurt ils font comme nos medecins et ensuite[162] se retirent et disant quil nen pouuoit pas Echaper cependant de quelque maniere quil en soit ces charlatans la ruinent et appauurisse[nt] La Cabanne ou la famille du malade

162. Two words omitted by Margry (110).

[68]

in this search, he jumps up, and utters a great joyful cry to show that the spell is lifted, and spits out that bone onto something. Thereupon all in attendance marvel at his art and cleverness, and the invalid begins to think himself healed.[97] In a word, all of the science consists in learning what the sick part is, which is declared to him by the one who is suffering. And then he says there is, in the affected part, a bone, a gun screw, a thorn, or a fishbone, or some hair, or something of the kind. But if the sick person does not improve and his [or her] illness continues and worsens, the surgeon continues, consequently, to juggle. He always picks out of him some bewitched piece of something, and the apothecary, on his side, works with his medicines. And when the patient dies, they do like our doctors and quickly withdraw, and say that he could not escape [his fate]. However, whichever way it turns out, these charlatans ruin and impoverish the cabin or family of the sick person,

97. For most of this passage, the reference is to a generic sick person, and nothing about what has been described is necessarily limited to the treatment of men.

[69]

Car sil guerit il leur donne tout ce quil possede, et toute la famille en fait de même, et sil meurt on ne laisse pas que de leur faire vn present tres considerable

Ces sortes de gens sont respetez et estimez parmy toutes les nations ils ont ladresse meme de se distinguer des autres en leurs manieres et en leurs actions qui sont exterieurem[en]t mieux reglee et plus moderees, leur demarches est aussy plus graue et plus composée que celle des autres, lors quils vont quelque part, ou quils sortent de leurs cabannes, ils portent autour de leur cou, Sur lepaule, ou sur le bras, vne peau de loutre ou de quelques autres betes bien enjoliuée, et cest par cette marque qu'on connois ces docteurs la, comme on remarque les chanoines par laumusse, cela fait voir que par tout le monde les vns abusent les autres, et qu'il y a des trompeurs et des charlatans surtout dans Ecole de Gallien et dJipocrate

vne[163] Chose est neanmoins tres certaine

163. The 1727 copy (415) again matches that of 1718 at this point.

[69]

for if he recovers, he gives them all that he possesses, and the whole family does likewise. And if he dies, they do not fail to make them[98] a very considerable present.

These sorts of men are respected and esteemed among all the nations. They even have the cleverness to distinguish themselves from the rest in their manners and in actions, which are outwardly more regular and more restrained; their gait is also more studied and more solemn than that of the others. When they go anywhere, or if they leave their cabins, they wear round their necks, on their shoulder, or on their arm, the skin of an otter or of some other beast, prettily decorated; and it is by this sign that one recognizes the doctors there, just as one recognizes monks by their amices.[99] This shows that throughout the world some [people] abuse others, and that there are cheats and charlatans, especially in the school of Galen and Hippocrates.

One thing, nevertheless, is quite certain

98. That is, the shamans.

99. A fur-lined hood carried on the left arm by members of certain religious orders when on their way to perform their offices.

[70]

que tous les sauvages sont tres habiler et tres experts pour guerir toutes sortes de playe et blessures de quelque Nature quelles puissent etre, et cela par la vertu des simples, dont ils ont vne merueilleuse[164] connoissance, ils ont aussy pour la brulure, la geleure, pour les piqureues et la morsure des serpens et autres animaux venimeux, mais le bon de laffaire cest quils envoient et repoussent par ce moyen le mal aussy promptement quil est venu; ils sont tres bons anatomistes, cest pourquoy lors quils ont des os rompus et frascasseé, ils y procedent auec beaucoup de sagesse de dexterité et dhabileté, et lexpérience fait voir quils guerissent plustos vn blessé en 8 jours que nos chirurgiens en 30, soit parce que ces premiers ont des meilleurs remedes et sont de meilleure foy, et que[165] les autres ont plus de malice pour faire valoir le talent, a legard des maux veneriens ils sen moquent car ceux qui en sont attaquez se guerissent

164. Margry (111) transcribed this as *meilleure*. It is as here in the 1727 copy (415).

165. Changed to *ou soit que* in 1727 copy (416).

[70]

[and it is] that all the *sauvages* are very skilled and expert in healing all kinds of sores and wounds, of whatever kind they may be, and that [is] by virtue of [medicinal] herbs, of which they have a marvelous knowledge. They also have them[100] for burns, frostbites, for the stings and bites of snakes and other venomous animals; but the best of it is that they dispatch and drive out, by that means, the illness as quickly as it came. They are very good anatomists, which is why, when they have bones that are broken and fractured, they proceed with great wisdom, dexterity, and cleverness. And experience shows that they can cure a wounded person better in eight days than can our surgeons in thirty—whether because these former have better remedies and are of better faith,[101] or whether [because] the others[102] maliciously seek to exploit their talent.[103] Regarding venereal disease, they make light of it, for those who are attacked are healed

100. That is, they also have herbal remedies.

101. That is, are more intent on fixing the problem, or more trustworthy, than are French doctors.

102. That is, French surgeons.

103. Literally, "have more malice to have their talent valued."

[71]

dans dix ou douze jours, au plus tard, en prenant de certaines poudres qui n'ont nul gout, quils aualent auec de leau Chaude, et cest pour cette raison qu'on ne voit point de veroleé parmy eux, mais ils ont la malice de ne vouloir point enseigner leurs secrets aux françois quoi quils ne leur en refusent point au besoin[166]

Tous ces peuples sans exception ont par la tradition connoissance du deluge, on va uoir quelle est leur jdee sur ce Sujet ils disant quil tomba vne grande quantité de neige et de pluye, et que toutes les eaux setant ramasser ensemble elles surpassoient les plus hautes montagnes en sorte qu'on alloit par tout en Canots et que la terre fut changee en vn grand Lac; mais ils pretendent que dans cette jnnondation universelle ou tous les ho[mm]es perrirent,[167] vn ancien de chaque nation fut reSerué auec toute sa famille parce quils eurent[168] lesprit voyant croistre les eaux de faire vn tres grand Caunot ou ils mirent des vivres, et des animaux

166. Margry (111) here created a new chapter, number "IV," and titled it *Traditions des Sauvages*. In the 1727 copy (416) there is a title, in large letters, but no chapter number: *ILs ont connoissance du Deluge*.

167. Word deleted in 1727 copy (417) and replaced with *perdirent La vie*.

168. Inserted here in the 1727 copy (417): *La prévoyance et*.

[71]

in ten or twelve days at the latest, by taking certain tasteless powders, which they swallow with hot water, and it is for this reason one never sees any syphilitics among them.[104] But they maliciously refuse to teach their secrets to the French, although they do not refuse [to treat] them in case of need.

All of these peoples, without exception, have by tradition, knowledge of the Flood; we shall see what their ideas are on this subject.[105] They say that a great quantity of snow and rain fell, and that all the waters, being gathered together, they rose higher than the highest mountains, so that one went about everywhere in canoes and that the land was changed into a vast lake. But they claim that in this universal flood, where all men perished, an elder of each nation was saved, with all his family, because they had the foresight and wit, seeing the waters rising, to build a very large canoe in which they put provisions and animals

104. This is a fairly unique observation in accounts of Great Lakes Indians' medicinal practices and knowledge. Until the development of penicillin there was no known "cure" for venereal disease, although there were treatments of varying efficacy for dealing with the outbreaks of the sores that accompanied it.

105. What follows is an amalgam of Algonquian and Iroquoian creation stories. The latter were recorded, as here, because they were thought to be of interest to European readers, as part of making a case either about the "superstitions" of Indians or about how their traditions revealed some familiarity with Christian traditions. The Jesuits' annual relations provide numerous such stories (e.g., *JR*, 72:321–22, for a partial listing) and they were recorded by numerous other observers. For Native peoples, sharing such accounts was a way to explain to others their sense of their origins, their connections to the places they occupied and used, and their relationship to the natural and spiritual worlds around them.

[72]

de diuerses especes, et quapres auoir eté pendant plusieurs jours en grand ennuy ils jeterent hors du Canot, vne loutre pour uoir si elle ne pourroit point prendre terre quelque part, mais a ce quils disent la loutre se Noya, car au bout de quelque jours on la vue floter sur les eaux le ventre en haut, au bout de quelque temps le vieillard enuoya vn Castor pour voir sil ne decouuriroit point la terre dun autre costé celui cy disent ils rencontrerent vne espece de digue de bois Sec, mais parce quil jeunoit il retourna au canot, et raporta[169] auec luy vn gros chicot, ce qui fit presumer a lancien que les eaux commancoient a diminuer,[170] et pour lors ils menerent leur canot vers lendroit, d'ou ils auoient vû reuenir le Castor, si bien qu enfin ils aperceurent de loin vn gros tas de bois qui cetoit ramassé en cette maniere

ILs disent; quil tomba du ciel vne

---

169. *apporta* in 1727 copy (418).

170. Margry (111) changed this word to *baisser*. It is as here in the 1727 copy (418).

[72]

of different kinds. And after having been many days in great *ennui*,[106] they threw out of the canoe an otter to see if she could not get to land somewhere. But, according to them, the otter drowned, for after several days, they saw her floating on the water, belly up. At the end of some time, the old man sent a beaver to see if he could not find land on another side. That one,[107] they said, encountered a kind of dam of dry wood, but, because he was hungry, he returned to the canoe and brought back with him a big stump, which made the elder assume that the waters were beginning to fall. And then they maneuvered their canoes toward the place from which they had seen the beaver return, and so, at length, they perceived from a distance a great heap of wood that had been piled up in this manner:

They say that there fell from the sky an

106. This word, then and now, can be translated as boredom, weariness, disquiet, and annoyance. Any one of these choices changes the meaning of the sentence and there is no way to determine which sense of the word the author meant to convey.

107. That is, the beaver.

[73]

Tortuë dune grandeur exceSiue qui flottoit entre deux eaux, et comme il y auoit aux environs quantité de bois sec et dautres arbres auec leurs branches et leurs racines qui alloient au gré du vent et des eaux ceux qui rencontroient la tortuë si acrochoient, et demeuroient la si bien quen peu de temps il Sy en accumula vne Si grande quantité qu'on sy promenoit comme Sur vn radeau ce que leur ancien aiant vu, il y debarqua ou aiant trouué vn peu de terre a la racine des arbres, il la ramassa et en fit vn Sacrifice au soleil qui la secha et ensuite le vieillard layant reduite en poudre[171] la jetta et Sema sur les eaux, tellement quelle but leau dont la terre etoit couuerte, or chaque nation pretend que la tortue qui tomba du Ciel sarreta sur la plus haute montagne qui est dans leur païs de sorte quils ne conuiennent point du lieu

Si[172] on veut faire cette attention sur les remarques[173] raportees dans ce chapitre on pourra penser comme moy que tous ses

171. *pouSsiere* in 1727 copy (418).

172. In the 1727 copy (419) this paragraph is preceded by a title, in large letters: *Origine des sauvages*.

173. Margry (113) rewrote this as: *Si on veut faire quelque attention aux remarques*. It is also altered in the 1727 copy (419): *Si on veut faire attention sur Les marques*.

[73]

excessively large turtle, which floated between two waters. And as there was in the environs a quantity of dry wood, and other trees with their branches and their roots, which were carried at the mercy of the wind and the water, the ones that lit upon the turtle attached to it and remained there, so that in a short time such a large quantity accumulated that one could walk on it as on a raft. When their elder saw it, he disembarked on it, where having found a little earth on the roots of the trees, he collected it and made a sacrifice to the sun, which dried it. And afterwards, the old man, having reduced it to dust, threw it and scattered it over the waters, so much so that it drank up the water with which the earth was covered. Now each nation claims that the turtle that fell from the sky stopped on the highest mountain that is in their country, so that they do not agree about the location.

If one considers with close attention the remarks set forth in this chapter, one may think, as I do, that all of these

[74]

peuples descendent des hebreux, et sont originaires juifs, ce qui se peut encore obseruer par les termes dont ils Se Seruient soit dans les conversations soit dans les harangues et manieres

Les juifs sappeloient entre eux[174] freres et compagnons, les sauuages en font de même les juifs huiloient et parfumoient leurs cheveux, les sauuages huilent et graissent les leurs, les juifs combattoient en deesperer et a la debandade pour la conSeruation de leur liberté, et aimoient mieux tuer leurs peres et meres Femmes et enfans et de ce defaire eux mêmes que de tomber viuans entre les mains de leurs ennemis les sauuages sont si jaloux de leur liberté quils la defendent jusqua la mort et ne concouie rien au monde qui soit si indigne de lhomme que la Seruitude, cest pourquoy on ne laisse rien au pouuoir[175] des prisonniers qui puisse contribuer a leur destruction, car ils se tuent dés que loccasion Sen presente, et lors quils sont au milieu des tourmens ils les soutiennent auec vne fermeté

174. Margry (113) replaced these two words with *autrefois*. It is as here in the 1727 copy (419).

175. Margry (113) rewrote this as: *C'est pourquoy on ne laisse rien aux mains des*. It is as here in the 1727 copy (420).

[74]

peoples descend from the Hebrews and are originally Jews, which may also be observed from the terms they use, whether in conversation, [or] in their speeches and customs.[108]

The Jews, amongst themselves, called each other brothers and companions; the *sauvages* do the same. The Jews oiled and perfumed their hair; the *sauvages* oil and grease theirs. The Jews fought desperately and in complete disorder to preserve their liberty, and preferred to[109] kill their fathers and mothers, wives and children, and be cut to pieces themselves rather than to fall alive into the hands of their enemies. The *sauvages* are so jealous of their liberty that they defend it unto death, and can conceive of nothing in the world that is so shameful to man as bondage. That is

108. European intellectuals, and others, were startled when Christopher Columbus bumped into "Indians" in 1492. The problem for them was to explain the existence of a place and people that seemed to have been overlooked in the Bible. European thinkers ran through a number of explanations for the apparent omission of Indians, quickly abandoned any that did not conform with Christian orthodoxy, and concluded that since all humans were derived from Adam and Eve, and Indians were human, then so too were Indians descendants of the first man and woman. Indians were most likely descendants of peoples mentioned in the Bible, possibly one of the Lost Tribes of Israel, and were not readily recognized as such because of cultural degradation due to long separation from the originating culture. This theory was fairly popular, and many European observers in North America used it to account for Indians and some of their practices. For a discussion of this problem and its resolution, see Robert Berkhofer Jr., *The White Man's Indian: Images of the American Indian from Columbus to the Present* (New York: Alfred A. Knopf, 1978), 33–69. For examples from this period, see Pierre-François-Xavier Charlevoix, *Histoire et description generale de la Nouvelle France avec le Journal Historique d'un Voyage fait par ordre du Roi dans l'Amérique Septentrionale*, 6 vols. (Paris: Chez Pierre-François Giffart, 1744), 6:72–73; "Remarques Sur l'origine des Peuples de l'Amerique par Mr. Bobé prestre de la Mission," Ayer MS 293, 3:1–109. Bobé summarized the debate in Europe (descendants of Adam and Eve? a species of human somewhere between humans and ape? a second Adam and Eve—one specific to the Americas?), and concluded that Indians are human, descendants of the one Adam and Eve and, like the rest of the world, the descendants of Noah (ibid., 3:1–3). Bobé then traced the way that may have happened and sought to link specific Indian groups to known nations around the world: Sioux to Chinese (35), Ottawa to the Chananéns from Mesopatamia (36), etc. The Jesuit missionary Joseph-François Lafitau, *Moeurs des sauvages ameriquains comparée aux moeurs des premiers temps*, 2 vols. (Paris: Saugrain l'aîné, 1724), devoted two volumes to the question.

Much of what follows is little more than a set of selective and sweeping generalizations about both Indians and ancient Hebrews, but it shows some learning on the author's part and familiarity with the Old Testament, biblical history, and that of the Jews. The latter seems to derive from the works of Flavius Josephus, whose *Antiquités judaïques* had existed in French since at least the mid-1500s. On this point, see the discussion below in the notes for page 84 of the manuscript.

109. Literally, "loved better to."

6. Female captive fastened to stake in preparation for torture and her "volunteer" executioner.

7. Medicine men engaged in curing a patient.

BOTH IMAGES: Louis Nicolas, Codex Canadensis, ink on paper, 13¼ × 8½ in. (33.7 × 21.6 cm), p. 22, GM 4726.7. Gilcrease Museum, Tulsa, Oklahoma.

why one leaves nothing in reach of the prisoners that could contribute to their destruction, for they kill themselves once the opportunity presents itself. And when they are in the midst of torture, they support it with a steadfastness

[75]

qui etonnent ceux qui les font soufrir, les juifs etoient jnquiets, remuant seditieux jaloux de la prosperite de leurs voisins, quoi que de meme race et de meme lignee, cest aussy le vray caractere des sauuages.

Les Juifs aimoient la guerre, les assembleé les conseils, les harangues, et toujours sous quelque beau pretexte ils faisoie[ent] des perfidies, des trahisons, et des massacres horribles, les sauuages ne peuuent vivre sils ne festinent souuent, les conseils et les assembleés sont leur pain quotidien, et dans le temps quils font semblant de negocier de bonnes affaires et negocier[176] des alliances auec leurs amis ou ennemis, ils epient loccasion de faire vn bong[177] coup a leur mode cest a dire de les destruire tout a fait a leur mode[178]

Les juifs ajoutoient foy aux reves et aux songes, et les sauuages croyent que cest vn Esprit protecteur qui leur fait voir pendant leur Sommeil, leur destineé, et ce qui doit leur arriuer sur

176. Two words omitted in Margry (114); *negocier* is replaced with *rechercher* in the 1727 copy (420).

177. *bon* in 1727 copy (420).

178. Three words missing in 1727 copy (421).

[75]

that astonishes those who make them suffer. The Jews were uneasy, restless, seditious, jealous of the prosperity of their neighbors—even if of the same race and same lineage. This is also the true character of the *sauvages*.

The Jews loved war, assemblies, councils, speeches, and always, under some fine pretext, they carried out perfidies, treasons, and horrible massacres. The *sauvages* cannot live if they do not feast often; councils and assemblies are their daily bread; and while they pretend to negotiate important matters and negotiate alliances with their friends or enemies, they watch for an opportunity to strike a good blow in their fashion, that is to say, of destroying them utterly.

The Jews attached credence to dreams and visions, and the *sauvages* believe that it is a guardian spirit that shows them, in their sleep, their destiny and what is to happen to them, above

[76]

tout dans leurs entreprises de guerre,

Les juifs epousoient plusieurs femmes et les repudioient quand la fantaisie Les en prenoit, les sauuages obseruent la meme chose, lors quun juif marié decedoit sans enfans sa veuue alloit trouuer le Cadet pour Sauoir sil vouloit lEpouser, sil la refusoit il[179] secouoit ses souliers sur le Seuil de[180] sa porte et lui crachoit au visage, si vn homme veuf mespriSe et rejette la femme que Sa parenté luy destine, elle lui dit des jnjures, brise pille et emporte ce quelle trouue dans la Cabanne du veuf, le juif puisne etpouSoit[181] la femme[182] de son ainé sil descedoit sans enfans, le sauuage epouse en pareil cas la veuue de son frere les femmes juiues apres leur accouchem[en]t netoient purifieé et nentroient dans le temple quau bout de quarante jours, les sauuagesses[183] n'aiant point de maison de prieres ne rentrent dans leurs cabannes que quarante jours apres quelles ont acouché pour coucher auec leurs maris, les juives

179. *elle* in 1727 copy (421).

180. Three words missing in 1727 copy (421).

181. *espouse* in 1727 copy (421).

182. *veuve* in Margry (114) and as here in 1727 copy (421).

183. Margry (114) changed this to *les sauvages* and, thus, had to make more changes for the rest of the sentence to make any sense: *Les sauvages n'ayant point de maison de prières, les femmes ne rentrent.* It is as here in the 1727 copy (421).

[76]

all in their war forays.

The Jews married several women, and repudiated them when the fancy took them. The *sauvages* observe the same practice. When a married Jew died without children, his widow went to find his younger brother to learn if he would marry her. If he refused her, she shook her shoes[110] on the threshold of his door and spat in his face. If a widowed [Indian] man[111] scorns and rejects the woman whom his relatives choose for him, she insults him, shatters, pillages, and carries off what she finds in the cabin of the widower. The younger Jew married the wife of his older brother if he died without children. The *sauvage* marries, in like cases, his brother's widow. Jewish women, after giving birth, were not purified and did not enter the temple until the end of forty days. The *sauvagesses*,[112] having no house of prayer, do not reenter their cabins until forty days after their delivery to sleep with their husbands. Jewish women

110. Should be read as "she shook the dust from her shoes."

111. What follows here refers to Native practices (see pp. 54–55 above), but the author did not make that clear because he failed to add, as was needed, *sauvage* at this point.

112. This is the French term for Indian woman used in the plural here: "Indian women."

[77]

qui auoient leurs fleures, et les hommes qui perdoient leur semence, nentroient point dans le temple. les sauuagesses qui ont cette jncommodité decampent de leurs cabanne, en font vne separeé sans auoir aucune communication[184] ny auec les hommes ny auec dautres femmes.

Les Juives enceintes ne couchoient point et nauoient aucun commerce auec leurs maris, les sauuagesse dans le meme cas font lit a part, les Juifs honoroient infiniment leurs morts et etoient tres soigneux du droit de sepulture, les sauuages, nont rien de sy precieux, que les ossement de leurs defunts et ils les conSeruent comme des reliques, les juifs faisoient des festes et prieres a Dieu, et jntercedoient pour ceux qui etoient decedés, et les sauuages font des fetes des festins des presens et des sacrifices au soleil et a la lune, pour les ames de leurs parens, les juifs prioient dieu de porter les oeuvres[185] de leurs parents dans lEden, cest a dire dans le jardin, ou paradis de delices

Les sauuages prient le Soleil de Conduire

---

184. *converSation* in 1727 copy (422).

185. Margry (115) replaced this with *âmes*. It is *oeuures* in the 1727 copy (422).

[77]

who are having their flowering [of womanhood], and men who lost their seed, did not enter the temple; the *sauvagesses* who are indisposed in this way leave their cabins, make one apart, and hold no communication either with men or with other women.

Jewish women, when with child, did not sleep with their husbands or have any commerce with them; the *sauvagesses*, in the same situation, have separate beds. The Jews honored their dead immeasurably, and were very careful about the rules of burial; the *sauvages* have nothing so precious as the bones of their dead, and preserve them as relics. The Jews held feasts and [made] prayers to God, and interceded for those who were deceased; and the *sauvages* have feasts and festivals and [make] presents and sacrifices to the sun and moon for the souls of their relatives. The Jews prayed to God to take the works[113] of their relatives to Eden, that is, to the garden or paradise of delights. The *sauvages* pray to the sun to guide

113. This word seems to make little sense here as the comparison being made is to beliefs about souls—as is stated in the sentences before and after this one. But it is *oeuvres* in both the 1718 copy and in that of 1727. It may have been used in the sense of "good works" or "good deeds."

[78]

et Eclairer celle de leur nation pendant le voyage jusqua ce quelles soient arriveé dans la demeure agreable de leurs anciens.

La sexte des esseniens parmy les juifs croyoient que les ames en se Separant des corps, trauersoient la mer occidentale, et alloient faire leur sejour dans des Jles rauissantes, ou le sucre et toutes sortes de douceurs etoient en abondance, ou l'air etoit doux et temperé, et bien epuré, et que la elles etoient exemptes de toutes les miseres qui se rencontrent dans la vie humaine, et les sauuages croyent que leurs ames vont dans vne region qui est[186] dans lorient ou tout y abonde sans quil y fasse jamais ny froid ni chaud, et que cest vn pais tout tapissé de robes de martres et de toutes sortes de Pelleteries

La Seste des sadduceens parmi les juifs nyoit que les ames fussent tourmentees

186. Margry (115) deleted these two words and inserted *située.*

[78]

and light those of their nation during their journey until they reach the happy dwelling place of their ancestors.

The sect of the Essenes[114] among the Jews believed that souls, on separating from their bodies, crossed the western sea and went to dwell on islands of rapture, where sugar and all sorts of pleasant things abounded, where the air was soft and mild and exceedingly pure, and that they were exempt there from all the misery encountered in human life; and the *sauvages* believe that their souls go to a region that is in the east, where everything abounds, without it being ever cold or hot, and it is a country carpeted with the robes of martens and all kinds of furs.

The sect of the Sadducees[115] among the Jews denied that souls were either tortured

114. Ancient Jewish ascetic sect believed by some today to have authored the Dead Sea Scrolls. Among their principal beliefs was the immortality of the soul and its return after death.

115. A sect, or party, from the time of Christ that held the beliefs described here.

[79]

ni honoreés, aussi bien que la resurrection, et les sauuages ne veulent pas seulement entendre parler des peines de lenfer, et disent que ce sont des mensonges, et des choses inventeés pour faire peur, ne pouuant point comprendre que ce qui est vne fois[187] mort puisse, ressusciter ny reuiure, les juifs parloient par paraboles et metaphoriquement,[188] et les sauuages ne parlent jamais presque autrement, enfin si cest par les juifs quon scait de quelle maniere le deluge est arriué, on voit aussi que les sauuages en ont connoissance, mais ils ne faut point setonner de leurs fables sur ce sujet et sur tant dautres, puisque les juifs qui ont eté si proche de Dieu, si soigneux pour lhistoire, nont pas laissé que de segarer, et si tant dautres peuples qui ont eu lEcriture pour suppleer au defaut de memoire se sont jettez dans vn abime de chimeres, et comment les Sauvages qui ne Sauent Ny lire ny Ecrire pourroient ils auoir retenu ce que tant de Siecles

187. Two words omitted by Margry (116). As here in 1727 copy (424).

188. Margry (116) rendered this as *métaphysiquement*. It is as here in 1727 copy (424).

[79]

or honored, as well as [denying] the resurrection; and the *sauvages* do not even want to hear of the pains of hell, and say that those are lies, and things invented to inspire fear, not being able to understand that he who is once dead can rise and live again. The Jews spoke in parables and metaphorically, and the Indians scarcely ever speak otherwise. Finally, if it is from the Jews that we know how the deluge came, we also see that the Indians know about it. But there should be no surprise at their fables about this subject and so many others, since if the Jews, who were so near to God, so attentive to history, could not help going astray, and if so many other peoples who have had writing to supply for the defects of memory have plunged into an abyss of fanciful imaginings, how could the *sauvages*, who don't know how to read or write, have retained that which so many centuries

[80]

ont effacé,[189] apres tout, je croy que, sur les obseruations que je viens de deduire plusieurs pourroient penser quils sortent et sont jssus de la race judaïque, puisq[ue] leurs coutumes manieres et ceremonies sont plus conformes a celles des juifs qu'a aucune autre nation, on verra encore en plusieurs differens endroits de ce detail dautres obseruations qui confirmeront celles quon vient de voir et acheueront de prouuer autant quil Se peut mon opinion, mais scauoir par quel passage ces nations se sont repandues dans ce nouueau monde, cest la le secret.

On pourroit penser que si les sauvages descendoient veritablement des Juifs, ils auroient a tous le moins retenu la langue, nestant pas naturel que les enfans oublient naturellment[190] ce que leurs peres et meres leurs ont enseigné des quils ont commanceé a beguayer etant bien plus probable

189. Two words omitted in 1727 copy (424).

190. Word deleted by Margry (116) and changed to *abSolument* in 1727 copy (425).

[80]

have effaced? After all, I believe that, from the observations I have inferred, many might think that they[116] come from, and are descended from, the Jewish race, since their customs, manners, and ceremonies more closely conform to those of the Jews than to those of any other nation. We shall see, again, in several different places in this account, other observations that will confirm those just seen and will finish proving, as far as possible, my opinion. But to find out by what route those nations have spread into the New World, that is the secret.

It might be thought that if the *sauvages* are truly descended from the Jews they would at least have retained the language, it not being natural that children should forget entirely what their fathers and mothers taught them from when they began to stammer. And it is much more probable

116. That is, the Indians.

[81]

que les coutumes, pratiques et manieres se peuuent plustos Evaporer que les operations de notre ame qui ne scauroient etre exprimeé ny connues que par la voye des signes, ou de la parole[191] qui ne Se perd que par la ruine des organes qui composent le corps humain

On peut sil me semble repondre a cette objection quun langage mal soigné se roüille et deperit entierement comme font toutes autres choses par succession de temps, la raison et lexperience nous aprennent quune langue se defigure Et s'affoiblit, a proportion et a mesure q[uel]le est negligeé et meprisée, il est Evident que la latine si estimee dans le monde seroit perduë et abolie si de tous temps on n'auoit pris soin d'en conserver la pureté par le moyen[192] des liures et volumes que la fureur du temps a epargné et dont on a jouy jusqu'a present, mais si des temps[193] des Cesars on auoit generalement brulé et aneanty tous les Ecrits

191. Word missing in 1727 copy (425).

192. Inserted here in the 1727 copy (426): *et la voye*.

193. Two words deleted by Margry (117) and replaced with *à l'époque*. As here in 1727 copy (426).

[81]

that customs, practices, and manners could, rather, disappear than the operations of the mind, which cannot be expressed or known but by means of signs or words, and which are not lost except by the decay of the organs that make up the human body.

One may, it seems to me, reply to this objection, that a language poorly attended to[117] rusts and perishes completely, as does everything else in the course of time. Reason and experience teach us that a language is disfigured and weakened in proportion to, and to the degree that, it is neglected and disdained. It is evident that Latin, so esteemed in the world, would have been lost and would have disappeared if, through the ages, care had not been taken to preserve its purity by means of books and volumes that the ravages of time have spared and that we enjoy to the present. But, if at the time of the Caesars there had been a general burning and annihilation of all texts

117. That is, not studied, well taught, or used on a regular basis by those who can speak it.

[82]

Latins et quensuite on eut pu composer en cette langue, il parroit que lusage en seroit deuenir[194] si corrompu et si changé que si les originaires et anciens Latins[195] resuscitoient et[196] parloient a ceux d'aujourdhuy, ils ne sentendroient point entre eux, aussi il nest point surprenant quvn peuple errant et vagabon depuis tant de Siecles degarny en tout usage dEcriture et de Lecture qui sont les meres nourrices d'une langue, l'ont tellement abatardie et barbarisee, quils nen reste plus quasi aucuns vestiges, et si lon voit tant de langues differentes parmy les sauuages, il ne faut pas sen etonner puis quil est Constant que Jerusalem etoit remplie de toutes sortes de nations, qui etoient soumises a la Circoncision et qui etoie[nt] compriSes dans celle des Juifs, comme on le voit dans la harangue que fit Eleazar au peuple en Masada,[197] et comme on peut le remarquer aux Actes des apotres Ch. 2 ou il est dit quil y auoit dans cette ville[198] toutes sortes de

194. Changed to *demeuré* by Margry (117) and *deuenu* in 1727 copy (426).

195. Three words deleted in 1727 copy (426).

196. Five words deleted by Margry (117).

197. Margry (117) deleted *en Masada*.

198. Word deleted in 1727 copy (427) and replaced with *sainte Cité*.

[82]

in Latin, and it had not been possible to write in that language, it appears that its use would have become so corrupted and changed that if its originators and ancient Latins were resuscitated, and were to talk to those of the present age, they would not understand one another at all. Also, it is not surprising that a people, wanderers and vagrants for so many centuries, stripped of all usage of writing or reading—which are the wet nurses of a language—should have so debased and barbarized it that nothing remains but a few vestiges of it. And if we see so many different languages among the *sauvages*, there should be no cause for surprise, for it is evident that Jerusalem was full of all sorts of nations who had submitted to circumcision and that were part of that of the Jews, as we see in the speech made by Eleazar[118] to the people of Masada, and as may be observed in the Acts of the Apostles, chapter 2, where it is said that there were in that city all sorts

118. Likely Eleazar ben Azariah, a first-century Mishnaic sage.

[83]

nations qui habitent sous le ciel, Parthes, Medes, Elamites, etc. on peut conjecturer de la que les juifs remfermes a legard de lobseruance de toutes les loix et coutumes auec les Etrangers circoncis qui ne faisoient quvn meme corps ne laissoient pas neanmoins dauoir jntroduit dans leurs frerie[199] la diuersité des langues qui peuuent auoir eté abolies par les habitans du nouueau monde[200]

Comme jay parlé de MissilimaKinaK dans le premier chapitre, il seroit inutile den parler dauantage je diray Seulement que le mot de Vavaës[201] signifie en notre langue nation des nez percez parce quils percent leurs nez, par ou ils attachent vne petite[202] pierre bien enjoliueé qui leur tombe dans le milieu de la bouche, entre les deux lévres; cest vne mode parmy eux et ils ne croiroient pas etre bien ornez, si cela leur manquoit; il y a quelques anciens pourtant qui pretendent que cest vn preServatif contre la medecine

199. Margry (118) rendered this as *livres*. It is *frerie* in the 1727 copy (426).

200. Margry (118) inserted here yet another chapter division not in the original. This one, chapter "V," he titled *Nations Habitant Dans Le Gouvernment de Lamothe Cadillac*. In the 1727 copy (427) the title, without number and in large letters, is *Nez Percez*.

201. A corruption of the French name for the Ottawa (Odawa) Indians. It is spelled *Vatavaes* in the 1727 copy (427).

202. Word missing in 1727 copy (427).

[83]

of nations who lived under the sun, Parthians, Medes, Elamites, etc. It may be conjectured from there that the Jews, close-mouthed concerning the observance of all the laws and customs with the circumcised foreigners who all formed but one body [with them], had not, nevertheless, failed to introduce into their friary[119] a diversity of languages that may have been done away with by the inhabitants of the New World.

As I have spoken of Michilimackinac in the first chapter, it would be useless to say any more about it. I will say only that the word Ottawa means, in our language, "Nation of the Pierced Noses," because they pierce their noses to which they attach a small stone prettily ornamented, that falls down to the middle of their mouth, between their two lips. It is a fashion among them, and they would not consider themselves well-adorned if they were missing that. There are some elders, however, who claim that it is a charm against medicine,

119. The word is used here in the sense of community of shared beliefs or practices.

[84]

Cest a dire contre les sortileges que leurs ennemis et autres maljntentionnees pourroient jetter sur eux pour les empoisonner ou faire mourit ce qui prouue encore que cest vne jdee des anciens juifs, car on voit dans lhistoire quvn nommé Eleazar delivra des gens possedes par le demon en presence de LEmpereur Vespasien, de son fils, plusi[eurs] Princes et autres princes[203] et seigneurs de sa Cour; et il en vsoit ainsi, il perçoit Le nez au possedé et il faisoit passer vn anneau creusé au dedans dans lequel il enchassoit vne herbe,[204] et que[205] dés que le demon venoit a le Sentir il jettoient et renversoient par terre le corps du possedé et senfuyoient sans oSer y rentrer dauantage, ce que le meme Eleazar faisoit aussy souuent au nom de Salomon de sorte que ces nations sauuages peuuent bien auoir retenu la coutume de percer leurs nez et auoir oublié pour quelle Raison ils lont jntroduite[206]

203. Three words omitted by Margry (119) and in 1727 copy (428).

204. *simple* in 1727 copy (428).

205. Word missing in Margry (119) and in 1727 copy (428).

206. Inserted after this paragraph is a title, in large letters, *Essalon*.

[84]

that is to say, against the spells that their enemies or other ill-intentioned persons might cast upon them to poison them or cause them to die. This proves, again, that it is an idea from the ancient Jews, for we see from history that one named Eleazar delivered people possessed by the demon in the presence of the Emperor Vespasian,[120] his sons, several princes, and other princes and lords of his court. And he dealt with it thus: he pierced the nose of the possessed [person], and pulled through it a hollow ring in which he enclosed an herb; and as soon as the demon smelt it, he threw the possessed over onto the ground and fled, without daring to reenter him. This same Eleazar often did this in the name of Solomon,[121] so these *sauvage* nations may very likely have retained the custom of piercing their noses, and have forgotten the reason for which it was introduced.

120. Titus Flavius Caesar Vespasianus Augustus, Roman emperor from A.D. 69 to 79.

121. King of Israel from 970 to 931 B.C. and credited with building the First Temple in Jerusalem. Compare the above with the following: "Bringing up to the nose of the demonized person a ring that had under its seal a root from among those prescribed by Solomon, he [Eleazar] would draw out the demonic [presence] through the nostrils, as the man sniffed. Upon the man's immediately falling down, he adjured the demonic [presence] not to return to him again, making mention of Solomon" (Steve Mason, gen. ed., *Flavius Josephus, Translation and Commentary: Judean Antiquities* (Leiden: Brill, 2000), 5:15) The similarities in the passage from Mason and that in the memoir seem to be too striking to suggest a source other than Josephus.

[85]

Il y a vn lieu, qui est proche de MissilimaKinacK, apellé Essolon, lors que jy ay passé je fis attention sur ce nom et m'estant jnformé a quelques sauuages pour quelle raison on auoit ainsi nommé cet endroit la, ils me repondirent que cetoit leurs anciens qui lui auoient donné ce nom, mais quils nen scauoient point le sujet, sur quoy on peut faire reflexion que Ruben auoit 4 fils, henoc, phalé, esron[207] et charmis, comment donc les sauuages ont ils donné a la rivière le Nom dEssolon, sil nen auoient jamais ouy parler, et il nest pas vray semblable que ce soit par hazard, ou par cas fortuit,[208] mais bien plutos, parce que la coutume des Juifs etoit de porter le nom de leurs terres ou bien de faire porter le leur a celle qui etoit en leur possession[209]

Les outavois et hurons, onts les cheveux fort Courts parce quils disent que par ce moyen ils donnent

207. *Essalon ou Esaron* in 1727 copy (429).

208. Four words omitted by Margry (119) and found in 1727 copy (429).

209. Inserted following here in the 1727 copy (429), in large letters, is the title *Outavois et hurons.*

[85]

There is a place, that is near Michilimackinac, called Essolon.[122] When I passed through there, I noted this name and, seeking to inform myself from some *sauvages* for what reason they had so named that place, they replied that it was their elders who had given it this name, but they did not know more about it. On this point one might consider that Reuben had four sons, Hanoch, Phallu, Hezron, and Carmi.[123] How, then, is it that the *sauvages* gave the river the name of Essolon if they had never heard speak of it? And it is not likely that it was by chance or luck, but more probably because the custom of the Jews was to carry [with them] the name of their lands, or to give their own [names] to lands that were in their possession.

The Ottawas and Hurons have their hair very short, because, they say, in this way they give

122. A "Rivière de Tessalon" appears in a 1670 map by Dollier and Galiné, while a "Pointe aux Tessalons" appears on Guillaume Delisle's 1718 *Carte de la louisiane et du cours du Mississipi* and on Nicolas Bellin's 1744 *Carte des lacs du Canada*. It is today Thessalon, Ontario, and is located on the south shore of the North Channel, at the mouth of the St. Mary's River, in Lake Huron.

123. Reuben, founder of the Tribe of Reuben, which is one of the Lost Tribes of Israel. His sons are correctly identified, but the point being made may be lost due to translation: Hezron is rendered in French as Esron or Essalon. See the note at this point in the transcription.

[86]

moins de prises a leurs ennemis ils laissent vne houpe au sommet de la teste, comme les mahomettans; dans toutes les affaires jmportantes les hurons ne parlent quasi[210] quau nom de Sataresky comme sil etoit leur veritable Roy, Les outauois ne sont pas jaloux de leurs femmes, les hurons le sont encore moins et elles sont absolument les maitresses, en sorte que les hommes ne font quasi rien sans leur consentement, elles ne se font point vne affaire de changer de mary, ou sans en changer de coucher auec ceux que bon leur Semble sans que leur mary s'en embarrasse du tout, disant quelles sont maitresse de leurs corps et quelles en peuuent disposer comme elles veulent tellement que lon peu dire De cette nation que les femmes et les enfans sont en Commun comme elles[211] etoient en Lacedemone les hurons ne sont amis des outauois que par necessité etant les plus foibles

210. Word deleted in 1727 copy (429).

211. Margry (120) changed this to *ils*.

[86]

less to their enemies to take hold of. They leave a crest [of hair] on the top of the head, like the Mahometans.[124] In all matters of importance the Hurons almost never speak but in the name of Sataresky,[125] as if he were their true king. The Ottawas are not jealous of their wives; the Hurons are even less. And the women are absolutely the mistresses, so that the men hardly do anything without their consent. They think nothing of changing husbands or, without changing them, of lying with whomever they choose, without their husbands being at all disturbed by it, saying that they are mistresses of their bodies and can dispose of them as they wish; so much so that it may be said of this nation that the women and children are held in common, as they were in Lacedemonia.[126] The Huron are not friends of the Ottawa but by necessity, being much the weaker,

124. A reference to followers of Mohammed and a word replaced by "Muslim" in current usage.

125. Also known as Kondiaronk, and by the French as "Le Rat," he was a respected Petun-Huron headman at Michilimackinac. He died from an illness contracted during the 1701 Montreal peace negotiations between the French, their Native allies, and the Iroquois. See William N. Fenton, "Kondiaronk," *DCB*, 2:320–23.

126. Lacedaemon was an ancient city state in Greece whose main settlement was Sparta.

[87]

car les autres les ont tellement tueés[212] & maltraiteé ils font ordinairem[en]t La guere a Ljroquois, aux Scious, et aux nations du sud au dela des Illinois

Maintenant on va[213] voir, quelles sont les nations qui sont autour du lac de Missiguan,[214] contigu et joint au lac huron, comme jay fait la carte de tous les lacs qui nen font quvn seul, a le bien prendre, et que jay marqué les lieux[215] dun endroit a vn autre, je cru quil seroit jnutile de les raporter icy.

Je Commancerai seulement par les jsles du Castor; ily a la quelques famille cabanees, et qui ont leur champ de bled djnde

LIsle des pouës est encore habitez par les Poutouätamis ce qui fait que nous les apellons les pouës parce que la première sillabe

212. Margry (120) rewrote this section as: *tant les autres les on tuez.* In the 1727 (430) copy this is rendered as: *car les autres Les Souvent tuez et Maltraitez.*

213. Beginning here in the 1727 copy (430) the copyist starts to adopt the practice found in the 1718 copy of making the first few words of a new paragraph larger as a way to distinguish a new topic. The words are not set apart as proper section titles, although he does create proper titles in other instances.

214. *Michigan* in 1727 copy (430).

215. *Lieuës* in 1727 copy (431).

[87]

for the others often kill and mistreat them. They generally make war against the Iroquois, the Sioux,[127] and the nations in the south, beyond the Illinois.

Now we will see which are the nations that are around Lake Michigan, next to, and contiguous with, Lake Huron. As I have the made of map of all the lakes, which are best taken [to be] but one, and as I have marked the locations[128] from one place to another, I believe that it would be useless to report them here.[129]

I begin only[130] with the Beaver Islands.[131] There are a few families encamped there, and who have fields of Indies' wheat.

The Island of the Poues is still inhabited by the Potawatomi. What leads us to call them the Poues is because the first syllable

---

127. The name Sioux, which is how the Ojibwa identified them to the French, usually refers to a group made up of distinct nations that in this period lived in an area from Mille Lacs, Wisconsin (in the northern reaches of the Mississippi River), west to the Missouri. The groups were, running east to west, the Santee, the Yankton and Yanktonai, and the Teton Sioux. The latter call themselves the Lakota, while three more eastern groups call themselves the Dakota. See Raymond J. DeMallie, "Sioux until 1850," *Handbook*, 13:718–60.

128. Quaife (p. 63) has rendered this as "leagues." He seems to have read the French word here, *lieux*, (also written as such in Margry, p. 120) as the plural for *lieue*, meaning league. And the copyist of the 1727 version of the document did, in fact, change the word to *lieuës*. However, the author, or copyist, of the 1718 version has been consistent in using *lieuës* as the plural form for league (*lieue*). The word *lieux* here, then, means place, or spot, or location. To the degree that scholars have relied on Quaife's translation to look for "Cadillac's" map (based on the view that this document was written by him), they have been misled into looking for a map that has leagues marking distances from one Indian nation to another.

129. The reference is to the placement of the Native groups on the map. The sentence might be best understood as: "As I have made a map of all the lakes, which are best taken to be one great lake, and as I have marked from one place to another on the map the locations of the groups, I believe it would be useless to report the locations here." In what follows there is, in fact, little effort to report the locations of groups other than in general terms as being upon some river or other.

130. In the sense of "simply."

131. Located in Lake Michigan, southwest of Michilimackinac. After this the author's "journey" follows the western side of the lake southward, then around the bottom of the lake and northward along the eastern side back to Michilimackinac. The groups mentioned can be found, for the most part, in Louvigny's *Carte du fleuue mississipi* . . . . (see p. li). For a distillation of Native group locations from a variety of sources, and placed on a modern map of the Great Lakes region, see Richard Colebrook Harris, ed., *Historical Atlas of Canada*, vol. 1, *From the Beginning to 1800* (Toronto: University of Toronto Press, 1985), plates 37–38. In a remarkable scholarly achievement, Conrad Heidenreich, author of the plates, locates and traces the movement over time of almost all the groups in the region.

[88]

de leur nom se prononce ainsi, cette nation est tres guerriere et[216] ennemie de LJroquois, et fait souuent de bons coups, elle ne garde de mesure auec personne, quoy quelle soit moins nombreuSe que beaucoup dautres leur jsles est abondante en graines et bien tempereé

La nation des Noquets est maintenant avilie,[217] il en reste si peu quelle ne doit pas porter vn nom de distinction puis quelle est jncorporeé en plusieurs autres

Les Malominy ou folles auoines sont ainsi apelleé a cause de la riuiere[218] leur village est situee qui produit vne quantité prodigieuSe de folle auoine, quils recüeillent et ramassent, comme nous faisons nos bleds, ils la font bouillir auec du Gibier ou de la Graisse cette nourriture est seine, il ny a point de nation ou les hommes soient

216. Word deleted in 1727 copy (431) and replaced with *fort*.

217. *abolie* in 1727 copy (431).

218. The word *ou* is missing here and is needed to make sense of the sentence. Margry (121) added the word, as did the copyist of the 1727 version (431).

[88]

of their name is pronounced thus.[132] This nation is very warlike and an enemy of the Iroquois, and often makes successful attacks on them.[133] It shows no fear of anyone,[134] although it is less numerous than many others. Their island abounds in grains and is very temperate.

The Noquet nation is now abolished.[135] There remain so few that it is not entitled to a distinct name, since it is incorporated into a number of other nations.

The Menominee or Wild Ricers[136] are so called because of the river where their village is situated, which produces a prodigious quantity of wild rice, which they reap and gather up as we do our wheat. They boil it with game or with grease. This food is wholesome. There is no other nation where the men

---

132. This group, part of the Algonquian language family, formerly occupied parts of southwest Michigan, around the St. Joseph River valley, but moved to the Dorr Peninsula, in Wisconsin, after the Iroquois wars of the 1640s. The island in question is likely Rock Island. By this period, groups of Potawatomis had begun moving back to the St. Joseph River area, around the fort of that name established there by the French in 1691. See James A. Clifton, "Potawatomi," *Handbook*, 15:725–42.

133. Literally, "often strike them well."

134. Literally, "does not keep a sense of moderation," but meaning they fear to attack no one.

135. An Ojibwa group that met the fate described here.

136. Part of the Algonquian language family, they occupied parts of the area around Green Bay. See Louise S. Spindler, "Menominee," *Handbook*, 15:708–24.

[89]

si bien fais, ny si bien tournez que dans celle cy, ils ne sont pas si bazaneés que les autres, et sils ne se graissoient point ils surpasseroie[nt] les francois en blancheur, les fem[m]es sont aussi aSSez Jolies et plus humaine que celles de leurs voisins,[219]

La nation des SaKis est ainsi apelleé parce que Saky signifie lentree de la riviere,[220] cette nation est guerriere et inquiète[221] Ljroquoise, elle etoit autrefois nombreuSe, mais les illinois auec qui ils eurent autrefois quelque piques auec[222] la destruisirent en partie lors quils y pensoient le moins[223]

Les Puans portent ce nom a cauSe de leur riviere dont leau est fort trouble, elle est si remplie de toute sorte de poissons quil est difficile de le pouuoir comprendre, si bien que pendant les Chaleurs de leste, soit a cauSe de la qualite de leau

219. Following here in the 1727 copy (432): *Les sakis* is inserted in large letters as a title.

220. Inserted here in the 1727 copy (432): *ainSi les Sakis veulent autant que les Gens qui Sont a l'entrée de la Riuiere.*

221. Added here in 1727 copy (432) is *souuent.*

222. This word, deleted by Margry (121) and the 1727 copyist (432), makes little sense here, but it is part of the text and not crossed out. Indeed, none of the words repeated in the 1718 copy are ever crossed out.

223. Inserted following here in the 1727 copy (432), in large letters, is the title *Les Puants.*

[89]

are so well-built or so graceful as in that one. They are not as swarthy as the others, and if they did not grease themselves they would be whiter than the French. The women are also very pretty, and more courteous[137] than those of their neighbors.

The nation of the Sauk[138] is so called because Saky means the mouth of the river, and so Sauk means the people who are at the mouth of the river. This nation is warlike and often harasses the Iroquois. They were once numerous, but the Illinois, with whom they once had several quarrels, destroyed them in part when they least expected it.

The Puans[139] have this name due to their river, whose water is very muddy. It is so full of all kinds of fish that it is difficult to be able to conceive of it, so that, during the heat of summer, due either to the quality of the water

137. The French word here (*humaine*) today means human. In this period it also meant gentle, courteous, affable, or civil.

138. The Sauks, yet another member of the Algonquian language family, spoke a dialect similar to that of the Kickapoo and the Fox. At this point in their history, the Sauks were located in the Green Bay region. See Charles Callender, "Sauk," *Handbook*, 15:648–53.

139. This French term, "stinkers" or "stinkards," shows up in the historical record dating to the mid-1600s. They are better known as Winnebago, which is likely derived from Potawatomi, and today call themselves Ho Chunk. They are part of the Siouan language family and in this period lived south of Green Bay and along the Fox River. See Nancy Oestrich Lurie, "Winnebago," *Handbook*, 15:690–707.

[90]

soit a cause de la trop grande quantité de poisson, on en voit leau toute couuerte et comme il est dans vn jnstant pourry et corrompu on ne peut quasi approcher les riuage a cause de la puanteur et par consequant leau en est tres mauvaise et[224] tres degoutante voila pourquoy cette nation est appelleé les puants, car de leurs personnes et de leurs manieres, ce sont les gens les plus propres qui soient parmy les Sauuages, et leurs femmes sont les moins saloper,[225] et ont vn tres grand Soin de tenir leur Cabannes bien[226] nette, et bien rangeé, ce qui nest guere le tallent des autres sauuageSSes.

Les outagamis, cest a dire la nation des renards est[227] ainsi apelleé parce que cest vne nation rusée et maline ils sont située sur une tres belle riuiere et dans un tres bon païs pour toutes choses, cette nation se rend puissante, et cest pour cette raison quelle

224. Three words omitted by Margry (121). In the 1727 copy (433) the words *mauvaise* and *degoutante* are in reverse order.

225. Margry (121) substituted *sales*. It is as here in the 1727 copy (433).

226. *très* in Margry (121) and as here in the 1727 copy (433).

227. *sont* in Margry (121) and as here in the 1727 copy (433).

[90]

or to the very great quantity of fish, the water is all covered with them. And as they in an instant become rotten and putrid, one can hardly approach the shore due to the stench; and consequently the water is bad and very disgusting. That is why this nation is called the stinkers, for in their persons and habits these are the cleanest people found among all the *sauvages*, and their women are the least slatternly, and take great care to keep their cabins clean and tidy, which is hardly a talent of other *sauvagesses*.

The Outagamis, that is to say the Fox nation,[140] is so called because it is a cunning and malicious nation. They are situated on a very fine river and in a very good country in every way. This nation is making itself powerful, and it is for this reason that it

140. The Foxes, who call themselves Mesquaki, share an Algonquian dialect with the Sauk and Kickapoo. At the time of this writing, they were based around the Wolf and Fox Rivers in Wisconsin, but they had ranged widely before settling there and would do so again in the early decades of the seventeenth century. See Charles Callender, "Fox," *Handbook*, 15:636–47.

[91]

deuient tous les jours jnsolente, et je pense que si nous nauions pas eu la guerre de Ljrroquois sur les bras, on auroit pris des mesures pour lhumilier, car elle a deja insulté et pillé plusieurs fois les francois, les traitans dailleurs indignement, ils ne font point la guerre a ljrroquois au contraire il y a quelque espece dalliance entre eux et cest la politique de cet ennemi commun de toutes les nations du nouueau monde dauoir pu tenir dans la neutralité, vne nation au milieu de toutes les autres qui auroit pu beaucoup ljncomoder, si elle lui auoit fait la guerre, Cela fait grand bien a ljrroquois, parce que par le moyen du renard, il mange Souuent la poule, car lors que les affaires vont mal celui cy sentremet pour les negotiations, et russit Souuent si bien[228] que ljrroquois prend haleine dans cet interuale, par ce qui luy a point de

228. Inserted here in the 1727 copy (434): *pendant*.

[91]

daily is becoming [more] insolent. And I think that if we had not had the war with the Iroquois to deal with,[141] we would have taken measures to humiliate them, for it[142] has many times assaulted and robbed the French, indeed treating them shamefully. They do not make war on the Iroquois. On the contrary, there is some kind of alliance between them, and it shows the shrewdness of this common enemy of all of the nations of the New World, to have been able to keep neutral one nation, among all the others, that could have greatly troubled them if it had made war upon them. This has been a great boon to the Iroquois, because by means of the Fox it often eats the hen. For when matters are going badly, the latter intervene with negotiations, and often are so crafty that the Iroquois regain their breath in the interval; for there is no

141. Literally, "war with the Iroquois on our arms."

142. That is, the Fox nation.

[92]

nation[229] qui ne sestime heureuse et qui ne tienne a grand honneur d'estre rechercheé dun ennemy, qui fait tout trembler, en sorte quon ne luy refuse point la paix lors quil la demande mais cest toujours dans ces pourparlers quil prend son temps pour destruire les nations, qui par vn malheureux sort ont toujours la SotiSe de demeurer dans ljndolence, lors que leur ennemy leur propose la treue, ou la paix, sans que lexperience les puisse reueiller ny sortir de leur assoupissement, les renards sont malpropres tout a fait, grands voleurs,[230] et il faut plutos prendre garde a leurs pieds qu a leurs mains, car ils sen seruant fort adroitement pour derober, ils font la guerre aux Chioux et aux Sauteurs et font de bons coups sur leurs ennemis ils sont si peut jaloux de leurs femmes[231] et de leurs filles quils ne les refusent point aceux qui les leur demandent en leur donnant

229. Six words deleted in 1727 copy (434).

230. Two words omitted in 1727 copy (435).

231. Four words omitted by Margry (123) and found as here in 1727 copy (435).

[92]

nation that does not deem itself fortunate, and that is not greatly honored, to be sought out by an enemy who makes everyone tremble, so that they are never refused peace when they ask for it. But it is always during these negotiations that they[143] take their opportunity[144] to destroy the nations who, by some unhappy fate, are always foolish enough to remain idle when their enemy proposes a truce, or a peace, to them, without experience being able to rouse them from their slumber. The Foxes are altogether slovenly, great thieves, and one should rather watch their feet than their hands, for they use them very adroitly for stealing. They make war on the Sioux and the Sauteurs and strike good blows upon their enemies. They are so little jealous of their wives and of their daughters that they never refuse them to those who ask for them, if they give them a

143. That is, the Iroquois.

144. Literally, "take their time" to destroy others.

[93]

quelques bagatelles[232]

Le poste de chigagou, vient ensuite[233] le mot signifie la riviere de L'ail a cause quelle en produit naturellement sans aucun soin une tres grande quantité,[234] il y a la vn[235] village de Miamis qui sont des gens fort bien fais, ils sont bons guerriers et extremement alertes se sont de vrais et veritables levriers ils jnquietent beaucoup ljrroquois et en tout temps ils luy arrache[236] poils ou plumes ce nation est nombreuSe, mais elle est diuiseé en diuerse[237] villages, par la jalousie des plus considerables qui ne peuuent pas compatir ensemble, et co[mm]e ils sont fiers et guerriers, ils font la guerre quasi contre tous les autres, mais parce quils sont diuiseé leurs ennemis les detruisent Sy souuent, que sils ne se reunissent pas ils risquent detre entierem[en]t anneantis, ce seroit bien dommage car ce sont de braves gens aSSez humains et ciuils, et les plus portees a ce que je croy a ecouter la uoye de lEvangile ils ne sembarrassent point du libertinage

232. Inserted here in 1727 copy (435), in large letters, is the title *Les Miamis.*

233. Two words deleted in 1727 copy (435).

234. Rewritten in the 1727 copy (435) as: *beaucoup sans aucun soin.*

235. Margry (123) changed this word to *le.* This both distorts the original author's meaning (it was one of several villages) and makes little sense in light of what follows, which makes clear that the Miamis had more villages elsewhere. It is as here in the 1727 copy (435).

236. Rewritten in the 1727 copy (435) as: *et en tout jls luy en arrachent toujours.*

237. Margry (123) substituted *plusieurs.* It is as here in the 1727 copy (436).

[93]

few trifles.

The post at Chicago comes next. The word means Garlic River, because it produces naturally, without any care, a very large quantity of it. There is there a village of the Miami,[145]who are very well-formed people. They are very good warriors and extremely agile—they are really and truly greyhounds. They trouble the Iroquois greatly, and are always plucking their hair or feathers. This nation is numerous, but is divided into various villages due to the jealousy of its most eminent [people], who cannot get along together. And as they are proud and warlike, they make war upon almost all the others. But because they are divided, their enemies destroy them so often that, if they do not reunite, they risk being completely annihilated. This would be a great pity, for they are a *brave*[146] people, affable and polite enough and the most disposed, in my belief, to listen to Gospel ways. They are not disturbed at the licentiousness

145. The Miamis had occupied southwest Michigan, around the St. Joseph River—which was first known as the River of the Miamis—but they moved south and west after the Iroquois wars. By this period some were located around Chicago, some back along the St. Joseph, while others were moving into Indiana. Part of the Algonquian language family, their dialect most closely resembled that of the Illinois. See Charles Callender, "Miami," *Handbook*, 15:681–89.

146. This word has multiple meanings in French and can be translated as brave, courageous, fine, and decent, among others. Any of these, or others, could have been intended by the author.

[94]

des filles, mais alegard de leurs femmes ils en sont tres jaloux, et des quil y en a quelquune convaincue djnfidelité et dadultere, le mary luy fait raser la teste, lui coupe le nez et les oreilles et la met hors de sa Cabanne apres quoy elle va ou elle veut et les parens ny trouuent rien adire, par ce que la loy de cette nation est telle, ils en ont vne autre[238] jnfame pour punir ladultere le mary prend sa femme et la mene au milieu du village il publie ahaute voix ce crime dont elle est coupable, et il jnvite en meme temps toute la jeuneSSe de luy aider ala punir, il la renuerSe au meme jnstant pour la Connoitre le premier ensuite tout le reste y passe si bien quils sont quelquefois 2 ou 300 hommes[239] qui ne sont point fachez de se trouuer[240] les bourreaux dune telle expedition, la plupart du temps la Criminelle en meurt elle en

238. Inserted here in the 1727 copy (436) is *maniere*.

239. This is changed to *deux ou trois hommes* in the 1727 copy (437). It should be noted here that there are, due to an error in pagination, three pages numbered 437: the original, one 437 *bis*, and another 437 *bis bis*. I have followed these designations. *Bis* is Latin for twice.

240. Three words deleted in 1727 copy (437) and replaced with *d'estre*.

[94]

of girls, but with regard to their wives, they are very jealous, and if one of them is convicted of infidelity and adultery, the husband shaves her head, cuts her nose and ears, and turns her out of his cabin. After which she goes where she wishes, and the relatives find nothing to say [against it], for such is the law of this nation. They have another infamous way to punish the adulterer: the husband seizes his wife and takes her into the midst of the village; he proclaims in a loud voice the crime of which she is guilty and, at the same time, invites all the youths to help him punish her. Then he throws her down to have [carnal] knowledge of her first. Afterwards, all the others follow suit, sometimes as many as two or three hundred men, who are not sorry to find themselves the executioners in such an undertaking.[147] Most of the time the criminal woman dies. She

147. This is changed to two or three men in the 1727 copy. The Degannes/Deliete memoir, covering this same practice, puts it differently, noting that 30 or so youths wait in ambush along a path that the women usually take when they go to the forest. When the accused woman approaches, her husband accosts the accused woman and says: *comme jay scay que tu aime les hommes, je ten fait festin . . . plusieurs la tienne et l'un apre l'autre* (as I know that you like men, I am throwing you a party [*festin*] . . . and many have her, one after the other). "Memoire concernant le pays Illinois," 1721, Ayer MS 293, 3:264–362, quote at p. 300.

[95]

rechaper Souuent aussy. ils pretendent que cette punition est conforme au uices dune femme jnfidele, et que puis quelle est si affamez il est juste de la rassasier cependant les françois ont tant fait par leurs reproches que maintenant, ils nexercent que tres[241] rarement ce dernier chatiment.

on trouve ensuite la riuiere de Saint Joseph. il y auoit la vn fort et garnison FrancoiSe et il y a vn village de Miamis de méme nation; ce poste est la clef de toutes les nations, qui bordent le nort du Lac Michigan, car au sud il ny a aucun village a cause des jncursions des Irroquois, mais dans la profondeur des terres du costé du nort, il y en a plusieurs en tirant vers louest, comme ceux des macoutains, Mesrains penguiseins[242] Peauguisians, Peaouarias, KiKapoux, Ayouez, Scious, et Tinions[243]

Les scioux et[244] vne nation fiere et orgueuilleuSe qui fait la guerre a toutes les autres, elle surpasse ljrroquois en brauoure et en courage se

241. *fort* in Margry (124) and as here in 1727 copy (437).

242. Margry (124) omitted these last two groups.

243. These groups are listed in the 1727 copy (437) as follows: *Mascoutins, Merains, PenguiSains, Peauguizia, Peaouarias, KiKapoux, ayouez, Scioux, et Tintons.* Added in the 1727 copy (437) after this paragraph, in large letters, is the title *Les Sçioux.*

244. *sont* in Margry (124) and *est* in 1727 copy (437).

[95]

often also recovers. They claim that this punishment befits the vice of an unfaithful woman and that, since she is so ravenous, it is reasonable to satiate her. However, the French have reproached them so much that now they but very rarely inflict this last punishment.

One next finds the river of Saint Joseph. There once was a fort there, with a French garrison, and there is a village of the same Miami nation.[148] This post is the key of all the nations that border the north of Lake Michigan, for to the south there are no villages due to the raids of the Iroquois; but in the interior country of the northern part, and towards the west, there are many, including the Mascouten,[149] Mesrains,[150] Peanguiseins, Peaugisians,[151] Peaouarias,[152] Kikapoux,[153] Ayouez,[154] Sioux, and Tintons.[155]

The Sioux is a proud and haughty nation that makes war on all the others. It surpasses the Iroquois in valor and courage. They

---

148. The fort, which came to be known as Fort St. Joseph, was established by Frontenac in 1691 and closed by royal decree in 1696. It was reopened, officially, in the 1710s. See José António Brandão and Michael S. Nassaney, "A Capsule Social and Material History of Fort St. Joseph and Its Inhabitants (1691–1763)," *French Colonial History* 7 (2006): 61–75.

149. The Mascouten are an Algonquian group that lived and hunted, in this period, around Chicago and the southern end of Lake Michigan. Their territory was "coextensive" with that of the Kickapoo. See Ives Goddard, "Mascouten," *Handbook*, 15:668–72.

150. The Missouria. They, like the Iowa, were Siouan speakers who shared a mutually intelligible dialect of the Chiwere language. In this period a group was located at the junction of the Missouri and Grand Rivers, in Northwest Missouri. See Marjorie M. Schweitzer, "Otoe and Missouria," *Handbook*, 13:447–61.

151. Names of Miami groups or villages.

152. Peorias, one of the three larger Illinois groups.

153. The Kickapoo, an Algonquian group who moved widely across, mostly, prairie habitats. In this period they may have been along the upper Rock River in Wisconsin. See Charles Callender, Richard K. Pope, and Susan M. Pope, "Kickapoo," *Handbook*, 15:656–67.

154. The Iowa, a Siouan-speaking group that, in the 1600s and early 1700s, had villages along the Mississippi River, and its tributaries, about where modern-day La Crosse, Wisconsin, is located. They eventually moved further west, and it is likely the latter location that is being referenced here. See Mildred Mott Wedel, "Iowa," *Handbook*, 13:432–46.

155. The Teton, one of the three main groups of the Sioux.

[96]

sont des hommes vigoureux, vigilans,[245] mefians, et veritablement guerriers, et lon peut dire quils ne dorment quun pied en lair, aiant toujours la dague pendue au poing, leurs arcs et leurs carquois leur sert de cheuet, lors quils ne sont point surpris, ils sont quasi jnvincibles, mais lors quils le sont, ils ce battent jusqua la mort, et il est rarement arriveé quun scioux ait eté pris en vie, par ce que des quils voyent quils ne peuuent plus resister, ils se tuent eux memes estimant quils sont jndignes de vivre, sils ont eté vne fois liée, vaincus et fais esclaues, il est assez surprenant que des gens aussi braves et autant martiaux que ceux la, ayent cependant les larmes a Commandement, mais dune si grande force, quon ne pourroit peut etre Se L'jmaginer, et je pense quon ne sauroit le croire sans le voir, car on les voit quelquefois, rire, chanter et Se diuertir et dans le meme jnstant[246] on diroit que leurs yeux sont des Goutieres, baignee

245. Word missing in 1727 copy (437 *bis*).

246. *moment* in the 1727 copy (437 *bis*).

[96]

are active, vigilant, and distrustful men, and true warriors. One might say that they only sleep with one foot in the air, having a knife always hanging from their wrist. Their bows and quivers serve them as pillows. When they are not surprised they are almost invincible, but when they are [surprised] they fight to the death. And it has rarely happened that a Sioux has been taken alive, because once they see that they can no longer resist, they kill themselves, believing that they are unworthy to live once they have been bound, conquered, and made slaves. It is rather surprising that people as brave and martial as they are have, however, tears at the ready—but in such volume that no one could perhaps imagine. And I think that one would not be able to believe it without seeing it, for sometimes one sees them laughing, singing, and amusing themselves, and at the same moment, one would say that their eyes were gutters,

[97]

de quelque grand Orages, et aussitos quils ont pleuré ils rentrent dans leur premiere joye vraye ou fausse[247] le principale sujet de leurs larmes Cest lors que leurs ennemis ont tué quelquevns de leurs gens pour lors ils sadressent a leurs aliez ou au commandant des françois en sjnclinant sur la teste,[248] ils font des heurlemens horribles en versant vn deluge de larmes, apres cela[249] ils cessent de pleurer et de heurleur et Leurs yeux sont aussi secs que sils n'auoient point pleuré,[250] ils exposent ensuite lEtat de leurs affaires[251] sorte que lon diroit, que ce sont les memes juifs qui habitoient les montagnes de GariSein,[252] que lon apelloit les pleurans, parce quils auoient le don des larmes il y a dans leur païs plusieurs mines de plomb tres[253] abondantes

mer de L'ouest[254]

IL y a aussi chez cette nation vne riuière connuë dans la profondeur des terres jusqua millle lieues elle nest point rapide et porteroit

247. Three words missing in 1727 copy (437 *bis*).

248. *terre* in 1727 copy (437 *bis bis*).

249. Eight words deleted in the 1727 copy (437 *bis bis*) and the following inserted in their place: *et la moüille de Larmes en Sorte qu'en un jnstant ils degoute L'eau comme s'ils sortoient d'un puits apres qu'ils l'on ainSi ondoyé.*

250. Two words deleted in 1727 copy (437 *bis bis*) and replaced with *Jamais Coulé une larme.*

251. A word is needed here. Margry (125) provided *en* and the 1727 copyist (437 *bis bis*) added *de.*

252. *Garizim* in 1727 copy (437 *bis bis*).

253. *fort* in 1727 copy (437 *bis bis*).

254. Margry (125) added a chapter number, "VI," to this existing title. It is *Mer de l'oüest* in the 1727 copy (437 *bis bis*).

[97]

flooded by some great storm. And as soon as they have cried, they return to their former joy, real or false. The main reason for their tears is when their enemies have killed some of their people, and then they address themselves to their allies or to the commandant of the French. Bowing, they utter horrible howls and pour out a deluge of tears. After that they cease weeping and howling, and their eyes are as dry as if they had not shed a tear. They then relate the state of their affairs, such that one might say that they were the same Jews that dwelt on the mountain of Gerizim, who were called the Weepers because they had the gift of tears. There are, in their country, several lead mines that are very rich.

The Western Sea

There is also among this nation a river,[156] in the depths of the [interior] lands, that is known for up to 1,000 leagues.[157] It is not fast-flowing and it would carry

156. Most likely the Missouri River. See Delisle's 1718 *Carte de la louisiane et du cours du mississipi*. A much less developed sketch of the river is found on Louvigny's map, where it is called the river of the "Missorins"—that is, the Missourians. Quaife (p. 73) identifies this as the Minnesota River, based on the reference below to the St. Pierre River, which, he notes, the Minnesota River was sometimes called in this period. However, at 332 miles in length, and running in a north-south direction, it does not fit the description here, and below, of a much longer river that cuts into the western interior. The St. Pierre also does not connect with the Mississippi anywhere near the Illinois River, as noted below by the author. Moreover, as Delisle's 1703 map shows, it is the Missouri that has the potential to connect with the Western Sea—something that is suggested in Louvigny's map. Cornelius Jaenen (*The French Regime in the Upper Country of Canada during the Seventeenth Century* [Toronto: Champlain Society, 1996], 43 n. 48) identifies this river, without further comment, as the Missouri.

157. The Missouri River is over 2,000 miles long.

[98]

vne barque partout, elle est bordee, des deux costeé de prairies, dont on ne voit pas la fin, auec quelques bouquets de bois, sa source n'est pas encore connuë, la riviere coure[255] et descend du costé de L'ouest et vient se joindre a celle du Missicipi qui va a la mer du sud, ma pensee est quon pourroit par cette riuiere, decouurir la mer de louest, car lexperience fait voir a ceux qui voyage dans ce pais la que toutes riuieres prennent leurs sources de quelque lac scitué sur vne montagne, ou[256] hauteur de terre en equilibre qui a deux pentes qui forment quasi toujours deux ou plusieurs riuieres ce quon voit meme aisement a lacadie ou vn bras de riuiere va tomber dans la mer du costé du sud et lautre costé du nort, cest pourquoy ceux qui vont a quebec montent par des lacs ou riuieres jusqua vne certaine elevation des terres apres quoy on va toujours en descendant ensuite[257] jusqua la mer,[258] ors la meme obseruation doit etre faite generalement partout comme lors quon vient de

255. Margry (126) rendered this as *coule*. It is as here in the 1727 copy (438).

256. Two words deleted in 1727 copy (438).

257. Word omitted by Margy (126).

258. Four words deleted in 1727 copy (438). Inserted in their stead is: *Et ceux qui viennt de Quebec a lacadie montent par eau jusqu'a une certaine hauteur Et deScendant enSuite jusqu'a la mer.*

[98]

a boat throughout. It is bordered on both sides by prairies, the ends of which cannot be seen, with a few clumps of trees. Its source is not yet known. The river runs and descends from the western parts and comes to join that of the Mississippi, which flows into the Southern Sea.[158] My thinking is that one could, by this river, discover the Western Sea, for experience shows those who travel in that country that all rivers take their rise from some lake situated on a mountain, or high level ground, which has two slopes that form, almost always, two or more rivers, which one can easily see in Acadia, where one arm of a river falls into the sea on the southern side and the other on the northern side. That is why those who go to Quebec ascend by lakes or rivers up to a certain elevation of the land, after which one continually descends to the sea.[159] And those who come from Quebec to Acadia ascend by waterways up to a certain height of land and then descend to the sea.[160] Now, this same observation ought to be made generally throughout, for in coming from

158. The Gulf of Mexico which then connects to both the North and South Atlantic oceans

159. This is either meant to be read as "sea level," or a reference to the St. Lawrence River, which connects with the Gulf of St. Lawrence and then to the Atlantic Ocean.

160. Either the Bay of Fundy or Gulf of St. Lawrence, both of which connect to the Atlantic Ocean.

[99]

Montreal au païs des Outauois, on monte la moitié du chemin vn peu plus, ensuite au portage de varles[259] la riviere descend jusque dans le lac des Nipissimgues ou elle Semble se perdre, et qui forme la riuiere des francois qui se va degorger dans le lac huron par ou lon va jusqua chiKapou[260] ou il y a vne riuiere qui vient et descend de la profondeur des terres par ou lon monte ensuite, et[261] on descend aux jllinois, et de la par la riviere de Missicipi a la mer du sud,[262] si bien que lon pourroit dire que de chicagou a vne certaine eleuation des terres, et dans la pente du nort au sud, le chemin en seroit partagé[263] par eau a la mer du Sud et vers quebec, a la mer du nort en venant par le lac de missigan, par le lac huron par le lac Erié, et par celui de pontario au fort de Fontenac ce qui prouue aSSez clairement[264] quil ny a rien de si aisé au monde que davoir la communication des deux mers, par les lacs et riuieres en trauersant la profondeur des terres

259. *Vaches* in 1727 copy (439).

260. Chicago. This word is spelled as here in the 1727 copy (439).

261. Inserted here in 1727 copy (439) is *ensuite.*

262. Margry (126) left out a section of this description, beginning with the word *terres* and ending here.

263. Inserted here in 1727 copy (439): *pour deScendre.*

264. *fortement* in 1727 copy (439).

[99]

Montreal to the country of the Ottawas, one ascends for a little more than half the route, then at the *Vaches* portage,[161] the river descends into the lake of the Nipissings, where it seems to lose itself, and which forms the river of the French [French River]. It discharges into Lake Huron, over which you can go as far as Chicago, where there is a river[162] that comes from, and descends from, the depths of the [interior] lands, [and] by which one can then ascend, and descend, to the Illinois and, from there, by the Mississippi River, to the Southern Sea. So that one might say that from Chicago to a certain elevation of the land, and sloping from north to south, the route would be divided to descend by water towards the Southern Sea and towards Quebec to the Northern Sea,[163] coming through Lake Michigan, Lake Huron, Lake Erie, and from that of Ontario to Fort Frontenac.[164] Which proves clearly enough that nothing in the world is easier than to find a communication between the two seas by [way of] the lakes and rivers, [and by] traversing the depths of the [interior] lands

161. Possibly at present day Mattawa, Ontario, where there is a bend in the Ottawa River. A number of eighteenth-century French maps give names to the various portages along the Ottawa River, but none that I have found list a Varles or Vache portage. Dollier and Galiné's 1670 *Carte du lac Ontario* lists a "Vase" river for the last section of waterway flowing into Lake Nipissing, and there is a portage indicated at that point.

162. One would need to travel through Lake Huron, then via Michilimackinac to Lake Michigan, to arrive at Chicago by water routes alone. The river alluded to here may be either the Chicago or Fox, although the former did not connect directly with Lake Michigan in this period and neither come from deep in the interior regions The reference might also be to the Kankakee River, on the southeastern side of Lake Michigan. It could be reached by portage from the St. Joseph, which discharged into Lake Michigan. All of the latter rivers, even if by portage, connected to the Illinois River and, via it, to the Mississippi River.

163. Presumably, the North and South Atlantic oceans or the gulfs of St. Lawrence and Mexico.

164. Modern-day Kingston, Ontario.

[100]

jus qua 12 ou 1500 lieues et en prenant la riuiere de Saint pierre qui se joint a celle du Missicipi, dont la source est au sud ouest a 48 degres de latitude et a 276 de longitude,[265] et qui passe aux scioux, on peut la suiure en courant a l'ouest jusqua 1000 lieues, si bien que si la riuiere de St. pierre aussi grande et aussi belle que celle de Missicipi prend sa source de quelque lac situé et assis sur vne Eleuation de terre qui donne deux pentes comme Il arriue en tous les autres jl est euident quil faut que cette autre riuiere aille tomber dans la mer de l'ouest, ou dans quelque autre mer, car il est clair que ce ne peut etre dans la mer de lEst et il est tres dificile de Conceuoir que ce puisse etre dans la mer du Nort

Quand a la source de la riuiere du Missicipi nous venous de dire que sa Source est a 48 degrez de latitude et a 276 de longitude il y a appa

265. The section on the source of the Mississippi, from that word to here, is missing in the 1727 copy (439).

[100]

up to 1,200 or 1,500 leagues. And by taking the St. Pierre River, which joins that of the Mississippi, the rise of which is to the southwest at 48° latitude and 276° longitude, and which passes through the Sioux [country], one can follow it westward for 1,000 leagues.[165] Hence, if the St. Pierre River, as large and fine as that of the Mississippi, takes its rise from some lake situated on some height of land that has two slopes, as is the case with all the others, it is evident that this other river must fall into the Western Sea, or some other sea, for it is clear that it cannot be into the Eastern Sea, and it is very difficult to conceive that it can be into the Northern Sea.

As to the source of the Mississippi River, we have just said that its rise is at latitude 48° and longitude 276°.[166] It

165. The coordinates cited here would, if plotted on Delisle's *Carte de la louisiane*, mark the northwestern reaches of the Missouri River, not the St. Pierre/Minnesota. Henry Rowe Schoolcraft, Superintendent of Indian Affairs, and based in Michilimackinac, determined in 1832 that Lake Itasca, in present-day Minnesota, is the source of the Mississippi. The lake is located at 47 degrees north and 95 degrees west. Plotting the latter location on Delisle's map would put the headwaters of the Mississippi at about 48° latitude and 285° longitude.

166. As noted at this point in the transcription, these coordinates were not found at this point in the 1727 copy. In their place is a sentence indicating that the source is yet unknown but "likely some lake" followed by the rest of this sentence as here. A few pages later in the 1727 copy, the coordinates were added along with additional information about the source of the St. Lawrence. As noted in the Introduction, these coordinates may not have been in all versions of the document that came to be copied in 1718.

[101]

rance quelle prend sa source[266] de quelque Lac qui forme vne autre riviere qui va au Nord ce decharger dans le grand lac des assinioboels qui forment des riuieres sans fin qui vont se degorger vers le fort Nesson, et dans ces autres grandes bayes, ce lac[267] est appellé par les sauvages le grand pere de tous les lacs, voulant dire par cette expression quil est jncomparablement plus grand que tous les autres, Les Assiniboels raportent quapres auoir trauersé par les lacs et riuieres pendant cent jours de marche en allant vers le soleil couchant, on trouue la mer[268] salleé apres quoy ils disent quil ny a plus de terre, cela etant ce ne pourroit etre que la mer de louest,[269]

Enfin il faut obseruer quon peut nauiguer dans la profondeur des terres dedans leau douce en barque ou nauire, en faisant ce qui suit, scauoir, de construire des batimens au fort de fontenac qui peuuent aller jusqua la Galette cest a dire a deux journees de Montreal et ensuite reuenir audit fort et par le lac Ontario venir jusqua Niaraga il faut batir des autres barques au dessus

266. Margry (127) wrote *naissance* here. In the 1727 copy (440) the eighteen words after *Mississippi* to about here are deleted and replaced with the following: *elle eSt encore jnconnüe, mail il y a apparence qu'elle la prend de quelque lac.*

267. Two words deleted in 1727 copy (440) and replaced with *Le Lac des aSsimpoels.*

268. *L'eau* in the 1727 copy (441).

269. Inserted here in the 1727 copy (441), indented on the page, are two short paragraphs: one adds information missing at page 100 above, and the second adds information about the St. Lawrence not found in the 1718 copy. They read as follows:

Notta

On a découuers la Sourçe du MiSsiSspi elle est au Sud oüest du lac de aSsimboels au 48 degré de latitude Et au 276 de Longitude.

On a auSsi reconnu La Source du fleuue St Laurent, elle et a 100 Lieuës ou enuiron a L'oüest du Lac des aSsemboels.

[101]

appears that it takes its rise from some lake that forms another river going north to discharge into the great lake of the Assiniboine,[167] which forms rivers without end that disgorge toward Fort Nelson and into these other great bays. This lake is called by the *sauvages* the grandfather of all the lakes, by which they mean that it is incomparably larger than all the others. The Assiniboine report that after traversing lakes and rivers for one hundred days, towards the setting sun, one finds the salt sea.[168] After that, they say, there is no more land. That being true, it can only be the Western Sea. The source of the St. Lawrence is also known; it is about 100 leagues west of the lake of the Assiniboines.[169]

Finally, it should be observed that one can navigate the depths of the [interior] lands on fresh water in a boat or ship by proceeding as follows, that is, by building vessels at Fort Frontenac, which can go up to La Galette,[170] that is to say, two days from Montreal, and then return to the said fort and, by Lake Ontario, go as far as Niagara. It is necessary to build other boats above

167. The Assiniboines, in this period, occupied the area around Lake of the Woods, Ontario, which also borders Minnesota and Manitoba. That lake is often marked on maps as Lake Assiniboine, but it does not fit the description offered here, and what is being referred to is more likely Lake Winnipeg in Manitoba, Canada. A group of Assiniboines also occupied that region. On the Assiniboines, a Siouan speaking group, see Raymond J. DeMallie and David Reed Miller, "Assiniboine," *Handbook*, 13:573–95.

168. Presumably, the Pacific Ocean.

169. Since the Great Lakes flow into each other and, eventually, out to sea via the St. Lawrence, and given how many watersheds flow into the different lakes, this is an odd thing to contemplate, let alone try to pinpoint. Still, it is of a piece with the author's view that all the lakes are "one sea." Given the latter view, it might be logical, if somewhat implausible, to try to pinpoint an origin for the St. Lawrence.

170. Modern-day Johnstown, Ontario, where a fortified storehouse was built in the 1670s.

[102]

dela chute qui peuuent venir par la riuiere, par le lac Eriè, par le lac huron jusqu au pied du Saut de Sainte Marie, et de la jusqua Chicagou jusqua la baye et jusqu aux misamis et audessus du saut de Sainte Marie il y faut dautres barques pour nauiguer dans le lac superior si bien quen faisant vne barque sur la riuiere de missicipi en transportant les Effets de Chikagou en canots, ou chariots dans cette riuiere, et conduire ensuite la barque jusqua la mer du Sud, on peut sans contredit nauiguer 2300 lieues de païs en faisant des batimens en 3 endroits Seulement

Au reste ce sont les plus belles terres quon puisse jamais voir elles sont rompues par vne infinité de tres belles et grandes riuieres qui vont abreuuer tous les lacs, dont jay fait mention elles sont couuertes de beaux bois francs; comme ormes, noyers, chatengniers, chesnes, merisiers, Noisetiers, on y voit de grandes allees de

[102]

the falls that can go by the river, by Lake Erie, [and] Lake Huron up to the foot of Sault Saint Marie, and from there to Chicago, Green Bay, and the Miamis. Above Sault Saint Marie other ships are needed to navigate Lake Superior. So that by making a boat on the Mississippi, while transporting goods from Chicago, in canoes or wagons, to the Mississippi, and then taking the ship as far as the Southern Sea, one can, without a doubt,[171] navigate through 2,300 leagues of country by building vessels in only three places.

Moreover, these are the finest lands one can ever see. They are broken up by an infinitude of very beautiful and large rivers that replenish all the lakes I have mentioned. They are covered with fine hardwood[172] forests, such as elm, walnut, chestnut, oak, cherry, and hazel. One sees long avenues of

171. Literally, "without contradiction."

172. John McDermott (*A Glossary of Mississippi Valley French, 1673–1850* [St. Louis: Washington University Studies—New Series, Language and Literature, No. 12, 1941], 28) indicates that the French term here (*bois franc*) is how the French described any forest that was not mostly made of coniferous trees. What follows is, indeed, a list of hardwood tree varieties.

[103]

pommiers et pruniers, comme si on les auoit arrangez, des vignes qui produisent des grappes des raisins dvne grosseur excessiue, des beaux paysages des prairies sans fin, on y uoit vne infinité de bestes, comme biches, cerfs, origninaux, Chevreuils, ours, Castor, boeufs, sauuages peSant 6 ou 700 [livres] toute sorte de gibier y abondent, comme outardes, oyes, canards, cercelles, tourterelles, perdrix, cailles, faisant djnde et le reste[270]

La nation jllinoiSe est nombreuse ce Sont des hommes bien tournée la signification du nom le fait voir clairement car illinois veut dire veritable hommes ceux ceux[271] ont la meme méthode ques les mis amis.[272] ainsi il seroit inutile den parler d'auantage leur village est scitué sur une riuiere qui se degorge a 8 lieues du fort, dans celle de Missicipi celle cy est bordees des deux costez dun grand nombre, et diuerSes nations le village des Naké[273] merite

270. Inserted here in the 1727 copy (443), in large letters, is the title *Illinois*.

271. Word repeated by copyist. It is replaced with *ils* in the 1727 copy (443).

272. Miamis. It is spelled correctly in the 1727 copy (443).

273. The four preceding words, in large print and with Natchez spelled properly, form a topic sentence for a new paragraph in the 1727 copy (443).

[103]

apple and plum trees, as if they had been arranged [thus]; vines that produce bunches of grapes of prodigious size; beautiful landscapes [and] prairies without end. One sees an infinite number of animals there, like deer, elk, moose, bears, beavers, and wild oxen weighing 600 or 700 pounds. All sorts of small game abound: bustards, geese, ducks, teal, partridges, turtledoves, quail, Indian pheasants,[173] and others.

The Illinois nation is a large one. They are well-formed men. The meaning of their name clearly shows this, for "Illinois" means "real men." They have the same customs as the Miami, and it would therefore be useless to say any more [on the subject]. Their village is situated on a river that discharges eight leagues from the fort[174] into that of the Mississippi. The latter is bordered, on both sides, by a large number of nations. The village of the Natchez[175] deserves

173. That is, turkeys.

174. Given how many groups made up the Illinois, it is difficult to precisely identify that being referred to here, possibly a reference to the Peoria group based along the Illinois River.

175. The Natchez included the Taensa, and Avoyel—Theolel in some sources. They shared a cultural heritage, which included a hierarchal structure and an "elaborate veneration of the sun." Infant heads were flattened. See Patricia K. Galloway and Jason Baird Jackson, "Natchez and Neighboring Groups," *Handbook*, 14:598–615.

[104]

neamoins quon le distingue des autres, puisque ce peuple est gouuerné par vn souuerain, a qui ils obeissent auec beaucoup de respect et de Soumission il est parfaitement bien logé et autant que la comodité du pais le peu permettre, il a diuers appartemens, personne nentre dans le sien, sans quil en soit auerti est sans sa permission ce quil naccorde jamais qua 5 ou 6 vieillards des plus considerables de la nation qui sont de son conseil.

Cest luy Seul qui decide de la paix ou de la guerre et de toutes les afaires jmportantes qui regardent le public et voicy les termes dont se Sert celuy qui publiè ses ordres, LEsprit dit il fait la guerre et la declare a vne telle nation quon se tienne prest pour vn tel temps, ou bien il fait la paix ainsi il ne prend point dautre qualité que celle la, destre[274] lesprit

274. Changed to *dont* in the 1727 copy (444).

[104]

however, that one distinguish it from the rest, since this people is governed by a sovereign whom they obey with great respect and submission. He is perfectly well lodged, as far as the comfort of the country will allow him. He has various apartments [and] no one enters his without his being informed and without his permission, which he never grants except to five or six elders from [among] the most considerable of the nation, who belong to his council.

It is he alone who decides about peace or war, and about all the important matters that concern the public. And these are the terms used by the person who proclaims his orders: "The Spirit," he says, "makes war and declares it upon such-and-such a nation. Be ready at such a time." Or, he makes peace thusly. He does not take any authority or title except that of the Spirit

[105]

qui gouuerne, et qui donne le mouvement a tout ce quil ordonne, est[275] sans aucune opposition

IL a Cent garde du Corps, qui font faction dans[276] les postes quil leur prescrit Lors quil sort de sa maison, si quelquun luy veut parler il met un genou en terre et il appuye son coude sur tout ce costé[277] en portant la main deuant Sa face en baissant la teste, et les yeux vers la terre, cest en cette posture quon luy parle, soit[278] pour luy demander justice ou quelq[ue] fauueur, au moment quil sort de sa maison le peuple fait de grands cris et des heurlemens leuant les mains vers le Ciel comme cy cetoit vne diuinité, qui se fait voir a leurs yeux; lors quil ua a la promenade, il trouue son chemin tout preparé cest a dire bien balayé, net, arroSé et couuert de nattes tres propres bien tendues, et parsemeé de fleurs dun bout a lautre il ny a que luy qui marche dessus ceux qui le suiuent marche des deux Costez[279] comme sils craignoient de prophaner ses pieds

275. Inserted here in 1727 copy (444) is *toujours recue.*

276. *devant* in Margry (129) and as here in 1727 copy (444).

277. Three words omitted in 1727 copy (444) and replaced with *Sur L'autre.*

278. Word missing in Margry (129) and found in 1727 copy (444).

279. Inserted here in 1727 copy (445): *de son alleé.*

[105]

who governs and who sets everything in motion. Whatever he orders is always received without any opposition.

He has one hundred bodyguards who are on sentry duty at such posts as he stipulates. When he leaves his house, if anyone wishes to speak to him, he kneels on the ground [on one knee], supporting his elbow on the other, putting his hand before his face, his head lowered, and eyes fixed on the ground. It is in this posture that they speak to him, be it to ask for justice or for some favor. The moment he leaves his house the people utter loud shouts and howls, raising their hands toward heaven as if it were a divinity showing itself to them. When he goes for a walk he finds his route all prepared—that is to say, well-swept, clean, watered,[176] and covered with clean mats, stretched tight and strewn with flowers from one end to the other. None but he walks on them; those who follow him walk on either side of his path, as if they feared to profane his feet

176. Presumably to keep down the dust from the dirt.

[106]

en marchant sur ses pas. il a plusieurs femmes et concubines qui ont leurs appartemans sans qu'il soit permis a personne de les visiter, ny de leur parler, lors quils meure on casse la teste a ses fauoris et a ceux quil a[280] le plus aimé pendant sa uie[281] principalement ceux qui ont eu la garde de sa personne. afin disent ils de luy faire compagnie dans son voyage, et ces fols sestiment tres heureux de cette destineé et se font vn grand honneur dun si funeste choix, on tue meme jus quaux Chiens, et aux cheuaux dont il faisoit plus de Cas

Dans le village il y a vn temple proprement natté auec vn pillier dans le milieu, ou il y a vn arc et vn carquois auec diuerses peaux et figures de serpens, vers le milieu il y a au costé droit vne espece dautel de terre, auec vn grand pot[282] de terre ou il y a de leau dedans, et proche de la porte il y en a vn autre, ou il y a

280. Added here in the 1727 copy (445): *temoigné auoir.*

281. Three words omitted by Margry (130).

282. Added here in the 1727 copy (446) is *aussi.*

[106]

by walking in his footsteps. He has several wives and concubines, who have their own apartments, [and] no one is allowed to visit them or speak to them. When he dies they break the heads[177] of his favorites and those to whom he showed the most love during his life, especially those who guarded his person, in order, they say, that they may keep him company on his journey. And those fools consider themselves very happy with this fate, and highly honored by such a deadly selection. They kill even the dogs and horses he thought most of.

In the village there is a temple, neatly matted, with a pillar in the middle, where there is a bow and quiver with various skins and figures of snakes. Towards the middle, on the right side, there is a type of altar made of earth with a large pot, also made of earth, in which there is water; and near the door there is another where there is

177. Rather than simply write that favorites were killed, the author chose this phrasing, which points to a particular method of killing. The Jesuit missionary Jacques Gravier, who also mentioned this practice, noted that those killed were garroted. *JR*, 65:141.

[107]

du feu, qui y est entretenu par vn homme, continuellement, qui en a le soin et la garde luy en est remiSe,[283]

Il y a vn village a 4 lieues de Naké[284] apellé n[oe]ma,[285] ou la fille de ce chef gouuerne, et commande auec autant d'autorité que son pere, et[286] comme jndependamment de luy

Le nom de ce village ma fait faire reflexion que ce nom est juif car Tobel[287] fils de sella eut vne fille nommee Noema qui etoit unique il Se peut faire que ces descendant ont toujours tenu ce nom, et lont eu en veneration, si bien que par cette raison on peut auoir donné au village le nom de cette dame juiue, et comme elle etoit vnique et sans doute estimee, on peut par cette raison auoir determiné que ce seroit la fille aineé de ce capitaine qui gouuerneroit en chef dans son village qui est tres considerable et

283. Margry (130) combined the above, and the following few lines, into one paragraph. Inserted here in the 1727 copy (446), in large letters, is the title *Le Village de Noema*.

284. *Natché* in 1727 copy (446).

285. This is one of the few words in the manuscript that is partially illegible. The two letters in brackets may be "oe" or "ox." The latter makes little sense, and since the name is repeated below with the "oe" clearly written, it seemed logical to conclude that this was the same letter combination here. It is clearly *Noema* in the 1727 copy (446).

286. Word deleted in 1727 copy (446) and replaced with *que son pere fait ailleurs*.

287. *Thobel* in 1727 copy (446).

[107]

a fire, which is maintained continually by a man who looks after it and is given the responsibility of guarding it.

There is a village four leagues from Natchez called Noema where the daughter of this chief governs and commands with as much authority as her father does elsewhere, and as if independently of him.

The name of this village has led me to consider that it is Jewish, for Thobel, son of Sella, had an only daughter called Noema.[178] It may be that her descendants have always kept this name, and have held it in veneration so that, for this reason, they may have given the village the name of this Jewish lady. And as she was an only daughter and no doubt esteemed, they may for this reason have determined that it should be the eldest daughter of this captain who should govern their village, which is very considerable and

178. This is correct. If the author had known that one of the Natchez groups were known as the "Theolel," he might have been more persuaded of his connection. In reality, however, while the Natchez chief's sister commanded respect, this story (as noted in the discussion in the Introduction) relates to the Houma Indians. On the latter, see Jack Campisi, "Houma," *Handbook*, 14:632–41. The Houma shared many of the cultural features attributed to the Natchez.

[108]

quasi en etat de resister a celui de Nackque,[288] il est bon aussi de sauoir Que cette gouuernante porte le nom de son village je scay bien que lon peut dire que le hazard peut se rencontrer ordinairement dans ljmposition des noms, soit pour des raisons solides et necessaires, ou memes extrauagantes, mais aussi fautil auouer, quil y a de beaux noms qui ne sont tels que parce quils ont eté proposeé depuis leur naissance, ainsi si lon ueut alleguer, que cest vn pur hazard que le village dont je viens de parler porte le nom de la fille de thobel, pourquoy pourroit y trouuer mauuais aussi que je pense que ce meme village a eté ainsi nom[m]é en memoire de cette fille pour eterniSer son nom, dautant plus que tout contribue a tombes dans cette oppinion surtout par la pratique du gouuernement, aiant toujours la fille ainée dun souuerain, je lappelle ainsi parce quenfjn il est absolu respeté et tres bien obei pour luy refuser ce titre

288. *Natché* in 1727 copy (447).

[108]

almost in a state to resist that of Natchez. It is also good to know that this governess bears the name of her village. I am well aware that it may be said that chance is generally a factor in the giving of names, whether for reasons solid and necessary, or even extravagant [ones]. But it must also be acknowledged that there are beautiful names that are so only because they have been put forward as such since they originated. So if one wants to allege that it is a mere chance that the village of which I have just spoken bears the name of the daughter of Thobel, why should anyone find it amiss that, as well, I think this same village was so named in memory of that girl, to perpetuate her name? Especially since everything lines up in support of this opinion, and, above all, by the custom of governance having the eldest daughter of a sovereign [as ruler]. I call him thus because he is, in fact, absolute, respected, and too well obeyed to refuse him this title.

[109]

Lors que le soleil se leue, tout ce peuple sort de ses maisons, et se tournant vers ce bel astre, ils font leurs prieres en leuant leurs mains vers le ciel mais cest en heurlant comme des loups.

Les hommes ont le front et la teste sy platte quils semble que leurs ceruelle en doit etre Ecraseé, et cest leur beauté, ils trauaillent beaucoup et ne souffr[ent] point que leurs femmes fassent des ouurages penibles, on peut dire que Se sont les sauuageSSes qui sont les moins fatigueés, elles nont point la teste plate comme les hommes, elles sont aSSez jolies et fort propres, elles sont habillees com[m]e les Egyptiennes, elles font leurs etoffes et leurs toiles auec des Ecorces d'orme, quelles mettent par paquets ou par poignees, comme on fait le Chamvre, elles les mettent tremper dans leau pendant quelque temps et les rendent plus blanc que le Cotton dont elles font des jupes, auec des broderies fort jolies et de diferentes couleurs car elles ont toutes sortes de teintures elles portent sur leurs Epaules plusieurs glans, comme on portoit

[109]

When the sun rises, all of these people leave their houses and, turning towards this beautiful star, say their prayers, lifting their hands to the sky, while howling like wolves.

The men have foreheads and heads so flat that it seems [as though] their brains would be crushed, and this is their [idea of] beauty. They work hard and do not suffer their wives to do heavy tasks. It may be said that they are the least fatigued [of all] *sauvagesses*. They do not have flat heads like the men. They are rather pretty and very tidy. They are dressed like Egyptian women. They make their cloths and stuffs from elm bark, which they make into packets or bunches, as one does with hemp. They put them to soak in water for some time and turn them whiter than cotton, which they make into skirts with very pretty embroidery, and of different colors, for they have all sorts of dyes. They wear several tassels on their shoulders as was

[110]

autre fois[289] en france, leurs cheueux sont laSSez auec vn ruban et tracees autour de leurs testes, en vn mot elles sont passablement bien faites ce pais la est vne terre de promission

Quelquvn pourroit sjmaginer quon est bien indolent de nauoir pas appris de ces peuples connus, les raisons de leurs Ceremonies et coutumes, et certaines autres choSes dont on ne parle qu tatons, mail cela nest pas si aiSé quon le pense, car ils arriue ou quils n'en sauent rien eux memes ou bien que ceux qui voyagent nayant pas le don des langues ne peuuenṭ Senoncer ny Sufisamment Conceuoir ce quon leur veut faire entendre, et ainsi il y a de lembarras de part et d'autres, dailleurs ce Sont de barbares et tres mechantes nations et il nest pas de la prudence de trop les questionner dans les premieres entreuuës, il s'agit seulement de les menager dabord et de les humaniSer jnsensiblement a quoy on ne reussit pas mieux que par la voye de la Societé et de la conversation, mais on narriue pas a

289. Four words deleted in 1727 copy (448) and replaced with *comme la mode en eStoit anciennment.*

[110]

the custom in the past in France. Their hair is bound with a ribbon and wound around their heads. In a word, they are moderately good-looking. That country is a promised land.

Some may think that we are quite indolent not to have found out from these known people the reasons for their ceremonies and customs, and various other matters of which one speaks but hesitantly. But that is not so easy as one might think, for it [sometimes] happens that either they themselves know nothing [about them], or that travelers, not having the gift of languages, cannot express themselves or clearly understand what they[179] want them to comprehend, and so there is difficulty on both sides. Moreover these are barbarous and very malicious nations, and it is not prudent to question them too much in the first interviews; it is a matter of approaching them with care at first and gradually humanizing them, for which there is no better method than by associating and conversing with them. But one does not arrive at

179. That is, the Indians.

[111]

ce but de plain saut, on ne possede pas tant de langues diferentes en un seul jour, ces beaucoup faire que de pouuoir Senoncer, dans ce qui est preciSement necessaire pour paruenir et toucher l'objet quon s'est propoSe

ce 21e Juillet 1718

[111]

this goal in one bound. One cannot gain knowledge of so many different languages in a day. It is doing much to be able to express oneself using what is precisely necessary for reaching and attaining one's intended objective.

This 21st of July, 1718

Louis Nicolas, Codex Canadensis, ink on paper, 13¼ × 8½ in. (33.7 × 21.6 cm), p. 15, GM 4726.7. Gilcrease Museum, Tulsa, Oklahoma.

8. The tools of summer fishing, including canoes, nets, and spears.

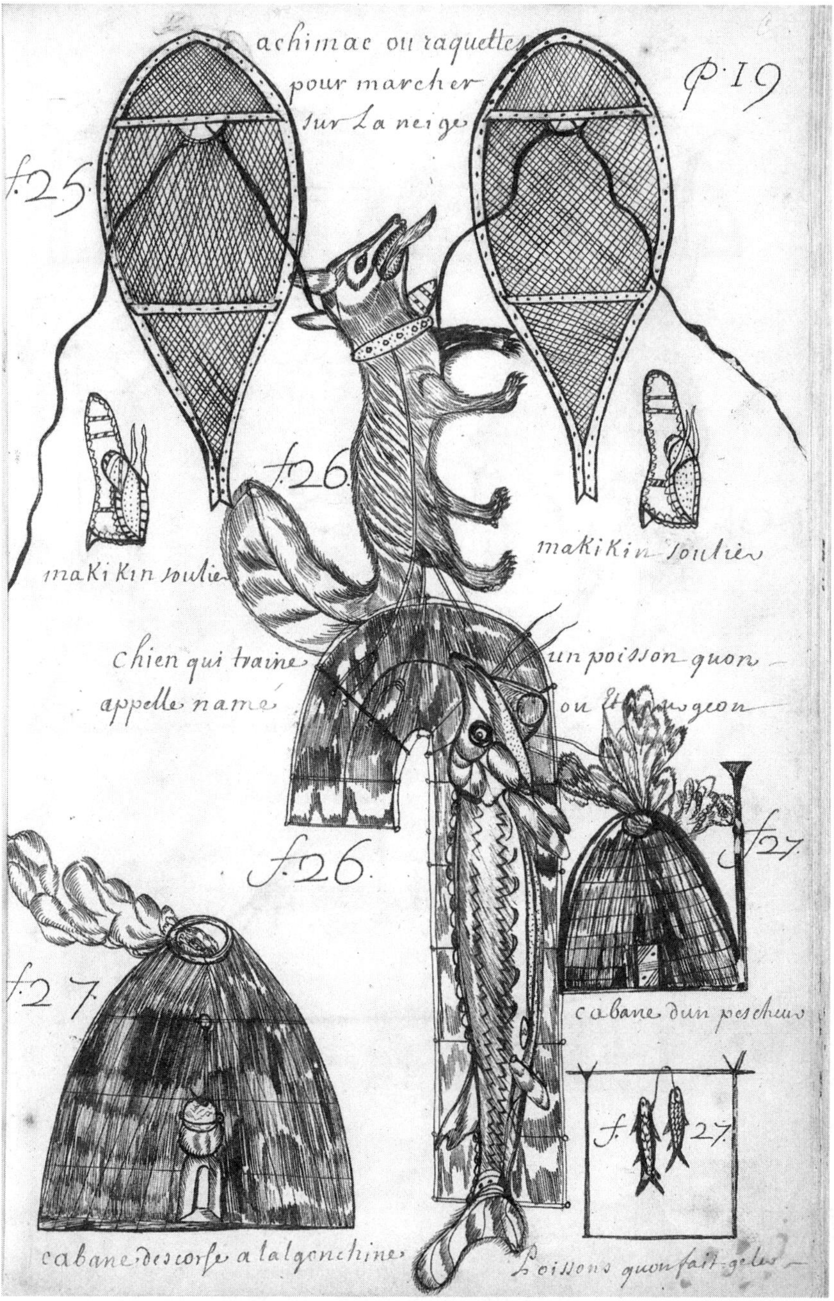

9. Scenes from winter fishing, featuring snowshoes, a dog pulling a large sturgeon on a sled, a fishing cabin, and fish hung up to freeze.

Louis Nicolas, Codex Canadensis, ink on paper, 13¼ × 8½ in. (33.7 × 21.6 cm), p. 19, GM 4726.7. Gilcrease Museum, Tulsa, Oklahoma.

D'Aigremont's

Mémoire

[D'Aigremont's Mémoire]

[folio 68r]

Apres[1] auoir Sejourné[2] 19 Jours au Detroit j'en partis le 3e aoust pour aller a MissilimaKinac[3] qui en est esloigné de 130 lieues ou je n'arriuay que le 19 du dit mois a cauSe des vents contraires. Je n'y ay Sejourné que quatre jours pendant les quels j'ay remarqué que cest le plus considerable de tous les postes auances du Canada, tant par raport a Sa Situation auantageuSe a cause dela[4] dificulté qu'jl y a d'y venir Sans estre decouuert que par le commerce qu'on y peu faire. Ce poste est le rendez vous de toutes le nations qui descendent du Lac Superior dela Baye des[5] Puants, dela Riuiere de St. Joseph, et Topicaniche C'est le passage des nations qui pourroient auoir dessein de se faire la guerre, estant facile aux Outavis d'arrester leur hache e destre les mediateurs de touts leurs differens, comme jls lont esté par le passé. Jl est Jnaccessible aux plus puissants de leurs ennemies qui Sont les miamis est les ouyatanons n'estant point gens de canot.

1. In the margin, opposite this first word of the new paragraph, and in the same hand as the rest of the document is *MissilimaKinac*. The word is added here to indicate to the reader that the subject to follow was now another post, and not Detroit.
2. D'Aigremont, or his scribe, wrote the letter "s," when it was at the start of a word, as if a block letter and not a script "s." As a result, it appears as if each word that starts with an "s" is capitalized. Because the block "s" is the same size and shape each time, whether at the start of a word or the first word in a sentence, it is virtually impossible to determine when a capital letter is intended and when the scribe has simply fallen into a pattern of writing the letter that way. For the sake of consistency, the transcription follows the practice in the original text.
3. In the margin, in pencil, opposite this word: *le plus considerable de tous les postes avancés du Canada*. This and other subsequent penciled comments in the margin are in a hand different from the rest of d'Aigremont's *mémoire*. This sort of marginalia in official documents was added, usually, by the Minister of the Marine. The comments served to mark matters that would be stressed in reports to the king, or that would need to be addressed in letters and instructions sent back to officials in New France. Sometimes the comments just reflected the reader's reaction to something written in the document. Jérôme Phélypeaux de Pontchartrain was Minister of the Marine from 1699 to 1715. His father, Louis Phélypeaux de Pontchartrain, held the office from 1690 to 1699.
4. Word added above the line of text at this point.
5. In the margin opposite this word: *son importance*.

[D'Aigremont's Mémoire of 14 November 1708]

[68r]

After having stayed at Detroit nineteen days, I left there on the 3rd of August to go to Michilimackinac, which is at a distance of 130 leagues; where I did not arrive but the 19th of the said month due to contrary winds. I did not stay there but four days, during which I noted that it was the most considerable of all the advance posts of Canada, as much on account of its advantageous position (due to the difficulty that there is of approaching it without being discovered) as for the trade that can be done there. This post is the meeting place of all the nations that come down from Lake Superior, from the Bay of[1] the Stinkers [Green Bay], from the St. Joseph River, and from Topicaniche.[2] It is the passage for nations that might plan to make war, [it thus] being easy for the Ottawas to stay their axes and be the mediators of all their quarrels—as they have been in the past. It is inaccessible to the most powerful of their enemies, who are the Miamis and the Onyatatanous,[3] not being people of the canoe.[4]

1. In the margin: "its importance."

2. Timothy Kent, *Rendezvous at the Straits: Fur Trade and Military Activities at Fort de Buade and Fort Michilimackinac, 1669–1781*, 2 vols. (Ossineke, MI: Silver Fox Enterprises, 2004), 1:172), identifies this as a "native gathering place on the northern shore of Lake Huron."

3. Likely a reference to one of the Miami subgroups better known as the Wea. See Charles Callendar, "Miami," *Handbook*, 15:689. In both the Sheldon translation (*Early History of Michigan*, 289) and that in WHC (16:257), the names of these groups are omitted.

4. That is, since the Miamis do not have a cultural tradition of using canoes to travel long distances, the Ottawas' distant location helps protect them from the Miamis.

[68v]

La[6] pesche y est tres abondante et du plus excellent poisson qu'il y ait au monde qu'on nomme poisson blanc. Jl est dautant meilleur qu'il ny faut aucun assaisonment que du Sel.

Les[7] terres n'y Sont pas bonnes, cependant on y peu faire venir du bled d'Jnde autant qu'il en faut pour les Sauuages et pour les Francois qui y pourroient aller. Jl est certain, Monsiegneur, et tout le monde en conuient que le commerce du nord du lac Superieur est le Seul bon qu'il y ait en Canada par la bonne qualité des pelleteries[8] qu'on en peut tirer. On ne peu faire ce commerce, ny aucune entreprise de ce coste la Si ce poste nest estably, parce qu'on ne peut porter des viures que ce qu'jl en faut pour aller jusques la.

Jl a esté remarqué cy deuant que tout le castor qui va au Detroit est porté chez les anglois. Jl est donc necessaire pour empescher cela d'arrester le Sauuages a MissilimaKinac. Cela ne Se peu faire qu'en y mettant vn commandant auec vne garnison de xxx[9] hommes Seulment comme les outuois le demandent.

6. In the margin: *pesche abondante.*

7. In the margin: *mauvaises terres.*

8. In the margin: *poste importante a y établir pour garantir le commerce du Nord du lac Superieur.*

9. It is not clear if d'Aigremont is using "X's" here because he is unwilling to be precise about the size of the garrison needed, or if he has, for some reason, decided to use Roman numerals rather than the Arabic ones he has used before. A few pages later on in the document, this same pattern of using "X's" and Arabic numbers appears again.

[68v]

The[5] fishing there is very abundant, and of the most excellent fish that there is in the world, which is called whitefish. It is so good that it need not be seasoned but with salt.

The[6] soils there are not good; however one can grow as much Indies' wheat as needed for the *sauvages* and for the French people who may go there. It is certain, My Lord,[7] and everyone agrees, that the trade from the north of Lake Superior is the only good [one] there is in Canada due to the good quality of the furs[8] that one can take [from there]. This trade cannot be carried on, nor any enterprise in that direction, if this post is not established, because one cannot carry more provisions than the quantity necessary for going up there.[9]

It has been noted before that all the beaver that goes to Detroit is taken among the English.[10] It is therefore necessary, to prevent that, to stop the *sauvages* at Michilimackinac. That cannot be done but by putting a commandant[11] there with a garrison of thirty men,[12] just as the Ottawas are requesting.

5. In the margin: "abundant fishery."
6. In the margin: "bad soils."
7. The French word here, *Monsiegneur*, translates as "My Lord," or "My Liege," and is used to acknowledge a client relationship to someone of superior status or to mark deference to a person. Its origins lie in the French feudal system of vassalage known as the seigneurial system. *Monsieur*, used below, is sometimes translated as Mr. or Sir, but really is not equivalent in this period. *Monsieur* is a more polite form of *sieur*, which is also used below, and usually used to address someone of noble birth or superior social standing, but it does not necessarily denote a formal title. At the same time, Mr. does not convey the same sense of deference to, or recognition of, noble birth or superior social status. The latter two French terms are, thus, left in French.
8. In the margin: "important post to establish there to guarantee the trade from the north of Lake Superior."
9. That is, Michilimackinac is needed as a reprovisioning spot because it is not possible to carry enough provisions all the way from Montreal to trade into Lake Superior.
10. This observation is part of the scathing critique of Cadillac and Detroit that precedes this section on Michilimackinac. See *MPHSC*, 33:424–46, esp. 431.
11. A title used in both French and English to refer to an officer, of any rank, who served as commander of a post or fort.
12. On this number, see the discussion at this point in the transcription.

[69r]

Jl ne faudroit pas que la garnison y Semast aucune graines parce que cela Seroit Souuent cause qu'il arriueroit des disputes entre les Soldats de cette garnison et les Sauuages. Ces derniers faisoient cy deuant beaucoup de pelleteries auec leur bled d'Jnde qu'ils traittoient aux Sauuages den haut; mais depuis qu'ils ont esté Solicitez par M$^{r.}$ de la Mothe de S'aller establir au Detroit plusieurs de leurs gens ont esté dans vne continuelle jncertitude, et ont employé presque tout le tems en alléer et venuir ce qui a esté cause qu'ils n'ont fait que tres peu de bled d'Jnde, et qu'il y est extraordinairement cher. Cette cherté vien encores de ce que le hurons n'y Sont plus, lesquelles y faisoient aussy beaucoup de bled d'Jnde, estans ceux de tous les Sauuages qui s'attachent le plus a la culture des terres. Jls n'auroient jamais abandonné MissilimaKinac S'il y auoir eu vn Commandant François, et jls nont quité ce poste que par l'auersion naturelle qu'jls ont par les Outauis, et que ceux cy les tenoient dans vne espece d'esclauage, ce qui n'auroit pas esté S'jl y auoir eu vn Commandant lequel

[69r]

The garrison there should not sow any grains because that would often lead to disputes arising[13] between the soldiers of that garrison and the *sauvages*. These latter, before, used to obtain many pelts with their Indies' wheat, which they sold to the *sauvages* of the upper [country]; but since they were entreated by *Monsieur* de Lamothe to go and establish themselves at Detroit, many of their people were in a continuous [state of] uncertainty, and have employed nearly the whole time going and coming, which was the reason that they grew but very little Indies' wheat, and that it is extraordinarily dear there. This dearness arises, moreover, from the fact that the Hurons, who used to grow so much Indies' wheat, being those of all the *sauvages* who apply themselves most diligently to cultivating the land, are no longer there. They would never have abandoned Michilimackinac if there had been a French commandant there, and would not have left this post but for the natural aversion they have for the Ottawas, and [this] because the latter held them in a sort of slavery—which would never have been [the case] if there had been a commandant there who

13. Literally, "that would be the reason that disputes would come."

[69v]

auroit pris connoissance de tous leurs differens et en auroir esté le mediateur. Si ce poste estoit estably jls y reuiendroi[ent][10] bien viste. Je ne juge cela que parce qu'jls m'ont dit au Detroit qu'jls estoient beaucoup mieux a Missilimakinac. Je crois, Monseigneur, que Si on restablissoit ce poste jl faudroit en bonne les y faire reuenir, car outre que ce sont des gens tres labrieux, Jl est certain que l'auersion qu'jls on pour les outauis les attacheroit tout a fait aux françois, ce qui feroit qu'jls Servient plus absolus dans ce poste, quoy que cependant jl n'y ait rien a aprehender de la part des outauis ces gens la me paroissant aimer les Francois.

Si on ne met pas vn Commandant et vne garnison a MissilimaKinac jl est a craindre que les hurons ne S'establissent auec les Jroquois par le mecontentement qu'jls ont de M^r. de la Mothe. Et jls y Seroient desja Si les Jroquois auoient voulu qu'jls eussent fait vn village, ne voulant les receuoir qu'a condition qu'jls S'establissent dans les villages des cinq nations Jroquois et que la leur y Soit confondue et le nom huron estain.

10. Word cut off by the binding process. The loose folio sheets that made up the correspondence from and to New France were later bound into volumes for the sake of storage and record keeping. In the process, words written near the edges of sheets of paper often disappear when that edge is stitched to another as part of the binding process. In future instances the missing portions of the words, when it is possible to deduce them, are added in brackets as here.

[69v]

would have taken cognizance of all their differences and would have been the mediator [between them]. If this post were established, they would return there very quickly. I only judge that because they told me at Detroit that they were much better off at Michilimackinac. I believe, My Lord, that if this post were reestablished it would be good to make them return to it, for beside [the fact] that they are very industrious people, it is certain that the aversion they have for the Ottawas would attach them completely to the French, which would lead them to serve most loyally at this post; although, however, there is nothing to be feared on the part of the Ottawas, those people appearing to me to be fond of the French.

If a commandant and a garrison are not placed at Michilimackinac, it is to be feared that the Hurons will not [but] establish themselves among the Iroquois due to the displeasure they have of *Monsieur* de Lamothe. And they would be there already if the Iroquois had wanted them to form a village [there], not wanting to receive them except on the condition that they settle in the villages of the five Iroquois nations, and that there they be merged [with them], and the Huron name become extinct.[14]

14. Leaving their foes to form communities of their own among them was not uncommon for the Iroquois. The bulk of the population of the Huron villages of St. Michel and St. Jean Baptiste, as they were known to the Jesuits, moved to Seneca Iroquois territory about 1651 and by 1657 made up a village of their own. See *JR*, 36:141–43; 44:21; 57:193.

[70r]

Depuis qu'il ny a plus François a MissilimaKinac ou du moins qu'jl ny a plus que quelques Fugitifs la plus grande partie des pelleteries du nord sont portéer a la baye dhudson chez les anglois[11] parce que le Sauuages qui font ces belles pelleteries lesquels Se nomment Crices et gens des terres, les apportoient cy deuant a l'embouchure de deux riuieres qui tombent dans le lac Lemepigon, a l'embouchure de celles de Manestigoyac et du Picqui tombent dans le lac Superior, et dans le fond de la baye de Michipicoton, ou les françois les alloient chercher, Mais depuis qu'jls ne vont plus ces Sauuages sont obliger de les porter aux Anglois. Cette traitte ne peu estre faite par les outavis par deux raiSons le premiere est que ces Sauuages du Nord Sont extremem[ent] timides et les craignet beaucoup, cela n'est pas mesme Sans raison, car jls les on Souuent piller, ou du moins ne leur ont donné pour leur castor que tres peu de choSe, La 2e est que les outauis n'ont pas assez d'oeconomie pour leur deuoir confier des marchandiSes. Jl est donc certain qu'on ne peu auoir ces pelleteries qu'en les

11. An "x" is inserted here and in the margin. There, in ink and in the same hand as the rest of the document, is: [*jl*] *en passe pour plus de [10]0^{m} escus par an.*

[70r]

Since there are no more French left at Michilimackinac, or at least that there are no more than a few fugitives, the greatest part of the furs from the north are carried to Hudson's Bay among the English;[15] for the *sauvages* who obtain these beautiful furs, who are called the Crees and "people of the land,"[16] used to take them, formerly, to the mouth of two rivers that fall into Lake Lemipigon, and to the mouth of the Manestigoyac and Le Pic Rivers, which fall into Lake Superior, and the end of Michipicotin Bay where the French went to seek them.[17] But as they no longer go,[18] these *sauvages* are obliged to take them to the English. This trade cannot be done by the Ottawas for two reasons: the first is that these *sauvages* from the north are extremely timid and fear them greatly. That is not altogether without reason, for they have often plundered them, or at least have given them very little for their beaver. The second is that the Ottawas do not have enough [trading] skill[19] to entrust them with goods.

It is certain, therefore, that we cannot have those furs but by going

15. In the margin: "it surpasses 100,000 *écus* per year." An *écu*, usually translated as a "crown," varied in value depending on whether the reference was to a gold or silver version of the coin. A silver *écu* was worth 3 *livres*, 6 *sols* and a gold one was valued at 6 *livres*, 12 *sols*. It is not clear which version of the coin is meant. A *livre* was both a unit of weight and a basic unit of accounting in France and New France. It was akin to the dollar today, but did not exist as actual currency. Twenty *sols*, actual coins, equaled one *livre*. As a unit of weight, a *livre* was about one English pound.

16. That is, the Cree were also called "People of the Land" by the French. The Cree, an Algonquian culture group, occupied a vast swath of land east and west of James and Hudson Bays, all the coasts of the latter, and into the Canadian Prairies. They spoke their own language, Cree, but there were numerous dialects of it. The group most likely being referred to here is the Swampy Cree (part of the West Main Cree grouping), from the southwest area of James Bay. See John J. Honigman, "West Main Cree," *Handbook*, 6:217–30.

17. Lake Nipigon and the rivers mentioned are on the north shore of Lake Superior in northwestern Ontario, Canada.

18. That is, the French.

19. *Oeconomie*, the French word used here, refers to an ability to manage the expenses of running a household. In this context, then, it means that the Ottawas are not skilled enough at trading—do not have enough business acumen or bargaining ability—to be trusted to return a good profit for the goods they might be given to trade on behalf of the French.

[70v]

allant chercher. Jl Seroit necessaire pour cela de donner Seulment[12] douze congez aux François pour la premiere année par ce qui tous les Sauuages qui pourroient venir dans ces lieux la ny viendroient pas cette premiere année attendu qu'jls ne pourroient estre tous auertir du dessien qu'on auroit d'y all[er]. Jl faudroit par cette raison dans la Suit vn plus grand nomber de congez, Jl pourroit mesme aler jusques a vingt, mais jl ne faudroit pas qu'jl passast ce nombre lequel suFFeroit pour auoir autant de castors qu'on en voudroit. Ces congez Seroient vendus a vn prix fixé et le prouenu deliuré a de pauures familles comme jl estoit fait cy deuant.

Jl faudroit encores qu'jl fust tres expressement deffendu a M[r.] le Gouuerneur general de donner aucunes autres permissions Sous quelques pretexte que ce pust estre, Car Sous le pretexte Specieux de Seruice du Roy ces permissions Se multipleroient de telle Sort que les congez ne vaudroient plus rien, et donneroient lieu a mille abus.

Mais, Monsiegneur, comme le castor du Nord est

12. This word was added in the margin. It seems as if it was omitted when the document was written and added when it was reviewed for accuracy.

[70v]

to fetch them. For that it would be necessary to grant only twelve *congés*[20] to the French for the first year, for all of the *sauvages* who could come to those places would not come this first year, seeing that they could not all be notified of the plan we would have of going there. For this reason, afterwards, a much larger number of licenses would be required—it might even go up to twenty, but it would not be necessary that it exceed this number, which would be sufficient for obtaining as many beaver as we wish. These *congés* would be sold at a fixed price, and the proceeds handed over to poor families, as was formerly done.

It would also be necessary that *Monsieur* the governor-general[21] be expressly prohibited from giving any other passes, under any pretext whatsoever, for under the specious pretext of service to the King, these passes would multiply in such a way that the *congés* would not be worth anything, and give way to a thousand abuses.

But, My Lord, as the beaver from the north is

20. See the discussion in the Introduction.

21. The governor-general was the leading authority in New France with oversight on all matters of policy, including war—albeit the latter should only be pursued with approval from France. In time some of his powers were shared with a governing council (first called the Sovereign Council) and the intendant who was responsible for justice, public order, and law. The overlapping, if not actually shared, powers ascribed to the offices of governor and intendant often led to clashes when the two men holding the office did not agree on a course of action or overall policy. (A good summary of New France's evolving system of governance is André Vachon's "The Administration of New France," *DCB*, 2:xv–xxv.) Philippe de Rigaud, Marquis de Vaudreuil served, during a long and decorated career in New France, as governor-general of the colony from 1703 until his death in 1725. See Yves Zoltvany, "Philippe Rigaud de Vaudreuil," *DCB*, 2:565–74. Vaudreuil's long career, his policies during his governorship, and his quarrels with others are covered in greater detail in Yves Zoltvany, *Philippe de Rigaud de Vaudreuil: Governor of New France, 1703–1725* (Toronto: McClelland and Stewart, 1974).

[71r]

beaucoup meilleur que celuy du Sud, on pourroit mesme auancer que celuy la est valut deux liures de celuy cy, Jl Seroit bien rasonnable que les Traitans en donnassent plus de xxx^{s} de la liure.[13]

Jl est certain que S'jls en vouloient donner 40^{s} la liure jls auroient autant de ce beau castor qu'jls voudroient.

Comme tout le castor de cette traite arriueroit a MissilimaKinac, Jl faudroit pour empescher ceux qui Seroient charger de le conduire a Montreal d'enuoyer aux Anglois par le moyen de nos Sauuages domiciliez, que le Commandant de ce poste fist vn estat bien exact de la quantité de castor qui Seroit chargée dans chaque Canot lequel estat enuoyé a M$^{r.}$ l'Jntendant, et par ce moyen chaque canot ne pourroit Se dispenser de fournir au bureau toute la quantité qui y auroit este chargée a MissilimaKinac. Comme jl ne Seroit pas juste que ce Commandant prist cette peine la pour

13. It is again not clear if d'Aigremont is failing to commit to fixing a number to something, in this case the number of *sols* per pound of pelts, or using Roman numerals to offer a number value. In the following sentence, and using Arabic numbers, he suggests a price above 30^{s} that would ensure good trade.

[71r]

much better than that from the south[22] (it might even be suggested that the former is worth two *livres* of the latter), it would be very reasonable that the traders give more than 30 *sols* a *livre* for it.[23]

It is certain that, if they would give 40 *sols* a *livre* for it, they would have as much of this beautiful beaver as they wanted.

As all the beaver from this trading would come to Michilimackinac, it would be necessary, to prevent those who are charged with taking it to Montreal from sending it to the English by means of our domiciled *sauvages*,[24] that the commandant at this post make a most careful list of the quantity of beaver to be loaded into each canoe; which list would be

---

22. Similar claims were made starting in the mid-1600s when colonial officials in New Netherland, New York, and New France sought to justify expanding the fur trade, and historians have accepted this notion to help explain Iroquois wars against French Indian allies—that is, the Iroquois needed better furs from the north and sought access to the lands bearing them. In reality, however, the climatic differences between the southern and northern Great Lakes regions were not great enough to produce thicker furs in the north. See William A. Starna and José António Brandão, "From the Mohawk-Mahican War to the Beaver Wars: Questioning the Pattern," *Ethnohistory* 51, no. 4 (Fall 2004): 730, 744–45, notes 43–48.

23. As noted above, the *livre* was a unit of both weight and money. In the first part of the sentence d'Aigremont seems to be saying that the northern furs are valued at a two-to-one ratio in terms of weight, while in the second part of the sentence he is suggesting a price per pound of weight.

The fur trade in New France was heavily regulated, and furs were either to be traded to a private firm approved by the Crown to handle the trade and collect taxes for the Crown, or run by the Crown itself. In this period the monopoly was held by the Company of the Farm and prices that would be paid for furs set by them, with distinctions made for *castor gras* (greasy beaver) and *castor sec* (dry beaver). From 1706 to 1710 the price was 20 *sols* for greasy and 30 *sols* for dry—an unusual reversal of value as the greasy beaver, both before and after this period, was worth more than the dry. Prices did increase starting in 1710, and by 1715 greasy beaver was again worth about twice as much as the dry—about 57 to 80 *sols* for greasy and 28–32 *sols* for dry. On the prices, see Louise Dechêne, *Habitants et marchands de Montréal au XVIIe siècle* (Montreal: Librairie Plon, 1974), table 14, p. 141. On the different sorts of beaver pelts, see Harold Innis, *The Fur Trade in Canada*, rev. ed. (Toronto: University of Toronto Press, 1956), 14.

24. French missionaries had created reserves along the St. Lawrence as a way to isolate nascent converts from the "negative" influences of those who wanted to adhere to their traditional worldviews and cultural practices. Those on the reserves were called domiciled Indians by the French. The Mohawks at Kanawake (Caughnawauga), among others, were actively involved in the illegal trade to Albany. See Jean Lunn, "The Illegal Fur Trade out of New France, 1713–1760," *Canadian Historical Association Report* (1939): 61–76; Thomas E. Norton, *The Fur Trade in Colonial New York, 1687–1776* (Madison: University of Wisconsin Press, 1974), 121–51.

Louis Nicolas, Codex Canadensis, ink on paper, 13¼ × 8½ in. (33.7 × 21.6 cm), p. 8, GM 4726.7. Gilcrease Museum, Tulsa, Oklahoma.

10. King of the great nation Nadouessiouek, an unnamed Sioux headman.

sent to the intendant,[25] and by this means each canoe could not avoid furnishing to the agency the whole quantity that had been loaded in it at Michilimackinac. As it would not be right that the commandant should take that trouble for

25. From 1705 to 1710, Antoine-Denis Raudot held the post jointly with his father Jacques Raudot, who was well connected at the court of Louis XIV, but too frail to do the job of intendant unassisted. Both Raudots clashed with Vaudreuil over matters of policy, in particular French-Native relations, but Antoine-Denis shared Vaudreuil's and d'Aigremont's view on the need to restore the *congé* system. See Donald J. Horton, "Antoine-Denis Raudot," *DCB*, 2:549–54, and "Jacques Raudot," ibid., 2:554–61.

[71v]

rien, Jl faudroit que le Traitant du castor luy fist tous les ans quelque petite gratification, laquelle ne Seroit asseurement pas mal employ[ée.] Jl y a encores, Monseigneur, a MissilimaKina 14 ou 15 François ou jls ne pourroient Subister Si plusieurs marchands de Montreal ne leurs enuoyoient des marchandises par toutes les occasions qu'ils en trouuent Soit Francois ou Sauuages pour lesquelles jls leur font des retour de castor.

Ces marchands ne Sont pas les Seuls qui enuoyent des marchandises as ces fugitifs. Depuis 1703 jl a esté enuoye plusieurs Canots Sous diuers pretextes qui y ont tout porté leur charge de marchandiSe. Comme Ceux qui ont conduit ces canots estoient la plus grande partie Creatures de M^r.^ le Marq[uis] de Vaudreuil jl est certaine qu'il a eu beaucoup de part a ce commerce. Je n'entreray pas Monseign[eur] dans vn plus grand detail que je ne Sache

[71v]

nothing, it would be necessary that the beaver trader make him some small payments every year, which would assuredly not be ill-applied. There are still, My Lord, at Michilimackinac, fourteen or fifteen French, where they could not subsist if several merchants from Montreal did not send them goods by every opportunity they find, whether by French or *sauvages*, for which they give them beaver in return.

These merchants are not the only ones who send goods to these fugitives. Since 1703 many canoes have been sent under various pretexts—all of which have taken their load of goods there. As those who conduct these canoes have been, for the most part, creatures of the Marquis de Vaudreuil, it is certain that he has had a large share in this trade.[26] I will not enter, My Lord, into more detail, without knowing

26. The problem of illegal trading to the western posts, supported by government officials and under various pretexts, was an old one. It became a serious breach after 1696 when the king ordered the closing of the posts and prohibited trade at them. See, for example, Joseph L. Peyser and J. A. Brandão, eds. and trans., *Edge of Empire: Documents of Michilimackinac, 1671–1716* (East Lansing/Mackinac Island: Michigan State University Press/Mackinac State Historic Parks, 2008), 112–26. Still, as d'Aigremont notes below, and Bégon repeats in his 1713 *mémoire*, which follows this one, this trading did serve French interests by maintaining Indian alliances, among other things.

[72r]

auparauant Si vous Souhaitez que je le fasse Cependant je crois Monseigneur, estre obligé de vous dire que le nommé Boiseau Canadien soldat de la Compagnie d'Esgly a traitté dans la Baye des Puans a 80 lieues de MissilimaKinac l'hiuer dernier pour enuiron 500 escus de march. Il estoit monte l'automme auec le S$^{r.}$ de St. Pierre Lieutenant, et Jnterpreter dela langue outaoiSe pour aller au Detroit et MissilimaKinac pour engager les outaois a luy remttre le PeSant pour le mener a M$^{r.}$ de la Mothe. Jl y a aparence que le dit Boisseau ne put traitter les marchandises qu'il auoit portés pendant le peu de tems que le S$^{r.}$ de St. Pierre resta a MissilmaKinac n'estant pas reuenu auec luy Son pretexte de rester fut qu'il estoit malade. La mere du dit Boisseau estant venue a Montreal lors que le S$^{r.}$ de St. Pierre arriua, laquelle luy ayant demandé des nouuelles de Son fils est le dit S$^{r.}$ de St. Pierre repondu qu'jl estoit resté malade

[72r]

beforehand if you wish that I do so. However, I think, My Lord, I am obliged to tell you that a [man] named Boisseau,[27] a Canadian and a soldier in d'Esglis's company,[28] traded last winter at Green Bay, 80 leagues from Michilimackinac, for about 500 écus[29] [worth] of goods. He had gone up in autumn with the *sieur* de Saint-Pierre,[30] a lieutenant and interpreter of the Ottawa language, to go to Detroit and Michilimackinac to induce the Ottawas to deliver Le Pesant[31] to him to take him to *Monsieur* de Lamothe. It appears that the said Boisseau could not sell the goods he had taken during the short time the *sieur* de Saint-Pierre remained at Michilimackinac, not having come back with him. His pretext for remaining was that he was ill. The mother of the said Boisseau, having come to Montreal when the *sieur* de Saint-Pierre arrived, she asking him for news of her son and the said *sieur* de Saint-Pierre replying that he had remained, sick

27. Possibly Vincent Boisseau, from Verchères. See René Jetté, *Dictionnaire généalogique des familles du Québec, des origines à 1730* (Montreal: Les Presses de l'Université de Montréal, 1983), 121.

28. François Mariauchau d'Esglis. He came to New France in 1689 and was made a lieutenant in a company of the regular troops in 1696 and in 1703 secured his own company. By 1705 he held the rank of captain in Vaudreuil's guards. See Hervé Biron, "François Mariauchau d'Esglis," *DCB*, 2:456–57. He went on to command at Fort Chambly, where he was accused of allowing illegal trading (ibid., 456).

29. As noted above, a silver *écu* was worth 3 *livres*, 6 *sols*, and a gold one was valued at 6 *livres*, 12 *sols*. It is not clear which version of the coin d'Aigremont meant.

30. Jean-Paul Legardeur de Saint-Pierre, who had been sent to Michilimackinac to apprehend Le Pesant. Legardeur de Saint-Pierre went on to reestablish the French post at Chequamegon Bay in Lake Superior, where it is believed he died in 1722–23. See Donald Chaput, "Jean-Paul Legardeur de Saint-Pierre," *DCB*, 2:386–87.

31. Le Pesant (the Heavy One) was an Ottawa headman from the Sable division of that nation. He had, at the behest of Cadillac, moved his people to Detroit, where the failure of Cadillac's promises led to discontent, ill will among the various nations settled there, and eventually, hostilities that ended with numerous deaths. Among the dead were a French priest and a soldier. Le Pesant and others fled back to Michilimackinac. See Donald Chaput, "Le Pesant," ibid., 414–15.

[72v]

a MissilimaKinac, fut fort alarmée et a la trouuer M$^{r.}$ le Marquis de Vaudreuil qui la consola beaucoup en l'asseurant que Son fils n'en mourroit pas et que Sa maladie estoit peu de chose.

Celuy de tous les marchands de Montreal qui fait le plus de commerce auec les françois qui Sont a Missilimackinac est le S$^{r.}$ Soumande. J'ay mesme trouué en reuenant de MissilimaKinac a Montreal a vne pointe ou je mis pied a terre, vne lettre que le [no]mmé[14] Chasles luy a escrit par laquelle jl lui demande de plusieurs marchandises et luy marque les noms de Sauuages outauis a qui jl peut leur donner. Jl y a aparence que cette lettre auoit esté oubliée la par vn Sauuage.

Jl est cependant vray, Monseigneur, de dire que Si ces françois n'estoient point la, jl ne viendroit presque point de castor a Montreal car on n'auroit que celuy que les outauis y aporteroient[15] qui Seroit en petite quantité parce qu'j[ls] en traitteroient en descendant plus de la moité a nos

14. The first two letters of this word are missing in the original.
15. The preceding two words were repeated and crossed out.

[72v]

at Michilimackinac, [she was] much alarmed and went to the Marquis de Vaudreuil, who consoled her greatly by assuring her that her son would not die, and that his illness was a small matter.

He of all the Montreal merchants who does the most trade with the French who are at Michilimackinac, is the *sieur* Soumande.[32] I even found, on returning from Michilimackinac to Montreal, at a spot where I set foot on land, a letter that someone named Chasles[33] wrote to him, by which he asks him for a number of goods, and indicates to him the names of the Ottawa *sauvages* to whom he may give them. It appears this letter had been forgotten there by a *sauvage*.

It is nonetheless true, My Lord, to say that if these French were not there, hardly any beaver would come to Montreal, for we should not have but what the Ottawas might bring, which would be a small quantity because they would sell, along the way, more than half of it to our

32. Probably Jean-Pascal Soumande, a Montreal merchant. He was one of eight children of Jean Soumande, who was a well-known fur trade merchant in Quebec. Jetté, *Dictionnaire généalogique*, 1056.

33. Possibly Jacques Chasle, *dit* Duhamel, a soldier in the DuCruzel company. Ibid., 238.

[73r]

Sauuages domiciliez lesquels le portent ensuite chez les anglois. Je tire de la vne consequence qu'il est absolument necessaire de mettre vn Commandant a MissilimaKinac auec vne garnison de xxx hommes, et de donner les 12 congez dont jl est parlé cy deuant, au moyen de quoy et en prenant les precautions qui y sont marquées on aura tout le beau castor du Canada. Car puis qu'jl n'est pas possible dempescher qu'on n'enuoye tous les ans Sous diuers pretextes des marchandises a ces fugitifs, Jl vaut bien mieux donner des congez. Jl en resulteroit au moins ce bien cy qui Seroit que les pauures familles profiteroient d'vne partie de ce commerce, ce qui les Soulageroit d'autant au lieu que Sur le pied que Sont les choses, ceux qui le font Sont les plus en estat de s'en passer.

Par tout ce qui a esté dit cy deuant on peu connoistre que MissilimaKinac est le poste le plus auantageuse qu'jl y ait en Canada, et pour faire voir l'auantage que celuy y a Sur le Detroit, Je dis que quand tous

[73r]

domiciled *sauvages*, who then take it to the English.[34] I draw from that one conclusion: that it is absolutely necessary to place a commandant at Michilimackinac with a garrison of thirty men, and to issue the twelve *congés* spoken about above, by which means, and by taking precautions noted there, we will have all the fine beaver of Canada. For, as it is not possible to prevent goods from being sent to these outlaws every year, under various pretenses, it would be much better to grant *congés*. One advantage, at least, would result—which would be that the poor families would profit from a part of this trade, which would relieve them to that extent; whereas, as things stand, those who engage in it[35] are those most able to do without it.

By all that was said above, one can understand that Michilimackinac is the most advantageous post that there is in Canada. And to show the advantage that it has over Detroit, I say that even if all

34. On furs shipped from Michilimackinac disappearing before arriving at their intended destinations, see the case of Louis Ouakouts in Peyser and Brandão, *Edge of Empire*, 3–20. This problem, as the other cases found in the latter source attest, was a common one.

35. That is, those who are trading illegally.

[73v]

les Sauuages du Canada y Seroient establis on en tireroit pas la 10^{e} partie du castor de ce qu'on peu tirer de MissilimaKinac parce qu'jl passeroit presque tout chez les anglois par le moyen des Jroquois et des hurons et mesme de plusieurs autres Sauuages qui ont pris celle route, Je dis mesme quand on pourroit donner a ces Sauuages au dit lieux du Detroit les marchandiSes au mesme priz qu'on les leur donner a Montreal, et la plus grande preuue qu'on en puisse donner, est que nos Sauuages domiciliez viennent tous les jours en la ville de Montreal traitter auec des marchandiSes angloises le castor des marchands pour le por[ter] ensuite a orange, ce qui doit encores vne fois faire conclure, Monseigneur, que le Detroit est vn poste tres desauantageux a la Colonie a cauSe de la facilité que les Sauuages ont daller chez les anglois par le moyen des Jroquois.

[16]Jl y a, Monseigneur, vne remarque a faire sur la traitte qu nos Sauuages domiciliez viennent faire a

16. In the margin, in ink: *N.a*—possibly an abbreviation for *nota*, short for *nota bene*, which is Latin for take note or note well.

[73v]

the *sauvages* in Canada were to settle there, we should not obtain a tenth part of the beaver that we can get from Michilimackinac, for it would almost all go to the English by means of the Iroquois and the Hurons, and even many other *sauvages* who have taken that route. I [would] say the same even if we were able to give these *sauvages*, at the said post of Detroit, goods at the same price as we give them at Montreal. And the most significant proof that can be given [of this] is that our domiciled *sauvages* come every day into the town of Montreal to trade with English goods for the beaver of [Montreal] merchants, to then carry them to Orange;[36] which should, once more, lead us to conclude, My Lord, that Detroit is a very disadvantageous post to the colony due to the ease it gives the *sauvages* to go to the English by means of the Iroquois.

There[37] is a point to be made, My Lord, about the trade that our domiciled *sauvages* come to make at

36. The French term for Albany, New York, formerly the site of Fort Orange during the period of Dutch occupancy in the region.

37. See the comment at this point in the transcription. It would seem that this entire paragraph is intended to be a parenthetical statement to emphasize, again, the need for better prices for furs and the dangers to French imperial politics if corrective action is not taken.

[74r]

Montreal du castor des marchandes auec des marchandises angloises qui me paroist tres jmportente, laquelle est qu'on ne Sauroit empescher ces Sauuages de faire cette traitte qu'en leur faissent beaucoup de violence et jl est a craindre que cela ne les Jritent de telle Sort qu'jls ne Se declarent contre nous pour peu qu'ils trouuent les Jroquois disposez a nous faire la guerre, ce qui Seroit vn extreme malheur pour cette colonie. Jl n'y a Monseigneur, qu'un remede a cela qui Seroit d'obliger les tratittans du castor d'en donner 40$^{s.}$ dela liure car Si cela estoit non Seulment nos Sauuages domiciliez ne viendroient plus traitter le castor des marchands de montreal, mais encore jls leurs apporteroient celuy de leur chasse, Et on oterois par la aux anglois vn moyen presque Sur de brouiller tous les Sauuages auec nous, Et jl ny a pas a douter qu'ils n'en viennent a bout si le prix du castor reste a 30$^{s.}$

La veille que je partis de MissilimaKinac, les

[74r]

Montreal for the beavers of the merchants using English goods, which seems to me most important; that is, that we are unable to prevent these *sauvages* from carrying on this trade except by doing them great violence, and it is to be feared that would but so irritate them that they would declare against us if ever they find the Iroquois ever so little disposed to make war upon us, which would be extremely unfortunate for this colony. There is not, My Lord, but one remedy for that, which would be to compel the beaver traders to give 40 *sols* a *livre* [for them]; for if that were to be [done], not only would our domiciled *sauvages* no longer come to trade for the beaver of the Montreal merchants, but they would then bring them those from their hunting. And we should, in that way, remove from the English a nearly sure means of [making] all the *sauvages* fall out with us. And it is not to be doubted that they will but attain that end if the price of beaver skins remains at 30 *sols*.

The eve before I left Michilimackinac the

[74v]

outauis qui estoient descendus a Montreal y arriu[rent.] Jls y ont aporté plus de cinq barriques d'eau de vie. Jls S'enyurerens tous Si fort pendant la nuit qu'jls mirent le feu dans leurs cabannes dont jl y en eut Sept de brulées et l'auroient este toutes Sans les francois fugitifs et mes canotiens qui y acouruent et qui estoignirent le feu. Ces Sauuages estoient yures a vn tel point quils voulerent les battre, et les empes[cher] des tiendre le feu. Les Missionaires y furent aussy lesquels furent pareillment tres mal traittez et chargez d'Jnjures. Ces Sauuages auront Sans doute brule les nuits suiuantes le reste de leurs Cabannes et leur fort car jl leur restoit encores beaucoup deau de vie. Je Vous asseure Monseigneur, que ces Missionaires sont tres exposer dans ces terres la. On pourroit empescher a Montreal que ces Sauuages n'importasSant vne Si grand quantité deau de Vie. On ma dit qu'jl ne leur auoit este permis d'en emporter vne Si grande quantité qu'a condition qu'ils feroient de gros presens a M^r.^ le Gouuerneur general. Je ne Scay pas Si cela

[74v]

Ottawas who had gone down to Montreal arrived there. They brought more than five barrels of brandy.[38] They all got so drunk during the night that they set fire to their cabins, seven of which were burned down—and they would all have been burned but for the French fugitives and my canoemen who came running and who put out the fire. These *sauvages* were so drunk that they wanted to fight them and prevent them from putting out the fire.[39] The missionaries who were there were also very badly treated and laden with insults.[40] These *sauvages*, no doubt, burned the rest of their cabins and their fort on the following nights, for they still had a great deal of brandy left. I assure you, My Lord, these missionaries are very exposed [to danger] in these lands. These *sauvages* might be prevented, at Montreal, from taking away such a large quantity of brandy. I was told that they had not been permitted to take such a large quantity except on condition that they make large presents to *Monsieur* the governor-general. I do not know if that

38. Literally, *eau de vie* (water of life), but the name, even today, for what is in English called brandy.

39. Natives in the Great Lakes region did not use alcohol before it was introduced to them by Europeans. Without the social and cultural strictures that accompanied alcohol use in other cultures, Indians adapted it to suit their own purposes, among which was getting drunk to achieve a state that allowed one to do what was not normally permitted in one's own society. Once in that state, as is true for everyone who drinks too much, and especially among those without built-up tolerance to alcohol, individuals lost control of their actions. The documents of the period are filled with such cautionary tales, but for an overview of the issue see Peter C. Mancall, *Deadly Medicine: Indians and Alcohol Use in Early America* (Ithaca, NY: Cornell University Press, 1995), especially pp. 127–54 for the situation in New France.

40. The fire seems to have been a major catalyst in the Ottawas' abandoning the north side of the straits and relocating to the south side, where, by 1716, a new French fort was established. See Brandão and Peyser, *Edge of Empire*, xxxii–xxxiv.

[75r]

est vray, Mais je Scay de bonne part que les presens qui luy on este faire cette année par les Sauuages valent plus de cinq cens pistoles. Les Jnterprettes qui Sont chargez de negocier ces choses auec les d[it][17] Sauuages s'en preualent extremement Sans qu'on ose le trouuer mauuais, c'est a dire qu'ils traittent aux d[it] Sauuages autant d'eau de vie qu'jls en veulent jndependament de celle que M$^{r.}$ le Gouuerneur general leur permet de porter. Jl arriue de cecy, Monseigneur, beaucoup de mal dont le plus grand n'est pas de donner lieu a ces Sauuages de S'enyuir quoy qu'il Soit fort grand, puis qu'estant en ces estat jls Se portent a bruler leurs Cabanes, a se manger le nez, a Se dechirer, a Se tuer et enfin a toutes les plus mauuaises actions dans les hommes puissent estre capables. Jl en arriue vn autre dont les Suittes Sont encores plus facheuses qui est que ces Sauuages ayant consommé en presens et en eau de vie la plus grand partie de leurs pelleteries, le reste ne leur Suffit pas a beaucoup pres pour auoir

17. The last letters of the word are left out. Only the "d" and a flourish, indicating something akin to "read the rest of the word as usual" is written.

[75r]

is true, but I know from a good source that the presents that have been made to him this year by the *sauvages* are worth more than 500 *pistoles.*[41] The interpreters who are charged with negotiating these matters with the said *sauvages* take very great advantage [of it] without anyone daring to find it objectionable—that is to say, they sell to the said *sauvages* as much brandy as they like, independently of that which the governor-general permits them to take. From this comes, My Lord, a great deal of harm, of which the worst is not that it gives these *sauvages* occasion to get drunk—although this is very great since, being in this state, they take to burning their cabins, biting each other,[42] tearing at each other, killing one another, and, finally, the most evil acts of which men can be capable. Another [evil] arises, the outcomes of which are still more distressing, which is that the *sauvages*, having consumed the greater part of their furs on presents and brandy, the remainder is not sufficient, by a great deal, to get

41. Another term used in accounting, but not actual currency. A *pistole* was the equivalent of 10 *livres*.

42. Literally, "eating each other's noses."

[75v]

les choses qui leur Sont necessaires qui Sont des couuertures, des mitasses, des Fusils, de la poudre, du plomb, du tabac et des chaudieres, et qu'jls tombent dans vne extreme misere, ce qui les portent a tenir des discours tres licencieux de M[r.] le Gouuerneur ge[neral] et jusques la mesme que c'est vn auare qui les a pillez. Jl peut arriuer de ce mepris les plus grand[s] malheur a cette Colonie. Ce que je dis donc leur est arriué cette année, car je scay qu'ils n'ont pas remporté de la traitte de leurs pelleteries le tiers de ce qui leur estoit necessaire.

Jl est encores enuoyé beaucoup de marchandiSes a MissilimaKinac par les canots qui portent aux Missionaires les choses qui leur Sont neceSSaire non pas que ces bons Peres ayant aucune part a cela ces marchandiSes appartenant aux Canoteurs qui y Sont mis de la part de M[r.] le Gouuerneur general.

Le nommé Reynant gendre de M[r.] de Lobiniere estoit descendu de MiissilimaKinac auant que je partiSe

[75v]

the things that they need—which are blankets, leggings, guns, powder, lead, tobacco, and kettles—and they fall into extreme wretchedness; which leads them to make very scandalous comments about *Monsieur* the governor-general, and even that he is a miser who has robbed them. From this contempt may arise the greatest misfortune for this colony. What I am saying has, accordingly, happened to them[43] this year, for I know they have not brought back from the trading of their furs one third of what they needed.

Much merchandise is still sent to Michilimackinac by the canoes that take the missionaries the things they need—not that these good fathers have any share in that; these goods belong to the canoemen who are put there on behalf of *Monsieur* the governor-general.

The [man] named Reynant,[44] son-in-law of *Monsieur* Lobiniere,[45] had descended from Michilimackinac before I departed

43. That is, to the Ottawas.

44. Possibly Arnauld, a contraband trader. Peyser and Brandão, *Edge of Empire*, 112, 113 n. 3.

45. Possibly René-Louis Chartier de Lotbinière, who had a long career in New France and was, in 1703, appointed chief councilor of the Superior Council of New France. See André Vachon, "René-Louis Chartier de Lotbinière," *DCB*, 2:135–39.

[76r]

de Montreal. Le S^r. Boudor estoit descendu aussy mais jl y en retourné Sans permission et je l'y ay trouué ou jl commerce comme les autres pour pouuoir Subsister. Je luy ay ordonné de la part du Roy de s'en retourner chez luy Sous peine de desobeissance, Jl ma repondu qu'jl estoit dans le desobeissance, et de plus qu'jl auoit eu auis qu'on auoit procedé contre luy, que cependant Si je voulois luy donner parole jl ne luy seroit rien fait jl descendroit, mais je nay pas cru deuoir m'engager a cela, dont jl m'aparu tres mortiFié et mesme au despoir de sa faute. Je croire pouuoir repondre que Si vous vouliez bein, Monseigneur, luy pardonner, jl ne retomberoit de sa vie dans vne pareille. Suiuant le temoignage de tout ce qu'jl y a d'honnestes gens dans la Colonies cet homme a tres bien Seruy dans toutes les guerres qu'on a eu de son tems contre les anglois et contre les Jroquois, et mesme S'y est Signalé. Il me paroist estre encores

[76r]

from Montreal. The *sieur* Boudor[46] had also come down, but he returned without permission and I found him there where he trades, like the others, to be able to subsist. I ordered him, on behalf of the king, to return home on pain of disobedience.[47] He replied to me that he was already in disobedience and, moreover, that he had been advised that they had proceeded against him; that, however, if I wanted to grant him a parole,[48] nothing would be done against him [and] he would descend [to Montreal]. But I did not believe that I needed to involve myself in that, about which he appeared to me very mortified, and even in despair over his offense. I believe I can say that if you were willing, My Lord, to pardon him he would not fall into the same error in a like situation. According to the testimony of all the honorable people in the colony, that man has served very well in all the wars of his days against the English and the Iroquois, and has even distinguished himself. He appears to have, still,

46. Jean Boudor, a Montreal merchant who shows up in various records in association with illegal trading. Peyser and Brandão, *Edge of Empire*, 112, 113 n. 4, 128–38.

47. That is, on pain of being found to be in disobedience of the king's orders.

48. This word, the same in French and English, meant release and also referred to an act of swearing allegiance—that is, of giving one's word. It is not clear how it is being used here, since if the latter, it would be Boudor who would be swearing allegiance. It seems to be a request for a release from the charges against him or, as made clear below, a request for a pardon of the same.

[76v]

toutes ces dispositons.

Ouaouyelo outauis Kiscacon qui demeuroit cy deuant au Detroit et qui est presentment a MissilimaKinac dit qu'il a laissé au Sr. de Grandmenil commis de Mr. de la Mothe vn collier de porcelaine et vne grande chaudiere de festin, que Mr. de la Mothe refus de luy faire rendre quoy qu'jl aye offert dix castors a ce Commis pour la valeur de cinq dont jl luy auoir fait credit et pour Seureté de laquelle cette chaudiere et ce colier luy auoit esté donnez. Ce Sauuage dit que quand jl a dema[ndé] ce colier et cette chaudiere a Mr. de la Mothe, jl luy a repondu qu'jl les auoit donnez aux Miamis pour leur parler.

Que Mr. de la Mothe l'auoit Jnuité d'aler au Detroit et que n'ayant pas voulu y aler, jl croit que c'est par cette raison qu'jl a refusé de luy faire rendre cette chaudiere et ce colier.

Que mesme jl le menace auec plusieurs autres de sa nation que S'jls ne retournoient pas S'establir

[76v]

all of these inclinations.

Onaouyelo,[49] a Kiscacon Ottawa, who used formerly to live at Detroit and who is presently at Michilimackinac, says that he left with *sieur* de Grandmesnil,[50] *Monsieur* de Lamothe's agent, a large porcelain necklace[51] and a great feast kettle, which *Monsieur* de Lamothe refuses to have returned to him, although he offered to the agent ten beaver for the five's worth for which he had given him credit and as security for which his kettle and necklace had been given to him. This *sauvage* says that when he asked *Monsieur* de Lamothe for this necklace and kettle, he replied to him that he had given them to the Miamis to speak to them.[52]

[He said] that *Monsieur* de Lamothe had invited him to go to Detroit, and as he would not go there, he believes it is for that reason that he refused to give him back the kettle and collar.

[He also said] that he threatened him and many others of his nation that if they did not go back to settle at Detroit

49. It has not been possible to identify this person.

50. Étienne Véron de Grandmesnil. He served, as noted here, as Cadillac's secretary and agent. He became a notary in 1706 and acted in that capacity until 1720. See Roland Auger, "Étienne Véron de Grandmesnil," *DCB*, 2:647–48.

51. Natives in the Great Lakes region used wampum, a marine shell and, later, glass beads to form "belts" (*ceintures*) and "necklaces" (*colliers*). These items were not, in reality, worn as the terms might suggest. Rather, the terms, in French and English, described as best observers could, the shape of items used as mnenomic devices in Indian diplomacy. *Colliers*, sometimes translated as necklaces, collars, or strings, referred to single strands of beads and stood in distinction to the "belts," which averaged 4 to 6 inches in width and could be several feet in length. See for examples *Handbook*, 15:423, 429.

52. That is, had used the items he held in collateral for the loan as gifts to be used, as was native custom, when beginning some sort of conference.

[77r]

au Detroit jls mouroient tous. Jl est vray Monseigneur, qu'jl leur a dit cela parce qu'jl Scait qu'jls Sont tres Supersticieux. Si Bien qu'jls croyent presentment que tous ceux de leurs gens qui meurent c'est M$^{r.}$ de la Mothe qui les fait mourir. Jl y en a mesme beaucoup qui pour euiter cette pretendüe mort ont estre S'establir au Detroit.

Voila Monseigneur, toutes les remarques que jay pû faire dans mon voyage. Jl y en a quelques vnes qui sont contre mon jnclination et ce dautant plus que je n'ay en mon particulier aucun sujet de me plaindre des personnes sur qui elles sont faites. Jl ne faloit par moins qu'un ordre de vous, Monseigneur, pour mobliger a le faire. La bonté que Vous auez a eue de me marque que vous ne me commettriez pas ne m'a point porté a m'y determiner auec plus de facilité. Je Scay trop que je dois vous obeir Sans aucune conditions

[77r]

they would all die. It is true, My Lord, that he told them that, for he knows they are very superstitious, so that presently they believe that of all their people who die, it is *Monsieur* de Lamothe who causes their death. There are even many who have gone to settle at Detroit in order to avoid their supposed death.

Behold, My Lord, all the observations that I have been able to make on my journey. There are some that are against my inclination, and this all the more because I have, of my own, no reason to complain of the persons about whom they are made. It needed no less than an order from you, My Lord, to compel me to do it. The kindness that you had in telling me that you would not expose me did not induce me to make up my mind to it more easily; I know too well that it is my duty to obey you without any conditions.

[77v]

aussy quand jl sagira de le faire ne suiuray je point d'autre regle que vostre volonté pour laquelle j'auray toute ma vie vne obeissance aueugle et respecteuSe.

Je suis auec vn tres profond respect
Monsiegneur
Votre tres humble, tres obeissance, et
oblige Seruiteur [signed] Daigremont

[In the margin, opposite Votre:]

a Quebec le 14.
Nouembre 1708.

[77v]

Therefore, when it is a question of doing that, I shall follow no rule but your will to which, all my life, I shall have a blind and respectful obedience.

I am, with the most profound respect, My Lord, your most humble, most obedient, and obliged servant.

[signed] D'Aigremont
Quebec, the 14th of November, 1708

Mémoire on the Establishment of Michilimackinac

[folio 128r]

Memoire sur l'Etablissement de MichilimaKina

Jl paroist par la lettre du 19 Juillet dernier du Pere Marest missionnaire dela compangnie de jesus que ce poste a esté abandonné par l'Etablissement du Detroit, et que le retablissement de MichilimaKina seroit util a la Colonie Que M.r de Louuigny y est attendu pour plaçer le sauuages les rassembler et les y amner par la confiance qu'ils ont enluy.

Et par la lettre aussy de Mr. delignery du 20 juillet dernier il marque qu'il jnformera de cequi sera passé entre les nations qui sont allées en guerre contre les Renards lors qu'elles seront de retour a MichilimaKina, sans marquer qu'il y ait a present aucun ordre a donner sur ce sujet

Que si on veut restablir ce poste jl est necessaire d'y auoir vne garnison sans quoy il n'y auroit pas d'agrement pour vn commandant

[Bégon's September 20, 1713, Mémoire]

[f. 128r]

Memoir on the Establishment of Michilimackinac

It appears by the letter of 19 July last, from Father Marest,[1] missionary of the Society of Jesus, that this post was abandoned due to the establishment of Detroit, and that the reestablishment of Michilimackinac would be useful to the colony; that *Monsieur* de Louvigny[2] is awaited to settle the *sauvages*, assemble them and lead them, due to the trust they have in him.

And also by the letter of *Monsieur* de Lignery[3] of 20 July last, he notes that he will report on what has happened among the nations who went to war against the Foxes when they[4] have returned to Michilimackinac, without noting that at present he has any orders to give on the subject.

That if one wants to reestablish this post it is necessary to have a garrison; without which there would be no attraction for a commander,

1. Probably Father Joseph-Jacques Marest, who served as missionary to the Indians at Michilimackinac and was, from 1706 to 1721, the superior of the mission. He was a vocal critic of Cadillac's efforts to relocate his charges to Detroit. Joseph's brother, Father Pierre-Gabriel Marest, worked among the Illinois and also reported on matters in the region of Michilimackinac. See Maud M. Hutcheson, "Joseph-Jacques Marest," *DCB*, 2:453–54, and "Pierre-Gabriel Marest," ibid., 454–55. On the Jesuit critique, led by Father Joseph Marest, of Cadillac and his plans, see the *Michigan Pioneer and Historical Society Collections*, vol. 33 (1904): 102–60, and vol. 34 (1905): 285–91.

2. On Louvigny see the introduction to this volume and the sources cited there.

3. Constant le Marchand de Lignery, lieutenant and captain in New France, who twice commanded at Michilimackinac. In 1715 he was charged with leading an expedition out of the fort against the Fox Indians. See Yves F. Zoltvany, "Constant le Marchand de Lignery," *DCB*, 2:389–90. The expedition did not take place.

4. That is, the nations that went to war against the Fox Indians.

[f. 128v]

y ayant apresent 40 fuyards les quels font tout ce qui leur plait, n'ayant en ueuë que leur jnterests.

Qu'il attend auec jmpatience Mr. de Louugny estant bien persuadé qu'il n'y viendra pas sans vne garnison, moyen enquoy il estant qu'il ne paroîtra pas vn de ces fuyards.

Le resultat de ces deux lettres est que le retablissem[ent][1] de MichilimaKina sera fort util au commerce de la Colonie que M. de Louuigny y est attend[u][2] auec jmpatience pour rassembler les Sauuages et les exiiter de venir s'y establie par la confi[ance[3]] qu'ils ont enluy, et qu'il est necessaire pour contenir les fuyards qui y sont au nombre de 40 qu'il y aille auec vne garnison au moyen de laquelle on les empeschera d'y venir.

Il ne paroist pas par ces lettres que la guerre que les nations font aux Renards merittent a present beaucoup d'attention de ce costé cy d'autant que Mr. de Lignery marque qu'a

1. Part of this word was cut off due to the binding process.
2. Word is cut off due to the binding process.
3. Word cut off due to binding process.

[f. 128v]

there being at present forty deserters [there] who do all that they please, having nothing in sight but their interests.

That he awaits *Monsieur* de Louvigny with impatience, being well persuaded that he will not come without a garrison; things being the way they are, not one of those deserters will appear.

The outcome[5] of these two letters is that the reestablishment of Michilimackinac will be very useful to the commerce of the colony; that *Monsieur* de Louvigny is awaited with impatience to gather the *sauvages* and excite them to come and establish themselves due to the trust they have in him; and that it is necessary, in order to contain the deserters who are there to the number of forty, that he sail with a garrison, by which means one can prevent them from coming there.

It does not appear by these letters that the war that the nations are waging with the Foxes merits, at present, very much attention from this side, inasmuch as *Monsieur* de Lignery noted that, upon

5. In the sense of "the conclusion to be drawn" based upon the information in the letters.

[f. 129r]

leur retour de MichilimaKina jl jnformera de ce qui sera passé entr'eux et on jugera alors de cequil y aura faire pour le printems prochain, ainsy cette guerre n'oblige jusques a ce tems la aucune mesure.

JI reste presentement a Examiner si lutilité qu'il ya lieu desperer qu'on retirera du retablissement de MichilimaKina est vne raison suffisante pour y enuoyer Mr. de Louugny presentment auec des troupes ou sans, On ne peut y enuoyer a present des troupes par cequ'il en couteroit beaucoup pour leur habillment qui doit arriuer cet automme et pour toutes les autres depenses a faire sur les quelles jl n'y a point d'ordre.

Il ne paroist pas plus conuenable d'y enuoyer presentement Mr. de Louuigny sans troupes puisque suiuant la lettre de Mr. delignery le principal fruit du voyage de Mr. de Louuigny

[f. 129r]

their return from Michilimackinac, he will report on what has happened among them; and we will decide then what we will need to do for the following spring. Thus, this war does not, at this time, require any measures [from us].

It presently remains to examine if the usefulness that one may rightly expect to derive from the reestablishment of Michilimackinac is a sufficient reason to send *Monsieur* de Louvigny there presently—with troops or without. One cannot send troops there at present because it will cost a great deal for their clothing, which should arrive this fall, and for all of the other needed expenses, about which there are no orders.

It does not appear advisable to send *Monsieur* de Louvigny there, at present, without troops since, according to the letter of *Monsieur* de Lignery, the principal fruit of *Monsieur* de Louvigny's voyage

[f. 129v]

Seroit qu'amenant vne garnison auec luy jl sera en estat des chasser 40 coureurs de bois qui seront les maitres d'y rester tant qu'il n'y aura point de troupes.

C'est ce qui fait juger qu'il n'y a rien de pressé Sur le voyage de Mr. Louuigny qui se fera beau[coup][4] plus vtilment au printems prochain que cet hiuer puis qu'il ne pourroit partir qu'entre cy e[t] le 15 du mois prochain, et que si cette année jl estoit deux mois amonter comme les canots de lannée dernier l'ont esté Mr. de Louuigny n'y arriuant que le 15 de Nouembre, les Sauuages seroient alors en chasse d'ou ils n'y seront de retour qu'au mois de may prochain, pour y faire leurs semence de bled d'jnde, et ce ne sera qu'alors que Mr. de Louuigny pourra parler auec [les][5] Sauuages pour les affaires dela Colonie.

Cependant Mr. de Louuigny ne pourroit

4. Word cut off by binding process.

5. This word is missing here but is needed.

[f. 129v]

would be that, bringing a garrison with him, he will be in a position to hunt [down] the forty *coureurs de bois* who have the power to stay there as long as there are no troops.

This is what suggests that there is nothing urgent about the voyage of *Monsieur* de Louvigny, which can be much more usefully made next spring than this winter, [especially] since he could not depart but between now and the 15th of the next month.[6] And that if, this year, he is two months ascending[7] as were the canoes of last year, *Monsieur* de Louvigny—not arriving there but by 15 November—the *sauvages* would then be hunting; from which they would not return until the following month of May to sow their Indies wheat, and it would not be but then that Mr. de Louvigny will be able to talk with the *sauvages* about the affairs of the colony.

However, *Monsieur* de Louvigny could not

6. October 15, 1713.

7. That is, ascending the rivers to the upper country.

[f. 130r]

entreprendre ce voyage y allant a ses frais en luy donnant deux Canots sans qu'ils en cousta a sa Majeste des presens pour ses sauuages, les quels presents on ne sera point obligé de faire si Mr. de Louuigny n'y va pas cette année, ainsy ce seroit vne augmentation de depense pour laquelle jl n'y a pas de fond, ce qui sera d'autant plus considerable qu'il n'y a rien dans les magazins et que toutes les marchandises sont hors de prix, et en y enuoyant seulment au printems prochain on pourra se seruir de celles que Sa Majesté enuoyera jcy cet automme.

D'ailleurs le principal objet du voyage de Mr. de Louuigny estant de restablir le poste de MichilimaKina ce que esté remis a la paix par ce qu'on n'a pas affoiblir la Colonie pendant la guerre, jl est necessaire auant de trauailler au rêtablissement de Sçauoir les jntentions de Sa Majesté sur la depense

[f. 130r]

undertake this voyage, going there at his expense [and] giving him two canoes,[8] without it costing His Majesty presents for the *sauvages*; which presents one will not be required to give if *Monsieur* de Louvigny does not go there this year. Thus, this[9] would be an added expense for which there are no funds, which will be even more considerable given that there is nothing in the [king's] stores, and that all the merchandise [that would need to be purchased] is overpriced. And sending him only next spring, one can use those[10] that His Majesty will send here this fall.

Moreover, the principal object of *Monsieur* de Louvigny's voyage being to reestablish the post of Michilimackinac, which is put off until the peace[11] so as not to weaken the colony during the war, it is necessary, before working towards the reestablishment, to know His Majesty's intentions about the

8. That is, he could not go even at his own expense and with two canoes provided to him by the Crown to defray his costs.

9. That is, the voyage to Michilimackinac.

10. That is, the goods designated as presents for the Indians.

11. The Treaty of Utrecht ended the War of Spanish Succession in Europe and its corollary fight in North America between England and France's colonies. The latter war is known in what came to be the United States as Queen Anne's War. The treaty was signed April 12, 1713, and Bégon may not have known this, as the ships with his orders may have sailed before the news was announced. He would, however, have known that a peace was coming, as negotiations had begun with a formal truce the previous year.

[f. 130v]

extraordinaire qui y sera faite tant pour les Officiers que pour la garnison et les presens a faire aux Sauuages tous les ans pour laqu[elle][6] il n'ya aucun fonds ordonné, ainsy auant de faire cette depense jl conuient de faire vn projet de tout ce qu'il en coûtera extraordinaire sur lequel jl plaira a sa Majesté ordonner les fonds necessaires par les depenses ne paroissant pas qu'elle ait voulu qu'il en fust fait aucune depense que les fonds n'en ait esté ordonnéer

Ainsy pour sy conformer, jl est apropos de faire vn projet pour le restablissement de MichilimaKina sans qu'il en coute rien a sa Majesté Soit en abandonnant le commerce de ce poste et des particuliers qui S'obligeront de payer a leur depens toute la depense Extraordinaire tant pour la

6. Word cut off by binding process.

[f.130v]

extraordinary expenses that will need to be made, as much for the officers as for the garrison, and the presents to be made to the *sauvages* each year, for which there are no funds ordered. Thus, before undertaking that expense, it is advisable to make a plan[12] of all that it will cost extra, [and] about which it will please His Majesty to order the funds necessary for the expenses, [it] not appearing that he wanted any expenditures be made unless the funds had been ordered for it.

Thus, to so conform,[13] it is appropriate to make a plan for the reestablishment of Michilimackinac without it costing His Majesty anything; be it in forsaking the commerce from this post and from private [parties] who will obligate themselves to pay, at their expense, all the extraordinary costs, as much for the

12. A call for a study or budget appears to be what is intended, but the former word seems not to be used in that sense in this era, and "budget" only came into common French usage in the second half of the eighteenth century.

13. That is, with the directive not to authorize expenditures for which funds have not already been specified.

[f. 131r]

Subsistence de 22 hommes de troupes que pour les deux officiers qui y Seruiront y fourniront les munitions de guerre pour la deffence du fort, les presens a faire aux Sauuages et feront generallement toutes les depenses soit en vendant des congez dont le produit Sera employé au payement des depenses de MichilimaKina en cas que Sa Majesté ne juge pas apropos d'accorder vn commerce exclusif.

Jl est necessaire de Sçauoir les jntentions de Sa Majesté sur l'une de ces deux propositions ou sur les fonds extraordinaires qu'elle voudra bien Ordonner pour MichilimaKina en cas qu'elle n'ait approuué aucune des deux proposition; Comme Mr. delignery est a MichilimaKina jl Suffit pendant l'hiuer dedans ce poste, dont le restablissement ne

[f. 131r]

subsistence of twenty-two men of the *Troupes [de Marine]* as for the two officers who will serve there, furnish the war munitions for the defense of the fort, the presents to be made to the *sauvages*, and pay all the usual expenses; [or] be it in selling *congés* whose profit will be used to pay the expenses of Michilimackinac, in the case that His Majesty does not judge it appropriate to allot an exclusive commerce.[14]

It is necessary to know the intentions of His Majesty about one of these two propositions, or about the extraordinary funds that he might wish to order for Michilimackinac in the case that he has not approved either of the two propositions. As *Monsieur* de Lignery is at Michilimackinac, it is enough [that he stay] during the winter in the post, whose reestablishment

14. That is, allot the trade at the post to one individual or group.

[f. 131v]

prejudicie pas plus a la colonie apresent qu'il fait depuis enuirons 8 ou 10[7] qu'il est abandonné

Il en est de mesme des coureurs de bois qui est vn mal qui dure depuis longtems et Sur lequel il est necessaire de Sçauoir le jntentions de Sa Majesté si elle leur accorde ou non vne amnistie a la paix ou s'il seront punit Suiuant la rigueur des ordannances, et jusque a ce qu'il y ait vne decision Sur leur Sujet jl ne paroist pas que le commerce qu'ils font a MichilimaKina porte plus de prejudice a la Colonie que celuy qu'ils feroient ailleurs, estant Egallement jnfractaires des ordonnances du Roy jl n'est pas plus permis a Mr. delignery et autres qui p[euuent?][8] auoir de permissions de Mr. Le gouuerneur general viseés de l'jntendant de faire comm[erce[9]] chez les nations d'enhaut qu'a ces coureurs de Bois y ayant vne ordonnance du Roy

7. Either the word *ans* is missing here, or the reference is to the number of winters that have passed since the post was to have been abandoned.

8. The only legible part of this word is the letter "p." The rest of the word is written in such tight and small script that it is just a blotch disappearing into the binding. Given the context, this seems a logical choice for what the word may be.

9. Word cut off by the binding process.

[f. 131v]

does not prejudice the colony any more now that it has for the approximately eight or ten [years] that it has been abandoned.

There is, too,[15] the *coureurs de bois*, which is an evil that has existed for a long time, and about which it is necessary to know the intentions of His Majesty: if he will grant, or not, an amnesty at the peace,[16] or if they will be punished in strict accordance with the ordinances. And until there is a decision on the subject, it does not appear that the trading they do at Michilimackinac brings more harm to the colony than that which they do elsewhere, being equally violations of the King's ordinances. It is no more permitted to *Monsieur* de Lignery and others who may have passes from *Monsieur* the Governor-General, designed by the Intendant,[17] to trade among the upper [country] nations than it is those *coureurs de bois*, there being an ordinance from the King

15. That is, "one must also consider the problem of the . . . ."

16. That is, at the formal conclusion of the anticipated peace.

17. Michel Bégon de la Picardière had a long career in the service of France. From 1712 to 1726 he was intendant of New France. He supported ending the fur trade monopoly—that is, of requiring all furs traded for in New France having to be sold to one purchaser appointed by the king to fill that role. At the same time, he opposed Governor Vaudreuil's efforts to reestablish Michilimackinac. See Yves Zoltvany, "Michel Bégon de la Picardière," *DCB*, 3:57–63.

[f. 132r]

qui deffend de donner ces permissions et ordonne peine Corporelle contre les voyageurs et confiscation de leur marchandises.

Toutes ces raisons font juger que rien ne periclite de remettre le Voyage de Mr. de Louuigny au printems prochain parce qu'on Sçaura alors si les congez Serron restablir ou non, et s'ils sont restably [illegible]][10] le pouuoir den donner et on sçaura si on le vendra et combien pour en employer le prix a la depense a faire pour MichilimaKina, n'y ayant a present aucun party certain a prendre, ce qui ne sera que lors que Sa Majesté se sera expliquée sur les congez et en mesme tems il Sera necessaire qu'elle marque ses jntentions Sur ceux qui seront accordés pour le detroit qui doiuent estre limités

Enfin jl est necessaire que Sa Majesté se determine de les retablir ou de former des

10. The ascension stamp of the Archives Coloniales: Marine et Colonies is used to mark pages at intervals and with no particular order of where it is put on a page. In most cases, it is possible to read the text beneath the stamp mark, but that is not the case here, where it looks as if there are two words: *on aura*.

[f. 132r]

that prohibits giving these passes and prescribes corporal punishment against the *voyageurs* and confiscation of their merchandise.

All of these reasons make one think that nothing will be jeopardized by putting off *Monsieur* de Louvigny's voyage until next spring, because we will know then if the *congés* will be reestablished or not; and if they are reestablished, [if] we will have the power to give them; and we will know if we will sell them, and how many to use the [sale] price [of] toward the expenditures for Michilimackinac, there not being, at present, any party certain to take them, which will not happen until His Majesty has explained himself about the *congés*. And, at the same time, it will be necessary for him to indicate his intentions about the ones that will be accorded for Detroit, which must be limited.

Lastly, it is necessary that His Majesty resolve himself to establish them or to create

[f. 132v]

Compagnies pour faire le commerce exclusif dans les postes quelle jugera apropos de faire establir sans quoy les Sauuages jront chez les Anglois ou les marchandises Sont a meilleur marché qu'a montreal, des qu'ils Seront oblig[er] de les aller chercher, ainsy jl faut de necessité leur emporter afin que les Sauuages en trouuant n'en aillent pas chercher chez les Anglois.

C'est ce qui fait juger que quoy que les coureurs de bois Soient punisables par leur desobeissa[nce] aux ordres du Roy, le commerce qu'ils font chez les nations d'enhaut ne laisse pas d'estr[e] auantageux a la colonie et de l'auoir Souten[t] pendant la guerre par les marchandises qu'ils ont traitté auec ces Sauuages pour des castors et pelleteries qui sont descendus a Montreal et qui sans doute, auroient esté chez les Anglois qui Seul auroient fait

[f. 132v]

companies to carry on the exclusive trade in the posts that he will judge appropriate to establish, without which the *sauvages* will go among the English, where the merchandise is better priced than at Montreal, once they are obliged to go search for it. Thus, necessity requires that we take it[18] so that the *sauvages*, in finding it, do not go looking for it among the English.

This is what makes one think that although the *coureurs de bois* are liable for punishment for disobeying the King's orders, the trading they do among the upper nations does not prevent them from being advantageous to the colony and from having sustained it during the war through the goods that they traded with those *sauvages* for beaver and [other] skins that came down to Montreal and that, without doubt, would have gone to the English, who alone would have been

18. That is, merchandise.

[f. 133r]

le commerce s'il n'estoit monté aucun francois d'en les pais d'Enhaut

Dailleurs la principale attention deuant estre dempescher l'jntelligence entre les outaoüois et les JroquoiS il S'ensuit qu'il faut que les françois leur portent chez eux leurs besoins pour qu'ils ne saccoutument pas a les tirer des Anglois estant a craindre que S'ils y estoient attirés premierement par la necessité et ensuite par la bon marché jl ne fust plus possible de les Empescher d y aller ce qui Feroit tomber en canada le commerce des pelleteries qui est le principal Sur lequel On puisse compter et cequi dans la Suitte pourroit faire ranger les Sauuages du costé de Anglois a la premiere guerre ny ayant pas lieu de douter qu'ils ne prennent toujours le party de ceux auec les quels jls

[f. 133r]

trading, if some French had not gone up to the upper country.

Furthermore, the principal goal needing to be to prevent communication between the Ottawas and the Iroquois, it follows that the French must take them what they need so that they do not become accustomed to getting it[19] from the English, it being feared that if they were attracted at first by need, and then by good prices, it would no longer be possible to keep them from going there, which would cause a decline in Canada of trade in skins, which is the one thing that one may count on, and which could, afterwards, make the *sauvages* align on the side of the English at the first [sign of] war, there being no reason to doubt that they will not take the side of those with whom they

19. That is, trade goods.

[f. 133v]

feront Commerce fait a Quebec le 20e Septembre 1713

[signed] Bégon

[f. 133v]

trade. Done at Quebec, the 20th of September, 1713

[signed] Bégon

Codex Canadensis. Ink on paper. Overall: 13¼ × 8½ in. (33.7 × 21.6 cm). p. 5. GM 4726.7. Museum, Tulsa, Oklahoma.

11. Captain of the Illinois Nation, an unnamed Illinois headman.

APPENDIX

Other Translated Documents That Relate to Michilimackinac and the *Pays d'en Haut* in This Period

SOURCES CONSULTED AND ABBREVIATIONS

AUL

Jones, Arthur E., ed. *The Aulneau Collection, 1734–1745*. Rare or Unpublished Documents 2. Montreal: Archives of St. Mary's College, 1893.

COL

Darlington, Mary Carson, ed. *Fort Pitt and Letters from the Frontier*. The First American Frontier, edited by Dale Van Every. 1892; repr., Arno Press and The New York Times, 1971.

IHC

Pease, Theodore Calvin, and Raymond C. Werner, eds. *Collections of the Illinois State Historical Library*. Vol. 23, *The French Foundations, 1680–1693*. French Series 1. Springfield: Illinois State Historical Library, 1934.

Pease, Theodore Calvin, ed. *Collections of the Illinois State Historical Library*. Vol. 27, *Anglo-French Boundary Disputes in the West, 1749–1763*. French Series 2. Springfield: Illinois State Historical Library, 1936.

Pease, Theodore Calvin, and Ernestine Jenison, eds. *Collections of the Illinois State Historical Library*. Vol. 29, *Illinois on the Eve of the Seven Years' War, 1747–1755*. French Series 3. Springfield: Illinois State Historical Library, 1940.

HIS

Krauskopf, Frances, trans. and ed. *Ouiatanon Documents*. Indiana Historical Society Publications, vol. 18, no. 2. Indianapolis: Indiana Historical Society, 1955.

LaV J&L

Burpee, Lawrence J., ed. *Journals and Letters of Pierre Gaultier de Varennes de la Vérendrye and His Sons: With Correspondence between the Governors of Canada and the French Court, Touching the Search for the Western Sea*. Facsimile edition. 1927; repr., New York: Greenwood Press, 1968.

MPA

Rowland, Dunbar, and Albert Godfrey Sanders, eds. and trans. *Mississippi Provincial Archives, 1729–1740: French Dominion*. Vol. 1, *French-English-Indian Relations: Wars with the Natchez and Chickasaw Indians*. 1927; repr., New York: AMS Press, 1973.

———. *Mississippi Provincial Archives, 1701–1729: French Dominion*. Vol. 2. 1929; repr., New York: AMS Press, 1973.

———. *Mississippi Provincial Archives, 1704–1743: French Dominion*. Vol. 3. 1932; repr., New York: AMS Press, 1973.

———. *Mississippi Provincial Archives: French Dominion, 1729–1748*. Vol. 4, revised and edited by Patricia Kay Galloway. Library of Southern Civilization, edited by Lewis P. Simpson. Baton Rouge: Louisiana State University Press, 1984.

———. *Mississippi Provincial Archives: French Dominion, 1749–1763.* Vol. 5, revised and edited by Patricia Kay Galloway. Library of Southern Civilization, edited by Lewis P. Simpson. Baton Rouge: Louisiana State University Press, 1984.

MPHC

Michigan Pioneer and Historical Society. *Historical Collections: Collections and Researches Made by the Michigan Pioneer and Historical Society.* Vol. 33. Lansing, MI: Robert Smith Printing, 1904.

Michigan Pioneer and Historical Society. *Historical Collections: Collections and Researches Made by the Michigan Pioneer and Historical Society.* Vol. 34. Lansing, MI: Wynkoop Hallenbeck Crawford, 1905.

NYCD

O'Callaghan, E. B., and Berthold Fernow, eds. and trans. *Documents Relative to the Colonial History of the State of New-York.* 15 vols. Albany, NY: Weed, Parsons, 1853–87.

PA

Linn, John Blair, and William Henry Egle, eds. *Pennsylvania Archives.* Second series, edited by Matthew S. Quay. Vol. 6. Harrisburg, PA: Lane S. Hart, 1877.

SHORTT

Shortt, Adam, ed. *Documents Relating to Canadian Currency, Exchange and Finance during the French Period.* 2 vols. Burt Franklin: Research Source Works Series, 235. 1925; repr., New York: Burt Franklin, 1968.

WCNP

Stevens, Sylvester Kirby, and Donald H. Kent, eds. *Wilderness Chronicles of Northwestern Pennsylvania.* Harrisburg: Commonwealth of Pennsylvania, Department of Public Instruction, Pennsylvania Historical Commission, 1941.

WHC

Draper, Lyman Copeland, and Reuben Gold Thwaites, eds. *Collections of the State Historical Society of Wisconsin*. 21 vols. Madison: State Historical Society of Wisconsin, 1855–1915.

FRENCH DOCUMENTS: PUBLISHED TRANSLATIONS

1631

1631. Abstract of the Discoveries in New France, as well as of those made by us as by the English, from the Virginias to Davis Straits, and of what they and we can claim, according to the report of Historians who have written thereof, which will enable every one to judge dispassionately of the whole. Champlain. In PA, 6:3–6.

1634

1634. Jean Nicolet's Visit to Wisconsin. From *The Jesuit Relation* of 1642–1643. In WHC, 16:1–3.

1638

February 10, 1638. Letter of King Louis XIII., on the subject of the limits of command between Messrs. Charnisay and de la Cour, in New France. In NYCD, 9:4–5.

1640

Between 1640 and 1660. Tribes and Tribal Wars about Green Bay. From Bacqueville de la Potherie, *Histoire de l'Amérique Septentrionale*, published at Paris in 1722, and again in 1753. In WHC, 16:3–10.

1651

June 20, 1651. Quebec. Letter of the Council at Quebec to the Commissioners of New England, respecting the Indians, &c. Commission of the Rev. Father

Druillettes and M. Jean Godefroy as ambassadors to New England. In NYCD, 9:5–7.

1653

1653–55. First Iroquois Raid into Wisconsin. From Nicolas Perrot, *Mémoire sur les moeurs, coustumes et relligion des Sauvages de l'Amérique Septentrionale*: written about 1715–18; published at Paris, 1864, with annotations by Rev. Jules Tailhan, SJ. In WHC, 16:10–13.

1654

July 18, 1654. Alterations in the Ratings of Coins. Registers of the Council. Signed Peuvret. In Shortt, 1:3–5.

1656

1656–62. The Ottawas and Hurons Flee to Wisconsin; Hostilities between Them and the Sioux. From Perrot, *Mémoire*. In WHC, 16:14–21.

1658

1658–62. Radisson and Groseilliers in Wisconsin: The Third Voyage of Radisson. In WHC, 11:64–71. The Fourth Voyage of Radisson. In WHC, 11:71–96.

1661

1660–61. Ménard's Labors and Death. From *The Jesuit Relation* of 1662–63. In WHC, 16:22–25.

June 2, 1661. First Jesuit Mission among the Ottawas. Letter of Father René Ménard to his superior at Quebec, Jerome Lalemant. In WHC, 16:21–22.

October 7, 1661. Alterations in the Ratings of Coins. Registers of the Council. Signed Peuvret. In Shortt, 1:5.

1662

Relations between the Wisconsin Tribes and the Sioux. From Perrot, *Mémoire*. In WHC, 16:25–31.

March 20, 1662. Alterations in the Ratings of Coins. Registers of the Council. Signed Peuvret. In Shortt, 1:5–7.

1663

1663. Memoir in relation to the fortifications necessary to protect Canada from the insults of the Iroquois. In NYCD, 9:20–21.

1663. Canada. Proposals for a special Canadian Currency. Unsigned. In Shortt, 1:9–11.

March 1663. Louis. Edict of the King, for the creation of a Sovereign Council, &c., in New France. In NYCD, 9:7–9.

May 1, 1663. Instructions for Sieur Gaudais sent by the King to Canada. In NYCD, 9:9–13.

August 4, 1663. Gaspé. Letter of M. Dubois d'Avaugour, Governor of Canada, to the Minister upon the state of affairs in the Colony, &c. In NYCD, 9:13–17.

November 19, 1663. Paris. Commission to Sieur de Prouville de Tracy, to be Lieutenant-general in America, during the absence of the Vice-Roy, the Count d'Estrades, &c. In NYCD, 9:17–19.

1664

April 17, 1664. Order of the Superior Council of Quebec, reducing liards to three deniers each. In Shortt, 1:11–13.

June 18, 1664. Request for Money instead of Supplies. The Sovereign Council Established at Quebec to Colbert. In Shortt, 1:13–15.

July 17, 1664. Liards to pass for two Deniers. In Shortt, 1:15.

November 15, 1664. Extracts of a Memoir from M. de Lyonne (Hugues), Minister of Marine, to M. de Tracy. In NYCD, 9:22.

1665

1665. Allouez Describes Lake Superior. From *The Jesuit Relation* of 1666–67. In WHC, 16:31–32.

1665–66. Perrot Visits the Wisconsin Tribes, and Induces Them to Become Allies of the French. From La Potherie. In WHC, 16:32–50.

1665–67. Religious Beliefs and Superstitions of the Upper Algonkin Tribes. From *The Jesuit Relation* of 1666–67. In WHC, 16:50–54.

1665–69. Allouez's Mission at Lake Superior. From *The Jesuit Relations* of 1666–67 and 1668–69. In WHC, 16:59–62.

March 23, 1665. Paris. Commission to the Sieur Talon, to be Intendant of Justice, Police, and Finance, in Canada, &c. In NYCD, 9:22–23.

March 27, 1665. Paris. Memoir of the King to serve as Instruction to Sieur Talon proceeding to New France as Intendant of Justice, Police and Finance. In NYCD, 9:24–29.

May 29, 1665. Regulation of Price of Wheat When Given in Payment. In Shortt, 1:15.

October 4, 1665. Quebec. Letter of M. Talon to the Minister, upon Canadian affairs. In NYCD, 9:29–36.

November 14, 1665. Prices of the Goods brought by the India Company's ships to be delivered to the Inhabitants of Quebeck. In NYCD, 9:36–37.

November 26, 1665. Order in Council directing the coining in the mint of Paris of coins to the amount of 100,000 livres to be current only in the territories granted to the West India Company, to wit: pieces of 20 and 10 sous of silver, nine-tenths fine. In Shortt, 1:17.

December 1, 1665. Explanation of the Eleven Presents of the Iroquois Ambassadors. In NYCD, 9:37–38.

December 13, 1665. Quebec. Treaty of Peace between the Iroquois and Governor de Tracy. In NYCD, 3:121–25.

1666

1666. An account of the nine Iroquois tribes, with illustrative drawings, &c. In NYCD, 9:47–51.

1666. Talon. Census of Canada: Abstract of the Roll of Families in the Colony of New France. In NYCD, 9:57–58.

April 5, 1666. Versailles. Letter of M. Colbert to M. Talon on Canadian affairs. In NYCD, 9:39–44.

May 25, 1666. Quebec. Treaty between the Senecas and the French. In NYCD, 9:44–45.

July 12, 1666. Quebec. Treaty between the Oneidas and the French. In NYCD, 9:45–47.

September 1, 1666. Quebec. Paper addressed by M. Talon, to Messrs. de Tracy and de Courcelles, on the question whether it is more advantageous to the King to make war or to be at peace with the "Agniez." In NYCD, 9:52–54.

November 13, 1666. Extracts of a Memoir on the Condition of Canada, addressed by M. Talon to M. de Colbert. In NYCD, 9:55–57.

1667

1667. Abstract of the census of Canada for the year 1667. In NYCD, 9:61.

January 10, 1667. The Council met . . . *Sols Marquez* to Circulate at 20 Deniers Each. In Shortt, 1:17–19.

January 31, 1667. The Council met . . . Extension of Time for Reduction of *Sols Marquez*. In Shortt, 1:19–21.

February 14, 1667. The Council met . . . Private Aid to meet Distress from Reduction of *Sols Marquez*. In Shortt, 1:21–23.

April 6, 1667. Saint Germain en Laye. Extracts of a Memoir of M. Colbert to M. Talon, about Canadian affairs. In NYCD, 9:58–59.

October 27, 1667. Extracts of a Memoir of M. Talon to M. Colbert, upon the affairs of Canada, &c. In NYCD, 9:60.

1668

1668. Abstract of the census of Canada for the year 1668. In NYCD, 9:61.

1669

[1669? or 1670?]. Proclamation of France on taking formal possession of the West. Signed Francois Dollier, priest of the diocese of Nantes in Brittany, and De Galinee, deacon of the diocese of Rennes in Brittany. In Ontario Historical Society Papers, 4:77, and MPHC, 33:36.

March 19, 1669. The Council met . . . Wheat to be taken in Payment at 4 livres per Minot. In Shortt, 1:23–25.

May 15, 1669. Extracts of a letter from M. Colbert to M. de Courcelles, upon Canadian affairs. In NYCD, 9:61–63.

1670

1670. Galinée and Dollier de Casson at Sault Ste. Marie. In WHC, 16:62–63.

1670. Jesuit Missions among the Wisconsin Tribes. From *The Jesuit Relation* of 1669–70. In WHC, 16:63–71.

1670. Dablon's Account of Copper Mines at Lake Superior. From *The Jesuit Relation* of 1669–70. In WHC, 16:72–76.

1670. Chequamegon a Center of Trade. From *The Jesuit Relation* of 1669–70. In WHC, 16:77–78.

1670–73. Jesuit Missions in the Lake Region; Tribal Migrations. From *The Jesuit Relations* of 1670–71, 1671–72, and 1672–73. In WHC, 16:78–88.

February 19, 1670. Declaration of the King that there shall be minted a special money for the Islands and Continent of America. In Shortt, 1:25–29.

March 24, 1670. Decree of the King's Council of State, respecting the Special Money for the Islands and Continent of America. In Shortt, 1:29–31.

April 9, 1670. St. Germain. Letter of M. Colbert to M. de Courcelles (extract). In NYCD, 9:63.

November 10, 1670. Quebec. Extracts of a Memoir addressed by M. Talon to the King on the affairs of Canada. In NYCD, 9:63–67.

November 10, 1670. Quebec. Extracts of a Memoir addressed to M. Colbert, by M. Talon. In NYCD, 9:67–70.

November 10, 1670. Quebec. Goods Preferred to Specie: Extracts from the Memoir addressed by M. Talon to Monseigneur Colbert. In Shortt, 1:31–33.

1671

1671. An Account of what occurred during the Voyage of Monsieur de Courcelles, Governor of New France, to Lake Ontario. In NYCD, 9:75–85.

February 1671. Extracts of a letter from M. Colbert to M. Talon—La Salle. In NYCD, 9:70.

February 11, 1671. Advisability of Sending Goods to Canada Instead of Money: From the Minister, Colbert, to M. Talon. From Archives of the Marine, King's Orders for the Indies Companies, 1671, fol. 22. In Shortt, 1:33.

March 11, 1671. Paris. Extracts of a letter from M. Colbert to M. de Courcelles. In NYCD, 9:70–71.

June 14, 1671. Saint-Lusson's Procès-Verbal. Original in Margry, *Découvertes et établissements des Français, 1614–1754* (Paris, 1876–85), 1:96–99. Translation from NYCD, 9:803–4, with some errors of nomenclature corrected. In WHC, 11:26–29.

November 2, 1671. Quebec. Extracts from the Memoir addressed by M. Talon to the King on the State of Canada. In NYCD, 9:71–73.

November 3, 1671. Quebec. Proposal for a Canadian Currency: Letters written to the King and to M. Colbert by M. Talon, Intendant in Canada, forwarded to M. de Bonrepaus, Envoy Extraordinary of the King, at London; Memorandum on Canada. In Shortt, 1:33–35.

November 11, 1671. Extracts of a Memoir addressed by M. Talon to the Minister, on the State of Canada. In NYCD, 9:74–75.

1672

January 25, 1672. Paris. Proposal for a Canadian Currency: Memorandum from Sr Patoulet requested by my Lord, 1672. In Shortt, 1:35.

April 7, 1672. Versailles. The King's Instructions to Count de Frontenac, whom his Majesty has chosen as his Governor and Lieutenant General in Canada. Signed Louis and Colbert. In NYCD, 9:85–88.

June 4, 1672. St. Germain. Extracts of a letter from the Minister to M. Talon, on Canadian affairs. In NYCD, 9:89–90.

June 4, 1672. St. Germain. Proposal for a Canadian Currency: M. Colbert to M. Talon. In Shortt, 1:35.

November 2, 1672. Quebec. Extracts of a despatch of M. de Frontenac to the Minister, upon the affairs of Canada, the Iroquois, &c. In NYCD, 9:90–94.

November 18, 1672. Decree of the Council of State respecting the circulation of silver coins in the French Islands and Continent of America. In Shortt, 1:37–39.

1673

1673. Journal of Count de Frontenac's Voyage to Lake Ontario in 1673. A detailed account of M. de Frontenac's voyage, &c., to Lake Ontario, interviews with the Indians, &c., in June, July, and August, 1673. In NYCD, 9:95–114.

1673. Joliet and Marquette Discover the Upper Mississippi. From a document in *The Jesuit Relations*. In WHC, 16:89–92.

1673–76. Jesuit Missions to Ottawas and Wisconsin Tribes. From *The Jesuit Relations* of 1673–74, 1675, and 1676–77. In WHC, 16:92–96.

June 13, 1673. Paris. Extracts of a letter of M. Colbert to M. de Frontenac, respecting the Iroquois, Jesuits, &c. In NYCD, 9:95.

1674

1674. Petition of Sieur de la Salle for a grant of Fort Frontenac. In NYCD, 9:122.

May 17, 1674. Paris. Extract of a letter from M. Colbert to M. de Frontenac. In NYCD, 9:114–16.

September 27, 1674. Order of the Superior Council of Quebec which decrees that Moose skins shall be current at the ordinary value and which forbids everyone to refuse them in payment of debts. Signed Frontenac. In Shortt, 1:39–41.

November 14, 1674. Quebec. Extracts of the General Memoir addressed by M. de Frontenac to the Minister upon Canadian affairs. In NYCD, 9:116–21.

1675

March 15, 1675. St. Germain en Laye. Extracts of a letter from M. Colbert to M. de Frontenac. In NYCD, 9:123.

May 13, 1675. Compeigne. Decree of the King, accepting the propositions made by M. de la Salle, respecting a Colony in Canada, and granting him Fort Frontenac. In NYCD, 9:123–24.

May 13, 1675. Compeigne. Patent of Nobility for Sieur Cavelier de la Salle. In NYCD, 9:125.

1676

1676–77. Allouez Begins the Illinois Mission. In WHC, 16:96–97. The mission to the Illinois tribes, which was founded by Marquette, was continued by Allouez (1676–77). His journal of the voyage thither is given in *Jesuit Relations* 60: 149–167. The original MS., written by him, rests in the archives of St. Mary's (Jesuit) College, Montreal.

April 15, 1676. St. Germain. Extracts of a letter from King Louis XIV., to M. de Frontenac, respecting new discoveries. In NYCD, 9:126.

October 6, 1676. Demand for Payment in Coin. Signed Duchesneau. In Shortt, 1:41.

1677

1677–79. Jesuit Missions to Ottawas and Wisconsin Tribes. From *The Jesuit Relations* of 1677–78 and 1679. In WHC, 16:97–99.

April 28, 1677. Dunkirk. Extracts of a letter from the King to M. de Frontenac—to be on good terms with the English, &c. In NYCD, 9:126–27.

April 28, 1677. Paris. Refusal to Send Money to Canada: To M. Duchesneau, Intendant of Canada. Unsigned. Archives of the Marine, King's Orders for the Indies Companies, 1677, fol. 7. In Shortt, 1:43.

1678

May 12, 1678. St. Germain en laye. Letters of the King, granting permission to M. de la Salle to make discoveries to the west of New France, &c. Signed Louis and Colbert. In NYCD, 9:127.

May 12, 1678. St. Germain en Laye. Extracts of a letter from the King to M. de Frontenac—the English—Iroquois, &c. In NYCD, 9:128.

1679

March 7, 1679. Order of the Council enacting regulations for the circulation of pieces of four sols and of sols marqués and the number of these pieces to be offered in payment. In Shortt, 1:43–45.

April 25, 1679. St. Germain en Laye. Extract of a letter from the King to M. de Frontenac—to maintain a good correspondence with the English, &c. In NYCD, 9:128.

April 29, 1679. Order in Council declaring that commencing from the 1st May, pieces of 4 sols shall stand reduced to 3 sols 6 deniers and sols marqués to 12 deniers. [Note only—no translated document]. In Shortt, 1:45.

May 16, 1679. Order in Council enacting that pieces of 3 sols 6 deniers shall be received in payment, as follows: payments of ten livres and below, in full; those from 10 to 500 livres, in half; from 500 to 3,000 livres, for one sixth; from 3,000 to 10,000 livres for one tenth; above 10,000 livres for one twentieth. [Note only—no translated document]. In Shortt, 1:45.

July 18, 1679. Ordinance of M. Duchesneau decreeing that, as to the refusal of various persons to take four sol pieces and sols marqués at the usual value, and according to their currency in this country, the said coins shall be current at their customary value until it is known by the first vessels what is the pleasure of His Majesty on this subject. In Shortt, 1:45–47.

November 6, 1679. Quebec. Extracts of a Memoir addressed to the King by M. de Frontenac—the Indians—Orange—Manhattan—Andros, &c. In NYCD, 9:129–30.

November 10, 1679. Quebec. Extracts of a Memoir by M. Duchesneau, Intendant, &c., of Canada, to the Minister—commerce with the Indians—census of Canada, &c. In NYCD, 9:131–36.

November 14, 1679. Quebec. Extracts of a Memoir of M. Duchesneau to the Minister—news from Albany—Manhattan, &c. In NYCD, 9:137–38.

November 14, 1679. Quebec, Letter of M. de Saurel to M. Duchesneau. In NYCD, 9:138–39.

1680

1680. La Salle on the Illinois Country. (Enclosed with the letter of Monsieur de Frontenac of November 9, 1680.) From Margry, *Découv. et étab.*, 2:93–102. In IHC, 23:1–16.

April 29, 1680. St. Germain. Extract of a letter from Louis XIV. to M. de Frontenac—rupture with England—precautions to be taken, &c. In NYCD, 9:139–40.

November 13, 1680. Quebec. Extracts of a Memoir of M. Duchesneau to the Minister—commerce with the Indians—census, &c. In NYCD, 9:140–45.

[November 28, 1680]. The Council met . . . Signed Duchesneau. In Shortt, 1:47–49.

December 2, 1680. The Council met . . . Signed Duchesneau. In Shortt, 1:49.

1681

1681–83. Fur Trade; Wisconsin Indians Atone to Jesuits for the Murder of their Servants. From La Potherie. In WHC, 16:99–105.

May 3, 1681. Versailles. Loss on Exchange: [Colbert] to Sr. Louis de Lubert. In Shortt, 1:49.

October 13, 1681. Quebec. Memoir to make known to my Lord the Indian Nations from whom we derive our peltries; their and our interests; the present condition of those Tribes; together with a brief description of the Country inhabited by the English, and of Acadia, adjoining thereunto. Signed Du Chesneau. In PA, 6:7–14.

September 17, 1681. Decree of the Superior Council ordering that the reals or dollars and all foreign coins, whether gold or silver, shall be taken according to their value by weight, with an advance of one third, according to the custom of the country. Signed Duchesneau. In Shortt, 1:51–53.

November 2, 1681. Quebec. Extracts of a letter of M. de Frontenac to the King—Iroquois—English, &c. In NYCD, 9:145–49.

November 13, 1681. Extracts of a letter of M. Duchesneau to the Minister, upon Canadian affairs, &c. In NYCD, 9:149–58.

November 13, 1681. Quebec. Extract of a paper annexed to the foregoing, respecting trade with the Indians, &c. Memoir of M. Du Chesneau on Irregular Trade in Canada. In NYCD, 9:159–60.

November 13, 1681. Quebec. Memoir of M. Duchesneau to the Minister upon the subject of the French and English trade with the Western Indians, &c. In NYCD, 9:160–66.

December 15, 1681. The Council met . . . Enforcement of the Circulation of Dollars. Signed Duchesneau. In Shortt, 1:53.

1682

1682. Description of Wisconsin Rivers; Accusations against Du Luth. From a letter by La Salle. In Margry, *Découv. et étab.*, 2:249–54. In WHC, 16:105–10.

1682. Memoir, to illustrate the situation in which Count de Frontenac left Canada, in regard to the Indians, and principally the Iroquois. In NYCD, 9:190–92.

[1682?]. Opinion of Francis Provost, Mayor of Quebec, regarding the Indian troubles of the Five Nations. In MPHC, 34:280.

[1682?]. James Du Chesneau's (Intendant of New France) opinion of the trouble with the Five Nations. In MPHC, 34:281–83.

[1682?]. Frontenac's advice regarding the trouble with the Five Nations. In MPHC, 34:283–85.

March 13 and 14, 1682. The Taking Possession of the Country Situated along the Ohio or St. Louis River, and the Mississippi or Colbert River. Official Report of This Taking Possession in the Country of the Akansas. From La Salle's Procès-Verbal. In WHC, 11:29–32. Original in Margry, *Découv. et étab.*, translated by Grace Clark, 2:181–85.

March 23, 1682. Extracts of the Opinions rendered at the Conference held at the House of the Jesuit Fathers on the subject of the news received from the Iroquois. In NYCD, 9:168–73.

March 23, 1682. Extracts from the opinions given at the conference held by the Reverend Jesuit Fathers, on the subject of the news which came from the Iroquois. Signed Thierry Bechefer, of the company of Jesus. In MPHC, 34:277–80.

May 10, 1682. Versailles. Instruction which the King desires to be placed in the hands of Sieur de la Barre, chosen by his Majesty as his Governor and Lieutenant in New France. In NYCD, 9:167–68, and IHC, 23:17–18.

July 28, 1682. Letter from M. Duchesneau to M. de Frontenac—Iroquois, &c. In NYCD, 9:174.

August 5, 1682. Montreal. Copy of Count de Frontenac's Answer to M. Duchesneau's letter of the 28th July, 1682 (cited above). In NYCD, 9:175.

August 13, 1682–August 20, 1682. Account of an interview between M. de Frontenac and the Ottawas, &c., at Montreal. In NYCD, 9:176–83.

September 11, 1682–September 12, 1682. Conference between Count de Frontenac and a Deputy from the Five Nations. In NYCD, 9:183–89.

September 16, 1682. Letter of Sieur Delaforest, Major of Fort Frontenac, to My Lord Count de Frontenac, on the departure of Niregouataron, the Iroquois deputy. In NYCD, 9:189.

September 20, 1682. Onondaga. Letter of Father de Lamberville to M. de Frontenac. In NYCD, 9:192–93.

October 10, 1682. Account of the Assembly held at Quebec, by M. de la Barre, &c., with the officers in Canada, the Jesuits, &c. respecting the Indians, &c. In NYCD, 9:194–95.

October 24, 1682. Ordinance of Messrs. Lefebvre de la Barre and de Meulles, enjoining the possession of fire-arms upon the inhabitants. Signed Regnault. In Shortt, 1:53–55.

November 4, 1682–November 12, 1682. Abstract of Letters received from Canada. M. de la Barre: Order for arms—power of Governors—Troops and Fortifications. In NYCD, 9:196–99.

1683

1683. Extract of the Memoir addressed to Messrs. the Partners of the Society *en Commandite* of the Farm and Trade of Canada, on the means of preventing the smuggling of beaver. In NYCD, 9:211–13.

[1683]. Representation on the Revenue and Trade of Canada. In Shortt, 1:63.

1683 and 1684. Memoir of expenses incurred for the king's service and the execution of the orders of Monsieur the General de la Barre by the Sieur de la Durantaye among the Ottawa. Signed Jean Bochart de Champigny, intendant of New France. In IHC, 23:60–67.

1683. Jesuit Missions in the Northwest. From Father Thierry Beschefer's report to his provincial, for the year 1683. In WHC, 16:113–14.

January 13, 1683. Decree of the Superior Council of Quebec determining that the dollars which are of full weight shall be marked with a fleur de lis, and those which are not of full weight shall be rated only according to the figures imprinted upon them. Signed De Meulles. In Shortt, 1:55–61.

April 26, 1683. Fort St. Louis. Grant of La Salle to Jacques Bourdon, Sieur d'Autray. From Otto L. Schmidt Collection, Chicago Historical Society. In IHC, 23:19–27.

May 31, 1683. Letter of Captain Brockholls to M. de la Barre. In NYCD, 9:199–200.

August 3, 1683. New York. Letter of Colonel Dongan to the French at Pemaquid. In NYCD, 9:263.

August 5, 1683. Fontainebleau. Extract of a letter from the King to M. de la Barre. In NYCD, 9:200–201.

August 11, 1683. Concession in fief by Robert Cavelier, Sieur de la Salle, to Pierre Prudhomme on the river of the Illinois. From notarial file of J. B. Adhémar, Palais de Justice, Montreal. In IHC, 23:28–36.

August 26, 1683. Missilimakinak. Affairs at Michillimackinac. Letter from Father Enjalran to Lefevre de la Barre, governor of New France. From Margry, *Découv. et étab.*, 5:3–7. In WHC, 16:110–13.

September 1, 1683. Chicago. La Salle to Messieurs Laurriet and Brossard and all the other inhabitants near Fort St. Louis in Louisiana. From Chicago Historical Society. In IHC, 23:36–41.

November 4, 1683. Quebec. Letter of M. de la Barre to the Minister—Iroquois—English, &c. In NYCD, 9:201–10.

November 4, 1683. Quebec. Dollars to Be Stamped According to Weight: M. de la Barre to M. de Seigneley. In Shortt, 1:61.

November 4, 1683. Quebec. Dollars to Be Stamped According to Weight: Letter from De Meulles to My Lord [Marquis de Seignelay]. In Shortt, 1:61–63.

December 2, 1683. Montreal. Contract of a concession given by M. de la Salle to Michel Disy. Done at the river of the Miami December 1, 1682. From notarial file of A. Adhémar, Palais de Justice, Montreal. In IHC, 23:42–44.

1684

1684. Memoir to render My Lord, the Marquis de Seignelay, an Account of the condition in which Sieur de Lasalle had left fort Frontenac during the time he was engaged on his Discovery, 1684. In NYCD, 9:213–16, and PA, 6:14–20.

1684. Representation of Sieur de la Salle of his outlay on Fort Frontenac, and of the Trade of that post. In NYCD, 9:216–21.

January 21, 1684. Fort St. Louis. Agreement of Tonti with the Inhabitants of Fort St. Louis. From Chicago Historical Society. In IHC, 23:45–46.

February 10, 1684. Letter from Father de Lamberville to M. de la Barre. In NYCD, 9:226–28, and PA, 6:21–24.

April 10, 1684. Versailles. Extract of a letter of the Minister to M. de la Barre—reproaching him for his bad conduct, &c. In NYCD, 9:221.

April 10, 1684. Versailles. Extract of a letter from the Minister to M. de Meules, Intendant in Canada. In NYCD, 9: 222–23.

April 10, 1684. Versailles. Extract of a letter from the Minister to M. de Meules. In NYCD, 9:223–24.

April 10, 1684. Versailles. Ordinances against Emigration from Canada to the British Colonies: Ordinance prohibiting all Frenchmen removing to Manhatte, Orange and other places belonging to the English and Dutch, on pain of death against those who will not be domiciliated, and Edict for the punishment of Frenchmen who will remove to Manatte, Orange and other places belonging to the English and Dutch. In NYCD, 9:224–25, and PA, 6:20–21.

April 10, 1684. Versailles. The King to La Barre. In IHC, 23:47–50.

April 12, 1684. Mischelimakinac. 1684: Indian Murderers Punished by Du Luth. Extract from a letter by Du Luth. In WHC, 16:114–25. The original MS. of this document, from which the present is a translation, is in the archives of the Ministère des Colonies, at Paris; press-mark, "Canada, Correspondence générale, vol. 6, c. 11, fol. 231."

April 14, 1684. Versailles. Commission from the King to M. de la Salle, to take command in the regions that shall become subjected to France, west of Canada, &c. In NYCD, 9:225.

May 5, 1684. Paris. Agreement between La Salle and François Plet. From Margry, *Découv. et étab.*, 2:416. In IHC, 23:51–52.

June 5, 1684. Quebec. Extract of a letter from M. de la Barre to the Minister (Seignelay). In NYCD, 9:226.

June 15, 1684. Montreal. Letter of M. de la Barre to Colonel Dongan. From New-York Papers, B. II. 20. In NYCD, 3:447–48.

June 24, 1684. Letter of Governor Dongan to M. de la Barre. From New-York Papers, B. II. 24. In NYCD, 3:448–49.

July 8, 1684. Quebec. M. de Meulles to M. de Seignelay. In NYCD, 9:228–32.

July 10, 1684. Letter from Father de Lamberville to M. de la Barre, dated Onondaga. In NYCD, 9:252.

July 11, 1684. Reverend Jean de Lamberville to M. de la Barre. In NYCD, 9:252–54.

July 13, 1684. Reverend Jean de Lamberville to M. de la Barre. In NYCD, 9:254–55.

July 18, 1684. Reverend Jean de Lamberville to M. de la Barre. In NYCD, 9:255–56.

July 25, 1684. Camp at Lachine. Letter of M. de la Barre to Governor Dongan. From New-York Papers, B. II. 22. In NYCD, 3:450.

July 25, 1684. Camp of Lachine. Instructions from Monsieur de La Barre to Monsieur de Salvaye. From New-York Papers, B. II. 13. In NYCD, 3:450–51.

July 31, 1684. Versailles. Extracts of a letter addressed by the King to Monsieur de la Barre. In NYCD, 9:232–33.

July 31, 1684. Versailles. M. de Seignelay to M. Barillon. In NYCD, 9:234.

August 14, 1684. Fort Frontenac. Return of officers and soldiers, militia and Indians, at a review held by the Governor of Canada at Fort Frontenac. In NYCD, 9:234–36.

August 17, 1684. Onnontague. Reverend Jean de Lamberville to M. de la Barre. In NYCD, 9:256–57.

August 28, 1684. Onnontagué. Reverend Jean de Lamberville to M. de la Barre. In NYCD, 9:257–58.

September 5, 1684. Interview between the Onondagas and M. De la Barre, at La Famine. In NYCD, 9:236–39.

September 20, 1684. Quebec. Engagement of Jean Pacquereau to Tonti. From Otto L. Schmidt Collection, Chicago Historical Society. In IHC, 23:53–54.

September 26, 1684. Montreal. Declaration of Monsieur Leger Hébert in favor of the Sieur Rolland against the Sieur Guillory. From notarial file of B. Basset, Palais de Justice, Montreal. In IHC, 23:54–56.

September 27, 1684. Onnontaé. Reverend Jean de Lamberville to M. de la Barre. In NYCD, 9:259–60.

October 1, 1684. Quebec. Memoir of M. de Labarre as to what had occurred and had been done regarding the War against the Senecas. In NYCD, 9:239–43.

October 7, 1684. Quebec. Letter of M. de la Barre to the Minister, complaining of Col. Dongan, &c. In NYCD, 9:244.

October 9, 1684. Onnontagué. Reverend Jean de Lamberville to M. de la Barre. In NYCD, 9:260–62.

October 10, 1684. Quebec. Letter of M. de Meules to the Minister—Iroquois—Ottawas, &c. In NYCD, 9:244–48.

October 14, 1684. Montreal. Engagement of Jean Baptiste Beauvais to Tonti. From Chicago Historical Society. In IHC, 23:56–59.

November 9, 1684. Montreal. Letter of M. de Callière, Governor of Montreal, to the Minister. In NYCD, 9:249–50.

November 10, 1684. Quebec. Interference in Canadian Affairs: De la Barre to Arnoul. In Shortt, 1:65.

November 12, 1684. Quebec. Complaint as to Money Supplies: Letter from de Meulles to M. Arnou. In Shortt, 1:65–67.

November 13, 1684. Quebec. Extract of a despatch of M. de la Barre to the King—difficulties with Colonel Dongan, &c. In NYCD, 9:250–51.

November 13 and 14, 1684. Extract of the Summary of Letters from Canada. In NYCD, 9:264.

November 14, 1684. Quebec. Extract of a letter from M. de la Barre to the Minister (Marquis de Seignelay). In NYCD, 9:263.

1685

1685. Resumé by the Minister of the letters received this year from Canada, and of the answers. In NYCD, 9:312–18.

1675–1685. Return of Beaver received from Canada from 1675 to 1685. In NYCD, 9:287.

February 18, 1685. Versailles. Extracts of the Summary of the Answers sent to the letters received from Canada. In NYCD, 9:270–71.

[February 25, 1685]. Memoir of Sieur de Callières for My Lord, the Marquis of Seignelay, on the encroachments of the English on the French Colonies in America. In NYCD, 9:265–68.

March 5, 1685. Quebec. Ordinance of M. de Meulles which prohibits all persons from either carrying or making use of money or bills of exchange in trading. In Shortt, 1:67–69.

March 10, 1685. Versailles. Instruction which the King desires to be placed in the hands of the Marquis de Denonville, chosen, by his Majesty, Governor and his Lieutenant-General in New France. In NYCD, 9:271–72.

March 10, 1685. Versailles. Instructions which the king wishes placed in the hands of the Sieur Marquis de Denonville, selected by his majesty as his governor and lieutenant-general in New France. In IHC, 23:68–78.

March 10, 1685. Versailles. Letter of the King to M. de la Barre, recalling him. In NYCD, 9:269.

March 10, 1685. Versailles. Extract of a letter from the King to M. de Meules, Intendant, &c. In NYCD, 9:269.

March 10, 1685. Versailles. Letter of the Minister to M. Barillon, Ambassador at London, complaining of the conduct of the Governor of New-York, &c. In NYCD, 9:269.

June 8, 1685. Quebec. Introduction of Card Money, Jacques de Meulles. In Shortt, 1:69–73.

August 20, September 3, and November 12, 1685. M. de Denonville to M. de Seignelay, and the latter's Answer. In NYCD, 9:273–79.

September 5, 1685. Quebec. Ordinance of Intendant de Meulles, announcing the redemption in coined money of the card money, eight days after publication. In Shortt, 1:73.

September 24, 1685. Quebec. Issue of Card Money justified. Signed de Meulle. In Shortt, 1:73–75.

October 13, 1685. Letter from Governor Dongan to M. de Denonville. In NYCD, 9:292–93.

November 12, 1685. Memoir on the present state of Canada, and the measures to be adopted for the safety of the country. In NYCD, 9:280–86, and PA, 6:24–33.

November 13, 1685. Denonville to Seignelay. In IHC, 23:78–81.

1686

1686. Memoir in proof of the Right of the French to the Iroquois country and to Hudson's Bay. In NYCD, 9:303–5, and PA, 6:33–36.

1686. Summary of Letters of Denonville, 1686, with Replies. In IHC, 23:89–90.

1686 (ca). Account of Detroit Post. Extract from a letter written apparently to Count de Pontchartrain, then intendant of finance in France. In WHC, 16:127–30. The original MS. is in the MSS. division of the Library of Congress, Washington.

February 9, 1686. Quebec. Ordinance of Nicholas Dupont, deputy of the Intendant, directing Mr de Verneuil to issue card money of 40 sols, and of 4 livres, and forbidding the refusal of these cards as payment, on pain of a fine of 150 livres. In Shortt, 1:75–77.

May 3, 1686. Account of a quarrel between Cadillac and Sabrevois written by René Hubert, Recorder in the marshal's court of this country. In MPHC, 33:36–39.

May 8, 1686. Quebec. Letter of M. de Denonville to the Minister. In NYCD, 9:287–92.

May 20, 1686. Albany. Governor Dongan to the Reverend Jean de Lamberville (Translated from the Latin). In NYCD, 9:311.

May 20, 1686. Extract from the replies to the letters received from Canada during the present year 1686: To M. de Denonville and To Sr. De Meulles. In Shortt, 1:79.

May 22, 1686. Albany. Letter of Governor Dongan to M. de Denonville, Governor of Canada. In NYCD, 3:455–56.

May 31, 1686. Versailles. The King to Tonti. In IHC, 23:82.

May 31, 1686. Versailles. Memoir of the king to the Marquis de Denonville in answer to his letters of August 20, September 3, and November 12 and 13, 1685. In IHC, 23:83–85.

June 5, 1686. Letter of M. de Denonville to Governor Dongan. From New-York Papers, B. II. 42. In NYCD, 3:456–58.

June 6, 1686. Villemarie. 1686: Governor Denonville Orders Du Luth to Establish a Post at Detroit. In WHC, 16:125–27. From MS. in archives of Ministère des Colonies, Paris; press-mark, "Canada, Corres. gén., vol. 8, c. 11, fol. 53."

June 6, 1686. Ville Marie. Letter to Monsieur Du Lhu. In MPHC, 33:40–41.

June 6, 1686. Copy of letter of Monsieur the Marquis de Denonville, governor-general of Canada, to Monsieur de la Forest, commandant of the Illinois. In IHC, 23:85–88.

June 12, 1686. Villemarie. Letter from M. de Denonville to the Minister—Indians—Colonel Dongan, &c. In NYCD, 9:293–96.

June 20, 1686. Letter of M. de Denonville to Governor Dongan. From New-York Papers, B. II. 34. In NYCD, 3:458–59.

July 26, 1686. Letter of Governor Dongan to M. de Denonville. From New-York Papers, B. II. 36. In NYCD, 3:460–61.

September 26, 1686. Quebec. Ordinance of Intendant Bochart, directing the inhabitants who have card notes to present them within two months, to receive the payment of them in money. In Shortt, 1:81.

October 1, 1686. Letter of M. de Denonville to Governor Dongan. From New-York Papers, B. II. 60. In NYCD, 3:461–62.

November 8, 1686. Quebec. M. de Denonville to M. de Seignelay: Memoir on the Present state of affairs in Canada, and the Necessity of waging war, next year, against the Iroquois. In NYCD, 9:296–303.

November 11, 1686. Quebec. Letter of M. de Denonville to the Minister—war with the Indians, &c. In NYCD, 9:306–8.

November 16, 1686. Quebec. Letter of M. de Denonville to the Minister. In NYCD, 9:308–10.

December 1, 1686. Letter of Governor Dongan to M. de Denonville. From New-York Papers, B. II. 38. In NYCD, 3:462–63.

December 4, 1686. Commission of Major McGregory to trade in the Ottawa Country. In NYCD, 9:318–19.

1687

1687–89. [Editor's Note: Hostilities between French and Iroquois.] In WHC, 16:132–33.

January 1687. Memoir for the Marquis de Seignelay Regarding the dangers that threaten Canada, the means of remedying them, and of firmly establishing religion, commerce and the King's power in North America. In NYCD, 9:319–22.

February 28, 1687. Versailles. Repayment of Bills of Exchange: Unsigned letter to Sr de Lubert. In Shortt, 1:83.

March 30, 1687. Versailles. Extracts from the letter of the King to Messrs. de Denonville and Champigny—Iroquois—the English, &c. In NYCD, 9:322–23.

March 30, 1687. Versailles. The king has received the following with the letters of the Sieurs Marquis de Denonville and de Champigny of May 8 and November 8, 10, 11, 16, and 17, last. In IHC, 23:91–122.

June 7, 1687. Endorsed—7th June 1687. [The] retaking possession of the lands in the neighborhood of the strait ("detroit") between Lakes Erie and Huron, by the Sieur de la Duranthais. In MPHC, 33:41–42.

June 8, 1687. English and Iroquois Intrigues among Northwestern Tribes. Part of a letter from Governor Denonville to the French Minister. In WHC, 16:130–32. The original MS. is in the Paris archives; we obtain our text from a transcript in the Dominion archives at Ottawa, Canada; press-mark, "Corres. gén., vol. 9, pp. 31–50."

June 8, 1687. Ville Marie. Letter of M. de Denonville to the Minister—Iroquois—Col. Dongan, &c. In NYCD, 9:324–30.

June 17, 1687. Versailles. Letter of the King to M. de Denonville, forbidding any efforts against the English, &c. In NYCD, 9:330.

June 25, 1687. Record of the Marriage of Antoine De La Mothe Cadillac and Marie Therese Guyon. In MPHC, 33:308–9.

July 16, 1687. Quebec. Account by M. de Champigny of the expedition of M. Denonville to Cataracouy, &c. In NYCD, 9:331–33.

July 19, 1687. Procès Verbal of the taking possession of the Senecas country by M. de Denonville. In NYCD, 9:334–35.

July 24, 1687. Quebec. Ordinance of M. Bochart Champigny which fixes the rating of louis d'or, half-louis, half-écus, etc., etc. In Shortt, 1:83–85.

July 31, 1687. Procès Verbal of the taking possession of Niagara by M. de Denonville. In NYCD, 9:335–36.

August 19, 1687. Montreal. Agreement between Monsieur de la Forest and the Sieur de Broyeux. From notarial file of A. Adhémar, Palais de Justice, Montreal. In IHC, 23:123–25.

August 19, 1687. Montreal. Agreement between Monsieur de la Forest and Dumay, accounting both for himself and Pichart. From notarial file of A. Adhémar, Palais de Justice, Montreal. In IHC, 23:126–28.

August 19, 1687. Montreal. Agreement between Monsieur de la Forest and Barette. From notarial file of A. Adhémar, Palais de Justice, Montreal. In IHC, 23:129–32.

August 21, 1687. Letter of M. de Denonville to Governor Dongan. From New-York Papers, B. II. 46. In NYCD, 3:466–68.

August 22, 1687. M. de Denonville's Remarks on Governor Dongan's Letter (of June 11, 1687). From New-York Papers, B. II. 50. In NYCD, 3:469–72.

August 25, 1687. Ville Marie. Letter of M. de Denonville to the Minister. In NYCD, 9:336–44.

August 25, 1687. Villemarie. Summary of M. de Denonville's Despatch and M. de Seignelay's Remarks thereupon. In NYCD, 9:345–46.

September 9, 1687. Governor Dongan to Monsieur de Denonville. From New-York Papers, B. II. 54. In NYCD, 3:472–75.

October 1687. Memoir of the Voyage and Expedition Undertaken Pursuant to the King's Orders, by the Marquis De Denonville, Governor of Canada, against the Senecas, Enemies of That Colony by M. De Denonville, 1687. In NYCD, 9:357–69.

October 2, 1687. Kebec. Monsieur de Denonville to Governor Dongan. From New-York Papers, B. II. 64. In NYCD, 3:512–13.

October 12, 1687. Quebec. Letter of M. de Denonville to Col. Dongan. In NYCD, 9:355–56.

October 12, 1687. Letter of Callières de Chasteauvilain. From Bibliothèque Nationale, Clairambault Collection, 1016:483–483v—C. In IHC, 23:132–36.

October 27, 1687. M. de Denonville to M. de Seignelay: Memoir on the present state of Affairs in Canada in reference to the Iroquois War. In NYCD, 9:346–54.

November 1687. Memoir by M. de Callière to the Minister, urging the necessity of war against the English in New-York, &c. In NYCD, 9:369–71.

December 13, 1687. Copy of the Memoir communicated by Messrs. de Barillon and de Bonrepaus to Messrs. the Commissioners of the King of England, . . . Concerning the right possessed by the King over the Iroquois. In NYCD, 3:507.

1688

1688–90. Disturbances among the Upper Tribes, Which Are Quelled by Perrot. From La Potherie. In WHC, 16:134–41.

March 8, 1688. Memoir to serve for Instruction to the Marquis de Denonville, Governor and Lieutenant-General of New France, respecting the information to be given on the subject of the differences between the French and English relative to the title to the Countries in North America. In NYCD, 9:371–72.

March 8, 1688. Extract of a letter from the Minister to M. de Denonville—Col. Dongan, &c. In NYCD, 9:372–73.

March 8, 1688. Extracts from the Summary of the answers to the letters received from Canada. To Messrs. de Denonville and de Champigny. In NYCD, 9:373–75.

March 8, 1688. Versailles. Memoir explanatory of the Right the French have to the property of the Countries of North America, especially the South part of Acadia, from Pantagouët to the River Kinibeky; of the Countries of the Iroquois and Hudson's Bay, with the posts occupied there by them and by the English, sent to the Court for its information by the Marquis de Denonville, the King's Governor and Lieutenant-General in New France. In NYCD, 9:377–84, and PA, 6:36–45.

March 8, 1688. Versailles. The King to Denonville and Champigny. In IHC, 23:136–44.

May 8, 1688. Project respecting the War to be waged against the Iroquois. In NYCD, 9:375–77.

May 14, 1688. Montreal. Engagement of Mousseaux, called Laviolette, to the Sieur Nicolas Perrot for the voyage to the Mascouten and Sioux. From notarial file of A. Adhémar, Palais de Justice, Montreal. In IHC, 23:145–47.

June 15, 1688. Declaration of the Iroquois in presence of Monsieur de Denonville at Montreal. In NYCD, 9:384–86.

July 5, 1688. Montreal. Engagement of Mathieu Rouillard and Jean Froment to La Forest. From notarial file of A. Adhémar, Palais de Justice, Montreal. In IHC, 23:147–50.

July 23, 1688. Montreal. Engagement of Antoine Morin to La Forest. From notarial file of A. Adhémar, Palais de Justice, Montreal. In IHC, 23:150–53.

July 24, 1688. Montreal. Engagement of Antoine Beaujean to La Forest. From notarial file of A. Adhémar, Palais de Justice, Montreal. In IHC, 23:154–56.

July 26, 1688. Montreal. Engagement of Jean Heurtebise to Monsieur de la Forest. From notarial file of A. Adhémar, Palais de Justice, Montreal. In IHC, 23:157–59.

July 29, 1688. Montreal. Engagement of François Tardif to Monsieur de la Forest. From notarial file of A. Adhémar, Palais de Justice, Montreal. In IHC, 23:159–61.

August 3, 1688. List of the merchandise delivered for the account of Madame Antaya, wife of François Pelletier, to the Sieur François Cottu, called Le Picard and De la Valtrie, Joseph Pelletier and Michel Pelletier. From Otto L. Schmidt Collection, Chicago Historical Society. In IHC, 23:162–69.

August 10, October 31, and November 6, 1688. Resumé by the Minister of the letters of Messrs. de Denonville and de Champigny, with notes thereon. In NYCD, 9:393–98.

September 15, 1688. Statement, showing the Condition in which the Fort of Niagara was left in 1688. In NYCD, 9:386–88.

October 30, 1688. Quebec. Relation of the Events of the War, and the difficulties with the Indians, Col. Dongan, &c. In NYCD, 9:388–93.

1689

1685–1689. Explanatory paper in relation to the defences necessary in Canada, the means of increasing the Indian trade, and the French influence, &c.: Government of M. de Denonville from 1685 to 1689. In NYCD, 9:399–401.

1686–1689. Memoir on the advantage of the establishment of a Fort at Niagara, from 1686–1689. In NYCD, 9:399.

1689. Paper showing the Differences in the Indian Trade between Montreal in Canada and Orange in New England, 1689. In NYCD, 9:408–9.

1689. Tariff of Prices at which the inhabitants of Canada might supply produce they may be able to send to France, in order that the Merchants of the Kingdom may be induced to import them from Canada in preference to all other countries, 1689. In NYCD, 9:409–10.

1689. Statement of what has been put on board the Ships *Le Fourgon* and *L'Embuscade*. In NYCD, 9:430–31.

January 1689. Memoir of Chevalier de Callières, Governor of Montreal, for My Lord, the Marquis de Seignelay: On the State of the Affairs of Canada. In NYCD, 9:401–4.

January 1689. Project of the Chevalier de Callières, of an expedition for the purpose of conquering New-York, &c. In NYCD, 9:404–8.

February 1689. Memoir of M de Callière to My Lord the Marquis de Seignelay upon his Project. In NYCD, 9:411–12.

February 1689. Memorandum of arms, ammunition and implements required for the expedition proposed by Chevalier de Callières, February, 1689. In NYCD, 9:412–13.

February 1689. Report to the Minister upon the foregoing Project and estimate. In NYCD, 9:413–15.

April 24, 1689. Versailles. Observations addressed to the Minister, upon the proposed plan for the conquest of New-York. In NYCD, 9:415–16.

May 1689. Memoir of Chevalier de Callières governor of Montreal, to the Marquis de Seignelay respecting the Expedition proposed by him against New-York, May, 1689. In NYCD, 9:420–22.

May 1, 1689. Versailles. Extract of a memoir of the King to the Marquis de Denonville and Sieur de Champigny, respecting the Indians—the English possessions in America, &c. In NYCD, 9:416–17.

May 1, 1689. Versailles. Extract of a despatch from M. de Seignelay to M. de Denonville. In NYCD, 9:417–18.

May 8, 1689. Canada, Bay des Puants. Perrot's Minute of Taking Possession, May 8, 1689: Minute of the taking possession of the country on the Upper Mississippi. Republished from NYCD, 9:418, in WHC, 11:35–36.

May 22, 1689. Memoir of Chevalier de Callières, respecting the proposed expedition against New-York. In NYCD, 9:419–20.

June 7, 1689. Instructions from the King to M. de Frontenac (appointed Governor of Canada) respecting the proposed conquest of New-York, giving full details of the views of the French government thereupon, &c. In NYCD, 9:422–26.

June 7, 1689. General Instructions from the King to the Count de Frontenac, appointed Governor and Lieutenant-general of the French possessions in North America. In NYCD, 9:427–28.

July 17, 1689. Accounts of the widow Antaya Cottu and Joseph Pelletier. From Otto L. Schmidt Collection, Chicago Historical Society. In IHC, 23:169–76.

July 27, 1689. Montreal. Protest by Monsieur François-Vienay Pachot against Monsieur de Tonti. From notarial file of B. Basset, Palais de Justice, Montreal. In IHC, 23:177–79.

July 29, 1689. Montreal. Settlement of Partnership Account between René Cuillerier and Michel Descaris. From notarial file of A. Adhémar, Palais de Justice, Montreal. In IHC, 23:179–80.

August 29, 1689. Montreal. Engagement of Jacques Filastreau, Louis Maillou (Malhiot or Mayot), Jean Cardinal, Joseph Fafart, and Antoine Morin to Monsieur de la Forest. From notarial file of A. Adhémar, Palais de Justice, Montreal. In IHC, 23:181–85.

October 5, 1689. Montreal. Engagements of Louis Maillou, Jean Cardinal, Antoine Morin, and Joseph Fafart to Sieur de la Forest. From notarial file of A. Adhémar, Palais de Justice, Montreal. In IHC, 23:185–86.

October 13, 1689. Montreal. Obligation undertaken to Monsieur de la Forest by Pierre Lespine, called Laviolette. From notarial file of A. Adhémar, Palais de Justice, Montreal. In IHC, 23:188–90.

October 15, 1689. Villemarie. Certificate of Denonville to Services of Tonti and La Forest. In IHC, 23:190–92.

November 1689. Algonkin, Huron, and Iroquois Politics; Synopsis of Letter of Étienne de Carheil, a Jesuit missionary, to Count Frontenac; written from Mackinac, probably in November, 1689. In WHC, 16:142.

November 1689. Extracts of the Minister's resumé of the letters received from Messrs. de Frontenac, de Denonville, de Champigny, and up to the sailing of the ships in 1689. In NYCD, 9:434–39.

November 8, 1689. Memoir addressed by Chevalier de Callieres to My Lord the Marquis de Seignelay: On the present condition of Canada. In NYCD, 9:428–30.

November 18, 1689. Extract from the Observations on the State of the Affairs of Canada at the departure of the ships. In NYCD, 9:431–34.

1690

1690–91: Perrot's Dealings with Wisconsin Tribes; He Establishes a Fort on the Mississippi, Near the Wisconsin. From La Potherie. In WHC, 16:143–60.

1690. Message of M. de Frontenac to be delivered to the Ottawas, to dissuade them from forming an alliance with the English, &c. In NYCD, 9:448–51.

1690. Memoir of Chevalier de Callières Governor of Montreal, for Mylord, the Marquis de Seignelay. In NYCD, 9:492–93.

January 1690. Extract of a Memoir by the Marquis de Denonville to the Minister, upon the situation of Canada—the expediency of the conquest of New-York, &c. In NYCD, 9:440–47.

February 15, 1690. Memoir by M. Duplessis upon the subject of the defence of Canada, war with the Indians, &c. In NYCD, 9:447–48.

March 7, 1690. The Council in Special Session . . . Conviction for Counterfeiting. Signed Bochart Champigny and R. L. Chartier de Lotbinière. In Shortt, 1:85–87.

May 5, 1690. Montreal. Authorization to François de Boisrondel to sign Engagements made by La Forest. From Chicago Historical Society. In IHC, 23:192–94.

May 5, 1690. Montreal. Engagement of Joseph Fafart, called La Fresnaye, to François de la Forest. From notarial file of A. Adhémar, Palais de Justice, Montreal. In IHC, 23:195–98.

May 7, 1690. Montreal. Engagement of Eustache and François Dumais to Monsieur de Boisrondel. From notarial file of A. Adhémar, Palais de Justice, Montreal. In IHC, 23:199–201.

May 8, 1690. Montreal. Engagement of Joseph and Louis Fafart (Fafard or Faffar) to Monsieur de Boisrondel, acting for Monsieur de la Forest. From notarial file of A. Adhémar, Palais de Justice, Montreal. In IHC, 23:202–6.

May 8, 1690. Villemarie. Engagement of Daniel-Joseph Amyot, Sieur de Villeneuve, to Monsieur de Boisrondel, acting for Monsieur de la Forest. From notarial file of A. Adhémar, Palais de Justice, Montreal. In IHC, 23:207–10.

May 8, 1690. Villemarie. Engagement of Joseph Besnard, Sieur de Carignan, to the Sieur de Boisrondel, acting for Monsieur de la Forest. From notarial file of A. Adhémar, Palais de Justice, Montreal. In IHC, 23:210–14.

May 8, 1690. Villemarie. Engagement of Jean Lelat to Monsieur de Boisrondel, acting for Monsieur de la Forest. From notarial file of A. Adhémar, Palais de Justice, Montreal. In IHC, 23:215–18.

May 10, 1690. Villemarie. Engagement of Pierre Le Boeuf to Monsieur Alphonse de Tonti. From notarial file of A. Adhémar, Palais de Justice, Montreal. In IHC, 23:218–20.

May 12, 1690. Agreement between Sieur François de Boisrondel and Sieur de la Forest granting Boisrondel general power of attorney. From notarial file of A. Adhémar, Palais de Justice, Montreal. In IHC, 23:186–88.

May 15, 1690. Villemarie. Engagement of Pierre Lelat to the Sieur de Boisrondel, acting for Monsieur de la Forest. From notarial file of A. Adhémar, Palais de Justice, Montreal. In IHC, 23:221–24.

May 16, 1690. Villemarie. Acknowledgment of debt by Monsieur de Boisrondel to the Sieur Jean Nafrechoux. From notarial file of A. Adhémar, Palais de Justice, Montreal. In IHC, 23:225–27.

July 14, 1690. Versailles. Extract of a despatch from King Louis XIV. to Count de Frontenac and M. de Champigny—cannot undertake the attack on New-York at present, &c. In NYCD, 9:452.

July 14, 1690. Further extract from the King's despatch to Messrs. de Frontenac and de Champigny—the Iroquois, &c. In NYCD, 9:452–55.

July 14, 1690. Versailles. Decree of the King's Council of State Confirming Grants made to Divers Individuals herein named (including grant of Fort St. Louis to Tonti and La Forest). In IHC, 23:228–30.

July 14, 1690. Versailles. Letters Patent from King Louis to Tonti and La Forest, confirming the Grants of Land made in above Decree of July 14, 1690. In IHC, 23:230–34.

October 10–24, 1690. Sir William Phips' Attack on Quebec: An Account of what occurred in Canada on the descent of the English at Quebec, in the month of October, 1690. In NYCD, 9:455–58.

November 1690. An Account of the most remarkable Occurrences in Canada from the departure of the Vessels in the month of November, 1689, to the month of November, 1690. Signed De Monseignat. In NYCD, 9:462–91.

November 12, 1690. Sieur De Louvigny's Expedition to Mackinac: Extract of a letter from M. De Frontenac to the Marquis De Seignelay, November 12th, 1690, relating to the exploits of Sieur De Louvigny. In WHC, 5:65–67.

November 12, 1690. Extracts of a letter of M. de Frontenac to the Minister—details of the military operations in Canada, &c. In NYCD, 9:459–62.

November 22, 1690. Quebec. Ordinance of M. Bochart Champigny, which fixes the rating of louis d'or, half-louis, etc., etc. In Shortt, 1:89–91.

1691

1691. Petition of M. de Callières to M. de Pontchartrain, for an allowance equal to that of other Colonial Governors. In NYCD, 9:507–8.

1691. Memoir on the present state of Canada, and the aid required to be extended to it for its preservation, 1691. In NYCD, 9:508–10.

1691. Remarks on what appears Important to the King's service for the preservation of New France, 1691. In NYCD, 9:510–12.

January 7, 1691. Quebec. Ordinance of M. M. de Frontenac and Bochart, announcing that a new issue of card money will be made of 4 livres, 2 livres, and 20 sols. In Shortt, 1:91–93.

February 13, 1691. Montreal. Ordinance of M. Fleury Deschambault: Since the Treasurer cannot, for the moment, change the cards of 1690 for new ones, which he has not yet received, the clerk may accept in exhange the notes of the Treasurer which have the same value as coined money. In Shortt, 1:93–95.

March 20, 1691. Villemarie. Cancellation of Engagement of Martin Soullard to La Forest. From notarial file of A. Adhémar, Palais de Justice, Montreal. In IHC, 23:234–36.

March 26, 1691. Villemarie. Engagement of Jean de Broyeux to La Forest. From notarial file of A. Adhémar, Palais de Justice, Montreal. In IHC, 23:236–38.

April 7, 1691. Camp before Mons. Extract of the King's despatch to Messrs. de Frontenac and de Champigny. In NYCD, 9:494.

May 10, 1691. Extract of a letter of M. de Frontenac to M. de Pontchartrain, the Minister—Indian affairs, &c. In NYCD, 9:495–96.

May 10, 1691. Extracts of a Memoir of M. de Champigny to M. de Pontchartrain, the Minister—Canadian affairs. In NYCD, 9:497–500.

May 10, 1691. Quebec. Necessity for new Issue of Card Money: Extract of the Memoir of M. de Champigny to the Minister. In Shortt, 1:95.

May 12, 1691. Quebec. Extract from the Memoir instructif annexed to M. de Champigny's despatch of the 10th May, 1691—upon Canada. In NYCD, 9:500–502.

May 12, 1691. Quebec. Letter of M. de Champigny to the Minister—attack of the Iroquois upon Montreal, &c. In NYCD, 9:503.

August 12, 1691. Letter of M. de Champigny to M. de Pontchartrain, the Minister—Indian troubles, &c. In NYCD, 9:503–4.

August 16, 1691. Villemarie. Engagement of Antoine Duquet, Sieur Madry, to Monsieur de la Forest. From notarial file of A. Adhémar, Palais de Justice, Montreal. In IHC, 23:239–41.

August 16, 1691. Villemarie. Engagement of François Roy to Sieur de la Forest. From notarial file of A. Adhémar, Palais de Justice, Montreal. In IHC, 23:241–43.

August 16, 1691. Villemarie. Engagement of Michel Pelletier Antaya to Sieur de la Forest. From notarial file of A. Adhémar, Palais de Justice, Montreal. In IHC, 23:244.

August 16, 1691. Villemarie. Engagement of Mathieu Raby (or d'Araby), called Villain. From notarial file of A. Adhémar, Palais de Justice, Montreal. In IHC, 23:244–45.

August 17, 1691. Villemarie. Engagement of Laurent Glory, called Labrière, to Sieur de la Forest. From notarial file of A. Adhémar, Palais de Justice, Montreal. In IHC, 23:245–46.

August 18, 1691. Villemarie. Engagement of Louis Pichart to Sieur de la Forest. From notarial file of A. Adhémar, Palais de Justice, Montreal. In IHC, 23:246–47.

August 18, 1691. Villemarie. Engagement of François Vaudry to Sieur de la Forest. From notarial file of A. Adhémar, Palais de Justice, Montreal. In IHC, 23:247.

August 22, 1691. Villemarie. Engagement of Pierre Hunaut (or Hénau) to Sieur de la Forest. From notarial file of A. Adhémar, Palais de Justice, Montreal. In IHC, 23:247–49.

August 23, 1691. Villemarie. Engagement of Sieur Claude Pinard to Sieur de la Forest. From notarial file of A. Adhémar, Palais de Justice, Montreal. In IHC, 23:249–51.

August 31, 1691. Villemarie. Engagement of Mathurin and Nicolas Rivard-Loranger and Joseph Moreau to Sieur de la Forest. From notarial file of A. Adhémar, Palais de Justice, Montreal. In IHC, 23:251–53.

October 12, 1691. Extracts from a Memoir annexed to Chevalier de Villebon's letter to My Lord de Pontchartrain, 12th October, 1691. In NYCD, 9:506–7.

October 12, 1691. Quebec. Alternative to Card Money: Extract of a Letter from Champigny. In Shortt, 1:97.

October 20, 1691. Extract of a letter from M. de Frontenac to M. de Pontchartrain, the Minister. In NYCD 9:505–6.

November 1691. An Account of the most remarkable Occurrences in Canada from the departure of the frigate *La Fleur de Mai*, on the 27th November, 1690, to the close Sixteen hundred and Ninety-one. In NYCD, 9:513–27.

1692

[1692]. King's Memorandum to the Sieurs Count de Frontenac and de Champigny. (Reply to Letter of October 12, 1691). In Shortt, 1:97–99.

1692. Notes by the Minister, upon the projected attack of the English Colonies upon Canada, and the means of opposing them, &c. In NYCD, 9:543–46.

1692. Extracts of a Memoir of M. de la Mothe Cadillac to the Minister, respecting Acadia, New England, New-York, and Virginia. In NYCD, 9:546–49.

1692. Extracts of a letter from the King to Frontenac and Champigny. In IHC, 23:254–64.

February 17, 1692. Extract of the Memoir on the Affairs of Canada, Acadia and Newfoundland. In NYCD, 9:527–30.

April 1692. Versailles. Despatch of M. de Pontchartrain to M. de Frontenac—M. de la Mothe Cadillac to be sent to France to give intelligence, &c. In NYCD, 9:530–31.

September 15, 1692. Extracts of a letter from M. de Frontenac to M. de Pontchartrain, the Minister—Boston—New-York—Port Royal, &c. In NYCD, 9:531–34.

September 15, 1692. Quebec. Occupying posts in the West: Letter from M.M. de Frontenac and de Champigny. In MPHC, 33:44–53.

October 5, 1692. Quebec. An Account of the Military Operations in Canada from the month of November, 1691, to the month of October, 1692, by M. de Champigny. In NYCD, 9:534–38.

November 11, 1692. Extract of a letter from M. de Frontenac to M. de Pontchartrain, the Minister. In NYCD, 9:538.

November 11, 1692. Memoir to M. de Pontchartrain on behalf of the Iroquois and other North American Indians, &c. Signed Champigny. In NYCD, 9:539–43.

1693

1693. An Account of what occurred in Canada from the month of September one thousand six hundred and ninety-two to the departure of the ships in 1693. In NYCD, 9:555–73.

March 28, 1693. Memoir of the King to Count de Frontenac, Lieutenant-General, and Sieur de Champigny, Intendant, of New France. In NYCD, 9:549–50.

April 19, 1693. François de la Forest Sells Half-interest to Michel Accault (Ako or Aco). From Otto L. Schmidt Collection, Chicago Historical Society. In IHC, 23:264–66.

April 27, 1693. Chicago. Power of Attorney to La Forest by Michel Accault. From Otto L. Schmidt Collection, Chicago Historical Society. In IHC, 23:266–67.

August 17, 1693. Quebec. An account of the Military operations in Canada against the English and the Iroquois, since the month of November 1692, by M. de Champigny. In NYCD, 9:550–55.

September 1693. Montreal. Engagement of Jean Baptiste Depeyras to Messieurs de la Forest and de Tonti. From notarial file of A. Adhémar, Palais de Justice, Montreal. In IHC, 23:292–94.

September 1693. Villemarie. Engagement of Nicolas le Tellier to de Tonti and de la Forest. From notarial file of A. Adhémar, Palais de Justice, Montreal. In IHC, 23:294–96.

September 1693. Villemarie. Engagement of Charles Dazé to de Tonti and de la Forest. From notarial file of A. Adhémar, Palais de Justice, Montreal. In IHC, 23:297–99.

September 1693. Villemarie. Engagement of Gabriel Benoist to Messieurs de la Forest and de Tonti. From notarial file of A. Adhémar, Palais de Justice, Montreal. In IHC, 23:299–301.

September 1, 1693. Villemarie. Engagement of François Picard to Alphonse de Tonti and De Laferté. From notarial file of A. Adhémar, Palais de Justice, Montreal. In IHC, 23:267–70.

September 1, 1693. Villemarie. Engagement between Monsieur de Tonti and the Sieur Pailleur Laferté. From notarial file of A. Adhémar, Palais de Justice, Montreal. In IHC, 23:270–72.

September 11, 1693. Villemarie. Engagement of Bertrand Viau, called Lespérance, to Messieurs de la Forest and de Tonti. From notarial file of A. Adhémar, Palais de Justice, Montreal. In IHC, 23:273–75.

September 12, 1693? With the letter of the Sieur de Tonti of September 12, 1693. [Montreal]. Monsieur de Tonti's Relation concerning the Illinois and for going among them along the Mississippi River by way of the Gulf of Mexico. In IHC, 23:276–82.

September 13, 1693. Villemarie. Engagement of Jacques Simon to Messieurs de Tonti and de la Forest. From notarial file of A. Adhémar, Palais de Justice, Montreal. In IHC, 23:283–85.

September 13, 1693. Villemarie. Bond assented to for Monsieur Charles Juchereau by Messieurs de la Forest and de Tonti, acting for themselves and for the Sieur Accault, in which the said bond is accepted from the aforesaid Sieurs on behalf of Mademoiselle Migeon. From notarial file of A. Adhémar, Palais de Justice, Montreal. In IHC, 23:285–89.

September 13, 1693. Villemarie. Bond assented to for Monsieur de la Forest by Monsieur de Tonti. From notarial file of A. Adhémar, Palais de Justice, Montreal. In IHC, 23:289–91.

1694

1694. Memoir of the Negotiations in Canada with the Iroquois, by M. de la Mothe Cadillac. In NYCD, 9:577–87.

1694. Report of the Minister on Operations against the English, 1694. In NYCD, 9:587–88.

May 8, 1694. Extract of a Memoir of the King to Count de Frontenac and Sieur de Champigny. In NYCD, 9:573.

August 20, 1694. Memoir of M. de Villebon to M. de Pontchartrain, on the proposed enterprise against Fort Pemaquid. In NYCD, 9:574–77.

September [October] 28, 1694. Montreal. The establishment of theaters in Quebec: A Letter from M. De La Mothe Cadillac. In MPHC, 33:54–71.

October 25, 1694. Quebec. Promotion of Cadillac. M. de Frontenac. In MPHC, 33:72.

November 5, 1694. Quebec. Coin in Canada not to be reduced. Signed Frontenac and Champigny. In Shortt, 1:99.

1695

1695. Northwestern Indians at Quebec; Huron Intrigues. From NYCD, 9:619–21. [This excerpt is part of a longer document in NYCD, 9:594–632, entitled "Narrative of the most remarkable Occurrences in Canada, 1694, 1695." According to a footnote this document was "Embodied in Letter IX., of the 4th Vol. of La Potherie's *Histoire de l'Amerique*"]. In WHC, 16:160–65.

1695. An Account of the most remarkable Occurrences in Canada from the month of September 1694 to the sailing of the Vessels in 1695. In NYCD, 9:594–632.

1695. Abstract of the Despatches from Canada, 1695: Memoir submitted to My Lord of the contents of the Canada despatches of 1695; of the requisitions for the support of the War, and of the disbursements to be made &c. in the present state of affairs in that country in regard to the Iroquois, the Upper Nations and the English. In NYCD, 9:633–34.

February 16, 1695. Versailles. Manner of paying Bills of Exchange: Letter to M. de Lubert. In Shortt, 1:101.

April 16, 1695. Versailles. Letter of M. de Pontchartrain, the Minister, to Count de Frontenac—negotiations with the Iroquois, &c. In NYCD, 9:588–90.

June 14, 1695. Versailles. Despatch of King Louis XIV. to Messrs. de Frontenac and de Champigny. In NYCD, 9:590–91.

November 2, 1695. Quebec. Letter from Frontenac to M. de Lagny. In Shortt, 1:101.

November 6, 1695. Memoir by Mons. de Champigny, concerning the fort at Cataracouy, &c. In NYCD, 9:591–94.

1696

February 25, 1696. Ministerial memorandum on the subject of the Canadian despatches, and the preparations necessary to be made thereupon. In NYCD, 9:634–36.

May 26, 1696. Versailles. Despatch of King Louis XIV. to Messrs. de Frontenac, and de Champigny—Indian troubles—the English, &c. In NYCD, 9:636–39.

October 25, 1696. Quebec. Letter of Count de Frontenac to the King Louis XIV.—expedition against the Onondagas, &c. In NYCD, 9:639–40.

October 26, 1696. Quebec. Request for additional Funds: Letter from Messrs de Frontenac and de Champigny. In Shortt, 1:103.

November 1696. An Account of the most remarkable Occurrences in Canada from the departure of the Vessels in 1695, to the beginning of November 1696. In NYCD, 9:640–59.

1697

1697. Northwestern Indians at Quebec; Frontenac's Policy toward them. From NYCD, 9:671–75. [This excerpt is part of a longer document in NYCD, 9:664–77, entitled "Narrative of the most remarkable Occurrences in Canada, 1696, 1697: An Account of the most remarkable Occurrences in Canada, from the departure of the Vessels in 1696 to the 15th of October 1697." According to a footnote this document is "Embodied in Letter VIII., of 3rd Vol. of La Potherie's *Histoire de l'Amerique Septentrionale.*"] In WHC, 16:166–73.

January 20, 1697. Paris. Plan of an Expedition against Boston and Manatte, presented by Mr. de Lagny to M. de Pontchartrain, the Minister. In NYCD, 9:659–62.

April 28, 1697. Versailles. Despatch of M. de Pontchartrain to M. de Frontenac—approving his conduct, &c. In NYCD, 9:662–64.

October 13, 1697. Quebec. Licenses to trade are revoked: Portions of a letter of M. de Champigny. In MPHC, 33:72–77.

October 15, 1697. Quebec. Plans to capture New York: Letter of the Comte de Frontenac; In MPHC, 33:77–86.

October 18, 1697. Quebec. An Account of the most remarkable Occurrences in Canada, from the departure of the Vessels in 1696 to the 15th of October 1697. In NYCD, 9:664–77.

October 19, 1697. Le Sueur's Mines on the Mississippi; Extract from a letter of Frontenac and Champigny (intendant of New France) to the French Minister, dated October 19, 1697. MS. in Ministère des Colonies, Paris; press-mark, "Canada, Corres. gén., vol. 15, c. 11, fol. 39." In WHC, 16:173–74.

November 23, 1697. Quebec. Compromise between Mon. dela Mothe Cadillac and Joseph Moreau and Louis Durant. Signed LaMothe Cadillac, Joseph Moreau, F Aubert, Haymard, Chambalon. In MPHC, 34:215–16.

December 10, 1697. Quebec. Judgment by arbitration between Mon. De La Mothe Cadillac and Joseph Moreau and Louis Durant. Signed F. Pachot, F. Hazeur, Chambalon. In MPHC, 34:216–18.

1698

1698. Memorandum respecting the Sovereignty of the King of France over the Iroquois, 1698. In NYCD, 9:689.

January 27, 1698. Quebec. Arbitration between Mon. dela Mothe Cadillac and Joseph Moreau and Ls Durand. Signed F. Hazeur, F Pachot, Chambalon. In MPHC, 34:218–19.

February 14, 1698. Quebec. Judgment showing discontinuance of Messres Hazeur and Pachot and myself (Chambalon) of the arbitration between Mon. dela Mothe Cadillac, Moreau and Durand. Signed F Pachot, F Hazeur, Chambalon. In MPHC, 34:219–20.

February 22, 1698. The Council in Special Session . . . Officers of Justice to receive Salaries, etc., in Money of France. Signed Bochart Champigny and Roüer De Villeray. In Shortt, 1:103–5.

March 12, 1698. Versailles. Despatch of M. de Pontchartrain to Count de Frontenac—news of peace of Ryswick, &c. In NYCD, 9:677.

April 22, 1698. New-York. Letter from the Earl of Bellomont, Governor of New-York, to the Count de Frontenac: On the question Whether the Five Iroquois Nations are subjects of the King of France or of England. In NYCD, 9:690.

May 21, 1698. Versailles. Extract of a despatch from M. de Pontchartrain to Count de Frontenac—Indians, &c. In NYCD, 9:678.

June 8, 1698. Quebec. Letter of Count de Frontenac in reply to the letter of the Earl of Bellomont (of April 22, 1698). In NYCD, 9:690–91.

July 3, 1698. Quebec. —A suit against Cadillac: Letter of M. de Champigny. In MPHC, 33:86–94.

July 14, 1698. Ville Marie. Collation of the account of Sieur dela Mothe. Signed Sorret. In MPHC, 34:220–21.

August 13, 1698. New-York. Letter of Lord Bellomont to Count de Frontenac. In NYCD, 9:692–93.

August 22, 1698. Letter of Lord Bellomont to the Count de Frontenac. In NYCD, 9:693.

September 21, 1698. Quebec. Letter of the Count de Frontenac to the Earl of Bellomont, in reply. In NYCD, 9:694–95.

October 10, 1698. Quebec. Frontenac praises Cadillac: Portions of a letter from the Comte de Frontenac. In MPHC, 33:94–96.

October 14, 1698. 1698: Illicit Fur Trade; Participation therein of French Soldiers; Complaints against Le Sueur. [Extracts from a letter of Champigny to the French Minister, Oct. 14, 1698. MS. in Ministère des Colonies, Paris; press-mark, "Canada, Corres. gén., vol. 16, c. 11, fol. 102"]. In WHC, 16:174–77.

October 20, 1698. An Account of the most Remarkable Occurrences in Canada from the departure of the Vessels in 1697 to the 20th October 1698. In NYCD, 9:678–88.

October 25, 1698. Letter of Messrs. de Frontenac and de Champigny to M. de Pontchartrain, the Minister. In NYCD, 9:695–97.

1699

1699. Memoir respecting the encroachments of the English upon the Territories of France in North America. In NYCD, 9:701–4, and PA, 6:45–49.

March 25, 1699. Versailles. Despatch of King Louis XIV. to M. de Frontenac, respecting the Indians, &c. In NYCD, 9:697–98.

April 27, 1699. Versailles. Despatch of King Louis XIV. to M. de Callières—directing him to observe the treaty of Ryswick, &c. In NYCD, 9:698–99.

[May 27, 1699]. Extract from a Memoir of the King to Chevalier de Callières—appointed Governor, &c., of Canada, in place of M. de Frontenac deceased—and to Sieur de Champigny, Intendant of Justice, Police and the Finances of New France. In NYCD, 9:699–701.

May 27, 1699. Versailles. Disapproval of the use of Card Money: Letter to Monsieur de Champigny. In Shortt, 1:105–7.

October 20, 1699. Reasons for Issue of Card Money: Letter from M. de Champigny. In Shortt, 1:107–9.

November 23, 1699. The Council met . . . Prohibition of Transport of Specie to America. Signed Dupont and Bochart Champigny. In Shortt, 1:109.

1700

1700. Le Sueur's Voyage up the Mississippi. [Bénard de la Harpe, an officer in Iberville's expedition to Louisiana (1698–99) left a MS. work entitled *Journal historique de l'établissement des Français a la Louisiane*; this was published at New Orleans and Paris in 1831. La Harpe compiled therein (pp. 22–25, 38–70), from Le Sueur's journal, an account of the latter's voyage. The concluding portion is given by Pénicaut in his *Relation*; see Margry, *Découv. et étab.*, 5:416–20. The portion given by La Harpe is translated by J. G. Shea, in his *Early Mississippi Voyages*; we reprint this, adding our own translation of Pénicaut's account]. In WHC, 16:177–94.

1700. Council held by M. de Longueuil French commandant of Detroit, with the Indians, respecting a declaration of war against the English (of Carolina). In NYCD, 9:704–7.

1700–02. Le Sueur's Fort on the Mississippi. From Pénicaut's Relation in Margry, *Découv. et étab.*, 5:414–21, 425, 426. In WHC, 16:194–200.

May 5, 1700. Despatch of the King to Messrs. de Callière and de Champigny—peace with the Indians, &c. In NYCD, 9:704.

May 5, 1700. Prohibition of Card Money: Extract from a letter from the Minister to M. de Champigny. In Shortt, 1:109–11.

June 19, 1700. Replies of M. de Longueuil to the speech of the White River Indians. In NYCD, 9:707–8.

July 18, 1700. Conference between Chevalier de Callières and the Iroquois at Montreal, 18th July, 1700. In NYCD, 9:708–11.

September 3–8, 1700. Conference between the Iroquois deputies and Governor de Callières at Montreal. In NYCD, 9:715–20.

September 24, 1700. Quebec. New Ratings for Coins: Ordinance of the Governor General and Intendant. Signed Le Chevalier de Callières and Bochart Champigny. In Shortt, 1:111–13.

October 15, 1700. Quebec. Current Accounts. Signed M. de Champigny. In Shortt, 1:113–15.

October 16, 1700. Treaty with Indian Tribes; Illicit Trading; Extract from letter of Governor Callières to Count de Pontchartrain, Oct. 16, 1700. In WHC, 16:200–203.

October 16, 1700. Quebec. Letter of M. de Callières to M. de Pontchartrain, the Minister,—the Iroquois—Mississippi—Lord Bellomont, &c. In NYCD, 9:711–15.

October 18, 1700. Quebec. Detroit is founded: Letter of M. de Lamothe Cadillac. In MPHC, 33:96–101.

November 6, 1700. Quebec. Sieur De Louvigny's Petition and Defence: Louis De la Porte, Sieur De Louvigny, "To our Lords of the Sovereign Council of Quebec." In WHC, 5:67–73.

November 7, 1700. Sieur De Louvigny's Disobedience of Orders: Extract of a letter of Chevalier De Callières to the Minister, November 7, 1700, informing him of the judgment which had been rendered in the affair of Sieur De Louvigny. In WHC, 5:73–76.

1701

[1701]. A report setting forth the necessity of a post at Detroit. In MPHC, 33:42–44.

[1701?]. Account of Detroit. C. M. Burton says that another translation of this document is printed in WHC, 16:127, with an intimation that it should be dated about 1686, but the text of this document shows that it is a description of Detroit probably written by Cadillac, since it is similar to an account by him sent to Paris in 1701. In MPHC, 33:131–32.

1701. Cadillac's Detroit Colony; Approved by Jesuits. [Letters of missionaries to Cadillac.MSS. (copies) in the archives of Province of Quebec, and in those of St. Mary's College, Montreal. The French text of most of these documents was published by Margry, in vol. 5 of *Découv. et étab.*] In WHC, 16:204–6. Listed below are the three letters printed—July 25, 1701, Missilimakinak, Etienne de Carheil to Cadillac. July 28, 1701, Missilimakinak, Joseph Marest to Cadillac. September 23, 1701, Fort Frontenac, François Vaillant to Cadillac.

1701. New Trading Posts to be Established in the West; Extract from a letter of the directors of the Company of the Colony of Canada. From Margry, *Découv. et étab.*, 5:360–62. In WHC, 16:208–10.

1701. Cabinet paper, containing details of a project for the conquest of New England, &c. In NYCD, 9:725–28.

1701. Memoir by M. d'Iberville, upon the situation of Boston, New-York, &c., and the project for attacking them. In NYCD, 9:729–35.

May 31, 1701. Versailles. Despatch of the King Louis XIV. to Messrs. de Callières and de Champigny—Iroquois—the Mississippi, &c. In NYCD, 9:721.

May 31, 1701. Versailles. Suppression of Card Money approved: Letter to M. de Champigny. In Shortt, 1:117.

July 25, 1701. Missilimakinac. Letter of Estienne de Carheil to M. de la Mothe. In MPHC, 33:102.

July 28, 1701. Missilimakina. Letter of Joseph J. Marest to M. de la Mothe. In MPHC, 33:103.

August 4, 1701. Montreal. Ratification of the Peace concluded in the month of September last between the Colony of Canada, its Indian allies and the Iroquois, in a General Meeting of the Chiefs of each of these Nations convoked by Chevalier de Callières Governor and Lieutenant-General for the King in New France. In NYCD, 9:722–25.

August 4, 1701. Biloxi. Letter of De Sauvole de La Villantray, the first governor of Louisiana under the French crown, to [Pontchartain?] relating the succession of the events that took place in the fort of Biloxi from the departure of the vessel for Santo Domingo on May 2, 1700. From Ministry of the Colonies, C. 13, vol. 1, pp. 315–22. In MPA, 2:9–18.

August 25, 1701. Quebec. Letter of Joseph Germain to M. de la Mothe. In MPHC, 33:104–5.

August 27, 1701. Montreal. Power of Attorney and Substitution: Madame dela Motte Cadillac to Mon. Hazeur. Signed Hatanville, Lamothe Cadillac, Rivet, Adhemar. In MPHC, 34:221–22.

August 30, 1701. Three Rivers. Letter of Enjalran. J. to M. de la Mothe. In MPHC, 33:105–6.

September 23, 1701. Fort Frontenac. Letter of Francois Vaillant. J. to M. de la Mothe. In MPHC, 33:106.

October 4, 1701. Quebec. Cadillac starts for Detroit: Letter of the Chev. de Callieres. In MPHC, 33:107.

October 5, 1701. Sieur De Louvigny's Disobedience of Orders: Extract from a letter from Messrs. De Callières and De Champigny to the Minister, October 5, 1701, concerning the Sieur De Louvigny, Major of the Three Rivers. In WHC, 5:76–77.

October 5, 1701. Quebec. Detroit in charge of the company of Canada: Letter of the Chev. de Callieré and M. de Champigny. In MPHC, 33:108–10.

October 5, 1701. Description of the River of Detroit by M. de la Mothe, the commandant there. Annexed to the letter from MM. de Callieres and de Champigny. In MPHC, 33:111–12.

October 8, 1701. Missilimakinak. Letter of Joseph J. Maret to M. de la Mothe. In MPHC, 33:112–14.

October 8 and 20, 1701. Michillimakinac and Detroit; Extracts from letters by the Jesuit missionary Joseph Marest to La Mothe Cadillac; dated at Michillimakinac, Oct. 8 and 20, 1701.MSS. (copies) in archives of Province of Quebec; press-mark "Mss. relat. N. France, series 2, vol. 9, pp. 5117–20." In WHC, 16:206–8.

October 20, 1701. Missilimakinak. Letter from Joseph J. Marest to M. de la Mothe. In MPHC, 33:114–15.

October 30, 1701. Quebec. Detroit given to the company of the Colony: Letter of M. de Champigny. In MPHC, 33:115–17.

October 31, 1701. Quebec. Transaction: His Grace the Governor and the intendant and Messres the Directors for the post at Detroit. Signed the Chevalier Decailliére, Bochart Champigny, Ruette D'Auteuil, R. L. Chartier de Lotbiniére, Fs. Hazeur, Peire—Gobin—Macart, Rageot, Chambalon. In MPHC, 34:222–25.

1702

[1702?]. Remarks Made by M. De La Motte Concerning the Board of Directors. In MPHC, 33:152–55.

[1702]. 2nd letter of Mr. De La Mothe, written to Reverend Father Maret, in reply to the 11th letter of the same Father, dated May 30, 1702. (See MPHC, 33:121.) In MPHC, 34:286–89.

April 19, 1702. Riviere St. Joseph. 1702: Miamis Intrigue with English Traders; Letter of Father Jean Mermet to Cadillac. From Margry, *Découv. et étab.*, 5:219–21. In WHC, 16:211–13.

April 19, 1702. St. Joseph River. Letter of Jean Mermet to M. de la Mothe. In MPHC, 33:118–19.

April 20, 1702. Quebec. Letter of M. Bonnart to M. de la Mothe. In MPHC, 33:120–21.

May 2, 1702. Letter of M. De La Mothe written to Father Maret, missionary to the Ottawas at Missilimakinak, concerning Cadillac's troubles with the Jesuits at Missilimakinak. In MPHC, 34:285–86.

May 3, 1702. Memoir of the King to Chevalier de Callières Governor and Lieutenant-General of New France in answer to his despatches and those of Sieur de Champigny formerly Intendant of said Country of the 5th and 31 October 1701. In NYCD, 9:735–36.

May 30, 1702. Missilimakinak. Letter of Joseph J. Marest to M. de la Mothe. In MPHC, 33:121–22.

June 4, 1702. River St. Joseph. 1702: Miamis Unwilling to go to Detroit; Letter from Aveneau to Cadillac. From Margry, *Découv. et étab.*, 5:239, 240. In WHC, 16:213–14.

June 4, 1702. St. Joseph River. Letter of Cl. Aveneau to M. de la Mothe. In MPHC, 33:123–24.

June 17, 1702. Missilimakinak. Letter of Etienne de Carheil to M. de la Mothe. In MPHC, 33:124–26.

July 23, 1702. Missilimakinak. Letter of J. J. Marest to M. de la Mothe. In MPHC, 33:126–29.

August 7, 1702. Montreal. Letter of Father Anjalran to M. de la Mothe. In MPHC, 33:129–30.

August 30, 1702. Evils attendant upon the Fur Trade; Demoralization of both French and Indians; Synopsis of Letter of Father de Carheil to the intendant of Canada, J. B. de Champigny. From *Jesuit Relations*, lxv, 18–21, 189–253; lxxi, 381. In WHC, 16:214–17.

September 23, 1702. Quebec. Contract: Mon. François Hazeur with Mon. dela Motte Cadillac. Signed F. Hazeur, La Mothe Cadillac, J. Phelippeaux, Huguet, Chambalon. In MPHC, 34:225–26.

September 25, 1702. Quebec. Description of Detroit: Advantages found there; The necessity and the means of perfecting this post; Letter of M. La Motte Cadillac. In MPHC, 33:133–51.

September 26, 1702. Quebec. Contract: Mon. Pierre Peire with Mon. dela Motte Cadillac. Signed La Mothe Cadillac, A. Lagarde, Huguet, Chambalon. In MPHC, 34:227.

September 27, 1702. Quebec. Power of Attorney: Mon. delamotte Cadillac to Mon. Lagarde. Signed Lamothe Cadillac, Huguet, Haymard, Chambalon. In MPHC, 34:228.

November 3, 1702. Quebec. The company of the colony proposes to surrender Detroit to Cadillac: Portions of a letter of M. de Callieres and M. de Beauharnois. In MPHC, 33:155–57.

November 4, 1702. Extract of a letter of M. de Callières to M. de Pontchartrain, the Minister—peace with the Indians—Orange—New-York, &c. In NYCD, 9:736–38.

November 4, 1702. Quebec. Cadillac makes arrangements with the Jesuits: Portions of a letter of the Chev. de Callieres. In MPHC, 33:158.

November 6, 1702. Extract of a letter from M. de Callières to M. de Pontchartrain, the Minister—Onondagas—Orange—New-York, &c. In NYCD, 9:739.

November 11, 1702. Quebec. Extracts of a letter of M. de Beauharnois, Intendant of Canada, to M. de Pontchartrain, the Minister—Indian affairs, &c. In NYCD, 9:740–41.

1703

1703. Succinct Detail of what composes the twenty millions (or thereabouts,) which the Colony of Canada produces yearly to the King and his subjects, 1703. In NYCD, 9:757–58.

May 12, 1703. Missilimakinak. 1703: Hurons refuse to go to Detroit; Extracts from letter of Father Joseph Marest to Cadillac. From Margry, *Découv. et étab.*, 5:247–50. In WHC, 16:217–18.

May 12, 1703. Missilimakinak. Joseph J. Marest to M. de la Mothe. In MPHC, 33:159–60.

May 30, 1703. Importance of Post at Detroit; Extract from letter of Louis XIV to Canadian officials; dated May 30, 1703. From NYCD, 9:742. In WHC, 16:218–19.

June 15, 1703. 3rd letter of M. De La Mothe, written to Father Maret Superior of the Ottawa missions, June 15, 1703, in reply to the 15th letter of the same Father. In MPHC, 34:290–91.

August 31, 1703. Fort Pontchartrain. Report of Detroit in 1703: Letter of M. de la Mothe Cadillac. In MPHC, 33:161–81.

August 31, 1703. Fort Pontchartrain. Cadillac has trouble with the Jesuits: Letter of M. de la Motte. In MPHC, 33:182–84.

September 27, 1703. Conference of Indian Envoys with Governor De Vaudreuil; Speeches of the Outaouaes of Misilimakinac, 27 September, 1703. These speeches are referred to in the November 14, 1703, document cited below. In WHC, 16:221–27.

November 7, 1703. Protested Bills of Exchange: Ordinance of M. de Beauharnois, Intendant of New France, on a petition of the merchants and settlers of the colony on the subject of the bills of exchange accepted by them to the profit of the Company of the Colony. In Shortt, 1:117–25.

November 14, 1703. Indian Intrigues; Detroit should be abandoned; Extract from letter of Governor de Vaudreuil to Count Pontchartrain; dated at Quebec, Nov. 14, 1703. From NYCD, 9:743–44. In WHC, 16:220–21.

November 14, 1703. Conference between M. de Vaudreuil and the Indians, &c., in July, September and October, and notes by the Minister thereon. In NYCD, 9:746–54.

November 15, 1703. De Louvigny's Projected Expedition: Extract of a letter from Messrs. De Vaudreuil and De Beauharnois, November 15th, 1703, concerning a proposition of De Louvigny relating to an Expedition beyond Lake Superior. In WHC, 5:77.

November 15, 1703. Abstract of certain parts of a Despatch from Messrs. de Vaudreuil and Beauharnois, and notes of the Minister thereon. In NYCD, 9:755–56.

November 25, 1703. Port Royal, Acadia. Card Money in Acadia: Letter from Monsieur de Brouillan. In Shortt, 1:125.

1704

January 30, 1704. Versailles. Letter from Pontchartrain to Bienville: Twenty girls and one hundred soldiers sent to Louisiana; Plantations. From Ministry of the Colonies, B, vol. 25, pp. 4–7. In MPA, 3:15–18.

February 13, 1704. Versailles. Letter from Pontchartrain to Bienville: The King changes his mind on the subject of the Canadians and is sending some provisions for their subsistence. From Ministry of the Colonies, B, vol. 25, pp. 10v–11. In MPA, 3:18.

April 29, 1704. Paris. Reflections on the present state of the settlement of Detroit in Canada: Letter of Riverin. In MPHC, 33:185–87.

June 4, 1704. [Versailles]. Disapproval of Card Money: Extract from a letter from the Minister to M. de Brouillan. In Shortt, 1:125–27.

June 14, 1704. Versailles. Memorandum to the Marquis de Vaudreuil and to M. de Beauharnois, Lieutenant-General for His Majesty and Intendant of Justice, Police and Finance in New France. Signed Louis Phelypeaux. In Shortt, 1:127.

June 14, 1704. Versailles. Endorsed letter from the Court or arrangement made by the King and M. D'Lamothe on account of Detroit: Letter from M. de Pontchartrain to M. de la Motte. In MPHC, 33:187–90.

July 30, 1704–August 7, 1704. Talk between the different Indian tribes at Detroit. In MPHC, 33:190–93.

August 31, 1704. Fort Louis of Mobile, Nicholas de La Salle, Census of Louisiana: Description of the condition of the colony of Louisiana, census of the population and enumeration of all the material for the defence of the country. From Ministry of the Colonies, C. 13, vol. 1, pp. 211–14. In MPA, 2:18–20.

September 6, 1704. Fort Louis, Mobile. Letter from Bienville to Pontchartrain: Bienville, St. Denis and Tonti lead force against Alabama Indians; English arm Chickasaws; Voyageurs on the Missouri; Wabash post; Peltries; Provisions and recruits; Animals, farmers, negroes, flour mill; Relations of English with Apalachees and Spaniards; Choctaws; Condition of forts; Pensacola provisioned; Death of Beccancourt, Levasseur, Juchereau and Tonti; Pierre Michel (p. 449). Colonies. From Ministry of the Colonies, C. 13, vol. 1, pp. 449–65. In MPA, 3:18–29.

November 7, 1704. Quebec. Fulfillment of contract between Cadillac and Pierre Peire, dated September 26, 1702. Signed La Mothe Cadillac, Huguet, Rageot, Chambalon. In MPHC, 34:227–28.

November 14, 1704. Quebec. Ramezay complains of the treatment of Cadillac: Portions of a letter of M. de Ramezay. In MPHC, 33:194–96.

November 16, 1704. Quebec. Extract of a letter from M. de Vaudreuil to M. de Pontchartrain, the Minister—Abenaquis—Iroquois—Detroit—Albany—Peter Schuyler, &c. In NYCD, 9:758–61.

November 17, 1704. Quebec. Extract of a letter of Messrs. de Vaudreuil and Beauharnois, to M. de Pontchartrain, the Minister—Indian affairs—Jesuits—the English—Schuyler, &c. In NYCD, 9:761–65.

November 17, 1704. Quebec. Portions of letters from MM. de Vaudreuil and de Beauharnois complaining about Cadillac. In MPHC, 33:196–98.

November 17, 1704. Quebec. The Colony's Agreement with Gay, Du Moulin and Mercier. Signed Messrs de Vaudreuil and de Beauharnois. In Shortt, 1:127–35.

November 19, 1704. Quebec. Memorandum of M. de la Mothe Cadillac concerning the establishment of Detroit from Quebec: La Mothe Cadillac gives an account of his conduct concerning the establishment of Detroit by questions and answers. In MPHC, 33:198–241.

December 8, 1704. Port Royal. Melting of Coins by de Brouillan. Signed Mathieu de Goutin. In Shortt, 1:135–37.

1705

May 5, 1705. Quebec. Attempt to prevent trouble between the Hurons and Outavois: Letter of M. de Vaudreuil. In MPHC, 33:242.

June 3, 1705. Melting of Coins by de Brouillan: Letter to Sieur de Loppinot. Unsigned. In Shortt, 1:137.

June 10, 1705. Versailles. Seizure of Beaver for Payment of Bills of Exchange: Letter to Jacques Raudot. Unsigned. In Shortt, 1:139–41.

June 17, 1705. Versailles. Extract of King Louis XIV.'s despatch to M. de Vaudreuil, in answer to the joint despatch written by him and Sieur de Beauharnois, on the 17th of November of last year.—the Miamis—Onondagas, &c. In NYCD, 9:765–66.

June 17, 1705. Posts of the Upper Countries: Extract from the letter of M. de Pontchartrain. In MPHC, 33:243.

August 16 and 17, 1705. Conference between M. de Vaudreuil and the Iroquois: Speeches of the Iroquois to the Governor-General, 16th of August, 1705; Delivered in the name of 4 Nations, by 4 Belts; Answer of the Governor-General to the Senecas and other Chiefs of the Four Nations, 17 August 1705. In NYCD, 9:767–69.

September 7, 1705. Quebec. Ordinance enacting that customs duties on spirits, wines, etc., are to be paid in money of France. Signed Raudot. In Shortt, 1:141.

September 28, 1705. Quebec. Agreement made between the directors and agents of the company of the colony of Canada and M. de Lamothe in concert with the Governor General and three intendants concerning Detroit or Fort Pontchartrain. In MPHC, 33:245–48.

October, 1705. Quebec. Draft of the Treaty to be concluded between the two Colonies of New France and New England, agreeably to the proposals Mr Veche submitted to M. de Vaudreuïl, governor-general of New France on the part of Mr Dudley, governor-general of New England. In NYCD, 9:770–72.

October 12, 1705. Quebec. Excess of Cards over Funds. Signed M. de Ramesay. In Shortt, 1:141–43.

October 13, 1705. Quebec. Hazeur fulfills the terms of contract made on September 23, 1702. Signed La Mothe Cadillac, Fr. Hazeur—Mirambeau—Rageot, Chambalon. In MPHC, 34:226.

[October 19, 1705]. [Quebec]. Explanation of the Issue of New Cards and the Colony's Difficulties with the Commissioners of the Company: Common Letter of Messrs. de Vaudreuil, de Beauharnois and Raudot to the Count de Pontchartrain. In Shortt, 1:149–55.

October 19, 1705. Quebec. Extracts of a letter from M. de Vaudreuil to M. de Pontchartrain, the Minister. In NYCD, 9:766–67.

October 19, 1705. Quebec. Conduct of the Directors of the Company of the Colony. Signed M. Raudot. In Shortt, 1:143–45.

October 24, 1705. Quebec. Ordinance Ratifying Cards. Signed Jacques Raudot. In Shortt, 1:145–47.

November 4, 1705. Marly. Letter from Pontchartrain to Bienville: Failure of his enterprise against the Alabamas; Assistance taken to Fort St. Augustine and to the Apalachees; Two priests sent to the Choctaws and to the Chickasaws. From Ministry of the Colonies, B, vol. 27, pp. 188–89. In MPA, 3:30–31.

November 29, 1705. Quebec. Destruction of Cards. Signed Raudot. In Shortt, 1:147.

December 5, 1705. Quebec. Ordinance enacting that pieces of four sols shall be current in this country for four sols, and sols of any kind whatsoever for fifteen deniers. Signed Jacques Raudot. In Shortt, 1:147–49.

1706

1706. 1504–1706. General Memoir, on the subject of the French dominion in Canada, from 1504 to 1706, with extracts from the despatches of the Governors, &c. In NYCD, 9:781–804.

1706. Proposals to be submitted to the Court that it may understand the importance of taking possession of Niagara at the earliest date, and of anticipating the English who design to do so, for if they were masters thereof, they would bar the passage and cut off our communication with, and attract, our Indian allies as well as the Iroquois, by their Trade, and dispose them at their will, to war against us, which would desolate Canada, and constrain us to abandon it. In NYCD, 9:773–75.

1706. List of the people who came to Detroit in 1706. According to C. M. Burton there is nowhere any list of the people who came to Detroit in 1706, after the exclusive control of the post was given to Cadillac. It was in that year that the greatest influx of newcomers came—second only, in number, to those who came in 1749. From the records in the notarial offices of Montreal, the archives of Quebec and the church records of Detroit, the following list has been compiled, which, if not complete, is much fuller than anything heretofore compiled in this line. In MPHC, 33:271–72.

January 27, 1706. Memorial of the S. de la Mothe Cadillac with the replies of M. de Vaudreuil in the margin. Annexed to the letter of the 30th Oct. 1706. In MPHC, 33:297–99.

January 29, 1706. Sale: Madme dela Forest to Mon. dela Mothe Cadillac. Signed C F Juchereau dela forest de St. Laurent, Lamothe Cadillac, Mirambeau, Rageot, Chambalon. In MPHC, 34:229–31.

March 18, 1706. Cadillac's requests to the Governor General regarding the settlement of Detroit: Memorandum by the Sr. de la Mothe Cadillac. In MPHC, 33:249–53.

March 20, 1706. Quebec. Reply to the memorial of the Sr. de la Mothe Cadillac. Annexed to the letter of the 30th Oct. 1706. In MPHC, 33:299–300.

March 31, 1706. Quebec. Monsieur de la Mothe Cadillac's memorial to the Governor-General and the Marquis de Vaudreuil's reply given at Quebec on April 7, 1706. In MPHC, 33:253–56.

April 10, 1706. Fort Louis, Mobile. Letter from Bienville to [Pontchartrain]: Spanish vessel lost in Pensacola harbor; Supplies; Canadians; Hostility of Illinois tribe; Spanish mines; Trade; Indian wars; Opposition to Jesuits; English among Choctaws; Pensacola-Mobile boundary dispute; La Salle degrades his office; Marginal notes by minister. From Ministry of the Colonies, C. 13, vol. 1, pp. 502–13. In MPA, 3:31–35.

April 28, 1706. Quebec. Extract of a letter of M. de Vaudreuil to M. de Pontchartrain, the Minister—Governor Dudley, &c. In NYCD, 9:775–76.

June 9, 1706. Marly. Royal Disapproval of Card Money: King's Memorandum to Messrs the Marquis de Vaudreuil, Governor and Lieutenant General and Raudot, Intendant of New France. Signed Louis and Phelypeaux. In Shortt, 1:155.

June 9, 1706. Versailles. 1706: Illicit Trade; French Policy toward Indian Tribes; Letter of Count de Pontchartrain to Governor de Vaudreuil. In WHC, 16:228–32, and a larger extract appears in NYCD, 9:776–79.

June 9, 1706. Extract from the letter of the said minister of the 9th of June 1706, at paragraph 6. In MPHC, 33:257.

June 15, 1706. Ville Marie. Power of Attorney: Mon. dela mot Cadillac to Madme dela Forest and substitution to Mon Joseph Riverin. Signed Lamothe Cadillac, Rivet, Claude Maurice, Adhémar. In MPHC, 34:231–32.

July 28, 1706. Mobile. Abstract of Letters from Bienville to Ponchartrain: On the condition of Louisiana for the year 1706, the provisions of which the inhabitants of Mobile have an urgent pressing need and the necessity that exists for sending some goods to be distributed as presents to the Indians. From Ministry of the Colonies, C. 13, vol. 1, pp. 514–44. In MPA, 2:20–29.

August 1, 1706. Talk between Marquis de Vaudreuil and Onaskin, chief of the Outavois. In MPHC, 33:258–62.

August 14, 1706. Michilimackinac. Detroit Attacked by Ottawas and Miamis; Jesuits Pacify Michillimackinac Savages; Letter from Father Joseph Marest to Governor Vaudreuil; translated from Cass MSS. (transcribed from documents in Paris archives), and published by Mrs. E. M. Sheldon in her *Early History of Michigan* (N.Y., 1856), pp. 206–17. In WHC, 16:232–38.

August 14, 1706. Mishilimakina. Letter from Father Marest to the Marquis de Vaudreuil. In MPHC, 33:262–69.

August 23, 1706, and August 25, 1706. Words of the Sonnoutouans to the Marquis de Vaudreuil on the 23rd of August 1706 and replies of the Marquis de Vandreuil to the four Iroquois tribes on the 25th of August, 1706. Annexed to the letter of the 4th Sept. 1706. In MPHC, 33:285–88.

August 27, 1706. Mishilimakina. Letter from Father Marest to the Marquis de Vaudreuil. In MPHC, 33:269–71.

August 27, 1706. Michilimackinac. Letter signed by Jos. J. Marest. In WHC, 16:238–39.

August 27, 1706. Detroit Pontchartrain. Copy of the letter written to the Marquis De Vaudreuil by the Sieur de la Mothe Cadillac. In MPHC, 33:272–85.

September 26, 1706. Speech of Miscouaky, chief of the Outavois, to Marquis de Vaudreuil. In MPHC, 33:288–94.

September 28, 1706. Replies of M. de Vaudreuil to Miscouaky, chief of the Outaouas. Annexed to the letter of the 4th Nov. 1706. In MPHC, 33:294–96.

September 29, 1706. Fort Pontchartrain. Amounts expended for the King's service by Cadillac. Antoine de la Mothe Cadillac, commandant. In MPHC, 33:296–97.

September 30, 1706. Quebec. Memorandum on the Cards of Canada. Signed Raudot. In Shortt, 1:157–59.

November 1706. The New Colonial Contract and Restriction of Issue of Card Money: Common Letter. Signed Vaudreuil and Raudot. In Shortt, 1:159–61.

November 4, 1706. Quebec. 1706: Intertribal Relations; French Policy; Part of a letter from Governor de Vaudreuil to Count de Pontchartrain, dated Nov. 4, 1706. In NYCD, 9:779–81, and WHC, 16:240–42.

November 4, 1706. Quebec. Report of Marquis de Vaudreuil, Governor General, regarding the condition of the colony. In MPHC, 33:301–14.

November 4, 1706. Quebec. Madame dela forest appoints Mon. Joseph Riverin to act in her place according to agreement between her and Cadillac dated June 15, 1706. Signed C F Juchereau dela forest de St Laurent, Delestaige, Lambert, Chambalon. In MPHC, 34:232.

December 22, 1706. Port Royal. Necessity for Card Money in Acadia. Signed de Goutin. In Shortt, 1:161–63.

1707

[1707?]. Memorandum on the posts of the upper country. According to C. M. Burton the document is not dated, but the text indicates that it was after the date of the trading grant given to Cadillac, 1704, and about the time of his first transfers of village lots, 1707. In MPHC, 33:243–45.

1707. Extract from the letter of M. de Pontchartrain 1707, at paragraph 2. In MPHC, 33:315.

February 20, 1707. Fort Louis, Mobile. Letter from Bienville to Pontchartrain: Shortage of supplies; Fort among Chickasaws; Need of Indian presents to overcome English influence; Indian slaves; Warehouse and transport boat at Massacre Island; Illinois Indians demand munitions; Indians kill Father

St. Cosme and four Frenchmen near Natchez; Desertion of sailors; Rumor of trouble with Spaniards; Bienville's trouble with La Salle and La Vente; Desires to visit France. From Ministry of the Colonies, C. 13, vol. 2, pp. 5–31. In MPA, 3:35–46.

March 10, 1707–June 28, 1710. Lists of the contracts granted by M. de La Mothe Cadillac to the inhabitants of Detroit, under the authority which he had received from His Majesty in 1704, 1705, and 1706. In MPHC, 33:373–82.

April 1, 1707. Fort Pontchartrain, Detroit. Statement of sums expended by order of M. de la Mothe for the Iroquis chiefs who came to speak to him. In MPHC, 33:314.

April 11, 1707. Paris. Points concerning Canada for the year 1707. Riverin. In MPHC, 33:316–17.

April 15, 1707. Versailles. Draft of the Measures Which Dauteuil, Procureur-Général of the King to the Superior Council of Quebec, Most Humbly Proposes to the Comte De Pontchartrain, Minister and Secretary of State for Canada. In MPHC, 33:318–19.

June 18, 1707, and June 20, 1707. Words of the Outavois, twelve of whom came down from Michilimakina; four Kiskakoua, 4 Sinago Outaouas and 4 of the La Fourche tribe; on the 18th of June 1707, to the Governor-General and the reply of the Marquis de Vaudreuil to Jean le Bland and twelve other chiefs, or men of importance, among the Outtavois on the 20th of June, 1707. In MPHC, 33:319–24.

June 21, 1707, and June 22, 1707. Words of the Outtavois from Michilimakina to the Governor-General on the 21st of June, 1707, and the reply of the Governor-General to the savages from Michilimakina on the 22nd of June, 1707. In MPHC, 33:324–26.

June 23, 1707. Words of Jean LeBlanc to the Governor-General, on the 23rd of June, 1707. In MPHC, 33:326–27.

June 30, 1707. Versailles. Extracts from a despatch of M. de Pontchartrain, the Minister, to M. de Vaudreuil—to keep at peace with the Indians, and harass the English at Boston, &c. In NYCD, 9:804–5.

June 30, 1707. Versailles. 1707: Louis XIV Orders Inspection of Western Posts; Instructions to Sieur Daigremont, subdelegate of Sieur Raudot, Intendant of New France, whom the King has selected to go to Fort Cataracouy, Niagara, Fort Detroit de Ponchartrain, and Missilimakinac. In NYCD, 9:805–8, and WHC, 16:242–47.

June 30, 1707. Versailles. 1707: Policy toward Indians; Illicit Trade; Memoir of the King to the Marquis de Vaudreuil, Governor and Lieutenant-General, and Sieur Raudot, Intendant of New France; dated at Versailles, June 30, 1707. In WHC, 16:247–48, and a larger extract appears in NYCD, 9:808–10.

June 30, 1707. Versailles. Letter from Pontchartrain to De Muy: Settlement of the accounts with the Spaniards; Investigation of the conduct of Messrs. de Bienville and de Chateaugué. Sieur de La Vente; Expenses of 1706 and 1707. From Ministry of the Colonies, B, vol. 29, pp. 258v–262. In MPA, 3:46–50.

June 30, 1707. Versailles. Memoir from the King to Sieur de Muy, Governor of Louisiana, to serve him when he arrives in that country. From Ministry of the Colonies, B, vol. 29, pp. 248v–258v. In MPA, 3:50–60.

June 30, 1707. Versailles. Order of the King to Sieur de Bienville, Commandant in Louisiana, to Return to France. From Ministry of the Colonies, B, vol. 29, pp. 263v–264. In MPA, 3:60–61.

June 30, 1707. Versailles. Memoir from King Louis XIV to Sieur d'Artaguette, an ordinary commissary of the navy whom the King has selected to go to Louisiana. From Ministry of the Colonies, B, vol. 29, pp. 266v–272. In MPA, 3:61–66.

June 30, 1707. Versailles. Letter from Pontchartrain to Bienville: Dissatisfaction on the subject of the commerce that he carries on with the King's vessels and crews. From Ministry of the Colonies, B, vol. 29, pp. 262–263v. In MPA, 3:67–68.

June 30, 1707. Versailles. Letter from Pontchartrain to De La Salle: Conduct of Mr. de Bienville; Expenses of the colony. From Ministry of the Colonies, B, vol. 29, pp. 264–266v. In MPA, 3:69–71.

June 30, 1707. Versailles. Letter from Pontchartrain to Boisbriant: Misunderstanding between Sieurs de Bienville and de La Vente. From Ministry of the Colonies, B, vol. 29, p. 272. In MPA, 3:72–73.

June 30, 1707. Versailles. Prohibition of Issue of New Cards: Pontchartrain to Raudot. In Shortt, 1:165.

June 30, 1707. Versailles. Prohibition of Issue of New Cards: King's Memorandum to Messrs the Marquis de Vaudreuil, Governor and Lieutenant General, and Raudot, Intendant of New France. Signed Louis and Phelypeaux. In Shortt, 1:165–67.

June 30, 1707. Versailles. Disapproval of Card Money in Acadia: Letter to M. de Subercase. In Shortt, 1:167–69.

July 5, 1707. Fort Pontchartrain. Sale by René Benard and Ls Gatinau to Jacque Lemoyne. Signed Bourjolly, Gastinaux, Lemoyne. Witnesses—Henry Bel Ile, Grandmesnil. In MPHC, 34:294.

July 6, 1707. Rochefort. Letter from D'Artaguette to Pontchartrain: Reply to Mr. de Pontchartrain's letter of the twenty-third of last July about the order that he has received to embark for Louisiana on board the *Renommée* for the purpose of conducting together with Mr. de Muy the investigation concerning the charges brought against Mr. de Bienville; Petitions to have a cabin for himself alone on board this ship in order to work during the voyage on the brief of Mr. de La Salle's complaints against Mr. de Bienville; Western Navy. From Ministry of the Colonies, C. 13, vol. 2, pp. 49–52. In MPA, 3:73–74.

July 23, 1707. Marly. Letter from Pontchartrain to De Muy: Further Complaints against Mr. de Bienville. From Ministry of the Colonies, B, vol. 29, pp. 277v–278v. In MPA, 3:74–76.

July 23, 1707. Marly. Letter from King Louis XIV to Deschilais: An order of his Majesty directing Sieur Deschilais in command of the *Renommée* to receive Sieur de Bienville on board his ship and to bring him back to France as a prisoner. From Ministry of the Colonies, B, vol. 29, pp. 277–277v. In MPA, 3:76.

July 23, 1707. Marly. Letter from Pontchartrain to D'Artaguette: Further complaints against de Bienville. From Ministry of the Colonies, B, vol. 29, pp. 278v–279v. In MPA, 3:76–77.

July 23, 1707. Marly. Letter from Pontchartrain to La Salle: Further complaints against de Bienville. From Ministry of the Colonies, B, vol. 29, p. 280. In MPA, 3:78.

July 24, 1707. Quebec. 1707: Policy toward Indian Tribes; Letter from Governor de Vaudreuil to Count de Pontchartrain; dated July 24, 1707. In NYCD, 9:810–11, and WHC, 16:249–50.

July 24, 1707. Quebec. The Ottawas come to Quebec in the spring of 1707: Letter of M. de Vaudreuil. In MPHC, 33:328–31.

August 6, 1707–August 9, 1707. Summary of the words of Monsieur de la Mothe Cadillac, Commandant of Fort Pontchartrain at Detroit, on the 6th through the 9th of August, 1707, to Jean le Blanc, Kinougé, Meatinan and Menukoueak four chiefs of the four Outtavois tribes, sent to him by the Governor-General. In MPHC, 33:331–36.

August 10, 1707. Versailles. Loss on old Card Money: Letter to Messrs Neret and Gayot. In Shortt, 1:169.

September 10 and 15, 1707, and October 1, 1707. Cadillac complains of Vaudreuil: Letters of Sieur de La Mothe Cadillac. In MPHC, 33:336–41.

September 11, 1707. Fort Ponchartrain. Inventory of household goods belonging to Mon. Delille. Signed Dufiguier, Jacques Lucas, Chesne. In MPHC, 34:294–96.

September 15, 1707. Quebec. Letter from MM. de Vaudreuil and Raudot. In MPHC, 33:342–46.

September 24, 1707. Words of the Outtavois to Monsieur de Lamothe. In MPHC, 33:346–50.

October 1, 1707. Fort Pontchartrain. Copy of Monsieur de la Mothe's letter written to the Marquis De Vaudreuil. In MPHC, 33:350–53.

[October 1, 1707]. Observation of the Marquis de Vaudreuil on the letter from De Lamothe of the 1st of October, 1707. In MPHC, 33:354–61.

October 4, 1707. Minutes: M. de Vaudreuil has put Sieur de Tonty in command of Fort Frontenac. In MPHC, 33:367.

October 7, 1707. Quebec. Words of Three Savages from Michilimakina, who arrived at Quebec on the 7th of October, 1707, with the Sr. de St. Pierre, to the Governor General. In MPHC, 33:362–65.

October 8, 1707. Quebec. Marquis de Vaudreuil's reply to Koutaoulibois, Sakima, and Makatepilé, who arrived from Michilimakina on the 7th October, 1707. In MPHC, 33:366–67.

October 22, 1707. Fort Pontchartrain. Marriage Contract between Jacques Langlois and Marie René Dussaut. Signed Marie Thereze Guyon de la Mothe, Jacques Langlois, Magdeleine La Mothe, Dufigiers, La Mothe Cadillac, Grandmesnil. In MPHC, 34:232–34.

November 1707. Quebec. General Assurances as to Card Money: Common Letter written to the Count de Pontchartrain by Messrs de Vaudreuil and Raudot. In Shortt, 1:175–77.

November 7, 1707. Fort Pontchartrain. Judgment rendered by the Council of war against Bertellemy Pichon a soldier of the Company of Cortemanche of the garrison of Pontchartrain. Signed La Mothe Cadillac, Derané, D'Argenteuil, Guignolet, Francoeur. In MPHC, 34:234–37.

[November 8, 1707?]. Report from Marquis de Vaudreuil. In MPHC, 33:368–70.

[November 10, 1707?]. Cadillac sends Sieur de la Forest to Quebec. In MPHC, 33:370–71.

November 11, 1707. Quebec. Loss on Bills of Exchange: Letter from Messrs Raudot written to the Count de Pontchartrain. In Shortt, 1:171.

November 12, 1707. Quebec. Objections to Bills of Exchange on Paris: Messrs Raudot's Letter to My Lord. In Shortt, 1:171–73.

November 12, 1707. Quebec. Loss in Salaries paid in Currency Notes: Private letter from Messrs Raudot. In Shortt, 1:173–75.

November 12, 1707. Quebec. Letter from M. de Vaudreuil expressing his contempt for Cadillac. In MPHC, 33:371–72.

1708

February 24, 25, 26, and 27, 1708. Mobile. Abstract of Testimony Taken by Mr. d'Artaguette against Mr. de Bienville: Statement of the examination of eight witnesses, all inhabitants of Mobile. From Ministry of the Colonies, C. 13, vol. 2, pp. 249–312. In MPA, 3:78–106.

February 25, 1708. Fort Louis, Mobile. Memoir by Mr. d'Artaguette concerning the reply to the complaints formulated by Mr. De La Salle on the first of October, 1706, against Mr. De Bienville, and which had been previously transmitted to Mr. de Pontchartrain. From Ministry of the Colonies, C. 13, vol. 2, pp. 71–75. In MPA, 3:107–10.

February 25, 1708. Fort Louis, Mobile. Letter from Bienville to Pontchartrain: Shortage of supplies; Canadians in King's service dismissed; Soldiers; Trouble with La Vente and La Salle; English activity among the Indians; English aggression against Spaniards and French; Indians quiet along the Mississippi; St. Denis' expedition against the Chitimachas; Opinion on Jesuits and Foreign Missions; Settlers and workmen; His personal indebtedness. From Ministry of the Colonies, C. 13, vol. 2, pp. 89–117. In MPA, 3:111–24.

February 28, 1708. Mobile. Letter from Boisbriant to Pontchartrain: Note on the subject of the complaints brought against Mr. de Bienville; About Mr. de St. Denis' mission to restrain the Indians; Requests that a new commission as major drawn up in proper form be sent to him. From Ministry of the Colonies, C. 13, vol. 2, pp. 159–60. In MPA, 3:125.

March 2, 1708. Fort Louis, Mobile. Letter from the Reverend Henri Roulleaux de La Vente, the first curate of Mobile, to Pontchartrain on the subject of the information that he has received from the superiors of the Foreign Missions, [and] of the complaints that Mr. De Bienville has made against him; He proposes the filling of Mr. De Muy's position and that the French of Mobile be forbidden to live in concubinage with Indian women. From Ministry of the Colonies, C. 13, vol. 2, pp. 160–64. In MPA, 2:29–31.

March 4, 1708. Massacre (Dauphine) Island. Letter from La Salle to Pontchartrain: Announces receipt of supplies and munitions; Despatch of fiscal reports; Death of de Muy; Discusses trouble with Bienville and his brothers; Shipment of furs; Arrival of Le Roux, carpenter, denounces Barrot, surgeon, as drunken and ignorant; Asks for promotion and place in army for his two sons. From Ministry of the Colonies, C. 13, vol. 2, pp. 154–58. In MPA, 3:125–27.

March 25, 1708. The Jesuits' complaint against Cadillac. In MPHC, 33:382–83.

April 14, 1708. Fort Pontchartrain. Sale of the house of Pierre Pichet, *dit* St Onge to Ls. Fs. Vieneau. Signed Henry Belile, Grandmesnil. In MPHC, 34:237.

April 15, 1708. Fort Pontchartrain. Sale by Antoine Dupuis and wife to Ls. Gatineau for his brother, J Bte. Duplessis. Signed Gastineau, Robert, Rober Janot. In MPHC, 34:238–39.

May 24, 1708. Onnontagué. Copy of a letter written by the Reverend Father d'Heu, Missionary of the Company of Jesus, to the Marquis de Vaudreuil. In NYCD, 9:815–16.

June 4, 1708. Letter from Father Joseph Marest to the Marquis de Vaudreuil. In MPHC, 33:383–87.

June 6, 1708. Versailles. Extract of a despatch from M. de Pontchartrain, the Minister, to M. Raudot, urging him to excite the Indians to a war with the English, &c. In NYCD, 9:811.

June 6, 1708. Versailles. Extracts of the King's despatch to Messrs. de Vaudreuil and Raudot—His Majesty does not recognize Queen Anne, &c. In NYCD, 9:811–12.

June 6, 1708. Versailles. Extract of a despatch of M. de Pontchartrain, the Minister, to M. de Vaudreuil—Instructions, &c. In NYCD, 9:812–13.

June 6, 1708. Extract from the letter of the said minister at paragraph 6. In MPHC, 33:387.

June 6, 1708. Versailles. Small Cards: Copper Coinage, etc.; Extracts of letter from Pontchartrain. In Shortt, 1:179–81.

June 6, 1708. Versailles. Disapproval of Increase of Card Money in Canada: King's Memorandum to Messrs de Vaudreuil and Raudot. In Shortt, 1:181.

June 6, 1708. Versailles. Prohibition of Card Money in Acadia: Letter to M. de Subercase. Unsigned. In Shortt, 1:183.

June 6, 1708. Versailles. Currency Notes to be redeemed: King's Memorandum to Sr de Vaudreuil, Governor and Lieutenant-General, and to Sr Raudot, Intendant, of New France. Signed Louis and Phelypeaux. In Shortt, 1:183.

June 10, 1708. Fort Pontchartrain. Sale by Antoine Terron and his wife to Pierre Herbin. Signed Pierre Mallett, Guignolet. In MPHC, 34:239–40.

[July 1708]. List of the officers who were in the expedition commanded by MM. de Leschaillons and Rouville. According to C. M. Burton this report refers to the attack on Haverhill, MA, in July 1708. In MPHC, 33:387–88.

July 7, 1708. Fort Pontchartrain. Sale by Charle Charon *dit* Laroze to Pierre Garreau *dit* St Onge. Signed Louis Normand, Alexis Lemoyne. In MPHC, 34:240–41.

July 9, 1708. Fort Pontchartrain. Sale by Jacques Demoulin and wife to Jean Le Sueur. Signed Alexis Lemoyne, Paul Guillet. In MPHC, 34:241–42.

July 15, 1708. Sale by Louis Normand *dit* Labriere and his wife to Allexsi Lemoine. Signed Louis Normand, Alexis Le Moyne, Francois Peltier, Claude Martel. In MPHC, 34:242.

July 23, 1708. Words of the Outtavois of Michilimakina to Monsieur de Vaudreuil, with his replies. In MPHC, 33:388–89.

August 12, 1708. Fort Louis, Mobile. Census of Louisiana by De La Salle: Census and enumeration of all the inhabitants composing the colony of Louisiana; List of the domestic animals of this colony. From Ministry of the Colonies, C. 13, vol. 2, pp. 225–27. In MPA, 2:31–32.

August 18, 1708. Fort Louis, Mobile. Letter from D'Artaguette to Pontchartrain: On the unhappy situation of the colony; The plots to desert that are being formed among the soldiers and sailors; The plans of the Indian allies of the English, and of several Englishmen who intend to destroy the French settlements of Louisiana; The plan he has to create an establishment near Biloxi on the upper part of the Mississippi River. From Ministry of the Colonies, C. 13, vol. 2, pp. 327–40. In MPA, 2:33–37.

September 4, 1708. Fort Ponchartrain. Sale by Jacob de Marsac and wife to Jean Barte, *dit* Belleville. Signed Alexis Le Moyne, Jacque Cardinal, De Marsac, Therese David. In MPHC, 34:243.

September 15, 1708. Remarks on letters of M. de la Mothe Cadillac at Detroit. In MPHC, 33:390–94.

September 26 (October 7), 1708. Orange. Copy of a letter from Mr Peter Schuyler to the Marquis de Vaudreuil. In NYCD, 9:818–19.

October 1708. Quebec. Card Money in small Denominations: Private letter of Messrs Raudot. In Shortt, 1:185–87.

October 12, 1708. Fort Louis, Mobile. Letter from Bienville to Pontchartrain: Proposition to exchange Indian slaves for negroes; Refusal of the Indian nations allied with the French to give passage to the English to come and attack Fort Louis; Mr. De Bienville, presenting the account of his services, makes allusion to the untrue complaints that Mr. De La Vente, the curate, was able to bring against him. From Ministry of the Colonies, C. 13, vol. 2, pp. 177–91. In MPA, 2:37–44.

October 25, 1708. Quebec. Letter from M. Raudot, Jr. In MPHC, 33:395.

November 5, 1708. Quebec. Extract of a letter of M. de Vaudreuil to M. de Pontchartrain, the Minister—Onondagas—Boston—New-York, &c. In NYCD, 9:814–15.

November 5, 1708. Quebec. Portions of a letter from M. de Vaudreuil. In MPHC, 33:395–99.

November 12, 1708. Quebec. Letter of M. de Vaudreuil to M. de Pontchartrain, the Minister. In NYCD, 9:816–18.

November 13, 1708. Quebec. Memorandum by MM. De Vaudreuil and Raudot, on the Proposal of the Sr. De La Mothe to Establish Four Companies of Savages at Detroit. In MPHC, 33:399–400.

November 14, 1708. Quebec. 1708: Rejection of Proposal to enroll Indians in Canadian Militia; Part of Sieur d'Aigremont's report to Count de Pontchartrain; dated Nov. 14, 1708. In WHC, 16:250–51, and a larger extract appears in NYCD, 9:819–24.

November 14, 1708. Quebec. Letter from Sr. d'Aigremont—in accordance with the orders given to him by the Count de Pontchartrain, dated the 30th of June and 13th of July, 1707—he set out from Montreal on the 5th of June, last, to go to the advance posts of Canada, and returned on the 12th of September, following—contains an account of Michilimackinac. In MPHC, 33:424–52.

November 14, 1708. Quebec. 1708: Summary of an Inspection of the Posts of Detroit and Michillimackinac, by D'Aigremont; Dated Quebec, Nov. 14,

1708; translated from Cass transcripts from Paris archives, and published in Sheldon's *Early Hist. Mich.*, pp. 280–94. In WHC, 16:251–60.

November 14, 1708. Quebec. MM. de Vaudreuil and Raudot report of the colonies and criticise Cadillac. In MPHC, 33:401–24.

November 14, 1708. Quebec. Loss on Currency Notes: Letter from Messrs de Vaudreuil and Raudot. In Shortt, 1:187.

November 14, 1708. Quebec. Request for more Funds: Letter from Messrs Raudot. In Shortt, 1:187–89.

November 26, 1708. Louisiana. Robert, an inhabitant, or colonist, of Louisiana, to Pontchartrain: Reply to the proposal made by Mr. De Bienville and Mr. D'Artaguette in order to facilitate for the colonists of Louisiana the exchange of Indians for negroes, and the profit that the English of Carolina and Pennsylvania derive from it. From Ministry of the Colonies, C. 13, vol. 2, pp. 359–62. In MPA, 2:45–46.

December 29, 1708. Port Royal, Acadia. Acadian Card Money withdrawn: Letter from de Goutin. In Shortt, 1:189.

1709

January 9, 1709. Fort Ponchartrain. Sale by Jean Barte, *dit* Belleville, to Louis Normand, *dit* Labriere. Signed Louis Normand, Alexis Lemoyne, Paul Guillet. In MPHC, 34:244.

January 30, 1709. Fort Ponchartrain. Sale by Ls Normand, *dit* Labriere, to Charles Charon, *dit* Larose. Signed Louis Normand, De rané, Alexis Le Moyne. In MPHC, 34:245.

February 12, 1709. Fort Pontchartrain. Sale by Guillaume Agnet, *dit* Sansquartier, to Leonar Bolegne, *dit* Boivin. Signed P. Guillet, P. du lude. In MPHC, 34:245–46.

March 21, 1709. Fort Pontchartrain. Exchange between René Lemoine Depin and Pierre Hemar. Signed René Lemoyne, Gastineau, Montandre. In MPHC, 34:246–47.

March 22, 1709. Fort Pontchartrain. Sale by Jean Ferland, *dit* Deloriers to Pierre Come, *dit* Lajeunesse. Signed Mathurin Rivar, Bajoune. In MPHC, 34:247–48.

March 27, 1709. Fort Pontchartrain. Exchange between Lamothe, *dit* Cadillac, and Jean Labatut, *dit* Champagne, and between the latter and Jean Casse, *dit* St Aubin. Signed Lamothe Cadillac, Henry Belile, Montandre. In MPHC, 34:255–56.

April 13, 1709. Fort Pontchartrain. Sale by Jacques Demoulin, *dit* Filis, and wife, to Jean Comptant. Signed Henry Belile, Louis Normand. In MPHC, 34:256–57.

April 27, 1709. Quebec. Letter of M. de Vaudreuil to M. de Pontchartrain, the Minister—Schuyler—Onondagas—Orange, &c. In NYCD, 9:824–25.

April 27, 1709. Memoir on the Colony of Louisiana by M. de Mandeville, ensign of the company of Vaulezard at Fort Louis of Louisiana: Memoir on the situation and the products of the soil of Louisiana; Narrative of his voyage from Louisiana to Rochefort. From Ministry of the Colonies, C. 13, vol. 2, pp. 471–80. In MPA, 2:46–52.

June 2, 1709. Examination of Samuel Whiting, taken prisoner by the French. In NYCD, 9:835–36.

June 10, 1709. Fort Pontchartrain. Inventory of the goods found in the house of Sansquartier. Signed Lamothe Cadillac. In MPHC, 34:257–58.

June 14, 1709. Bay of the Cayugas. Copy of a letter from Sieur de Joncaire to Sieur de la Frenière, the King's Commandant at Fort Frontenac. In NYCD, 9:838.

June 16, 1709. Onondaga. Copy of a letter from Father de Mareuil, Jesuit Missionary at Onondaga, to Father d'Heu, Missionary of the Senecas. In NYCD, 9:836.

June 21, 1709. Detroit. Sale by Paul Guillet to Alexis Germain. Signed Paul Guillet, Montandre, Carrier. In MPHC, 34:259.

June 24, 1709. Fort Pontchartrain. Sale by Louis Normand and wife to Alexis Le Moyne. Signed Louis Normand, Alexis Le Moyne, Michel Masse, Louis hubert. In MPHC, 34:259–60.

July 6, 1709. Versailles. Copper Currency: Extract of letter from Pontchartrain. In Shortt, 1:189.

July 6, 1709. Versailles. Extract of the King's despatch to Messrs. de Vaudreuil and Raudot—to act on the defensive, &c. In NYCD, 9:826.

July 6, 1709. Versailles. 1709: Decisions Regarding Northwestern Posts; Part of a letter from Count de Pontchartrain to Sieur d'Aigremont; dated July 6, 1709. In WHC, 16:260–62, and a larger extract appears in NYCD, 9:826–28.

July 6, 1709. Extract from the Letter of the Said Minister, Pontchartrain, paragraphs 8, 9, 11, and 18. In MPHC, 33:452–53.

July 11, 1709. Versailles. Letter from Pontchartrain to Bienville: Fort of Mobile; Alabamas; Chickasaws; Pensacola; Lack of provisions. From Ministry of the Colonies, B, vol. 30, pp. 181–83. In MPA, 3:127–29.

July 11, 1709. Versailles. Letter from Pontchartrain to D'Artaguette: Instructions in regard to the fort at Mobile; Quarrel between Sieurs de Bienville and de La Salle. From Ministry of the Colonies, B, vol. 30, pp. 184–86. In MPA, 3:130–32.

August 1, 1709. Examination of Querel Roulonse, by M. de Ramezay at Crown Point. In NYCD, 9:837.

August 12 and September 1, 1709. Bienville to Pontchartrain: Mr. de Bienville on the subject of his letters of August 12 and September 1, 1709, in which he related the refusal of the viceroy of Mexico and of the Spanish governor of Pensacola to grant him the assistance that he had asked of them; His apprehension about the approaching failure of provisions and munitions for the garrison; Indian policy of English in Carolina; Fortifications; About the activities of the curate de La Vente; He announces the end of the investigation carried on against him by Mr. d'Artaguette and alludes to the promotion that he has previously solicited. From Ministry of the Colonies, C. 13, vol. 2, pp. 415–25. In MPA, 3:132–35.

August 20, 1709. From the fort of Louisiana. Abstract of letter from Bienville to Pontchartrain: On the present condition of Louisiana; Pensacola without provisions; The French would be able to give only restricted aid to the Spaniards in conflict with the Indians allied to the French and to the English; The English are planning an expedition against the French establishments; Corruption of Mr. de La Vente, curate of Mobile. From Ministry of the Colonies, C. 13, vol. 2, pp. 405–14. In MPA, 3:135–38.

September 12, 1709. Quebec. Indemnity: Mon. and Madame Riverin to Mon. Dela Mothe Cadillac. Signed J. Riverin, Michelle Mars, Grandmesnil, J Lajus, André Jorrian, Chambalon. In MPHC, 34:248–49.

October 8, 1709. Decree providing for the sale of the 143 bales of beaver, which are in the storehouses in Paris, to pay the bills of exchange drawn by the Colony of Canada, which remain to be paid of the years 1703, 1705, 1707, 1708 (Register of Decrees at the Secretary's, last three months of 1709). In Shortt, 1:191–99.

October 19, 1709. Montreal. Letter of M. de Ramezay to M. de Vaudreuil—Schuyler—Crown Point, &c. In NYCD, 9:838–40.

November 1709. Memoir on the Condition of Canada in November, 1709. In NYCD, 9:840–42.

November 14, 1709. Quebec. Letter of M. de Vaudreuil to M. de Pontchartrain, the Minister—details about Schuyler—Lake Champlain, &c. In NYCD, 9:828–35.

November 14, 1709. Quebec. Letter from MM. de Vaudreuil and Raudot. In MPHC, 33:453–55.

November 14, 1709. Remarks on report of Raudot—endorsed M. Raudot and M. de Frontenac. In MPHC, 33:456.

November 14, 1709. Quebec. Letter from Raudot. In MPHC, 33:456–75.

November 26, 1709. Quebec. Fulfillment of the terms of Indemnity made between Mon. and Madame Riverin and Mon. Dela Mothe Cadillac, dated September 12, 1709. Signed Grandmesnil, J Riverin, J Lajus, Barrollet, Chambalon. In MPHC, 34:249–50.

1710

[1710?]. Extract from the letter of M. de la Forest, written to M. de la Mothe at Detroit, at paragraphs 1, 2, and 3. In MPHC, 33:486.

1710. Census of Detroit de Pontchartrain in the year 1710. In MPHC, 33:492–95.

1710. Fort Louis, Mobile. Bienville and De La Salle, Statement of food supplied to garrison by inhabitants of Louisiana. From Ministry of the Colonies, C. 13, vol. 2, pp. 529–30. In MPA, 3:156–57.

February 12, 1710. Port of Massacre [Island]. Letter from D'Artaguette to Pontchartrain: Letter on the situation of the colony of Louisiana; Hunting; Agriculture; Rivalry with Canada; The Missouri ought to be explored. From Ministry of the Colonies, C. 13, vol. 2, pp. 531–38. In MPA, 2:52–55.

April 28, 1710. Fort Ponchartrain. Marriage Contract between Jean Bte. Turpin and Marguerite Fafard. Signed Marguerite Macouse, Paul tessier, Jean Baptiste Turpin, Jacque Cardinal. In MPHC, 34:260–61.

May 1, 1710. Quebec. Letter of M. de Vaudreuil to M. de Pontchartrain, the Minister—Chambly—Lake Champlain—Schuyler going to England, &c. In NYCD, 9:842–44.

May 10, 1710. Marly. Extract of a letter from M. de Pontchartrain, the Minister, to M. de Vaudreuil—Onondagas, &c. In NYCD, 9:844.

May 10, 1710. Marly. Letter from Pontchartrain to Bienville: Assistance to the Spaniards; Alabamas; Supplies of provisions; Port Massacre; Dissoluteness with the Indian women; Nominations disapproved. From Ministry of the Colonies, B, vol. 32, pp. 36v–41. In MPA, 3:139–42.

May 13, 1710. Marly. Letter from Pontchartrain to Bienville: Appointment of Mr. de Lamothe Cadillac. From Ministry of the Colonies, B, vol. 32, pp. 57v–58. In MPA, 3:142.

May 13, 1710. Marly. Memoir from King Louis XIV to Sieur de Lamothe Cadillac, the governor of Louisiana, to serve him when he arrives in that country. From Ministry of the Colonies, B, vol. 32, pp. 58v–66. In MPA, 3:143–50.

[May 16, 1710]. The Council met . . . Payment of Bills of Exchange by Beaver Shipment to Holland. Signed Daguesseau. In Shortt, 1:199–201.

May 20, 1710. Versailles. Prohibition of Card Money in Acadia: Letter to M. De Subercase. In Shortt, 1:201–3.

May 23, 1710. Versailles. Copy of a letter written by Monseigneur de Pontchartrain to Monsieur Raudot. In MPHC, 33:475–76.

May 23, 1710. Versailles. Letter from Pontchartrain to D'Artaguette: About sending Sieur Jamin to take the place of Sieur de La Salle. From Ministry of the Colonies, B, vol. 32, pp. 111–111v. In MPA, 3:150.

May 30, 1710. The Council met . . . Beaver Shipment to Holland disallowed. Signed Daguesseau. In Shortt, 1:203.

June 1710. Notes by the Minister upon M. de Vaudreuil's letters, &c. In NYCD, 9:845–46.

June 7, 1710. Versailles. Letter from M. de Ponchartrain, the Minister, to M. de Vaudreuil—designs of the English, &c. In NYCD, 9:845.

June 7, 1710. Extract from a resolution passed as between M. de la Mothe and his settlers of Detroit on the 7th of June, 1710. In MPHC, 33:478–79.

June 20, 1710. Fort Louis, Mobile. Letter from D'Artaguette to Pontchartrain: Situation of the colony; Provisions and powder advanced by the Spaniards; Necessity of sending farm girls rather than girls from Paris who are good for nothing. From Ministry of the Colonies, C. 13, vol. 2, pp. 541–47. In MPA, 2:55–60.

June 21, 1710. Port of Massacre (Dauphine) Island. Letter from Bienville to Pontchartrain: Relating the events that took place in Louisiana from September 1709; The sufferings endured by the garrison as a result of the lack of provisions and clothes; Voyageurs; Mines; Indians; La Vente goes to France; Missionaries. From Ministry of the Colonies, C. 13, vol. 2, pp. 549–54. In MPA, 3:151–54.

June 27, 1710. Fort Pontchartrain. Marriage Contract between Michel Bizalion and Marie Marguerite Fafart. Signed Lamothe Cadillac, Marie Therese Guyon dela Mothe, Marie Magdelaine Jobin, Marie Françoisse, Magdeleine Lamothe, Marie Magdelaine Delorme, LaMothe Cadillac Jr., Henry Belile, Nicolas Rivard, Jacque Cardinal, Jean Baptiste Turpin. In MPHC, 34:261–63.

June 28, 1710. Fort Pontchartrain. Sale by Michel Massé to André Marsil *dit* Lespagnol. Signed Michel Massé, Alexis LeMoyne, Joseph rivard. In MPHC, 34:264.

July 3, 1710. Detroit, Pontchartrain. Sale by Michel Massé to Louis Saint Terny. Signed Michel Massé, Pierre Mallet. In MPHC, 34:264.

August 10, 1710. Versailles. Currency in Acadia: Letter to M. De Subercase. In Shortt, 1:203–5.

September 2, 1710. Extract from Report of MM. De Vaudreuil and Raudot. In MPHC, 33:477–78.

September 2, 1710. Marly. Letter from Pontchartrain to Bienville: Delay of the *Renommée*; Visit of the governor of Pensacola; Necessity for marking the boundaries of the colony. From Ministry of the Colonies, B, vol. 32, pp. 197–98v. In MPA, 3:154–55.

September 3, 1710. Necessity for re-establishing Mackinac. M. de Vaudreuil. In MPHC, 33:479–83.

September 9, 1710. Marly. Letter from Pontchartrain to Bienville: Passage to Louisiana of Sieur Valigny. From Ministry of the Colonies, B, vol. 32, p. 206. In MPA, 3:155–56.

September 13, 1710. Quebec. Memorandum of Vaudreuil: Cadillac appointed Governor of Louisiana and de la Forest commandant at Detroit. In MPHC, 33:483–84.

September 13, 1710. Memorandum of Vaudreuil: Dubuisson ordered to act as commandant at Detroit. In MPHC, 33:484.

September 13, 1710. Quebec. Memorandum given by Vaudreuil for Sieur Dubuisson. In MPHC, 33:485.

October 18, 1710. Quebec. Letter from Sr. D'Aigremont. In MPHC, 33:487–91.

October 22, 1710. Quebec. Reasons for further Issue of Cards. Unsigned. In Shortt, 1:205–7.

October 31, 1710. Quebec. 1710: Disturbances among Indians; Michillimackinac Should Be Reoccupied; Extract from letter of Governor de Vaudreuil to Count de Pontchartrain; dated Oct. 31, 1710. In WHC, 16:263–65, and a larger extract appears in NYCD, 9:846–51.

October 31, 1710. Quebec. Petition for pension for Captain de Grandville's widow. In MPHC, 33:492.

November 2, 1710. Quebec. Extract from Report of MM. De Vaudreuil and Raudot. In MPHC, 33:478.

November 3, 1710. Quebec. Extract of a letter from M. de Vaudreuil to M. de Pontchartrain, the Minister. In NYCD, 9:851–52.

November 18, 1710. Trading Licenses and Sale of Brandy; Extract from letter of Sieur d'Aigremont to Count de Pontchartrain; dated Nov. 18, 1710. In NYCD, 9:852–53, and WHC, 16:265–67.

December 28, 1710. Fort Pontchartrain. Marriage Contract between Prudent Robert and Magdelaine Fafard. Signed Marie Magdelaine Fafard, Marie Magdelaine Jobin, Madelene Marette, LaMothe Cadillac, Madelenne Parend, Marie Therese Guyon de Lamothe, Magdelaine Lamothe, Dubuisson, Lamothe Cadillac *fils*, St. Jean Pachot, Demeul, Gastineau, Jacques Laglois, Jean Baptiste Turpin, Henry Belile, Joseph du Tremblé, Mary Francoisse, wife of Belile, By me, Paul Guillot. In MPHC, 34:265–66.

1711

[1711]. Words of the Marquis de Vaudreuil to the savages who came down from the upper country. In MPHC, 33:503–6.

[1711]. Financial Straits of the Colony: Memorandum on Canada. In Shortt, 1:215–19.

January 10 and January 17, 1711. Fort Pontchartrain. Instructions given Dubuisson by M. de la Forest. In MPHC, 33:495–97.

February 23, 1711. Massacre (Dauphine) Island. Bienville and D'Artaguette, Memorandum of goods sent to Vera Cruz on the King's account to be exchanged for provisions. From Ministry of the Colonies, C. 13, vol. 2, p. 717. In MPA, 3:157.

March 10, 1711. Montreal. Memorandum to serve as instructions from the Marquis de Vaudreuil to the officers and voyageurs despatched to bring down to Montreal the savages of the upper country. In MPHC, 33:97–502.

March 20, 1711. Memorandum of new card money prepared in the year 1710, in accordance with the official report of September 29 of the same year, which cards have been signed in the same manner and stamped with the same dies, as those issued in accordance with the ordinance proclaimed by the Governor General and the Intendant on January 10 of the same year, 1710. Signed Daigremont. In Shortt, 1:207–11.

April 25, 1711. Quebec. Letter of M. de Vaudreuil to M. de Pontchartrain, the Minister—New-York—Port Royal, &c. In NYCD, 9:853–55.

June 15, 1711. Montreal. La Motte Cadillac to the Marquis de Vaudreuil, Governor and Lieutenant General of New France: Cadillac asks to know the will of His Majesty in regard to the letter which Vaudreuil wrote to him on 13 September 1710. In MPHC, 33:506–8.

July 1, 1711. Quebec. Cadillac tries to sell his personal effects to de la Forest. In MPHC, 33:508–10.

July 3, 1711. Quebec. Agreement made between MM. de la Mothe and de la Forest. Annexed to the letter of M. de Vaudreuil of the 7th and 8th of Nov. 1711. In MPHC, 33:510–12.

July 7, 1711. Marly. Despatch of M. de Pontchartrain, the Minister, to M. de Vaudreuil—approves his conduct in reference to New-York—Boston—Indians, &c. In NYCD, 9:856–57.

July 7, 1711. Marly. Extract from the Memorandum of the King concerning Canada. In MPHC, 33:476–77.

July 14, 1711. Montreal. Memorandum of M. de la Forest in which he asks permission to go to his post. Annexed to the letter of M. de Vaudreuil of the 7th and 8th November, 1711. In MPHC, 33:512.

July 16, 1711. Montreal. Answer of M. De La Mothe to the Memorandum of M. De La Forest of the 14th July 1711. In MPHC, 33:513–15.

July 17, 1711. Montreal. Reply [of M. de la Forest] to Cadillac's claims. In MPHC, 33:515–17.

August 24, 1711. Paragraph from the letter of the Revd. Father Cherubin de Nian, recollet and missionary at the fort of Detroit, written to M. de La Mothe, who was at Quebec. In MPHC, 33:517.

August 25, 1711. Fort Pontchartrain. Inventory of Cadillac's Detroit property. Signed in the original by Chesne and Magnant and certified by Fr. Cherubin Deniaux, Priest, Missionary, Recollet. In MPHC, 33:518–28, and MPHC, 34:267–77.

September 8, 1711. Quebec. Report from M. de Vaudreuil of the condition of the colony. In MPHC, 33:528–36.

October 1, 1711. Quebec. 50 and 100 livre Cards to be issued: Resolution of Messrs de Vaudreuil, Raudot, and Monseignat, for the production of a new card money for the sum of 450,000 livres, money of the country. In Shortt, 1:211–13.

October 25, 1711. Quebec. 50 and 100 livre Cards to be issued: Ordinance of Messrs de Vaudreuil and Raudot giving currency to new card money. In Shortt, 1:213–15.

October 25, 1711. Quebec. Letter of M. de Vaudreuil to M. de Pontchartrain, the Minister—Albany—New-York—Boston—Onondagas—Port Royal, &c. In NYCD, 9:857–61.

October 27, 1711. Port Dauphin. Letter from Bienville to Pontchartrain: Munitions and supplies; Name of Massacre changed to Dauphin; Indian allies, presents and slaves; Danger from English; Voyageurs; Growth of tobacco and wheat; Mines; Mobile-Pensacola boundary dispute, Marie Grisot's defense; Domestic animals. From Ministry of the Colonies, C. 13, vol. 2, pp. 567–602. In MPA, 3:158–71.

November 8, 1711. Necessity for Payment of Bills of Exchange: Extract of letter from M. de Vaudreuil. In Shortt, 1:219.

November 12, 1711. Quebec. Contract and agreement between the reverend ladies Ursulines and Mon. dela mothe Cadillac. Signed Charles Glandelet, Vicar general, Superior of the convent of the Ursulines at Quebec, Soeur Catherine of the Incarnation Superior, Soeur of St John the Evangelist ass't., Soeur J. of St Francis, zealot, Soeur Catherine of the Seraphs, guardian, Soeur Marie Anne of Ste Therese, Soeur Louise of Ste Catherine, Lamothe Cadillac, Fournier, Du Figuier, Boisseau, Chambalon. In MPHC, 34:250–53.

1712

1712. Another Account of the Siege of Detroit; Translated from *Collection de Manuscrits relatifs à la Nouvelle-France* (Quebec, 1883), pp. 622–25; authorship ascribed to Gaspard Chaussegros de Léry, chief engineer of Canada. In WHC, 16:293–95.

[1712]. Review of the Finances of Canada: Memorial on the Present State of Canada. Unsigned. In Shortt, 1:223–29.

March 2, 1712. Louisiana. Letter from Bienville to Pontchartrain: He informs him that he has been warned that the English are preparing to attack Louisiana by sea and by land. From Ministry of the Colonies, C. 13, vol. 2, pp. 691–94. In MPA, 3:171–73.

May 12, 1712. Bayonne. Memoir of D'Artaguette to Pontchartrain on present condition of Louisiana and the observations that have been made and reported in regard to this memoir. From Ministry of the Colonies, C. 13, vol. 2, pp. 803–9. In MPA, 2:60–67.

June 1712. Rochefort. Letter from Tivas de Gourville to Pontchartrain: Concerning the establishment of Louisiana and the advantages that France might derive from the products of this colony. From Ministry of the Colonies, C. 13, vol. 2, pp. 737–41. In MPA, 2:67–72.

June 15, 1712. Fort du Detroit, Pontchartrain. 1712: Siege of Detroit by Wisconsin Indians; Official Report, made by the commanding officer, Mr. Dubuisson, to the Governor General of Canada, [the Marquis de Vaudreuil], of the war which took place at Detroit, in 1712, between the French and their allies, and the Ottagamie and Mascoutins Indians. This document is reprinted from a rare pamphlet with the foregoing title, published in 1845 at Detroit (printed by Harsha & Willcox, but copyrighted by A. McFarren). The preface mentions the copies made by Gen. Lewis Cass of documents in the archives of Paris, and states that he "furnished the publisher with a translation of one of the most interesting of these papers," Dubuisson's report of the Indian attack on Detroit in 1712. We find it necessary to correct a few obvious typographical errors in the document; otherwise, it is produced *verbatim et literatim*. It was also published by William R. Smith, in his *History of Wisconsin* (Madison, 1854), vol. 3, pp. 315–36.—Ed. In WHC, 16:267–87, and MPHC, 33:537–52.

June 21, 1712. (Michilimackinac). Extract from a letter of Father Marest to Governor de Vaudreuil; dated June 21, 1712 (contains an entry from July 2, 1712). From Sheldon's *Early Hist. Michigan*, pp. 299–305. In WHC, 16:288–92.

June 21, 1712. Indians on the St. Joseph River: Letter from the Revd. Father Joseph Marest, missionary at Michillimakinac, to the Marquis de Vaudreuil. Annexed to the letter from the Marquis de Vaudreuil of the 6th Nov. 1712. In MPHC, 33:553–57.

June 26, [1712]. Marly. Financial Difficulties: Letter to Messrs Vaudreuil and Begon. In Shortt, 1:219–23.

June 28, 1712. Marly. Extracts of the despatch of M. de Pontchartrain, the Minister, to M. de Vaudreuil—precautions to be taken against the English, &c. In NYCD, 9:861–62.

July 2, 1712. Letter from Father Joseph Marest, missionary at Michillimakinac, to the Marquis de Vaudreuil—annexed to the letter from the Marquis de Vaudreuil of the 6th of July, 1712—complaints of the Indians. In MPHC, 33:557–59.

September 6, 1712. Reports from the upper country. P.S. dated November 6, 1712. Signed M. de Vaudreuil. In MPHC, 33:559–67.

September 8, 1712. Paris. Memoir of D'Artaguette to Pontchartrain: Against the disorder in morals in Louisiana and about twelve hundred buccaneers on the coast of Cartagena who ask permission to settle in Louisiana. From Ministry of the Colonies, C. 13, vol. 2, pp. 799–802. In MPA, 2:72–74.

October 14, 1712. Quebec. Statement of expenditures, made by Mr. Dubuisson, for the service of the king, to gain an influence over the nations and to secure them in his interest, in order to sustain the post of the Fort de Pontchartrain, of Detroit, against the Ottagamies and Mascoutins, who had been paid by the English to destroy it—to wit. Signed Dubuisson. In WHC, 16:287–88, and MPHC, 33:568.

October 15, 1712. Quebec. Fox Indians attack Detroit: Letter of the Marq. de Vaudreuil. In MPHC, 33:569–71.

October 31, 1712. Quebec. Fulfillment of the agreement between the Ursulines and Cadillac, dated November 12, 1711. Signed Soeur C. of the Incarnation Superior, Soeur M. A. of St John the Evangelist, Ass't, Soeur C. of the Seraphs Guardian, Soeur Jeanne of St Francis Xavier Zealot, Soeur Angelique of the Holy Ghost, Soeur Marie Anne of Ste Theresa, Soeur Louise Rose of

Ste Catherine, Fournier, Dufiguier, Dela Riviére, Boisseau, Chambalon. In MPHC, 34:253–54.

November 6, 1712. Letter of M. de Vaudreuil to M. de Pontchartrain, the Minister—Detroit—Onondagas—Fort Frontenac, &c. In NYCD, 9:862–65.

November 12, 1712. Quebec. Suggestions for improving the Credit of Card Money. Signed Michel Bégon. In Shortt, 1:229–31.

November 12, 1712. Quebec. Necessity for using Cards and paying the Bills of Exchange: Letter of Messrs de Vaudreuil and Bégon. In Shortt, 1:233–35.

December 21, 1712. Versailles. Letter from Pontchartrain to Bienville: Attitude that he must have toward Messrs. de Lamothe Cadillac and Duclos; Refusal to grant him land in fief. From Ministry of the Colonies, B, vol. 34, pp. 159v–160v. In MPA, 3:173–74.

1713

1713. M. Riverin's two Plans for Retirement of Card Money: Sr Riverin sends two plans for retiring the card money. In Shortt, 1:237–39.

June 6, 1713. Paris. M. Riverin's two Plans for Retirement of Card Money: Letter of Riverin. In Shortt, 1:235–37.

June 25, 1713. Versailles. Retirement of Card Money by Conversion into Securities: Memorandum of the King to Messrs the Marquis De Vaudreuil, Governor and Lieutenant-General and Bégon, Intendant of New France. In Shortt, 1:241–43.

June 28, 1713. Conversion and Reduction in Rating of the Cards: A letter from the Minister to the Marquis de Vaudreuil and M. Bégon. In Shortt, 1:243–45.

June 28, 1713. Rambouillet. Conversion and Reduction in Rating of the Cards: Memorandum of the King to the Marquis De Vaudreuil, Governor and Lieutenant General and M. Bégon, Intendant of New France. In Shortt, 1:245–47.

June 30, 1713. Rambouillet. Proposals for withdrawing the Cards: Letter to Marquis de Vaudreuil and M. Bégon. In Shortt, 1:249.

July 1, 1713. Versailles. Disposal of the various Issues of Card Money: Letter to M. Bégon. In Shortt, 1:249–53.

July 3, 1713. Versailles. Conversion of Cards still urged: Letter to M. Bégon. In Shortt, 1:253.

July 3, 1713. Versailles. Council . . . Proposed Reduction in the Rating of Card Money. In Shortt, 1:239.

July 4, 1713. Versailles. Extract of a despatch of M. de Pontchartrain, the Minister, to M. de Vaudreuil. In NYCD, 9:865.

July 10, 1713. Fort Louis, Mobile. Letter from Duclos to Pontchartrain. From Ministry of the Colonies, C. 13, vol. 3, pp. 113–22. In MPA, 2:74–78.

September 20, 1713. Quebec. 1713: Reëstablishment of Michilimackinac; Memorial written by the Intendant of Canada [Claude Michel Bégon]; dated at Quebec, Sept. 20, 1713. In WHC, 16:295–98.

October 1713. Louisiana. Abstracts of Letters from Cadillac, Dirigoin and Bienville to Crozat: Industries; The fort; Peltries; Private trade; Spanish trade; Supplies to Pensacola; Women; Hat-maker. From Ministry of the Colonies, C. 13, vol. 3, pp. 351–61. In MPA, 3:174–78.

October 9, 1713. Fort Louis, Mobile. Duclos to Pontchartrain: Memoir concerning the Province of Louisiana. From Ministry of the Colonies, C. 13, vol. 3, pp. 209–86. In MPA, 2:79–143.

October 12, 1713. Fort Louis, Mobile. Duclos to Pontchartrain, Statement of Expenses necessary for 1714. From Ministry of the Colonies, C. 13, vol. 3, pp. 287–310. In MPA, 2:143–62.

October 26, 1713. Fort Louis, Mobile. Letter from Lamothe Cadillac to Pontchartrain. From Ministry of the Colonies, C. 13, vol. 3, pp. 1–93. In MPA, 2:162–204.

November 15, 1713. 1713–14: Foxes are unruly and lawless; Should be destroyed; French Renegades; Extracts from letter of Vaudreuil and Bégon to the Minister; dated Nov. 15, 1713. Original MS. is in archives of Ministère des Colonies, Paris; pressmark, "Canada, Corresp. gén., vol. 34, c. 11, fol. 4." In WHC, 16:298–300.

November 15, 1713. Quebec. Necessity for Withdrawal of Card Money: Letter from Vaudreuil and Bégon. In Shortt, 1:255.

November 15, 1713. Quebec. Destruction of the Register of Cards issued: Letter from François Clairambault d'Aigremont. In Shortt, 1:255–57.

1714

1714. Memoir on Detroit; Plea for Troops. "Supposed to have been written by Captain de la Forest," is E. B. O'Callaghan's note on this document. From NYCD, 9:866–67. In WHC, 16:307–10.

[1714]. Disposal of the Cards: Memorandum of Several Things to Which It Is Necessary to Devote Attention This Year for the Well Being of Canada [1715]. In Shortt, 1:285.

[1714]. Memoranda re Card Money. In Shortt, 1:285.

[1714]. The Annual Appropriations to be provided in Coin: 1713 Canadian Cards. In Shortt, 1:287.

March 19, 1714. Versailles. Proposals for Reduction in the Rating of Cards: Letter to the Marquis de Vaudreuil and M. Bégon. In Shortt, 1:259.

March 22, 1714. Versailles. Conversion of Card Money into Securities: Letter to M. Bégon. In Shortt, 1:261–63.

March 22, 1714. Versailles. Reduction in Value of the Card Money: Letter to Messrs de Vaudreuil and Bégon. In Shortt, 1:263–65.

May 16, 1714. [Fort Louis, Mobile]. Letter from Cadillac to Pontchartrain: Dispute between Mr. de Lamothe and Mr. de Bienville as follows. From Ministry of the Colonies, C. 13, vol. 3, pp. 493–94. In MPA, 3:178–80.

May 17, 1714. Versailles. Payment of the Civil List: Letter to Claude de Bermen, Sieur de la Martinière. In Shortt, 1:265–67.

May 23, 1714. Versailles. Reduction of the Face value of the Card Money by one-half: Letter to Messrs de Vaudreuil and Bégon. In Shortt, 1:267–71.

May 23, 1714. Versailles. Formalities to be observed in reducing the Card Money by one half: Letter to M. Bégon. In Shortt, 1:271.

September 16, 1714. Quebec. Practical Results of reducing the Card Money: Letter from Vaudreuil. In Shortt, 1:273–75.

September 18, 1714. 1713–14: Foxes are unruly and lawless; Should be destroyed; French Renegades; Part of a letter from Claude de Ramezay to the Minister;

dated Sept. 18, 1714. (The copy of this document from which our translation is made, is dated 1711; but internal evidence shows that it must have been written in 1714.—Ed.). From "Canada, Corresp. gén., vol. 34, c. 11, fol. 354." In WHC, 16:300–303.

September 20, 1714. Plans for Campaign against the Foxes: Part of a letter from Vaudreuil and Bégon to the French Minister; dated Sept. 20, 1714. From "Canada, Corresp. gén., vol. 34, c. 11, fol. 288 (228?)." In WHC, 16:303–7.

[September 20, 1714]. Withdrawal of Card Money: Letter from Vaudreuil and Bégon. In Shortt, 1:275–79.

October 1, 1714. Quebec. Memoir showing the advantages of the post at the Detroit to the King, &c. In NYCD, 9:866–67.

October 23, 1714. Quebekie. 1714–15: Intrigues of English and Iroquois among Western Tribes; Foxes slay Frenchmen; Extracts from letters of Ramezay and Bégon to French Minister; dated Oct. 23 and Nov. 12, 1714. Original MSS. are in archives of Ministère des Colonies; press-mark, "Canada, Corresp. gén., vol. 34, c. 11, fol. 362." In WHC, 16:310.

November 1, 1714. Official Minute of the Destruction of Cards: Statement of cards returned to M. Bégon, Intendant, by Petit, agent in New France for Messrs de Fontanieu and Vanolles. Signed de Ramezay, Begon, Demonseignat, Daigremont and Petit. In Shortt, 1:279–81.

November 8, 1714. Quebec. Effects of Reduction in Value of the Cards: Letter from De Monseignat. In Shortt, 1:281–83.

November 12, 1714. Intrigues of English and Iroquois among Western Tribes; Foxes slay Frenchmen; Extracts from letters of Ramezay and Bégon to French Minister; dated Oct. 23 and Nov. 12, 1714. Original MSS. are in archives of Ministère des Colonies; press-mark, "Canada, Corresp. gén., vol. 34, c. 11, fol. 364." In WHC, 16:311.

November 12, 1714. Quebec. Death of La Forest: Letter from MM. de Ramezay and Begon. In MPHC, 33:571–72.

November 12, 1714. Quebec. Statement of new Card Money issued: Letter from Bégon. In Shortt, 1:283–85.

1715

[1715]. Canadian Cards—1715. In Shortt, 1:289–91.

[1715]. No place or date. Basis of present Arrangements with regard to Card Money. In Shortt, 1:307–11.

January 9, 1715. Versailles. Progress of withdrawing the Card Money: Letter from [Pontchartrain] to M. de Nointel. In Shortt, 1:287–89.

February 17, 1715. Versailles. Requests for Payment of Bills of Exchange drawn to retire Card Money: Letter from Pontchartrain to M. de Nointel. In Shortt, 1:289.

March 27, 1715. Versailles. Requests for Payment of Bills of Exchange drawn to retire Card Money: Letter from [Pontchartrain] to M. Desmaretz. In Shortt, 1:291–93.

March 31, 1715. Versailles. Consequences of the Non-Payment of Bills of Exchange drawn for the Card Money: Letter from [Pontchartrain] to M. de Nointel. In Shortt, 1:293–95.

June 15, 1715. Fort Louis, Mobile. Letter from Bienville to Pontchartrain: English activity among the Indians of Louisiana; Cadillac's trip to the Illinois. From Ministry of the Colonies, C. 13, vol. 3, pp. 827–31. In MPA, 3:181–84.

June 19, 1715. Marly. Bills of Exchange for the Pay of the Crew of H.M.S. "Le Héros": Letter to François de Beauharnois. In Shortt, 1:295–97.

July 2, 1715. Marly. Urgent Need for Payment of the Bills of Exchange: Letter to M. Desmaretz. In Shortt, 1:297–99.

July 10, 1715. Urgent Need for Funds for Canada and Ile Royale: Letter to M. Desmaretz. In Shortt, 1:299.

July 10, 1715. Marly. Instructions to Begon in Regard to Redemption of the Old and Temporary Issue of New Card Money: Letter to M. Bégon. In Shortt, 1:299–303.

July 17, 1717 [1715]. Marly. Judgments for Debt against M. Gaudion: Letter to M. Desmarets. In Shortt, 1:303.

July 31, 1715. Marly. Postponement of Payment of Bills of Exchange: Letter to François Mouchard. In Shortt, 1:303–5.

September 1715. Suspension of legal Action for Non-Payment of Bills of Exchange. In Shortt, 1:305–7.

September 1, 1715. Fort Louis, Mobile. Letter from Bienville to Pontchartrain: Loss of the *Justice*; Opposes being sent to the interior; Soldiers; Sailors; Fortifications; Jesuits in Illinois; Indians hostile to English; His relations with Cadillac; Asks for decorations and more pay. From Ministry of the Colonies, C. 13, vol. 3, pp. 779–88. In MPA, 3:184–89.

September 13 and 16, 1715. 1714–15: Intrigues of English and Iroquois among Western Tribes; Foxes slay Frenchmen; Extracts from letters of Ramezay and Bégon to the French Minister; dated Sept. 13 and 16, 1715. Original MSS. are in archives of Ministère des Colonies; press-mark, "Canada, Corresp. gén., vol. 35, c. 11, fol. 3, 71." In WHC, 16:311–22.

October 27, 1715. The Louvre. Petition *re* Payment of Bills of Exchange. Council of Marine. In Shortt, 1:311–13.

October 28, 1715. Quebek. Evil Effects of Non-Payment of the Bills: Letter from de Ramezay. In Shortt, 1:313.

November 3, 1715. Epidemic among Weas prevents them from aiding De Lignery; Should be removed to Chicago; Letter from Ramezay to the French Minister; dated Nov. 3, 1715. Original MSS. are in archives of Ministère des Colonies; press-mark, "Canada, Corresp. gén., vol. 35, c. 11, fol. 101." In WHC, 16:322–26.

November 6, 1715. Paris. Grant of Delay in Payment of Bills: Registration of Letters Written to La Rochelle and Rochefort since the Establishment of the Council of Marine. In Shortt, 1:313–15.

November 7, 1715. Military Preparations against Foxes; Traders and Voyageurs; Their lawlessness; Restrictions on Trade; English seek to control Fur Trade; French should establish new Posts; Letter of Ramezay and Bégon to French Minister; dated Nov. 7, 1715. MS. in archives of Ministère des Colonies, Paris; press-mark, "Canada, Corresp. gén., vol. 35, c. 11, fol. 15." In WHC, 16:327–38.

November 7, 1715. Quebec. Considerations as to Payment of Bills of Exchange: Letter from Messrs de Ramezay and Bégon. In Shortt, 1:315–17.

November 7, 1715. Quebec. Discussion of the Difficulties resulting from the Non-Payment of the Bills of Exchange given for the Card Money: Letter from M. Begon. In Shortt, 1:317–21.

November 7, 1715. Canada. Explanation of the present Position of the Card Money: M. Begon 25th Sept. 1715. In Shortt, 1:321–25.

December 9, 1715. Paris. General Account of the Card Money and its Consequences. In Shortt, 1:325–35.

December 22, 1715. Louvre. Legal Protection for M. Gaudion. Council of Marine. In Shortt, 1:335.

December 25, 1715. Dauphine Island. Letter from Duclos to Pontchartrain. From Ministry of Colonies, C. 13, vol. 3, pp. 815–26. In MPA, 2:205–9.

1716

[1716]. Paris. Letter from the Company of the West to the Navy Council: Requesting that L'Epinay and Captain Artus be recalled to France and Bienville and Boisbriant named for vacancies; Hubert to remain as Commissary. From Ministry of the Colonies, C. 13, vol. 4, p. 931. In MPA, 3:190.

1716. Charlevoix's Account of De Louvigny's Expedition. In WHC, 5:81–85.

[1716]. Urging Abolition of Card Money and Supply of Special Coinage: Memoir on the Present Situation of Canada. In Shortt, 1:361.

[1716]. Project for using the Profits on the Beaver Trade to retire the Card Money: New Administration of the Beaver Trade by the Colony Itself, Calculated on the Annual Consumption. [Riverin]. In Shortt, 1:363–65.

[1716?]. Remarks on the war with the Fox Indians. According to C. M. Burton, this document is neither signed nor dated, but Louvigny led an expedition against the Fox Indians in 1717, and evidently, this was written prior to the formation of that expedition. In MPHC, 33:579–82.

January 2, 1716. Fort Louis, Mobile. Letter from Bienville to Pontchartrain: His relations with Cadillac; Fort St. Jerome, Natchez; Upper part of the river of the Alabamas. From Ministry of the Colonies, C. 13, vol. 4, pp. 759–72. In MPA, 3:191–97.

January 20, 1716. Fort Louis, Mobile. Letter from Bienville to Raudot: Affairs of the Natchez; He complains of Mr. de Lamothe; Accounts in confusion since death of Nicolas La Salle; Asks for an accountant; Asks that Duclos be retained. From Ministry of the Colonies, C. 13, vol. 4, pp. 775–83. In MPA, 3:197–200.

January 20, 1716. Paris. M. D'Auteuil's Objections to M. Riverin's Plan for the Redemption of Card Money. Signed DAuteuil. In Shortt, 1:337–39.

February 1716. I. A Plan for the Redemption of Card Money. II. Advisability of purchasing Goods for Canada in France: Memoir of M. de Vaudreuil. In Shortt, 1:339–43.

February 1716. Extracts of a general Mémoir, addressed by M. de Vaudreuil, to the Regent, the Duke d'Orleans, upon the state of affairs in Canada. In NYCD, 9:868–72.

February 2, 1716. Dauphine Island. Letter from Cadillac to Pontchartrain: Complains of Messrs. de Bienville and de Boisbriant who have led a group of officers to protest against a disciplinary measure taken in regard to Lieutenant Latour; Deserters; Prices of Crozat's merchandise. From Ministry of the Colonies, C. 13, vol. 4, pp. 571–73. In MPA, 3:201–3.

March 26, 1716. Rochefort. S. le Vasseur de Neré's Proposal for a Special Coinage for Canada. In Shortt, 1:343.

March 28, 1716. Plans for settling Difficulties with Fox Indians; Lawlessness of Coureurs de Bois; Proceedings in French Council of Marine, March 28, 1716. Translated from a copy of document in Paris archives, made for archives of the Province of Quebec. Signed by L. A. de Bourbon, Maréchal d'Estrées and by the Council: La Chapelle. In WHC, 16:338–40.

March 28, 1716. The settlement at Detroit. By the Council, Lachapelle. In MPHC, 33:574–76.

April 1716. Paris. Loss sustained by Vaudreuil in giving Exchange for Card Money. In Shortt, 1:349–51.

April 22, 1716. Paris. Notice of Recoinage of Issue of 1709: Letter to Philippe de Costebelle and Pierre Auguste de Soubras. In Shortt, 1:345–47.

April 28, 1716. War against the Fox Indians and amnesty to the "*Coureurs de bois.*" By the Council, La chapelle. In MPHC, 33:573–74.

May 12, 1716. Louvre. Probable Payment of Bills of Exchange given for Card Money. Council of the Marine. In Shortt, 1:351.

June 7, 1716. Paris. Amounts of Cards supplied for the Expenditures in Canada: Letter to M. de Champigny, Treasurer. In Shortt, 1:351–53.

June 7, 1716. Dauphine Island. Letter from Duclos to Pontchartrain: Approves the conduct of Mr. de Bienville at the Natchez; Fort Rosalie; The Tunicas. From Ministry of the Colonies, C. 13, vol. 4, pp. 671–92. In MPA, 3:203–13.

June 16, 1716. Paris. Funds for the Future to be sent in Cash or Goods. Card Money forbidden: Letter to Messrs Vaudreuil and Bégon. In Shortt, 1:353.

June 16, 1716. Paris. Proceeds from Beaver Sales to be used in paying Bills of Exchange: Letter to Messrs Vaudreuil and Bégon. In Shortt, 1:355.

June 23, 1716. Fort St. Joseph at the Tunicas. Letter from Bienville to Cadillac: Copy of the letter of Mr. de Bienville on the subject of the peace with the Natchez. From Ministry of the Colonies, C. 13, vol. 4, pp. 693–96. In MPA, 3:213–15.

August 29, 1716. Paris, the Louvre. Minutes of the Naval Council: State of the colony according to Mr. De Lamothe Cadillac's letters of January 2 and 23, and February 7, 1716. From Ministry of the Colonies, C. 13, vol. 4, pp. 185–204. In MPA, 2:209–17.

September 1, 1716. Paris, the Louvre. Minutes of the Naval Council: Deliberation of the Navy Council. Marriage of Frenchmen with Indian women. From Ministry of the Colonies, C. 13, vol. 4, pp. 255–57. In MPA, 2:218–19.

September 20, 1716. Funds for Payment of Bills of Exchange: Letter to M. Le Couturier. In Shortt, 1:355.

October 5, 1716. Montreal. Montreal Merchants object to Disposal of Bills of Exchange for Beaver: Copy of the Letter Written by the Merchants of Montreal to the Merchants of Quebec. Signed Charly, Pier, etc. In Shortt, 1:355–61.

October 9, 1716. Paris, the Louvre. Minutes of the Naval Council: Account of the needs of Louisiana; Work necessary in the different posts; Price of products. From Ministry of the Colonies, C. 13, vol. 4, pp. 389–98. In MPA, 2:219–25.

October 14, 1716. Quebec. De Louvigny's Expedition against the Foxes: Sieur De Louvigny's letter, thanking the Council for having granted to him the

Lieutenancy, and giving an account of his Expedition against the Foxes, from the 13th of March to the 13th of October, 1716. In WHC, 5:78–80.

October 14, 1716. The Fox War: Louvigny's Expedition; Proceedings of Council Thereon; Letter of Governor de Vaudreuil to Council of Marine; dated Oct. 14, 1716. Done and decreed by the Council of Marine, Dec. 28, 1716. [Signed] L. A. de Bourbon, Maréchal d'estrées and by the Council: La Chapelle. MS. in archives of Ministère des Colonies, Paris; press-mark, "Canada, Corresp. gén., vol. 36, c. 11, fol. 279." In WHC, 16:341–44, and MPHC, 33:576–79.

October 15, 1716. Quebec. Report on the Fortification and Situation of the city of Quebec, the Capital of Canada: By M. Chaussegros de Lery, Engineer-in-Chief. In NYCD, 9:872–74.

October 28, 1716. Paris. Letter from the Navy Council to Bienville: Sends an order from the King to command in the absence of Sieur de L'Epinay. From Ministry of the Colonies, B, vol. 38, pp. 326v–327. In MPA, 3:215.

October 30, 1716. Quebec. De Louvigny's Services in the Fox War: M. De Vaudreuil's letter dated Quebec, October 30, 1716, relative to the services of M. De Louvigny. In WHC, 5:80–81.

November 7, 1716. Quebec. Memorandum by Messrs. de Ramezay and Begon to the Council of the Marine, approving M. de Vaudreuil's proposition respecting the fort at Niagara, &c. In NYCD, 9:874.

November 12, 1716. Quebec. Letter of M. de Vaudreuil to the Council of the Marine—Detroit—Albany, &c. In NYCD, 9:875.

November 18, 1716. Paris. Minutes of the Navy Council on the subject of the letter of Mr. de Chateaugué who recalls the services of Mr. de Bienville, his brother, and asks that the post of King's Lieutenant be maintained for him. From Ministry of the Colonies, C. 13, vol. 4, pp. 475–80. In MPA, 3:216–17.

December 1716. Paris. Royal Edict declaring that there shall be made in the Mint of Perpignan twelve hundred and fifty thousand marks of copper coins of six deniers and twelve deniers for the American Colonies. Signed Louis. In Shortt, 1:365–67.

Bibliography

MANUSCRIPT SOURCES

ARCHIVES NATIONALES DE FRANCE

(Consulted on microfilm, French Michilimackinac Research Project Collection, Western Michigan University Archives)

Archives des Colonies, Series C11A

Archives des Colonies, Series B

Archives des Colonies, Series C11E

Archives des Colonies, Series C11G

Archives des Colonies, Marine, Ser. B 1

NEWBERRY LIBRARY (CHICAGO)

Ayer Manuscript Collection

MS 130

MS 293, 4 vols.

Edward E. Ayer Papers, boxes 1–4

Map Photo, France AN, BN-BSH, 8 boxes

Map Photo, France AN, Delisle Sketches, vols. 1–7

PRINTED SOURCES

Adams, Percy G. *Travelers and Travel Liars, 1660–1800.* New York: Dover Publications, 1980.

Anonymous. *Americana: Autographes, manuscrits, pièces et documents historiques.* 2 vols. A copy in the Newberry Library: n.p. n.d.

Axtell, James. *After Columbus: Essays in the Ethnohistory of Colonial North America.* New York: Oxford University Press, 1988.

———. *The Invasion Within: The Contest of Cultures in Colonial North America.* New York: Oxford University Press, 1985.

Balteau, J., M. Barroux, M. Prevost et al., eds. *Dictionnaire de biographie française.* 21 vols. Paris-VI: Librairie Letouzey et Ané, 1932–.

Banks, Kenneth J. *Chasing Empire across the Sea: Communications and the State in the French Atlantic, 1713–1763.* Kingston, ON: McGill-Queen's University Press, 2002.

Basset, John Spencer. Explanatory Note to "Letters of Francis Parkman to Pierre Margry." In *Smith College Studies in History*, vol. 7, nos. 3–4 (April–July 1923): 123–26.

Berkhofer, Robert, Jr. *The White Man's Indian: Images of the American Indian from Columbus to the Present.* New York: Alfred A. Knopf, 1978.

Brandão, José António. *"Your fyre shall burn no more": Iroquois Policy towards New France and Its Native Allies to 1701.* Lincoln: University of Nebraska Press, 1997.

Brandão, José António, ed. and trans. (with K. Janet Ritch). *Nation Iroquoise: A Seventeenth-Century Ethnography of the Iroquois.* Lincoln: University of Nebraska Press, 2003.

Brandão, José António, and Michael S. Nassaney. "A Capsule Social and Material History of Fort St. Joseph and Its Inhabitants (1691–1763)." *French Colonial History* 7 (2006): 61–75.

Brandão, J. A., and William A. Starna. "The Treaties of 1701: The Triumph of Iroquois Diplomacy." *Ethnohistory* 43, no. 2 (Spring 1996): 209–44.

Broc, Numa. "Deux géographes 'révolutionnaires': Philippe Buache et Jean Nicolas Buache de La Neuville." In *Cartes, Cartographes et Géographes: Actes du 114e Congrès National des Sociétés Savantes, 1989*, 7–13. Paris: Editions du CTHS, 1990.

Brown, George W., et al., eds. *The Dictionary of Canadian Biography*. 14 vols. Toronto: University of Toronto Press, 1966–.

[Buache, Philippe.] *Considérations Géographiques et Physiques Sur les Nouvelles Découvertes au Nord de la Grande Mer, appellée vulgairement la Mer du Sud; Avec des Cartes qui y sont relatives*. Paris: l'Académie Royale des Sciences, 1752.

Burton, Patricia Owens. *Clarence Monroe Burton: Detroit's Historian*. Detroit: Burton Abstract and Title Co., 1953.

Butler, Ruth Lapham, comp. *A Check List of Manuscripts in the Edward E. Ayer Collection*. Chicago: Newberry Library, 1937.

Butler, Ruth Lapham, ed. and trans. *Journal of Paul du Ru [February 1 to May 8, 1700] Missionary Priest to Louisiana*. Chicago: Printed for the Paxton Club, 1934.

Campeau, Lucien, SJ. *Catastrophe démographique sur les Grands Lacs*. Montreal: Éditions Bellarmin, 1983.

Carpenter, John R. *Histoire de la littérature française sur la Louisiane de 1673 jusqu'à 1766*. Paris: A.G. Nizet, 1966.

Catalogue de la Bibliothèque de feu M. Michel Chasles. Paris: A. Claudin, 1881.

Catalogue des manuscrits français de la Bibliothèque nationale: Nouvelles acquisitions françaises. Vol. 3. Paris: Ernest Leroux, Éditeur, 1900.

Charlevoix, Pierre-François-Xavier. *Histoire et description generale de la Nouvelle France avec le Journal Historique d'un Voyage fait par ordre du Roi dans l'Amérique Septentrionale*. 6 vols. Paris: Chez Pierre-François Giffart, 1744.

Codignola, Luca. "The Battle Is Over: Campeau's *Monumenta* vs. Thwaite's *Jesuit Relations*, 1602–1650." In *Missionaries, Native Americans, and Cultural Processes*, edited by Sylvia S. Kaspyrcki. Special issue, *European Review of Native American Studies* 10, no. 2 (1996): 3–10.

Cormier, Ls-P., ed. *Lettres à Pierre Margry de 1844 à 1886*. Quebec: Les Presses de l'Université Laval, 1968.

Cotgrave, Randle. *A Dictionarie of the French and English Tongues*. 1611; reprint, Columbia: University of South Carolina Press, 1968.

Dawson, Nelson-Martin. *L'Atelier Delisle: L'Amerique du Nord sur la table à dessein*. Sillery: Les Éditions du Septentrion, 2000.

Dechêne, Louise. *Habitants et marchands de Montréal au XVIIe siècle*. Montreal: Librairie Plon, 1974.

Delanglez, Jean, SJ. "Antoine Laumet, alias Cadillac, Commandant at Michilimackinac: 1694–1697." *Mid-America: An Historical Review* 27 (1945): 108–32, 188–216, 232–56.

———. *Frontenac and the Jesuits*. Chicago: Institute of Jesuit History, 1939.

———. "A Mirage: The Sea of the West." Part 1. *Revue d'histoire de l'Amérique française* 1, no. 3 (December 1947): 346–81.

———. "A Mirage: The Sea of the West." Part 2. *Revue d'histoire de l'Amérique française* 1, no. 4 (March 1948): 541–68.

———. "The Sources of the Delisle Map of North America, 1703." *Mid-America: An Historical Review* 25 (October 1943): 275–98.

Deslandres, Dominique. *Croire et faire croire: Les missions françaises au XVIIe siècle*. Paris: Fayard, 2003.

Drapeyron, M. Ludovic. *Les deux Buache et l'éducation géographique de trois rois de France*. Paris: Institut Géographique de Paris, Ch. Delagrave, 1888.

[Dufossé, E]. *Americana: Bulletin du bouquiniste, américain et colonial, et de l'amateur de livres relatifs, à l'Asie, à l'Afrique, à l'Océanie, et au nord de l'Europe*. Paris: E. Dufossé, 1884.

DuVal, John, and Kathleen DuVal. "Are *Sauvages* Savages, Wild People, or Indians in a Colonial American Reader?" *Translation Review* 79 (Winter 2010): 1–17.

Eccles, W. J. *The Canadian Frontier, 1534–1760*. Albuquerque: University of New Mexico Press, 1978.

———. *Essays on New France*. Toronto: Oxford University Press, 1987.

———. "French Exploration in North America, 1700–1800." In *North American Exploration*, vol. 2, *A Continent Defined*, ed. John Logan Allen, 149–202.

Lincoln: University of Nebraska Press, 1997.

———. *Frontenac: The Courtier Governor*. Lincoln: University of Nebraska Press, 2003.

———. "The Fur Trade and Eighteenth-Century Imperialism." *William and Mary Quarterly*, third series, 40, no. 3 (July 1983): 341–62.

Edmunds, R. David, and Joseph L. Peyser. *The Fox Wars: The Mesquakie Challenge to New France*. Norman: University of Oklahoma Press, 1993.

Foster, William C., ed. *The La Salle Expedition to Texas: The Journal of Henri Joutel, 1684–1687*. Translated by Johanna S. Warren. Austin: Texas State Historical Association, 1998.

Gênet, Nicole, Luce Vermette, and Louise Décarie-Audet. *Les objets familiers de nos ancêtres*. Montreal: Les Éditions de l'Homme, 1974.

Giraud, Marcel Giraud. *A History of French Louisiana*. Vol. 2. Baton Rouge: Louisiana State University Press, 1993.

Harris, Richard Colebrook, ed. *Historical Atlas of Canada*. Vol. 1, *From the Beginning to 1800*. Toronto: University of Toronto Press, 1985.

Havard, Gilles. *Empire et métissages: Indiens et Français dans le Pays d'en Haut, 1660–1715*. Sillery/Paris: Septentrion/Presses de l'Université de Paris-Sorbonne, 2003.

———. *The Great Peace of Montreal of 1701: French-Native Diplomacy in the Seventeenth Century*. Montreal: McGill-Queen's University Press, 2001.

Heidenreich, Conrad. "Early French Exploration in the North American Interior." In *North American Exploration*, vol. 2, *A Continent Defined*, ed. John Logan Allen, 65–148. Lincoln: University of Nebraska Press, 1997.

Innis, Harold A. *The Fur Trade in Canada*. Rev. ed. Toronto: University of Toronto Press, 1956.

Jacobs, Wilbur, ed. *Letters of Francis Parkman*. 2 vols. Norman: University of Oklahoma Press, 1960.

Jaenen, Cornelius, ed. *The French Regime in the Upper Country of Canada during the Seventeenth Century*. Toronto: Champlain Society, 1996.

Jetté, René. *Dictionnaire généalogique des familles du Québec des origines à 1730*. Montreal: Les Presses de l'Université de Montréal: 1983.

Joutel, Henri. *Journal historique du dernier voyage que feu M. de laSale fit dans le Golfe de Mexique, pour trouver l'embouchure, & le cours de la Riviere de Missicipi, nommé à present la Riviere de Saint Loüis, qui traverse la louisiane . . . Par Monsieur Joutel, l'un des Compagnons de ce Voyage, redigé & mis en ordre par Monsieur de Michel.* Paris: Chez Estienne Robinot, 1712.

Kent, Timothy J. *Rendezvous at the Straits: Fur Trade and Military Activities at Fort de Buade and Fort Michilimackinac, 1669–1781.* 2 vols. Ossineke, MI: Silver Fox Enterprises, 2004.

Kinietz, Vernon. *Indians of the Great Lakes, 1615–1760.* Ann Arbor: University of Michigan Press, 1940.

Ladurie, Emmanuel Le Roy. *The Ancien Régime: A History of France, 1610–1774.* Oxford: Blackwell Publishers, 1998.

Lafitau, Joseph-François. *Moeurs des sauvages ameriquains comparée aux moeurs des premiers temps.* 2 vols. Paris: Saugrain l'aîné, 1724. [trans. as Lafitau, J. F. *Customs of the American Indians Compared with the Customs of Primitive Times.* 2 vols. Edited by W. N. Fenton. Translated by E. L. Moore. Toronto: Champlain Society Publications, vols. 48–49, 1974 and 1977.]

Lagarde, Lucie. "Le passage du Nord-Ouest et la Mer de l'Ouest dans la cartographie française du 18e Siècle: Contribution à l'étude de l'oeuvre des Delisle et Buache." *Imago Mundi* 41 (1989): 19–43.

Lahontan, Louis-Armand Lom D'Arce, Baron de. *Memoirs de l'Amerique Septentrionale, ou la suite des voyages de Mr. de la Hontan: Qui contiennent la Description d'une grande étenduë de païs de ce Continent . . . .* Amsterdam: Chez François l'Honoré, 1705.

Levron, Jacques. *La vie quotidienne a la cour de Versailles aux XVIIe et XVIIIe siècles.* Monaco: Librairie Hachette, 1965.

Littré, Émile. *Dictionnaire de la langue française.* Colombes: Gallimard et Hachette, 1958.

Lunn, Jean. "The Illegal Fur Trade out of New France, 1713–1760." *Canadian Historical Association Report* (1939): 61–76.

Mancall, Peter C. *Deadly Medicine: Indians and Alcohol in Early America.* Ithaca, NY: Cornell University Press, 1995.

Mapp, Paul W. *The Elusive West and the Contest for Empire, 1713–1763*. Chapel Hill: University of North Carolina Press, 2011.

Margry, Pierre, ed. *Découvertes et établissements des Français dans l'ouest et dans le sud de l'Amérique septentrionale, 1614–1754*. 6 vols. Paris: D. Jouaust, 1876–1886.

———. *Relations et mémoires inédits pour servir à l'histoire de la France dans les pays d'outre-mer*. Paris: Challamel Aîné, 1867.

Marie, Alfred, and Jeanne Marie. *Versailles au temps de Louis XV, 1715–1745*. Paris: Imprimerie Nationale, 1984.

Mason, Steven, gen. ed. *Flavius Josephus, Translation and Commentary: Judean Antiquities*, vol. 5. Leiden: Brill, 2000.

McDermott, John Francis. *A Glossary of Mississippi Valley French, 1673–1850*. St. Louis: Washington University Studies, new series, 1941.

McDonnell, Michael. *Masters of Empire: Great Lakes Indians and the Making of America*. New York: Hill and Wang, 2015.

Miquelon, Dale. "Ambiguous Concession: What Diplomatic Archives Reveal about Article 15 of the Treaty of Utrecht and France's North American Policy." *William and Mary Quarterly*, third series, 67, no. 3 (July 2010): 459–86.

Moogk, Peter. *Building a House in New France: An Account of the Perplexities of Client and Craftsmen in Early Canada*. Toronto: McClelland and Stewart, 1977.

Norton, Thomas E. *The Fur Trade in Colonial New York, 1686–1776*. Madison: University of Wisconsin Press, 1974.

Oxford Dictionary of English. 2nd edition. Oxford: Oxford University Press, 2003.

Petto, Christine Marie. *When France Was King of Cartography: The Patronage and Production of Maps in Early Modern France*. Lanham, MD: Lexington Books, 2007.

Peyser, Joseph L., and J. A. Brandão, eds. and trans. *Edge of Empire: Documents of Michilimackinac, 1671–1716*. East Lansing/Mackinac Island: Michigan State University Press/Mackinac State Historic Parks, 2008.

Pritchard, James. *In Search of Empire: The French in the Americas, 1670–1730*. Cambridge: Cambridge University Press, 2004.

Quaife, Milo Milton, ed. and trans. *The Western Country in the 17th Century: The Memoirs of Lamothe Cadillac and Pierre Liette.* Chicago: Lakeside Press, 1947.

[Raudot, Antoine-Denis]. *Relation par lettres de l'Amerique septentrionale.* Edited by Camille de Rochemonteix. Paris: Letouzey et Ané, Éditeurs, 1904.

Richter, Daniel K. *The Ordeal of the Longhouse: The Peoples of the Iroquois League in the Era of European Colonization.* Chapel Hill: University of North Carolina Press, 1992.

Robert, Paul. *Dictionnaire alphabétique & analogique de la langue française.* 6 vols. Paris: Société du Nouveau Littré, 1960–64.

Sayre, Gordon M. *Les Sauvages Américains: Representations of Native Americans in French and English Colonial Literature.* Chapel Hill: University of North Carolina Press, 1997.

Sheldon, Electa M. *The Early History of Michigan: From the First Settlement to 1815.* New York: A. S. Barnes and Co., 1856.

Sleeper-Smith, Susan, Richard White et al. "Forum: The Middle Ground Revisited." *William and Mary Quarterly*, third series, 62, no. 1 (January 2006): 3–96.

Starna, William A., and José António Brandão. "From the Mohawk-Mahican War to the Beaver Wars: Questioning the Pattern." *Ethnohistory* 51, no. 4 (Fall 2004): 725–50.

Stueck, Adam. "A Place under Heaven: Amerindian Torture and Cultural Violence in Colonial New France, 1609–1729." PhD diss., Marquette University, 2012.

Sturtevant, William, gen. ed. *Handbook of North American Indians.* 20 vols. Washington, DC: Smithsonian Institution, 1978–.

Thwaites, Reuben Gold, ed. *The Jesuit Relations and Allied Documents: Travels and Explorations of the Jesuit Missionaries in New France, 1610–1791.* 73 vols. Cleveland, OH: Burrows Bros., 1896–1901.

Tonty, Henri de. "An Account of Monsieur de La Salle's Last Expedition and Discoveries in North America Presented to the French King, and published by the Chevalier Tonty . . . Made English from the Paris Original. Reprinted from the London edition of 1698." *Collections of the New York Historical Society*, 2:217–341. New York: Van Winkle and Wiley, 1814.

———. *Relation de la Louisanne & du Fleuve Mississipi par le Chevalier de Tonty,*

Governeur du Fort Saint Louis aux Islinois. In *Recueil de Voyages au Nord, contenant Divers Memoires . . . .*, 5:35–195. Amsterdam: Chez Jean Frederic Bernard, 1734.

Tooley, R. V. *French Mapping of the Americas: The De l'Isle, Buache, Dezaucher Succession (1700–1830)*. Map Collectors' Circle, no. 33. London: Durrant House, 1967.

Trigger, B. G. *The Children of Aataentsic*. 2 vols. Montreal: McGill-Queens University Press, 1976.

Walton, Guy. *Louis XIV's Versailles*. Chicago: University of Chicago Press, 1986.

Weyhing, Richard. "'Gascon Exaggerations': The Rise of Antoine Laumet dit de Lamothe, Sieur de Cadillac, the Foundation of Colonial Detroit, and the Origins of the Fox Wars." In *French and Indians in the Heart of North America, 1630–1815*, ed. Robert Englebrecht and Guillaume Teasdale, 77–112. East Lansing and Winnipeg: Michigan State University Press and University of Manitoba Press, 2013.

White, Richard. *The Middle Ground: Indians, Empires and Republics in the Great Lakes Region, 1650–1815*. Cambridge: Cambridge University Press, 1991.

Witgen, Michael. *An Infinity of Nations: How the Native New World Shaped Early North America*. Philadelphia: University of Pennsylvania Press, 2012.

Zeller, Gaston. *Histoire des relations internationales*. Vol. 3, *Les temps modernes: De Louis XIV à 1789*. Paris: Librairie Hachette, 1955.

Ziegler, Gilette. *The Court of Versailles in the Reign of Louis XIV*. London: George Allen & Unwin Ltd., 1966.

Zoltvany, Yves F. *Philippe de Rigaud de Vaudreuil: Governor of New France, 1703–1725*. Toronto: McClelland and Steward Ltd., 1974.

Index

O

P

Q

R

S

T

V

W